The Longman Companion to
Britain in the Nineteenth Century
1815–1914

Longman Companions to History

General Editors: Chris Cook and John Stevenson

Now available

The Longman Companion to

Britain in the Nineteenth Century 1815–1914

Chris Cook

LONGMAN
London and New York

Pearson Education Limited
Edinburgh Gate,
Harlow, Essex CM20 2JE,
United Kingdom
and Associated Companies throughout the world

*Published in the United States of America
by Pearson Education Inc., New York*

First published 1999 by Pearson Education

ISBN 0 582 27991 7 CSD
ISBN 0 582 27990 9 PPR

Visit our world wide web site at
hhtp://www.awl-he.com

British Library Cataloguing in Publication Data

A catalogue record for this book is available from the British Library

Library of Congress Cataloging-in-Publication Data

Cook, Chris, 1945–
    The Longman companion to Britain in the nineteenth century,
    1815–1914 / Chris Cook.
        p.   cm. — (Longman companions to history)
    Includes bibliographical references and index.
    ISBN 0–582–27991–7. — ISBN 0–582–27990–9 (pbk.)
    1. Great Britain—History—19th century Handbooks, manuals, etc.
    2. Great Britain—History—1901–1936 Handbooks, manuals, etc.
    I. Title.   II. Title: Britain in the nineteenth century, 1815–1914.
    III. Series.
    DA530.C8   1999
    941.081—dc21   99–21551
                                                                            CIP

Set by 35 in 9½/12 pt New Baskerville
Produced by Addison Wesley Longman Singapore (Pte) Ltd.,
Printed in Singapore

Contents

List of Maps

Preface

This new publication has attempted to provide a convenient and accessible *Companion* for both students and teachers of British history from 1815 to 1914, years which constitute one of the most intensely studied periods of recent history. This *Companion* is naturally a much condensed work, bringing together a wealth of chronological, statistical and tabular information which is not easily found elsewhere within the confines of a single volume. The book covers not only political, diplomatic and imperial events, but also the broader fields of social and economic history. Such topics as industrialisation, the growth of railways and the development of education are to be found alongside parliamentary reform, elections and the rise of political parties. The *Companion* has thus been designed as a user-friendly, desk-top handbook for use by teachers as well as by sixth-formers, college and university students. No book of this type can be entirely comprehensive. Rather the intention has been to include those facts, figures and statistics most needed for courses covering this period.

As always, I am indebted to many individuals for their guidance in the preparation of this volume. In particular, I must thank John Stevenson for his assistance in preparing the bibliography, Linda Hollingworth for her labours typing the manuscript and James Robinson for his constant help.

Chris Cook
London School of Economics
February 1999

Acknowledgements

The publishers would like to thank the following for permission to reproduce copyright material:

Cambridge University Press for tables from *Abstract of British Historical Statistics* (pp. 6–7, pp. 471–3 and pp. 487–9) by B.R. Mitchell and P. Deane, 1962, and tables from *British Economic Growth, 1688–1959* (p. 23 and p. 25) by P. Deane and W.A. Cole, 1969; a table from C. O'Leary, *The Elimination of Corrupt Practices in British Elections, 1868–1911* (App. 1), 1962 by permission of Oxford University Press; Routledge Publishers for the table *Patrick Colquhoun's estimate of the social structure of the United Kingdom*, c. 1815 (pp. 203–4) and a table from *An Atlas of Irish History* (p. 129) by R. Dudley Edwards, Methuen, 1973; and Weidenfeld & Nicholson for a table from *Mid-Victorian Britain, 1851–1875* by G. Best, 1971.

Whilst every effort has been made to trace the owners of copyright material, in a few cases this has proved to be problematic, and so we take this opportunity to offer our apologies to any copyright holders whose rights we may have unwittingly infringed.

SECTION ONE

Political history

Political chronology
1815–1914

Background note

This chronology is intended to provide a broad overview of the period. More detailed chronologies of specific themes can be found in the relevant sections (e.g. on trade unions, riots and public order, Chartism, religion, the women's movement, etc.). Although this volume covers the period after 1815, there is an obvious case for beginning the first chronology at the start of Lord Liverpool's administration.

1812
June Liverpool administration formed. Principal figures: Earl of Liverpool (First Lord of the Treasury); Viscount Sidmouth (Home Secretary); Viscount Castlereagh (Foreign Secretary); Sir Robert Peel (Home Secretary). Orders in Council revoked.
July Wellington defeated French at Salamanca.

1813
June Wellington's victory at Vitoria.
Oct. Defeat of Napoleon at battle of Leipzig.

1814
Apr. Abdication of Napoleon.

1815
Mar. Napoleon returned from Elba, beginning of the 'Hundred Days'. Widespread petitioning movement and riots in London against passing of the Corn Laws, imposing a high protective tariff against imports of grain.
June Defeat of Napoleon at Waterloo. Peace of Vienna signed (see p. 227).

1816
Apr. Income tax abolished after government defeat in the House of Commons. Beginning of widespread riots against distress in East Anglia and manufacturing districts.
Oct. First cheap edition of Cobbett's *Political Register* issued, the 'twopenny trash'.

1817

Jan. Attack on Prince Regent's coach led to introduction of 'Gag Acts'; Habeas Corpus suspended, and restrictions placed on meetings.
Mar. March of the 'blanketeers' broken up by troops.
June Pentrich 'rising' in Derbyshire led by Jeremiah Brandreth.

1819

Aug. Reform meeting at St Peter's Fields, Manchester, broken up by troops, ('Peterloo'); followed by 'Six Acts' restricting meetings and the press, and allowing magistrates to seize arms and prevent drilling.

1820

Jan. Death of George III; accession of George IV.
Feb. Cato Street conspiracy uncovered.
June George IV's estranged wife Caroline returned to claim her rights as Queen.
Nov. Government forced to abandon its attempt to deprive Queen Caroline of her title and dissolve her marriage to the King after widespread popular opposition.

1821

Apr. House of Lords defeated Bill to remove Catholic disabilities.
May Motion for parliamentary reform (introduced by Lord John Russell) defeated in Commons.
July Coronation of George IV.
Aug. Riots in London at Queen Caroline's funeral.
Oct. William Cobbett began his Rural Rides. Congress of Verona: Britain represented by Duke of Wellington.

1822

Jan. Peel became Home Secretary in place of Lord Sidmouth.
Aug. Castlereagh committed suicide; George Canning became Foreign Secretary.

1823

Jan. William Huskisson became President of the Board of Trade; Reciprocity of Duties Act passed (see p. 200).
Mar. Greeks (in revolt against Ottoman rule) recognised as belligerents by Canning.
May Catholic Association formed by Daniel O'Connell in Ireland.
July Abolition of death penalty for a variety of offences (see p. 144).

1824

Feb. Act to repeal the laws relative to combinations (see p. 152).

1825

May Roman Catholic Relief Bill rejected by Lords.
June Hours of work for children under 16 in cotton mills limited to 12-hour working day.
July New Combination Act (see p. 153).
Sept. Opening of Stockton – Darlington railway.
Nov.–Dec. Financial crisis in England, widespread bankruptcies and commercial failures.
Dec. Second Act relating to combinations of workmen, amending Act of 1824.

1826

Feb. Expansion of British power in Burma with acquisition of Arakan peninsula.
Apr. Britain and Russia agreed to recognise Greek autonomy in St Petersburg Protocol.
Dec. Canning offered military aid to liberal government of Portugal against Spanish threat.

1827

Feb. Lord Liverpool paralysed by a stroke (17th).
Mar. Resignation of Lord Liverpool as Prime Minister (28th).
Apr. George Canning became Prime Minister.
Aug. Death of Canning. Succeeded by Goderich.

1828

Jan. Resignation of Goderich after internal Cabinet disputes with his colleagues. Wellington administration formed. Principal figures: Duke of Wellington (Prime Minister); Robert Peel (Home Secretary); Huskisson (Secretary of State for War and the Colonies).
Feb. Bill to repeal Test and Corporation Acts introduced by Lord John Russell and passed with minor amendments (May).
May Resignation of Huskisson and Canningites over failure of Parliament to approve the transfer of the franchises of Penryn and East Retford to Manchester and Birmingham. Catholic Emancipation Bill passed Commons but defeated in Lords.
July Election of Daniel O'Connell (in by-election in County Clare). Catholicism debarred him from taking seat.

1829

Feb. Wellington and Peel declared themselves in favour of Catholic Emancipation after election of Daniel O'Connell for County Clare. Widespread protests from 'Ultra' Tories.

Apr. Catholic Emancipation passed. Catholics admitted to Parliament and to almost all public offices. Irish freehold qualification raised from 40s. to £10.

Sept. Metropolitan Police Act came into operation. London given force of 3,314 professional police.

Formation of Birmingham Political Union.

1830

June Death of George IV; accession of William IV.

July Dissolution of Parliament for fresh elections.

Sept. Huskisson killed at inauguration of Liverpool & Manchester Railway.

Nov. Wellington declared against parliamentary reform (2nd); government defeated on a vote on the Civil List Accounts (15th); Wellington resigned (16th). *Grey administration* formed. Principal figures: Earl Grey (Prime Minister); Lord John Russell (Paymaster-General); Viscount Melbourne (Home Secretary); Viscount Palmerston (Foreign Secretary); H. Brougham (Lord Chancellor).

Swing Riots (see p. 290).

1831

Mar. First Reform Bill introduced into House of Commons by Lord John Russell. Passed second reading.

Apr. Government defeated on Gascoyne's amendment objecting to the reduction in numbers of MPs for England and Wales. Parliament dissolved.

June Whigs returned after general election and second Reform Bill introduced into Parliament.

July Reform Bill received second reading.

Sept. Reform Bill received third reading.

Oct. Reform Bill rejected by House of Lords (8th). Riots in Nottingham and Derby (8th–10th); riots in Bristol (29th–31st).

Dec. New Reform Bill introduced into Commons; passed second reading (18th).

1832

Jan. William IV agreed to creation of peers in order to obtain passage of Reform Bill.

Mar. Reform Bill passed third reading by 355 votes to 239 (22nd).

Apr. Reform Bill passed second reading in Lords.

May Government defeated on Lyndhurst's motion; resignation of ministers. 'May days' (9th–15th); Wellington asked to form an administration but unable to do so; the King forced to recall Grey and confirm assurances that peers will be created as necessary to ensure passage of Reform Bill.

June Reform Bill received third reading in Lords and royal assent (4th and 7th). (For provisions of Reform Act, see pp. 60–2).
July Scottish Reform Act passed.
Aug. Irish Reform Act passed.

1833
Apr. Irish Coercion Act passed.
Aug. Slavery abolished throughout British Empire; £20 million allocated as compensation to slave-owners.

1834
July Resignation of Earl Grey over question of extending Irish Coercion Act. Lord Melbourne became Prime Minister with leading ministers retaining places.
Aug. Poor Law Amendment Act passed, the 'New Poor Law'. Central board of commissioners appointed to administer system (for further details, see p. 121).
Nov. Ministry dismissed by the King and caretaker administration formed under Duke of Wellington. Principal figures: Duke of Wellington (Prime Minister and Secretary of State); Lord Lyndhurst (Lord Chancellor).
Dec. *Peel administration* formed. Principal figures: Sir Robert Peel (Prime Minister and Chancellor of the Exchequer); Lord Lyndhurst (Lord Chancellor); Duke of Wellington (Foreign Secretary). Parliament dissolved because majority in the Commons against the ministry. Peel issued 'Tamworth Manifesto' in an attempt to broaden base of support.

1835
Feb. New parliament met.
Apr. Sir Robert Peel resigned after Whigs and Irish members combined in the 'Lichfield House Compact' to defeat Peel on the use of surplus revenues from the Irish Church. *Second Melbourne administration* formed. Principal figures: Lord Melbourne (Prime Minister); Viscount Palmerston (Foreign Secretary); Lord John Russell (Home Secretary).
Sept. Municipal Corporations Act. Members of town councils to be elected by ratepayers; town councils to publish accounts and budgets.

1836
Aug. Commutation of Tithes Act. Tithes to be paid in money and calculated on basis of average price of corn in previous seven years. Registration of births, marriages and deaths introduced.

1837
Apr. Birmingham Political Union revived by Attwood.
June Death of William IV; accession of Queen Victoria.

July General election (see p. 74).
Oct. Britain took control of Aden.
Nov. *Northern Star* refounded by Feargus O'Connor. Outbreak of rebellion in Lower Canada.

1838
June Coronation of Queen Victoria.
July Irish Poor Law Act (following 1834 reform in England).
Aug. National Charter drawn up (for fuller details of the development of Chartism, see pp. 154–6).
Sept. Anti-Corn Law League set up at Manchester under the leadership of John Bright and Richard Cobden.
Oct. First Afghan War (see pp. 222–3).
Resignation of Lord Durham as Governor-General of British North America.

1839
Feb. Chartist National Convention in London.
Mar. Anti-Corn Law League now organised on countrywide basis.
Apr. Treaty of London guaranteed Belgian independence.
June 'Rebecca riots' (see p. 305).
July Opium War with China (see p. 222).
Nov. Chartist rising at Newport.

1840
Jan. Penny postage introduced.
Feb. Marriage of Victoria and her first cousin, Prince Albert of Saxe-Coburg-Gotha.
Aug. Municipal Reform Act in Ireland.

1841
Aug. Following defeat of the government, *second Peel administration* formed. Principal figures: Sir Robert Peel (Prime Minister); Duke of Wellington (Minister without Portfolio); Sir James Graham (Home Secretary); William Ewart Gladstone (President of the Board of Trade from 1843).

1842
May Chartist demonstration (see p. 154).
June New sliding scale of duties introduced to regulate the corn trade; duties on over 700 articles removed or reduced; income tax reimposed.

1843
Jan. Conquest of Sind by General Charles Napier.
Apr./May Gambia and Natal became colonies.

Oct. Clontarf rally for repeal banned.
Dec. Basutoland created British protectorate.

1844
May Bank Charter Act. Note-issuing and credit functions of Bank of England separated. Note circulation limited.
June Factory Act introduced 12-hour day for women.
Dec. First cooperative retail outlet opened by Rochdale pioneers.

1845
Oct. First effects of Irish potato blight felt. Beginning of the Irish famine.
Newman became Roman Catholic.
Dec. Peel resigned over desire to repeal Corn Laws (6th); resumed office (20th).

1846
Jan. Peel declared for a total repeal of the Corn Laws.
June Royal assent given to repeal of the Corn Laws; sliding scale abolished; duty retained until 1849; only a nominal duty of 1s retained thereafter. Resignation of Peel after defeat of government on Irish Coercion Bill.

1846
June *Russell administration formed.* Principal figures: Lord John Russell (Prime Minister); Lord Palmerston (Foreign Secretary); Thomas B. Macaulay (Paymaster-General).

1847
Apr. The Don Pacifico affair (Pacifico, a British citizen, had his Athens home wrecked in an anti-Jewish riot).
June 'Ten Hours' Factory Act (see p. 119).
July General election (see p. 76).
Dec. Bentinck forced out by Protectionist Tories from front bench.

1848
Jan. Dalhousie began term as Governor-General of India.
Feb. *United Irishman* published by John Mitchel.
Apr. Chartist demonstration at Kennington Common in support of third petition.
July Public Health Act passed (see p. 122).
Ballingary rising in County Tipperary by William Smith O'Brien.

1849
Feb. Disraeli became leader of Conservatives in House of Commons.
Mar. Punjab annexed by Dalhousie.
June Repeal of the Navigation Laws.

1850
June Palmerston's '*Civis Romanus sum*' speech in defence of Don Pacifico affair.
July Death of Peel. Aberdeen led Peelites.
Aug. Australia Government Act.
Irish Tenant League established.
Sept. Re-establishment of Roman Catholic hierarchy in England. Attack on Austrian General Haynau in Southwark.

1851
Feb. Russell announced intention of government to resign after defeat over Bill to reduce the county franchise to £10 (24th).
Mar. Russell announced that ministers to resume office after failure of attempts to form a new ministry.
May Opening of Great Exhibition in Hyde Park.
Aug. Ecclesiastical Titles Act (ineffective; repealed 1871).
Dec. Dismissal of Palmerston for interference with internal affairs of France.

1852
Jan. Transvaal Republic recognised by Sand River Convention.
Feb. *Earl of Derby's administration* formed. Principal figures: Earl of Derby (Prime Minister); Benjamin Disraeli (Chancellor of the Exchequer).
June Representative government introduced for New Zealand.
July General election (see p. 77).
Sept. Death of Duke of Wellington. (State funeral on 18 Nov.)
Dec. *Aberdeen administration* formed. Principal figures: Earl of Aberdeen (Prime Minister); Lord John Russell (Foreign Secretary); W.E. Gladstone (Chancellor of the Exchequer); Viscount Palmerston (Home Secretary).

1853
Apr. First free trade budget introduced by Gladstone as Chancellor.
June Growing crisis over Russian threats to Ottoman Empire.
July Constitution proposed for Cape Colony.
Dec. Resignation of Palmerston (14th); decision reversed (23rd).

1854
Mar. Alliance of Britain and France with Turkey.
Declaration of war by England and France on Russia (28th), beginning of Crimean War (for details, see p. 223).

Apr. Cholera epidemic swept London.
Sept. Anglo-French landings in the Crimea.
Oct. Inadequacies of army medical service exposed by *The Times.*

1855
Jan. Resignation of Lord Aberdeen after criticism of the conduct of the Crimean War.
Feb. *Palmerston administration* formed. Principal figures: Lord Palmerston (Prime Minister); W.E. Gladstone (Chancellor of the Exchequer).
May Administrative Reform Association formed to campaign against bureaucratic bungling.
June Stamp duty abolished on newspapers.
July Responsible government granted to Australian colonies (except Western Australia).
Limited Liability Act passed (see pp. 193–4).
Sept. Sebastopol entered by British and French troops.

1856
Feb. Annexation of Oudh.
Mar. Treaty of Paris concluded Crimean War.
July Natal became a Crown Colony.
Aug. Self-government granted to Tasmania, responsible government to New Zealand.
Oct. *Arrow* incident off Canton, China (see p. 289).

1857
Mar. Successful motion of censure moved by Cobden against Palmerston's China policy.
Apr. General election (for details, see p. 78).
May Revolt in Meerut. Beginning of Indian Mutiny (see p. 224).
June Albert created Prince Consort by Letters Patent.
Aug. Divorce Courts established by Matrimonial Causes Act.
Nov. Commercial crisis in England. Charter Act of 1844 suspended.
Dec. British recaptured Cawnpore.

1858
Feb. Rejection of Palmerston's Conspiracy to Murder Bill led to his resignation. *Second Derby administration* formed. Principal figures: Earl of Derby (Prime Minister); Disraeli (Chancellor of the Exchequer).
June Property qualification for Members of Parliament abolished.
July Jews admitted to Parliament. Act for the better government of India.

1859
Mar. Defeat of government on Reform Bill introduced by Disraeli.
Apr. Parliament dissolved.
May Government resigned after finding itself in a minority in new parliament.
June *Second Palmerston administration* formed. Principal figures: Lord Palmerston (Prime Minister); W.E. Gladstone (Chancellor of the Exchequer); Earl Russell (Foreign Secretary).

1860
Jan. Commercial treaty between Great Britain and France.
Mar. Pioneering Food and Drugs Act to combat food adulteration.
Oct. Further commercial concessions obtained in China by Treaty of Peking.

1861
Nov. '*Trent* incident'. Two Confederate commissioners, Mason and Slidell, taken from the British steamer *Trent* by Federal (USA) warship.
Dec. Death of Prince Albert.

1862
Jan. Queen Victoria's virtual nervous breakdown.
Mar. 'Cotton Famine' resulting from American Civil War.
July *Alabama* sailed from Birkenhead.
Oct. Army revolt in Greece; Britain evacuated King Otho.

1863
Jan. Opening of first underground railway in London, from Paddington to Farringdon Street.
May Beginning of second Maori War.

1864
Mar. Ionian Islands ceded to Greece by treaty.
Apr. Opening of London Conference on Schleswig-Holstein question.
June Failure of London Conference.
Sept. Bombardment of Kagoshima in Japan after expulsion of foreign traders.
Oct. Quebec Conference put forward plans for a Dominion of Canada.

1865
Feb. Poor Law Bill introduced to improve workhouse conditions.
May Colonial Laws Validity Act (colonial legislatures not permitted to pass laws conflicting with Westminster legislation).

July General election produced Liberal gains (see p. 80).
Oct. Death of Lord Palmerston; Earl Russell assumed premiership.
Morant Bay rebellion in Jamaica.
Nov. Earl of Clarendon appointed Foreign Secretary.
Dec. Recall of Edward Eyre, Governor of Jamaica, to London.

1866
Feb. Gladstone introduced a Reform Bill. Fenian campaign in Ireland.
Mar. The 'Cave of Adullam' formed (see Adullamites, p. 289).
May Financial crisis in England; widespread bank failures.
June Gladstone introduced Reform Bill to lower franchise qualifications
in the boroughs and the counties. Defeat of the Bill by the revolt of the
Adullamites led to the resignation of the ministry. *Third Derby administra-
tion* formed. Principal figures: Earl of Derby (Prime Minister); Disraeli
(Chancellor of the Exchequer).
July Demonstrations by Reform League in London; Hyde Park railings
broken down by crowds (23rd).
Oct. Trade union violence against non-union workers in Sheffield – the
'Sheffield outrages'.

1867
Feb. Disraeli introduced reform proposals. Fenians attempted to seize
arsenal at Chester Castle and released prisoners at Clerkenwell prison.
Rising in Ireland suppressed.
Mar. Series of Fenian risings in various Irish towns. 'Conference of Trades'
gathered in London.
May Reform demonstration held in Hyde Park in defiance of government
ban; resignation of Home Secretary, Spencer Walpole.
July New Brunswick, Nova Scotia, Ontario and Quebec united in Domin-
ion of Canada by British North America Act.
Aug. Second Reform Act passed (for details, see pp. 62–3).
Nov. Inaugural meeting of National Union of Conservative and Con-
stitutional Associations.
Dec. Fenian bombing of Clerkenwell gaol in escape attempt (12 dead).

1868
Jan. Expedition under Napier entered Abyssinia.
Feb. Resignation of Lord Derby; Disraeli became Prime Minister.
Mar. Annexation of Basutoland.
Apr. Magdala (capital of Abyssinia) stormed by Napier.
May Meeting at Manchester of first Trade Union Congress.
July Renewal of Maori Wars.
Irish Reform Act passed.
Nov. Liberal triumph in General Election (for details, see p. 81).

Dec. Resignation of Disraeli and Conservatives following the general election. *Liberal government* formed. Principal figures: William Gladstone (Prime Minister and Chancellor of the Exchequer); J. Bright (President of the Board of Trade); E. Cardwell (War Office).

1869
June Repeal of Corn Importation Act.
July Disestablishment and disendowment of the Irish Church.
Oct. Opening of Suez Canal.
Nov. Surrender of rights to Dominion of Canada by Hudson Bay Company.

1870
Jan. Bankruptcy Act came into force; imprisonment for debt ended.
May Home Government Association founded by Isaac Butt.
June Civil service reforms (see p. 108). First of Cardwell's reforms in Army Enlistment Act.
July Earl Granville became Foreign Secretary (following death of Lord Clarendon).
Aug. Irish Land Act passed, providing for compensation for outgoing tenants, loans to be spent on improvement, restraint on evictions and establishment of courts of arbitration. Forster's Elementary Education Act. Establishment of School Boards made compulsory where educational provision deemed inadequate (for further details, see p. 116). Married Women's Property Act (see p. 128).

1871
Jan. Opening of London Conference on revision of Treaty of Paris.
May *Alabama* claim referred to international tribunal.
June Abolition of religious tests at Oxford and Cambridge. Trade Union Act gave legal recognition to trade unions and protection of funds, though unions to remain liable to prosecution under provisions of 1825 Act.
July British Columbia created a province of Canada.
Aug. Purchase of commissions in the army abolished.

1872
Feb. National Agricultural Labourers' Union founded by Joseph Arch.
Apr. Disraeli's famous phrase in the Commons, that the government is a range of exhausted volcanoes.
July Ballot Act passed (see p. 70).
Aug. Licensing Act restricting sale of intoxicating liquors.
Sept. Britain required to pay compensation over *Alabama* claims.
Nov. New commercial treaty between Britain and France.

1873

Mar. Gladstone defeated on Irish University Bill and resigned, but resumed office in the same month. Judicature Act reformed central court structure in England.

Apr. Beginning of Ashanti War.

May Joseph Chamberlain Mayor of Birmingham.

Aug. Gladstone shuffled Cabinet; became his own Chancellor of the Exchequer.

1874

Feb. Gladstone resigned following losses in general election. *Conservative government* formed. Principal figures: Benjamin Disraeli (Prime Minister); Sir Stafford Northcote (Chancellor of the Exchequer); Earl of Derby (Foreign Secretary).

Mar. Peace concluded with the Ashanti.

July New Licensing Act passed.

Aug. Factory Act introduced maximum 56-hour working week.

1875

Jan. Gladstone resigned Liberal leadership. Succeeded by Lord Hartington.

June Artisans Dwellings Act.

Aug. Conspiracy and Protection to Property Act ended use of law of conspiracy in trade disputes and legalised peaceful picketing. Employers and Workmen Act limited penalties for breach of contract.

Dec. British government purchased shares in the Suez Canal Company owned by the Khedive of Egypt for £4,000,000.

1876

Jan. Proclamation of Queen Victoria as Empress of India.

Mar. Passage of Merchant Shipping Act, which provided for safety measures.

Apr. Under Royal Titles Act, Queen Victoria to be Empress of India.

June Press reports of Turkish atrocities in Bulgaria.

Aug. Disraeli elevated to House of Lords as Earl of Beaconsfield. He remained Prime Minister.

Sept. Publication of Gladstone's pamphlet *The Bulgarian Horrors and the Question of the East.*

Oct. Britain and France established dual control of Egyptian finances.

Dec. Opening of Constantinople Conference.

1877

Apr. Ottoman Sultan rejected reform proposals embodied in London Protocol.

Transvaal annexed by Sir Theophilus Shepstone, administrator in Natal.

July Obstructionist tactics begun in Commons by Irish Home Rule members.
Aug. Parnell became President of Home Rule Confederation of Great Britain.

1878

Jan. Annexation of Walvis Bay in southwest Africa.
Apr. Salisbury became Foreign Secretary (succeeding Earl of Derby).
June Under Cyprus Convention, administration of the island in British hands.
July Treaty of Berlin (for details, see p. 229).
Oct. British forces entered Afghanistan (see p. 222).
Dec. Ultimatum sent to King Cetewayo of the Zulus.

1879

Jan. Beginning of Zulu War in South Africa. Defeat of British at Isandhlwana (see p. 224). Battle of Rorke's Drift.
July Defeat of Zulus at Ulundi.
Sept. Reassertion of Anglo-French control of Egyptian finances.
Oct. General Sir Frederick Roberts' troops entered Kabul. Foundation of Irish National Land League.
Nov. First speech of Gladstone's Midlothian campaign.

1880

Feb. Dissolution of Parliament for general election.
Apr. Resignation of ministers following general election. *Liberal government* formed. Principal figures: W.E. Gladstone (Prime Minister and Chancellor of the Exchequer); Sir William Harcourt (Home Secretary); Earl Granville (Foreign Secretary).
May Charles Bradlaugh, MP for Northampton, refused to take the oath. Parnell became chairman of Irish Nationalist Party in House of Commons.
Aug. Relief of Kandahar in Afghan War.
Sept. Beginning of boycott movement in Ireland.
Oct. War with Boer Republic of Transvaal.

1881

Jan. Report of Bessborough Commission on Irish land problem. Enunciated 'Three Fs' – Fair Rent, Free Sale, Fixity of Tenure. Obstructionist tactics of Irish Nationalists disrupted Commons.
Mar. Irish Coercion Act.
Apr. Pretoria Convention recognised Kruger as President of independent Boer republic of Transvaal.

Death of Disraeli left Stafford Northcote leader in Commons, Salisbury in Lords.
Aug. Irish Land Act (for details, see p. 252).
Sept. Revolt of Arabi Pasha in Egypt.
Oct. Irish Land League declared illegal.

1882
May Kilmainham Agreement (see p. 252). Murder of Lord Frederick Cavendish in Phoenix Park, Dublin (see p. 252).
July Bombardment of Alexandria. Resignation of John Bright as Chancellor of the Duchy of Lancaster. New Irish Coercion Act.
Aug. Married Women's Property Act.
Sept. Egyptian forces defeated by Wolseley at Tel-el-Kebir.

1883
Jan. British adviser to be appointed to manage Egyptian finances.
Aug. Corrupt and Illegal Practices Act.
Oct. Publication of pamphlet *The Bitter Cry of Outcast London* raised awareness of social problems.
Nov. Anglo-Egyptian force in Sudan defeated at El Obeid.

1884
Jan. Birth of the Fabian Society.
Feb. Establishment of Royal Commission on the Housing of the Working Class.
Mar. Franchise Bill introduced.
July Franchise Bill blocked in the House of Lords.
Nov. Agreement reached between government and opposition on redistribution of seats. Third Reform Act passed (see pp. 63–4).
Berlin Conference on Africa.

1885
Mar. Redistribution Act passed (see p. 64).
June Resignation of Gladstone administration. *Conservative government* formed. Principal figures: Marquess of Salisbury (Prime Minister and Foreign Secretary); Lord Randolph Churchill (Secretary for India); J. Chamberlain (President of Local Government Board).
Nov. General election (see p. 84).
Dec. Results of general election left Liberals as largest single party. 'Hawarden Kite'; Gladstone's support for Home Rule for Ireland widely reported.

1886
Feb. *Liberal government* formed. Principal figures: W.E. Gladstone (Prime Minister); Earl of Rosebery (Foreign Secretary); H. Campbell-Bannerman

(Secretary for War). Gladstone announced intention to examine 'going nearer to the source and seat of the mischief' in Ireland. Lord Randolph Churchill in Belfast urged loyalists to resist attempts at repeal of the Union. Unemployed riots in London.

Mar. Resignation of Joseph Chamberlain and George Trevelyan from government.

Apr. Gladstone introduced Irish Home Rule Bill.

June Defeat of Home Rule Bill on second reading in Commons. Dissolution of Parliament and general election called.

July As a result of general election Gladstone resigned. *Conservative government* formed. Principal figures: Marquis of Salisbury (Prime Minister and Foreign Secretary); Lord Randolph Churchill (Chancellor of the Exchequer).

Sept. Parnell's Tenant Relief Bill defeated.

Dec. Resignation of Lord Randolph Churchill after disagreements over his Budget proposals. G.J. Goschen became Chancellor of Exchequer.

1887

Feb. Mediterranean Agreements with Italy.

Mar. Balfour became Chief Secretary for Ireland.

Apr. First Colonial Conference held in London.

Forged letter linking Parnell to Phoenix Park murders published in *The Times*.

June Celebration of Queen Victoria's Jubilee (21st).

Aug. Irish Tenants' Act and new Coercion Act passed.

Nov. 'Bloody Sunday'; meeting of Social Democratic Federation in Trafalgar Square broken up by police and troops.

1888

Mar. Protectorates established over Sarawak, Borneo and Brunei.

July Women match workers' strike in Bow.

Aug. County Councils Act (see p. 147).

Sept. Commission formed to investigate complicity of Parnell and his colleagues in outrages in Ireland.

Oct. Cecil Rhodes acquired concession of all mining rights in Matabeleland.

1889

Feb. *The Times* conceded Parnell letter a forgery.

May Naval Defence Act began concept of 'Two-Power Standard'.

Aug. Beginning of London dock strike led by Ben Tillett, Tom Mann and John Burns.

Sept. Dock companies conceded 'docker's tanner', ending strike.

1890

Feb. Parnell cleared of involvement in Irish outrages.
Nov. Parnell cited as co-respondent in O'Shea divorce. Calls for Parnell to resign as leader of Irish Party.
Dec. Irish Nationalist Party split, majority seceding from Parnell's leadership.

1891

June Jameson appointed administrator of South Africa Company in Salisbury (Harare).
Aug. Abolition of fees for elementary education.
Oct. Gladstone outlined 'Newcastle Programme'. Death of Parnell.
Nov. Chamberlain renounced hope of Liberal Unionists rejoining Liberal Party.

1892

Mar. India Councils Bill (admitted nominated Indian members to Legislative Councils).
July General election returned small Liberal majority over Conservatives, but in a minority against all other parties (see p. 86).
Aug. Conservative administration defeated on vote of confidence.
Liberal government formed. Principal figures: William Gladstone (Prime Minister); H.H. Asquith (Home Secretary); Earl of Rosebery (Foreign Secretary); H. Campbell-Bannerman (Secretary for War).
Oct. Anglo-German agreement over Cameroon's boundary (West Africa).

1893

Jan. Bradford Conference led to formation of Independent Labour Party.
Feb. Gladstone introduced Second Irish Home Rule Bill.
Mar. Responsibility for Uganda passed to Colonial Office.
May Self-government granted to Natal.
July Rising in Matabeleland.
Sept. Home Rule Bill passed third reading in the Commons by 34 votes (1st); defeated in the House of Lords by 419 votes to 41 (8th).
Dec. Anglo-French agreement over Siam (Thailand).

1894

Feb. Employers' Liability Act defeated in the House of Lords.
Mar. Local Government Act passed, creating elected parish councils, urban district and rural district councils. Resignation of Gladstone. Queen summoned Earl of Rosebery to take premiership. Death duties introduced in Harcourt's Budget.
Apr. Uganda became British protectorate.

July Anglo-Japanese Treaty gave acknowledgement of Japan's national sovereignty.

1895
May Oscar Wilde trial ended in jail sentence (see p. 132).
June Resignation of Liberal government after defeat on 'cordite' vote (see p. 87).
July General election returned Conservatives as largest single party. *Conservative government* formed. Principal figures: Marquis of Salisbury (Prime Minister and Foreign Secretary); A.J. Balfour (First Lord of the Treasury); Marquis of Lansdowne (Secretary for War); Joseph Chamberlain (Colonial Secretary).
Dec. Boundary dispute between British Guiana and Venezuela led to crisis in relations between Britain and the United States (settled by Treaty of Washington, 1897). Jameson raid launched in South Africa.

1896
Jan. Chamberlain repudiated Jameson raid; 'Kruger telegram' of support from German Emperor to President Kruger on defeat of Jameson raid (3rd).
May Irish Socialist Republican Party founded by James Connolly.
Aug. Protectorate declared over Ashanti (West Africa).
Sept. Advance of General Kitchener into Sudan.
Oct. Lord Rosebery resigned Liberal leadership; Sir William Harcourt became effective party leader.

1897
May Milner arrives in Cape Town as High Commissioner.
June Queen Victoria's Diamond Jubilee.
July Committee of House of Commons reported on Jameson raid, censuring Rhodes but acquitting Chamberlain and the Colonial Office.
Aug. Workmen's Compensation Act passed; accidents at work to be paid for by employers.

1898
Apr. Britain leased Wei-hai-wei, naval base in China.
June Anglo-French Convention settled colonial boundaries in West Africa. Britain leased New Territories near Hong Kong.
Sept. Defeat of dervishes at Omdurman and capture of Khartoum. Confrontation of French and British forces at Fashoda – the 'Fashoda Crisis'.
Nov. Marchand marched French forces away from Fashoda.
Dec. Campbell-Bannerman became leader of the Liberal Party, following departure of Harcourt and Morley from the leading circles of the party.

1899

Jan. Liberal leadership in Commons passed to Henry Campbell-Bannerman.

Mar. Anglo-French Convention resolved spheres of influence dispute concerning Congo and Nile basins.

Mar.–Apr. Inconclusive talks with Germany about possibility of an alliance.

May Hague Conference to discuss disarmament and peace, leading to revision of laws of war and setting up of Court of Arbitration.

May–June Conference between Milner and Kruger to resolve differences between Boers and Uitlanders broke down (31 May–5 June).

Oct. Outbreak of Boer War.

Nov. British overtures for an alliance with Germany rejected.

Dec. 'Black Week' (10th–15th); British defeats at Stormberg (10th), Magersfontein (11th) and Colenso (15th). Buller superseded by Lord Roberts with Lord Kitchener as chief of staff.

1900

Jan. Arrival in South Africa of Lord Roberts as Commander-in-Chief.

Feb. Relief of Ladysmith (28th). Labour Representation Committee (LRC) formed after a meeting at Memorial Hall in London, with aim of electing Members of Parliament 'sympathetic with the needs and demands of the Labour movement'; political levy from unions agreed. Irish nationalists recombined under the leadership of John Redmond.

May Relief of Mafeking; widespread rejoicing in England (17th).

June Despatch of British troops to Peking in face of Boxer rebellion (see p. 225).

Oct. General election, known as the 'Khaki' election. Conservatives returned with reduced majority (see p. 87).

Nov. Salisbury gave up Foreign Office and replaced by Lansdowne.

1901

Jan. Death of Queen Victoria; accession of Edward VII (22nd).

Feb. Breakdown of peace negotiations between Kitchener and Botha at Middelburg.

July Legal judgment in Taff Vale case dismayed trade unions (see p. 308).

Dec. Lloyd George, seen as pro-Boer, besieged at Birmingham Town Hall.

1902

Jan. Alliance signed between Britain and Japan.

Mar. Boers sue for peace. Education Bill introduced.

May Peace with Boers signed at Vereeniging.

July Salisbury succeeded as premier by A.J. Balfour.

Dec. Education Act passed (see p. 117).

1903

Feb. Britain agreed to arbitration at The Hague over Venezuela dispute.
Mar. Irish Land Purchase Act passed, sponsored by George Wyndham, Secretary for Ireland.
May Chamberlain announced his support for imperial preference at speech in Birmingham. Edward VII's visit to Paris opened way to more cordial relations with France.
Sept. Chamberlain and leading tariff reformers resigned from Cabinet to prosecute their campaign in the country at large. Cabinet reconstruction. Austen Chamberlain became Chancellor of the Exchequer; Alfred Lyttelton became Colonial Secretary.
Oct. Women's Social and Political Union (WSPU) founded at Manchester by Emmeline Pankhurst (see p. 278).

1904

Apr. 'Entente Cordiale' between Britain and France. Agreement over Morocco, followed by agreement over Siam, Egypt and Newfoundland.
Aug. Drink Licensing Act angered many Nonconformists and temperance campaigners.
Oct. Sir John ('Jacky') Fisher appointed First Sea Lord. Dogger Bank incident involving Russian fleet and British fishing vessels.

1905

Apr. Anglo-French military convention.
May Britain proposed conference on worsening Moroccan crisis.
Aug. Unemployed Workmen Act passed. Unemployed registers formed under auspices of local government boards. Expenses to be defrayed by voluntary contribution.
Nov. Sinn Fein Party founded in Dublin.
Dec. Resignation of Balfour. *Liberal government* formed. Principal figures: Campbell-Bannerman (Prime Minister); Asquith (Chancellor of the Exchequer); Sir E. Grey (Foreign Secretary); Lord Haldane (Secretary for War); Lloyd George (President of the Board of Trade).

1906

Jan. General election; Liberals returned with an overall majority of 84 (see p. 88). Twenty-nine Labour MPs elected. Algeçiras Conference began.
Feb. Parliament met.
Apr. Education Bill introduced.
July Joseph Chamberlain paralysed by a stroke; effective end of his political career.
Aug. Meeting of Edward VII and the Kaiser at Cronberg.
Oct. State opening of Parliament disrupted by suffragettes.
Dec. Trades Disputes Act passed, reversing Taff Vale decision.

Government dropped Education Bill after it had been mutilated by amendments in Lords.

1907

Mar. Third Imperial (Colonial) Conference in London.
May Introduction of the Territorial and Reserve Forces Bill to establish the Territorial Army.
June House of Commons approved Campbell-Bannerman's resolutions that if a Bill passed all its stages in the Commons three times it should become law, notwithstanding opposition by the Lords.
Aug. Anglo-Russian Agreement on Asia. Russia joined the Entente.
Sept. Creation of Dominion of New Zealand.
Nov. State visit of Kaiser Wilhelm II.

1908

Apr. Campbell-Bannerman resigned and Asquith became Prime Minister. Lloyd George became Chancellor of the Exchequer.
June Meeting of Edward VII and Tsar Nicholas II at Reval.
July Old Age Pensions Bill passed by Parliament.
Oct. Suffragette disturbances in Trafalgar Square. Opening of South African Constitutional Convention.
Nov. Lords rejected Licensing Bill.

1909

Jan. Payment of old age pensions began.
Mar. Introduction of Navy Bill, a result of alarm at German shipbuilding. Four keels to be laid at once and four more if needed.
Apr. Lloyd George introduced his 'People's Budget'.
July Laying of the other four Dreadnought keels (provided for by Navy Act) was sanctioned by the government.
Aug. Origins of secret intelligence service (MI5).
Sept. Force-feeding of suffragettes at Winson Green prison, Birmingham.
Nov. Lords rejected the Budget. House of Lords upheld Osborne Judgment (see p. 161).
Dec. Parliament dissolved.
Birth of Union of South Africa.

1910

Jan. General election. Minority Liberal government formed, dependent upon the support of the Irish Nationalist and Labour Parties.
Feb. Carson led Ulster Unionist Council.
Apr. Lloyd George Budget passed. Parliament Bill introduced with aim of reforming the House of Lords.
May Death of Edward VII. George V ascended the throne.

June Constitutional Conference between the leaders of the Liberal and Unionist Parties. A 'party truce' called while Conference tried to reach a compromise on the question of reform of the House of Lords.

Oct. Unionists rejected Lloyd George's suggestion of a coalition.

Nov. Conference dissolved, having failed to reach agreement. Asquith secured the King's pledge to create enough peers to pass the Parliament Bill if the Liberals won the election.

Dec. Liberals returned to power with very little change in the relative strengths of the parties (see p. 89).

1911

Jan. 'Siege of Sidney Street'. Troops used against anarchists.

Feb. Ramsay MacDonald elected chairman of Labour Party. Parliament Bill introduced to Commons.

May National Insurance Bill introduced by Lloyd George.

Aug. Parliament Act passed House of Lords. The Lords lost their power of veto. House of Commons resolved to pay MPs £400 p.a. Dock strike. Two-day railway strike.

Oct. Churchill became First Lord of the Admiralty.

Nov. Balfour resigned leadership of the Unionist Party and was succeeded by Andrew Bonar Law. Suffragette riots, entailing extensive damage to property in London's West End.

Dec. National Insurance Bill received royal assent. Delhi Durbar in India.

1912

Feb. Miners' strike began with the aim of securing a national minimum wage for miners.

Mar. Bill to establish minimum district wages for miners rushed through Parliament.

Apr. End of miners' strike. Introduction of third Irish Home Rule Bill.

May Strike of London dockers.

End of dockers' strike.

Sept. 200,000 Ulstermen signed a 'Solemn Covenant' to oppose Home Rule. Anglo-French naval convention.

Dec. St James' Palace Conference explored Balkan peace.

1913

Jan. Home Rule Bill rejected by House of Lords.

Founding of Ulster Volunteer Force.

Apr. 'Cat and Mouse' Act (see p. 129).

May Treaty of London between Ottoman Empire and Balkan states.

June Emily Davison, suffragette, killed during the Derby.

July Home Rule Bill again rejected by Lords.

Oct. Lloyd George began his 'Land Campaign' for reform of rural social conditions.
Nov. Irish Volunteers founded.

1914

Mar. Suffragette riots in London. Curragh officers resigned their commissions rather than act against Ulster resistance to Home Rule.
Apr. Gun-running widespread by the Ulster Volunteers.
May Third reading of Home Rule Bill and Welsh Church (Disestablishment) Bill in Commons.
June Third reading of Plural Voting Bill. Assassination of Franz Ferdinand at Sarajevo.
July Buckingham Palace Conference attempted and failed to reach compromise on the exclusion of Ulster from the Home Rule Bill.
Aug. Britain declared war on Germany and Austria.

The monarchy

The monarchs and their issue: 1820–1910

Summary

George IV	1820–1830
William IV	1830–1837
Victoria	1837–1901
Edward VII	1901–1910

George IV

Born 12 Aug. 1762, the son of George III and Charlotte. He acceded to the throne on 29 Jan. 1820 and died on 26 June 1830. In April 1795 he married Caroline, daughter of Charles, Duke of Brunswick-Wolfenbüttel. The marriage produced one child, Princess Charlotte. She was born on 7 Jan. 1796 and died on 6 Nov. 1817. She married on 2 May 1816 Prince Leopold, the third son of Francis, Duke of Saxe-Coburg-Saalfeld.

William IV

Born 21 Aug. 1765, 3rd son of George III and Queen Charlotte; entered Navy as a midshipman on *Prince George* in 1779; thereafter pursued a naval career and held various commands; retired from active service as rear-admiral, 1791; created Duke of Clarence, 1789, and provided with parliamentary annuity of £12,000, raised to £18,000 on marriage in 1818; 1791–1811 lived with Mrs Dorothy Jordan (1762–1816) by whom he had ten children of family name Fitzclarence; promoted Admiral of the Fleet, 1811; married 18 July 1818 Adelaide of Saxe-Coburg-Meiningen. The marriage produced

Charlotte: Born 27 Mar. 1819. She died the same day.
Elizabeth: Born 10 Dec. 1820. Died 4 Mar. 1821.

Succeeded to throne 26 June 1830; crowned 8 Sept. 1831; died 20 June 1837; no legitimate heirs.

(Alexandrina) Victoria

Born 24 May 1819 at Kensington Palace, only daughter of Edward, Duke of Kent (1767–1820) and Princess Victoria of Saxe-Coburg-Saalfeld (1786–1861), married 11 July 1818; succeeded to throne 20 June 1837 on death of her uncle, William IV; crowned at Westminster Abbey 28 June 1838; married 10 Feb. 1840, at Chapel Royal, St James's, Albert of Saxe-Coburg-Gotha, by whom she had nine children; widowed 14 Dec. 1861; declared Empress of India 1 May 1876; died at Osborne 22 Jan. 1901; buried at Frogmore.

The children of Queen Victoria

1. H.R.H. Princess Victoria (Princess Royal); born 21 Nov. 1840; married 25 Jan. 1858 Prince Frederick of Prussia, afterwards Kaiser Frederick III (died 1888); died 5 Aug. 1901.
2. H.R.H. Prince Albert Edward, Duke of Cornwall (1841), Prince of Wales (1841), King Edward VII (1901); born 9 Nov. 1841; married 10 Mar. 1863 Princess Alexandra, eldest daughter of Christian IX of Denmark; succeeded to throne 22 Jan. 1901; crowned 9 Aug. 1902; died 6 May 1910.
3. H.R.H. Princess Alice, born 25 Apr. 1843; married Grand Duke Ludwig of Hesse (1862); died 14 Dec. 1878.
4. H.R.H. Prince Alfred, Duke of Edinburgh (1866), Duke of Saxe-Coburg-Gotha (1893); born 6 Aug. 1844; married Grand Duchess Maria Alexandrovna of Russia, 1874, only daughter of Tsar Alexander II; died 30 July 1900.
5. H.R.H. Princess Helena, born 25 May 1846; married Prince Christian of Schleswig-Holstein, 1866; died 9 June 1923.
6. H.R.H. Princess Louise, born 18 Mar. 1848; married, 1871, Marquis of Lorne, 9th Duke of Argyll (1900), no children, died 3 Dec. 1939.
7. H.R.H. Prince Arthur, Duke of Connaught and Strathearn (1874), born 1 May 1850; married Princess Louisa of Prussia, 1879; died 16 Jan. 1942.
8. H.R.H. Prince Leopold, Duke of Albany (1881), born 7 Apr. 1853, married Princess Helena of Waldeck, 1882; died 28 Mar. 1884.
9. H.R.H. Princess Beatrice, born 14 Apr. 1857; married Prince Henry of Battenberg, 1885; died 26 Oct. 1944.

Edward VII

See above, under 2.

Total annuities to royal family at various times,
1830–1900

Year	Amount (£)	No. of persons in receipt
1830	213,788	15
1836	209,788	14
1837	311,788	12
1840	341,788	13
1850	173,788	10
1860	142,000	8
1870	111,000	10
1880	146,000	11
1889	152,000	12
1900	168,000	16*

* Includes 4 children of Prince of Wales.
Source: *Parliamentary Papers* (1889) xi.

Chronology of royal events, 1815–1914

1818   Marriage of William IV to Adelaide of Saxe-Coburg-Meiningen.
1819   Birth of Victoria (24 May).
        Birth of daughter, Charlotte, to William IV (27 Mar.). She died
        the same day.
1820   Accession of George IV (29 Jan.); death of Edward, Duke of
        Kent (father of Victoria); birth of daughter, Elizabeth, to William
        IV (10 Dec.). She died 4 Mar. 1821.
1821   Coronation of George IV (19 July).
        Death of Queen Caroline (8 Aug.).
1830   Accession of William IV (26 June).
1831   Coronation of William IV (8 Sept.)
1837   Death of William IV without legitimate heirs; accession of Queen
        Victoria (20 June), niece of William IV.
1838   Coronation of Queen Victoria (28 June).
1839   'Bedchamber Crisis' (see p. 290).
        Hostility to Victoria shown by general public.
1840   Marriage of Victoria to Albert of Saxe-Coburg-Gotha (10 Feb.).
        The marriage produced 9 children (see list, p. 27). The first
        child, Princess Victoria, was born on 21 Nov. 1840.
1841   Birth of future Edward VII (Prince Albert Edward, Duke of
        Cornwall).

1843   Victoria and Albert guests of King Louis Philippe. First courtesy visit to a French king since 1520.

1845   Osborne, on Isle of Wight, purchased.

1851   Osborne House completed by Thomas Cubitt.

1852   Estate of Balmoral in Scottish Highlands purchased by Prince Albert.

1855   State visit of Queen Victoria to Paris.

1857   Albert made Prince Consort.

1861   Death of Albert (14 Dec.); Victoria devastated: became the 'Widow of Windsor'.

1862   Queen Victoria's nervous collapse; royal duties exercised by Leopold of Belgium.

1863   Marriage of future Edward VII to Princess Alexandra, eldest daughter of King Christian IX of Denmark (10 Mar.).

1864   Birth of Albert, Duke of Clarence (died 1892).
        Beginning of Victoria's friendship with John Brown, a gillie from Balmoral.

1865   Birth of future George V.

1868   Disraeli became Prime Minister; close friendship developed.

1874   Prince of Wales visited France. First royal visit to a French Republic.

1876   Victoria proclaimed Empress of India (1 May).

1883   Death of Victoria's trusted friend, John Brown.

1887   Celebration of Victoria's Golden Jubilee.

1892   Death of Duke of Clarence (son of Edward VII).

1897   Celebration of Victoria's Diamond Jubilee.

1901   Death of Victoria at Osborne (22 Jan.). Victoria buried at Frogmore. Accession of Edward VII. Advent of House of Saxe-Coburg-Gotha (after 1917, House of Windsor).

1902   Coronation of Edward VII (9 Aug.).

1909   Refusal of Edward VII to promise to create additional peers until the electors had delivered their verdict in a second general election.

1910   Death of Edward VII (6 May); accession of George V, Edward's second son. George V sponsored Constitutional Conference (July) followed by secret pledge to create peers if such action were needed.

1914   Coronation of George V (22 June).
        George V sponsored Buckingham Palace Home Rule Conference (July).

Lists of principal ministers

Prime Minister

June	1812	Earl of Liverpool
Apr.	1827	George Canning
Aug.	1827	Viscount Goderich
Jan.	1828	Duke of Wellington
Nov.	1830	Earl Grey
July	1834	Viscount Melbourne
Nov.	1834	Duke of Wellington
Dec.	1834	Sir Robert Peel
Apr.	1835	Viscount Melbourne
Aug.	1841	Sir Robert Peel
June	1846	Lord John Russell
Feb.	1852	Earl of Derby
Dec.	1852	Earl of Aberdeen
Feb.	1855	Viscount Palmerston
Feb.	1858	Earl of Derby
June	1859	Viscount Palmerston
Oct.	1865	Earl Russell
June	1866	Earl of Derby
Feb.	1868	Benjamin Disraeli
Dec.	1868	William Ewart Gladstone
Feb.	1874	Benjamin Disraeli (1st Earl of Beaconsfield 1876)
Apr.	1880	William Ewart Gladstone
June	1885	Marquis of Salisbury
Feb.	1886	William Ewart Gladstone
July	1886	Marquis of Salisbury
Aug.	1892	William Ewart Gladstone
Mar.	1894	Earl of Rosebery
June	1895	Marquis of Salisbury
July	1902	Arthur James Balfour
Dec.	1905	Sir Henry Campbell-Bannerman
Apr.	1908	Herbert Henry Asquith

Lord President of the Council

June	1812	Earl of Harrowby
Aug.	1827	Duke of Portland

Jan.	1828	Earl Bathurst
Nov.	1830	Marquis of Lansdowne
Dec.	1834	Earl of Rosslyn
Apr.	1835	Marquis of Lansdowne
Sept.	1841	Lord Wharncliffe
Jan.	1846	Duke of Buccleuch
July	1846	Marquis of Lansdowne
Feb.	1852	Earl of Lonsdale
Dec.	1852	Earl Granville
June	1854	Lord John Russell
Feb.	1855	Earl Granville
Feb.	1858	Marquis of Salisbury
June	1859	Earl Granville
July	1866	Duke of Buckingham
Mar.	1867	Duke of Marlborough
Dec.	1868	Earl of Ripon (later Marquis)
Aug.	1873	Lord Aberdare
Feb.	1874	Duke of Richmond
Apr.	1880	Earl Spencer
Mar.	1883	Lord Carlingford
June	1885	Viscount Cranbrook
Feb.	1886	Earl Spencer
Aug.	1886	Viscount Cranbrook
Aug.	1892	Earl of Kimberley
Mar.	1894	Earl of Rosebery
June	1895	Duke of Devonshire
Oct.	1903	Marquis of Londonderry
Dec.	1905	Earl of Crewe
Apr.	1908	Lord Tweedmouth
Oct.	1908	Viscount Wolverhampton
June	1910	Earl Beauchamp
Nov.	1910	Viscount Morley
Aug.	1914	Earl Beauchamp

Lord Chancellor

Apr.	1807	Earl of Eldon
May	1827	Lord Lyndhurst
Nov.	1830	Lord Brougham and Vaux
Nov.	1834	Lord Lyndhurst
Apr.	1835	in Commission
Jan.	1836	Lord Cottenham
Sept.	1841	Lord Lyndhurst
July	1846	Lord Cottenham
June	1850	in Commission

July	1850	Lord Truro
Feb.	1852	Lord St Leonards
Dec.	1852	Lord Cranworth
Feb.	1858	Lord Chelmsford
June	1859	Lord Campbell
June	1861	Lord Westbury
July	1865	Lord Cranworth
July	1866	Lord Chelmsford
Feb.	1868	Lord Cairns
Dec.	1868	Lord Hatherley
Oct.	1872	Lord Selborne
Feb.	1874	Lord Cairns
Apr.	1880	Lord Selborne
June	1885	Lord Halsbury
Feb.	1886	Lord Herschell
Aug.	1886	Lord Halsbury
Aug.	1892	Lord Herschell
June	1895	Lord Halsbury
Dec.	1905	Lord Loreburn
June	1912	Viscount Haldane
May	1915	Lord Buckmaster

Lord Privy Seal

Mar.	1807	Earl of Westmorland
Apr.	1827	Duke of Devonshire
July	1827	Earl of Carlisle
Jan.	1828	Lord Ellenborough
June	1829	Earl of Rosslyn
Nov.	1830	Lord Durham
Apr.	1833	Earl of Ripon
June	1834	Earl of Carlisle
July	1834	Earl of Mulgrave
Dec.	1834	Lord Wharncliffe
Apr.	1835	Viscount Duncannon
Jan.	1840	Earl of Clarendon
Sept.	1841	Duke of Buckingham
Feb.	1842	Duke of Buccleuch
Jan.	1846	Earl of Haddington
July	1846	Earl of Minto
Feb.	1852	Marquis of Salisbury
Jan.	1853	Duke of Argyll
Dec.	1855	Earl of Harrowby
Feb.	1858	Marquis of Clanricarde
Feb.	1858	Earl of Hardwicke

June	1859	Duke of Argyll
July	1866	Earl of Malmesbury
Dec.	1868	Earl of Kimberley
July	1870	Viscount Halifax
Feb.	1874	Earl of Malmesbury
Aug.	1876	Earl of Beaconsfield
Feb.	1878	Duke of Northumberland
Apr.	1880	Duke of Argyll
May	1881	Lord Carlingford
Mar.	1885	Earl of Rosebery
June	1885	Earl of Harrowby
Feb.	1886	William Ewart Gladstone
Aug.	1886	Earl of Cadogan
Aug.	1892	William Ewart Gladstone
Mar.	1894	Lord Tweedmouth
June	1895	Viscount Cross
Nov.	1900	Marquis of Salisbury
July	1902	Arthur James Balfour
Oct.	1903	Marquis of Salisbury
Dec.	1905	Marquis of Ripon
Oct.	1908	Earl of Crewe
Oct.	1911	Earl Carrington
Feb.	1912	Marquis of Crewe
May	1915	Earl Curzon

Secretary of State for the Home Department

June	1812	Viscount Sidmouth
Jan.	1822	Sir Robert Peel
Apr.	1827	William Sturges-Bourne
July	1827	Marquis of Lansdowne
Jan.	1828	Sir Robert Peel
Nov.	1830	Viscount Melbourne
July	1834	Viscount Duncannon
Dec.	1834	Henry Goulburn
Apr.	1835	Lord John Russell
Aug.	1839	Marquis of Normanby
Sept.	1841	Sir James Graham
July	1846	Sir George Grey
Feb.	1852	Spencer Walpole
Dec.	1852	Viscount Palmerston
Feb.	1855	Sir George Grey
Feb.	1858	Spencer Walpole
Mar.	1859	Thomas Henry Sutton Sotheron Estcourt
June	1859	Sir George Cornewall Lewis

July	1861	Sir George Grey
July	1866	Spencer Walpole
May	1867	Gathorne Hardy
Dec.	1868	Henry Austin Bruce
Aug.	1873	Robert Lowe
Feb.	1874	Richard Assheton Cross
Apr.	1880	Sir William Vernon Harcourt
June	1885	Sir Richard Assheton Cross
Feb.	1886	Hugh Culling Eardley Childers
Aug.	1886	Henry Matthews
Aug.	1892	Herbert Henry Asquith
June	1895	Sir Matthew White Ridley
Nov.	1900	Charles Thomson Ritchie
Aug.	1902	Aretas Akers-Douglas
Dec.	1905	Herbert Gladstone
Feb.	1910	Winston Churchill
Oct.	1911	Reginald McKenna
May	1915	Sir John Simon

Secretary of State for Foreign Affairs

Mar.	1812	Viscount Castlereagh
Sept.	1822	George Canning
Apr.	1827	Viscount Dudley and Ward
June	1828	Earl of Aberdeen
Nov.	1830	Viscount Palmerston
Nov.	1834	Duke of Wellington
Apr.	1835	Viscount Palmerston
Sept.	1841	Earl of Aberdeen
July	1846	Viscount Palmerston
Dec.	1851	Earl Granville
Feb.	1852	Earl of Malmesbury
Dec.	1852	Lord John Russell
Feb.	1853	Earl of Clarendon
Feb.	1858	Earl of Malmesbury
June	1859	Lord John Russell
Nov.	1865	Earl of Clarendon
July	1866	Lord Stanley
Dec.	1868	Earl of Clarendon
July	1870	Earl Granville
Feb.	1874	Earl of Derby
Apr.	1878	Marquis of Salisbury
Apr.	1880	Earl Granville
June	1885	Marquis of Salisbury
Feb.	1886	Earl of Rosebery

Aug.	1886	Earl of Iddesleigh
Jan.	1887	Marquis of Salisbury
Aug.	1892	Earl of Rosebery
Mar.	1894	Earl of Kimberley
June	1895	Marquis of Salisbury
Nov.	1900	Marquis of Lansdowne
Dec.	1905	Sir Edward Grey
Dec.	1916	Arthur James Balfour

Chancellor of the Exchequer

June	1812	Nicholas Vansittart
Jan.	1823	Frederick John Robinson
Apr.	1827	George Canning
Sept.	1827	John Charles Herries
Jan.	1828	Henry Goulbourn
Nov.	1830	John Charles Spencer (called Viscount Althorp)
Dec.	1834	Sir Robert Peel
Apr.	1835	Thomas Spring Rice
Aug.	1839	Sir Francis Thornhill Baring
Sept.	1841	Henry Goulbourn
July	1846	Sir Charles Wood
Feb.	1852	Benjamin Disraeli
Dec.	1852	William Ewart Gladstone
Feb.	1855	Sir George Cornewall Lewis
Feb.	1858	Benjamin Disraeli
June	1859	William Ewart Gladstone
July	1866	Benjamin Disraeli
Feb.	1868	George Ward Hunt
Dec.	1868	Robert Lowe
Aug.	1873	William Ewart Gladstone
Feb.	1874	Sir Stafford Henry Northcote
Apr.	1880	William Ewart Gladstone
Dec.	1882	Hugh Culling Eardley Childers
June	1885	Sir Michael Edward Hicks Beach
Feb.	1886	Sir William Vernon Harcourt
Aug.	1886	Lord Randolph Churchill
Jan.	1887	George Joachim Goschen
Aug.	1892	Sir William Harcourt
June	1895	Sir Michael Hicks Beach
July	1902	Charles Thomson Ritchie
Oct.	1903	(Joseph) Austen Chamberlain
Dec.	1905	Herbert Henry Asquith
Apr.	1908	David Lloyd George

First Lord of the Admiralty

Mar.	1812	Robert Dundas
Apr.	1827	Duke of Clarence (William IV, advised by a Council)
Nov.	1830	Sir James Graham
June	1834	Lord Auckland
Dec.	1834	Earl de Grey
Apr.	1835	Lord Auckland
Sept.	1835	Earl of Minto
Sept.	1841	Earl of Haddington
Jan.	1846	Earl of Ellenborough
July	1846	Earl of Auckland
Jan.	1849	Sir Francis Baring
Feb.	1852	Duke of Northumberland
Dec.	1852	Sir James Graham
Mar.	1855	Sir Charles Wood
Mar.	1858	Sir John Pakington
June	1859	Duke of Somerset
July	1866	Sir John Pakington
Mar.	1867	Henry Thomas Lowry Corry
Dec.	1868	Hugh Culling Eardley Childers
Mar.	1871	George Joachim Goschen
Feb.	1874	George Ward Hunt
Aug.	1877	William Henry Smith
Apr.	1880	Earl of Northbrook
June	1885	Lord George Hamilton
Feb.	1886	Marquis of Ripon
Aug.	1886	Lord George Hamilton
Aug.	1892	Earl Spencer
June	1895	George Joachim Goschen
Nov.	1900	Earl of Selborne
Mar.	1905	Earl Cawdor
Dec.	1905	Lord Tweedmouth
Apr.	1908	Reginald McKenna
Oct.	1911	Winston Churchill
May	1915	Arthur James Balfour

Secretary of State for War and the Colonies

Nov.	1830	Viscount Goderich
Apr.	1833	Lord Stanley
June	1834	Thomas Spring-Rice
Dec.	1834	Earl of Aberdeen
Apr.	1835	Lord Glenelg
Feb.	1839	Marquis of Normanby
Aug.	1839	Lord John Russell

Sept.	1841	Lord Stanley
Dec.	1845	William Ewart Gladstone
July	1846	Earl Grey
Feb.	1852	Sir John Pakington
Dec.	1852	Duke of Newcastle

Secretary of State for the Colonies

June	1854	Sir George Grey
Feb.	1855	Sidney Herbert
Feb.	1855	Lord John Russell
July	1855	Sir William Molesworth
Nov.	1855	Henry Labouchere
Feb.	1858	Lord Stanley
June	1858	Sir E. Bulwer-Lytton
June	1859	Duke of Newcastle
Apr.	1864	Edward Cardwell
July	1866	Earl of Carnarvon
Mar.	1867	Duke of Buckingham
Dec.	1868	Earl Granville
July	1870	Earl of Kimberley
Feb.	1874	Earl of Carnarvon
Feb.	1878	Sir Michael Hicks Beach
Apr.	1880	Earl of Kimberley
Dec.	1882	Earl of Derby
June	1885	F.A. Stanley
Feb.	1886	Earl Granville
Aug.	1886	E. Stanhope
Jan.	1887	Sir H.T. Holland (Lord Knutsford)
Aug.	1892	Marquis of Ripon
June	1895	Joseph Chamberlain
Oct.	1903	Alfred Lyttelton
Dec.	1905	Earl of Elgin
Apr.	1908	Earl of Crewe
Nov.	1910	L. Harcourt

Secretary of State for War

June	1854	Duke of Newcastle
Feb.	1855	Lord Panmure
Feb.	1858	John Peel
June	1859	Lord Herbert
July	1861	Sir G.C. Lewis
Apr.	1863	Earl de Grey and Ripon
Feb.	1866	Marquis of Hartington
July	1866	John Peel

Mar.	1867	Sir John Pakington
Dec.	1868	Edward Cardwell
Feb.	1874	Gathorne Hardy
Apr.	1878	F.A. Stanley
Apr.	1880	H.C.E. Childers
Dec.	1882	Marquis of Hartington
June	1885	W.H. Smith
Feb.	1886	Henry Campbell-Bannerman
Aug.	1886	W.H. Smith
Jan.	1887	Edward Stanhope
Aug.	1892	Henry Campbell-Bannerman
July	1895	Marquis of Lansdowne
Nov.	1900	William St John Brodrick
Oct.	1903	H. Arnold-Forster
Dec.	1905	Viscount Haldane
June	1912	J. Seely
Mar.	1914	Herbert Asquith
Aug.	1914	Earl Kitchener

Secretary of State for India
See p. 247.

President of the Board of Control
See p. 246.

President of the Board of Agriculture

Sept.	1889	H. Chaplin
Aug.	1892	H. Gardner
July	1895	W. Long
Nov.	1900	R.W. Hanbury
May	1903	Earl of Onslow
Mar.	1905	A.E. Fellowes
Dec.	1905	Earl Carrington
Oct.	1911	Walter Runciman

Chief Secretary for Ireland

Aug.	1812	Robert Peel
Aug.	1818	Charles Grant
Dec.	1821	Henry Goulburn
Apr.	1827	William Lamb (Viscount Melbourne)
June	1828	Lord Francis Leveson Gower
July	1830	Sir Henry Hardinge
Nov.	1830	Lord Stanley
Mar.	1833	Sir John Cam Hobhouse

May	1833	E.J. Hatherton
Dec.	1834	Sir Henry Hardinge
Apr.	1835	Viscount Morpeth
Sept.	1841	Lord Eliot
Feb.	1845	Sir Thomas Francis Fremantle
Feb.	1846	Earl of Lincoln
July	1846	Henry Labouchere
July	1847	Sir William Somerville
Mar.	1852	Lord Naas
Jan.	1853	Sir John Young
Mar.	1855	Edward Horsman
May	1857	Henry Arthur Herbert
Mar.	1858	Lord Naas
June	1859	Edward Cardwell
July	1861	Sir Robert Peel
Dec.	1865	Chichester Fortescue
July	1866	Lord Naas
Sept.	1868	John Wilson-Patten
Dec.	1868	Chichester Fortescue
Jan.	1871	Marquis of Hartington
Feb.	1874	Sir Michael Hicks Beach
Feb.	1878	James Lowther
Apr.	1880	William Edward Forster
May	1882	Lord Frederick Cavendish
May	1882	George Otto Trevelyan
Oct.	1884	Henry Campbell-Bannerman
June	1885	Sir William Hart Dyke
Jan.	1886	William Henry Smith
Feb.	1886	John Morley
Aug.	1886	Sir Michael Hicks Beach
Mar.	1887	Arthur James Balfour
Nov.	1891	William Jackson
Aug.	1892	John Morley
July	1895	George William Balfour
Nov.	1900	George Wyndham
Mar.	1905	Walter Long
Dec.	1905	James Bryce
Jan.	1907	Augustine Birrell

Presidents of the Board of Trade

Nov.	1830	Lord Auckland
June	1834	C.P. Thomson
Dec.	1834	A. Baring
Apr.	1835	C.P. Thomson

Aug.	1839	Henry Labouchere
Sept.	1841	Earl of Ripon
May	1843	William Ewart Gladstone
Feb.	1845	Earl of Dalhousie
July	1846	Earl of Clarendon
July	1847	Henry Labouchere
Feb.	1852	J.W. Henley
Dec.	1852	Edward Cardwell
Mar.	1855	Lord Stanley of Alderley
Feb.	1858	J.W. Henley
Mar.	1859	Earl of Donoughmore
July	1859	T.M. Gibson
July	1866	Sir Stafford Northcote
Mar.	1867	Duke of Richmond
Dec.	1868	John Bright
Jan.	1871	C.S. Fortescue
Feb.	1874	Sir C.B. Adderley
Apr.	1878	Viscount Sandon
May	1880	Joseph Chamberlain
June	1885	Duke of Richmond
Aug.	1885	Edward Stanhope
Feb.	1886	A.J. Mundella
Aug.	1886	Lord Stanley of Preston
Feb.	1888	Sir Michael Hicks Beach
Aug.	1892	A.J. Mundella
May	1894	James Bryce
June	1895	Charles Ritchie
Nov.	1900	George Balfour
Mar.	1905	Marquis of Salisbury
Dec.	1905	David Lloyd George
Apr.	1908	Winston Churchill
Feb.	1910	Sydney Buxton
Feb.	1914	John Burns
Aug.	1914	Walter Runciman

Cabinets and administrations

Introductory note

The fullest details of ministerial appointments, including not only Cabinet Ministers but also a full listing of non-Cabinet ministerial posts can be found in three reference volumes: Chris Cook and John Stevenson, *British Historical Facts, 1760–1830* (London, 1980), Chris Cook and Brendan Keith, *British Historical Facts, 1830–1900* (London, 1975) and David Butler and Gareth Butler, *British Historical Facts, 1900–1994* (London, 1995). These volumes are probably too detailed except for the advanced student. The lists of Cabinets given below show the members of the Cabinet at date of formation. Key changes are given in chronological sequence on pp. 54–5.

1. Liverpool's Cabinet (formed June 1812)
Prime Minister and First Lord of the Treasury: Earl of Liverpool
Lord Chancellor: Lord Eldon (Earl 1821)
Lord President: Earl of Harrowby
Lord Privy Seal: Earl of Westmorland
Chancellor of the Exchequer: Nicholas Vansittart (Lord Bexley 1823)
Home Secretary: Viscount Sidmouth
Foreign Secretary: Viscount Castlereagh (Marquis of Londonderry 1821)
Secretary for War and Colonies: Earl Bathurst
First Lord of the Admiralty: Viscount Melville
Master-General of the Ordnance: Earl of Mulgrave
President of the Board of Control: Earl of Buckinghamshire
Master of the Mint: W. Wellesley-Pole (Lord Maryborough 1821)
Chancellor of the Duchy of Lancaster: C.B. Bathurst
Cabinet Minister without Office: Marquis of Camden

2. Canning's Cabinet (formed Sept. 1827)
Prime Minister and First Lord of the Treasury ⎱ George Canning
Chancellor of the Exchequer ⎰
Lord Chancellor: Lord Lyndhurst
Lord President of the Council: Earl of Harrowby
Lord Privy Seal: Duke of Portland
Home Secretary: W. Sturges Bourne

Foreign Secretary: Viscount Dudley
Secretary for War and Colonies: Viscount Goderich
President of the Board of Trade and Treasurer of the Navy: William Huskisson
President of the Board of Control: C.W.W. Wynn
Chancellor of the Duchy of Lancaster: Lord Bexley
Secretary at War: Viscount Palmerston

3. Goderich's Cabinet (formed Sept. 1827)

Prime Minister and First Lord of the Treasury: Viscount Goderich
Lord Chancellor: Lord Lyndhurst
Lord President of the Council: Duke of Portland
Lord Privy Seal: Earl of Carlisle
Chancellor of the Exchequer: J.C. Herries
Home Secretary: Marquis of Lansdowne
Foreign Secretary: Earl (formerly Viscount) Dudley
Secretary for War and Colonies: William Huskisson
Master-General of the Ordnance: Marquis of Anglesey
President of the Board of Trade and Treasurer of the Navy: Charles Grant
President of the Board of Control: C.W.W. Wynn
Master of the Mint: G. Tierney
Chancellor of the Duchy of Lancaster: Lord Bexley
First Commissioner of Woods and Forests: W. Sturges Bourne
Secretary at War: Viscount Palmerston

4. Wellington's Cabinet (formed Jan. 1828)

Prime Minister and First Lord of the Treasury: Duke of Wellington
Lord Chancellor: Lord Lyndhurst
Lord President of the Council: Earl Bathurst
Lord Privy Seal: Lord Ellenborough
Chancellor of the Exchequer: Henry Goulbourn
Home Secretary: (Sir) Robert Peel
Foreign Secretary: Earl Dudley
Secretary for War and Colonies: William Huskisson
President of the Board of Trade and Treasurer of the Navy: Charles Grant
President of the Board of Control: Viscount Melville
Master of the Mint: J.C. Herries
Chancellor of the Duchy of Lancaster: Earl of Aberdeen
Secretary at War: Viscount Palmerston

5. Grey's Cabinet (formed Nov. 1830)

Prime Minister and First Lord of the Treasury: Earl Grey
Lord Chancellor: Lord Brougham
Lord President of the Council: Marquis of Lansdowne
Lord Privy Seal: Lord Durham

Chancellor of the Exchequer: Viscount Althorp
Home Secretary: Viscount Melbourne
Foreign Secretary: Viscount Palmerston
Secretary for War and Colonies: Viscount Goderich
First Lord of the Admiralty: Sir James Graham
President of the Board of Control: Charles Grant
Chancellor of the Duchy of Lancaster: Lord Holland
Postmaster-General: Duke of Richmond
Cabinet Minister without Office: Earl of Carlisle

6. Melbourne's first Cabinet (formed July 1834)
Prime Minister and First Lord of the Treasury: Viscount Melbourne
Lord Chancellor: Lord Brougham
Lord President of the Council: Marquis of Lansdowne
Lord Privy Seal: Earl of Mulgrave
Chancellor of the Exchequer: Viscount Althorp
Home Secretary: Viscount Duncannon
Foreign Secretary: Viscount Palmerston
Secretary for War and Colonies: Thomas Spring Rice
First Lord of the Admiralty: Lord Auckland
President of the Board of Trade and Treasurer of the Navy: C.E. Poulett Thomson
President of the Board of Control: Charles Grant
Master of the Mint: J. Abercromby
Chancellor of the Duchy of Lancaster: Lord Holland
Secretary at War: E. Ellice
First Commissioner of Woods and Forests: Sir John Hobhouse
Paymaster-General: Lord John Russell

7. Wellington's provisional government (formed Nov. 1834)
Prime Minister: Duke of Wellington
Lord Chancellor: Lord Lyndhurst
Secretary of State: Duke of Wellington
Lords Commissioners for Executing the Office of Lord High Treasurer {
Duke of Wellington
Earl of Rosslyn
Lord Ellenborough
Lord Maryborough
Sir J. Beckett
J. Planta
}

8. Peel's first Cabinet (formed Dec. 1834)
Prime Minister and First Lord of the Treasury } Sir Robert Peel
Chancellor of the Exchequer
Lord Chancellor: Lord Lyndhurst
Lord President of the Council: Earl of Rosslyn

Lord Privy Seal: Lord Wharncliffe
Home Secretary: Henry Goulburn
Foreign Secretary: Duke of Wellington
Secretary for War and Colonies: Earl of Aberdeen
First Lord of the Admiralty: Earl de Grey
Master-General of the Ordnance: Sir George Murray
President of the Board of Trade }
Master of the Mint } A. Baring
President of the Board of Control: Lord Ellenborough
Secretary at War: J.C. Herries
Paymaster-General: Sir Edward Knatchbull

9. Melbourne's second Cabinet (formed Apr. 1835)

Prime Minister and First Lord of the Treasury: Viscount Melbourne
Lord Chancellor: Lord Cottenham (from January 1836)
Lord President of the Council: Marquis of Lansdowne
Lord Privy Seal }
First Commissioner of Woods and Forests } Viscount Duncannon
Chancellor of the Exchequer: T. Spring Rice
Home Secretary: Lord John Russell
Foreign Secretary: Viscount Palmerston
Secretary for War and Colonies: C. Grant (Lord Glenelg)
First Lord of the Admiralty: Lord Auckland
President of the Board of Trade: C.E. Poulett Thomson
President of the Board of Control: Sir John Hobhouse
Chancellor of the Duchy of Lancaster: Lord Holland
Secretary at War: Viscount Howick

10. Peel's second Cabinet (formed Sept. 1841)

Prime Minister and First Lord of the Treasury: Sir Robert Peel
Lord Chancellor: Lord Lyndhurst
Lord President of the Council: Lord Wharncliffe
Lord Privy Seal: Duke of Buckingham
Chancellor of the Exchequer: Henry Goulburn
Home Secretary: Sir James Graham
Foreign Secretary: Earl of Aberdeen
Secretary for War and Colonies: Viscount Stanley
First Lord of the Admiralty: Earl of Haddington
President of the Board of Trade: Earl of Ripon
President of the Board of Control: Lord Ellenborough (Earl 1844)
Secretary at War: Sir Henry Hardinge
Paymaster-General: Sir Edward Knatchbull
Cabinet Minister without Office: Duke of Wellington

11. Russell's first Cabinet (formed July 1846)

Prime Minister and First Lord of the Treasury: Lord John Russell
Lord Chancellor: Lord Cottenham
Lord President of the Council: Marquis of Lansdowne
Lord Privy Seal: Earl of Minto
Chancellor of the Exchequer: Sir Charles Wood
Home Secretary: Sir George Grey
Foreign Secretary: Viscount Palmerston
Secretary for War and Colonies: Earl Grey
First Lord of the Admiralty: Earl of Auckland
President of the Board of Trade: Earl of Clarendon
President of the Board of Control: Sir James Hobhouse (Lord Broughton 1851)
Chancellor of the Duchy of Lancaster: Lord Campbell
First Commissioner of Woods and Forests: Viscount Morpeth (Earl of Carlisle 1848)
Chief Secretary for Ireland: Henry Labouchere
Postmaster-General: Marquis of Clanricarde
Paymaster-General: T.B. Macaulay

12. Derby's first Cabinet (formed Feb. 1852)

Prime Minister and First Lord of the Treasury: Earl of Derby
Lord Chancellor: Lord St. Leonards
Lord President of the Council: Earl of Lonsdale
Lord Privy Seal: Marquis of Salisbury
Chancellor of the Exchequer: Benjamin Disraeli
Home Secretary: Spencer Walpole
Foreign Secretary: Earl of Malmesbury
Secretary for War and Colonies: Sir John Pakington
First Lord of the Admiralty: Duke of Northumberland
President of the Board of Trade: J.W. Henley
President of the Board of Control: J.C. Herries
First Commissioner of Works: Lord John Manners
Postmaster-General: Earl of Hardwicke

13. Aberdeen's Cabinet (formed Dec. 1852)

Prime Minister and First Lord of the Treasury: Earl of Aberdeen
Lord Chancellor: Lord Cranworth
Lord President of the Council: Earl Granville
Lord Privy Seal: Duke of Argyll
Chancellor of the Exchequer: William Gladstone
Home Secretary: Viscount Palmerston
Foreign Secretary: Lord John Russell
Secretary for War and Colonies: Duke of Newcastle

First Lord of the Admiralty: Sir James Graham
President of the Board of Control: Sir Charles Wood
First Commissioner of Works: Sir William Molesworth
Secretary at War: Sidney Herbert
Cabinet Minister without Office: Marquis of Lansdowne

14. Palmerston's first Cabinet (formed Feb. 1855)
Prime Minister and First Lord of the Treasury: Viscount Palmerston
Lord Chancellor: Lord Cranworth
Lord President of the Council: Earl Granville
Lord Privy Seal: Duke of Argyll
Chancellor of the Exchequer: William Gladstone
Home Secretary: Sir George Grey
Foreign Secretary: Earl of Clarendon
Secretary for War: Lord Panmure
Secretary for the Colonies: Sidney Herbert
First Lord of the Admiralty: Sir James Graham
President of the Board of Control: Sir Charles Wood
First Commissioner of Works: Sir William Molesworth
Postmaster-General: Viscount Canning
Cabinet Minister without Office: Marquis of Lansdowne

15. Derby's second Cabinet (formed Feb. 1858)
Prime Minister and First Lord of the Treasury: Earl of Derby
Lord Chancellor: Lord Chelmsford
Lord President of the Council: Marquis of Salisbury
Lord Privy Seal: Earl of Hardwicke
Chancellor of the Exchequer: Benjamin Disraeli
Home Secretary: Spencer H. Walpole
Foreign Secretary: Earl of Malmesbury
Secretary for War: General Peel
Secretary for the Colonies: Lord Stanley
First Lord of the Admiralty: Sir John Pakington
President of the Board of Trade: J.W. Henley
President of the Board of Control: Earl of Ellenborough
First Commissioner of Works: Lord John Manners

16. Palmerston's second Cabinet (formed June 1859)
Prime Minister and First Lord of the Treasury: Viscount Palmerston
Lord Chancellor: Lord Campbell
Lord President of the Council: Earl Granville
Lord Privy Seal: Duke of Argyll
Chancellor of the Exchequer: William Gladstone

Home Secretary: Sir G. Cornewall Lewis
Foreign Secretary: Lord John Russell (Earl 1861)
Secretary for War: Sidney Herbert (Lord 1860)
Secretary for the Colonies: Duke of Newcastle
First Lord of the Admiralty: Duke of Somerset
Secretary for India: Sir C. Wood (Viscount Halifax 1866)
Chancellor of the Duchy of Lancaster: Sir George Grey
Chief Secretary for Ireland: E. Cardwell
Postmaster-General: Earl of Elgin
President of the Poor Law Board: T. Milner-Gibson

17. Russell's second Cabinet (formed Oct. 1865)

Prime Minister and First Lord of the Treasury: Earl Russell
Lord Chancellor: Lord Cranworth
Lord President of the Council: Earl Granville
Lord Privy Seal: Duke of Argyll
Chancellor of the Exchequer: William Gladstone
Home Secretary: Sir George Grey
Foreign Secretary: Earl of Clarendon
Secretary for War: Earl de Grey and Ripon
Secretary for the Colonies: E. Cardwell
First Lord of the Admiralty: Duke of Somerset
Secretary for India: Sir Charles Wood
Chancellor of the Duchy of Lancaster: Earl of Clarendon
Postmaster-General: Lord Stanley
President of the Poor Law Board: C.P. Villiers

18. Derby's third Cabinet (formed June 1866)

Prime Minister and First Lord of the Treasury: Earl of Derby
Lord Chancellor: Lord Chelmsford
Lord President of the Council: Duke of Buckingham
Lord Privy Seal: Earl of Malmesbury
Chancellor of the Exchequer: Benjamin Disraeli
Home Secretary: Spencer H. Walpole
Foreign Secretary: Lord Stanley
Secretary for War: General Peel
Secretary for the Colonies: Earl of Carnarvon
First Lord of the Admiralty: Sir John Pakington
President of the Board of Trade: Sir Stafford Northcote
Secretary for India: Viscount Cranborne
First Commissioner of Works: Lord John Manners
Chief Secretary for Ireland: Lord Naas (Earl of Mayo 1867)
President of the Poor Law Board: G. Gathorne Hardy

19. Disraeli's first Cabinet (formed Feb. 1868)
Prime Minister and First Lord of the Treasury: Benjamin Disraeli
Lord Chancellor: Lord Chelmsford
Lord President of the Council: Duke of Buckingham
Lord Privy Seal: Earl of Malmesbury
Chancellor of the Exchequer: G. Ward Hunt
Home Secretary: Spencer H. Walpole
Foreign Secretary: Lord Stanley
Secretary for War: General Peel
Secretary for the Colonies: Earl of Carnarvon
First Lord of the Admiralty: Sir John Pakington
President of the Board of Trade: Sir Stafford Northcote
Secretary for India: Viscount Cranborne
First Commissioner of Works: Lord John Manners
President of the Poor Law Board: G. Gathorne Hardy

20. Gladstone's first Cabinet (formed Dec. 1868)
Prime Minister and First Lord of the Treasury: William Ewart Gladstone
Lord Chancellor: Lord Hatherley
Lord President of the Council: Earl de Grey (Marquis of Ripon 1871)
Lord Privy Seal: Earl of Kimberley
Chancellor of the Exchequer: Robert Lowe
Home Secretary: H.A. Bruce
Foreign Secretary: Earl of Clarendon
Secretary for the Colonies: Earl Granville
Secretary of State for War: Edward Cardwell
Secretary for India: Duke of Argyll
First Lord of the Admiralty: H.C.E. Childers
President of the Board of Trade: John Bright
Chief Secretary for Ireland: Chichester Fortescue
Postmaster-General: Marquis of Hartington
President of the Poor Law Board: G.J. Goschen

21. Disraeli's second Cabinet (formed Feb. 1874)
Prime Minister and First Lord of the Treasury: Benjamin Disraeli
Lord Chancellor: Lord Cairns (Earl 1878)
Lord President of the Council: Duke of Richmond
Lord Privy Seal: Earl of Malmesbury
Chancellor of the Exchequer: Sir Stafford Northcote
Home Secretary: R.A. Cross
Foreign Secretary: Earl of Derby
Secretary for the Colonies: Earl of Carnarvon
Secretary for War: G. Gathorne Hardy
Secretary for India: Marquis of Salisbury

First Lord of the Admiralty: G. Ward Hunt
Postmaster-General: Lord John Manners

22. Gladstone's second Cabinet (formed Apr. 1880)

Prime Minister and First Lord of the Treasury ⎱ William Gladstone
Chancellor of the Exchequer ⎰
Lord Chancellor: Lord Selborne (Earl)
Lord President of the Council: Earl Spencer
Lord Privy Seal: Duke of Argyll
Home Secretary: Sir William Vernon Harcourt
Foreign Secretary: Earl Granville
Secretary for the Colonies: Earl of Kimberley
Secretary for War: H.C.E. Childers
Secretary for India: Marquis of Hartington
First Lord of the Admiralty: Earl of Northbrook
President of the Board of Trade: Joseph Chamberlain
President of the Local Government Board: J.G. Dodson
Chief Secretary for Ireland: W.E. Forster
Chancellor of the Duchy of Lancaster: John Bright

23. Lord Salisbury's first Cabinet (formed June 1885)

Prime Minister ⎱ Marquis of Salisbury
Foreign Secretary ⎰
First Lord of the Treasury: Earl of Iddesleigh (Sir Stafford Northcote)
Lord Chancellor: Lord Halsbury (Sir Hardinge Giffard)
Lord President of the Council: Viscount Cranbrook
Lord Privy Seal: Earl of Harrowby
Chancellor of the Exchequer: Sir Michael Hicks Beach
Home Secretary: Sir R.A. Cross
Secretary for the Colonies: Sir F.A. Stanley
Secretary for War: W.H. Smith
Secretary for India: Lord Randolph Churchill
First Lord of the Admiralty: Lord George Hamilton
President of the Board of Trade: Duke of Richmond
Irish Viceroy: Earl of Carnarvon
Postmaster-General: Lord John Manners
Vice-President (Education): Hon.E. Stanhope
Lord Chancellor of Ireland: Lord Ashbourne

24. Gladstone's third Cabinet (formed Feb. 1886)

Prime Minister and First Lord of the Treasury ⎱ William Gladstone
Lord Privy Seal ⎰
Lord Chancellor: Lord (Sir Farrer) Herschell
Lord President of the Council: Earl Spencer

Chancellor of the Exchequer: Sir William Vernon Harcourt
Home Secretary: H.C.E. Childers
Foreign Secretary: Earl of Rosebery
Secretary for the Colonies: Earl Granville
Secretary for War: Henry Campbell-Bannerman
Secretary for India: Earl of Kimberley
Secretary for Scotland: George Trevelyan
Chief Secretary for Ireland: John Morley
First Lord of the Admiralty: Marquis of Ripon
President of the Board of Trade: A.J. Mundella
President of the Local Government Board: Joseph Chamberlain

25. Lord Salisbury's second Cabinet (formed Aug. 1886)

Prime Minister and First Lord of the Treasury: Marquis of Salisbury
Lord Chancellor: Lord Halsbury
Lord President of the Council: Viscount Cranbrook
Chancellor of the Exchequer: Lord Randolph Churchill
Home Secretary: Henry Matthews
Foreign Secretary: Earl of Iddesleigh
Secretary for the Colonies: Hon. Edward Stanhope
Secretary for War: W.H. Smith
Secretary for India: Viscount Cross
Chief Secretary for Ireland: Sir Michael Hicks Beach
First Lord of the Admiralty: Lord George Hamilton
President of the Board of Trade: Lord Stanley
Chancellor of the Duchy of Lancaster: Lord John Manners
Lord Chancellor of Ireland: Lord Ashbourne

26. Gladstone's fourth Cabinet (formed Aug. 1892)

Prime Minister and First Lord of the Treasury ⎫
Lord Privy Seal ⎬ William Gladstone

Lord Chancellor: Lord Herschell
Lord President of the Council ⎫
Secretary for India ⎬ Earl of Kimberley

Chancellor of the Exchequer: Sir William Harcourt
Home Secretary: Herbert Henry Asquith
Foreign Secretary: Earl of Rosebery
Secretary for the Colonies: Marquis of Ripon
Secretary for War: Henry Campbell-Bannerman
Secretary for Scotland: Sir George Trevelyan
Chief Secretary for Ireland: John Morley
First Lord of the Admiralty: Earl Spencer
President of the Board of Trade: A.J. Mundella
President of the Local Government Board: H.H. Fowler

Chancellor of the Duchy of Lancaster: James Bryce
Vice-President (Education): A.H.D. Acland
First Commissioner of Works: G.J. Shaw-Lefevre
Postmaster-General: Arnold Morley

27. Lord Rosebery's Cabinet (formed Mar. 1894)

Prime Minister and First Lord of the Treasury ⎱
Lord President of the Council ⎰ Earl of Rosebery

Lord Chancellor: Lord Herschell

Lord Privy Seal ⎱
Chancellor of the Duchy of Lancaster ⎰ Lord Tweedmouth

Chancellor of the Exchequer: Sir William Vernon Harcourt
Home Secretary: Herbert Asquith
Foreign Secretary: Earl of Kimberley
Secretary for the Colonies: Marquis of Ripon
Secretary for War: Henry Campbell-Bannerman
Secretary for India: H.H. Fowler
Secretary for Scotland: Sir G.O. Trevelyan
Chief Secretary for Ireland: John Morley
First Lord of the Admiralty: Earl Spencer
President of the Board of Trade: James Bryce
President of the Local Government Board: G.J. Shaw-Lefevre
Vice-President (Education): A.H.D. Acland
Postmaster-General: Arnold Morley

28. Lord Salisbury's third Cabinet (formed June 1895)

Prime Minister and Foreign Secretary: Marquis of Salisbury
First Lord of the Treasury: Arthur James Balfour
Lord Chancellor: Earl of Halsbury
Lord President of the Council: Duke of Devonshire
Lord Privy Seal: Viscount Cross
Chancellor of the Exchequer: Sir Michael Hicks Beach
Home Secretary: Sir Matthew White Ridley
Secretary for the Colonies: Joseph Chamberlain
Secretary for War: Marquis of Lansdowne
Secretary for India: Lord George Hamilton
Secretary for Scotland: Lord Balfour of Burleigh
Irish Viceroy: Earl Cadogan
First Lord of the Admiralty: George Goschen
Chancellor of the Duchy of Lancaster: Lord James of Hereford
President of the Board of Trade: C.T. Ritchie
President of the Local Government Board: Henry Chaplin
President of the Board of Agriculture: Walter Long
Lord Chancellor of Ireland: Lord Ashbourne
Commissioner for Works: A. Akers-Douglas

29. Balfour's Cabinet (formed July 1902)
Prime Minister and First Lord of the Treasury: Arthur Balfour
Lord Chancellor: Earl of Halsbury
Lord President of the Council: Duke of Devonshire
Lord Privy Seal
President of the Board of Education } Marquis of Londonderry
Chancellor of the Exchequer: C.T. Ritchie
Home Secretary: A. Akers-Douglas
Foreign Secretary: Marquis of Lansdowne
Secretary for the Colonies: Joseph Chamberlain
Secretary for War: Hon. St. John Brodrick
Secretary for India: Lord George Hamilton
Secretary for Scotland: Lord Balfour of Burleigh
Chief Secretary for Ireland: George Wyndham
First Lord of the Admiralty: Earl of Selborne
Chancellor of the Duchy of Lancaster: Lord James of Hereford
President of the Board of Trade: George Balfour
President of the Local Government Board: Walter Long
President of the Board of Agriculture: R.W. Hanbury
Lord Chancellor of Ireland: Lord Ashbourne
First Commissioner of Works: Lord Windsor (Earl of Plymouth)
Postmaster-General: Austen Chamberlain

30. Campbell-Bannerman's Cabinet (formed Dec. 1905)
Prime Minister and First Lord of the Treasury: Sir Henry Campbell-Bannerman
Lord Chancellor: Lord Loreburn
Lord President of the Council: Earl of Crewe
Lord Privy Seal: Marquis of Ripon
Chancellor of the Exchequer: Herbert Asquith
Home Secretary: Herbert J. Gladstone
Foreign Secretary: Sir Edward Grey
Secretary for the Colonies: Earl of Elgin
Secretary for War: Richard Haldane
Secretary for India: John Morley
Secretary for Scotland: John Sinclair
Chief Secretary for Ireland: James Bryce
First Lord of the Admiralty: Lord Tweedmouth
Chancellor of the Duchy of Lancaster: Sir Henry H. Fowler
President of the Board of Trade: David Lloyd George
President of the Local Government Board: John Burns
President of the Board of Agriculture: Earl Carrington
President of the Board of Education: Augustine Birrell
Postmaster-General: Sydney Buxton

31. Asquith's first Cabinet (formed Apr. 1908)

Prime Minister and First Lord of the Treasury: Herbert Asquith
Lord Chancellor: Lord (Earl) Loreburn
Lord President of the Council: Lord Tweedmouth
Lord Privy Seal: Marquis of Ripon
Chancellor of the Exchequer: David Lloyd George
Home Secretary: Herbert J. Gladstone
Foreign Secretary: Sir Edward Grey
Secretary for the Colonies: Earl of Crewe
Secretary for War: Richard (Viscount) Haldane
Secretary for India: Viscount (John) Morley
Secretary for Scotland: John Sinclair (Lord Pentland)
Chief Secretary for Ireland: Augustine Birrell
First Lord of the Admiralty: Reginald McKenna
Chancellor of the Duchy of Lancaster: Sir H.H. Fowler (Viscount
    Wolverhampton)
President of the Board of Trade: Winston S. Churchill
President of the Local Government Board: John Burns
President of the Board of Agriculture: Earl Carrington
President of the Board of Education: Walter Runciman
Postmaster-General: Sydney Buxton
First Commissioner of Works: Lewis Vernon Harcourt

Chronology of major Cabinet changes

1816 George Canning became President of Board of Control (June).
1818 F.J. Robinson entered Cabinet (President of the Board of Trade and Treasurer of the Navy) (Jan.).
1821 C.B. Bathurst became President of Board of Control (Jan.).
1822 Robert Peel became Home Secretary (Jan.).
   Canning appointed Foreign Secretary (Sept.).
1823 Robinson replaced Vansittart as Chancellor of the Exchequer (Jan.).
   Huskisson became President of the Board of Trade.
1827 Marquis of Lansdowne became Home Secretary (July).
1828 Earl of Aberdeen became Foreign Secretary (June).
1831 Lord John Russell became Paymaster-General and E.G. Stanley became Chief Secretary for Ireland (both entering Cabinet) (June).
1833 Stanley became Secretary for War and Colonies (Mar.).
1839 Sir F.T. Baring became Chancellor of the Exchequer; H. Labouchere became President of the Board of Trade (Aug.).
1843 Gladstone became President of the Board of Trade (May).
1845 Sidney Herbert became Secretary at War (May).
   Gladstone became Secretary for War and Colonies (Dec.).
1851 Granville succeeded Palmerston as Foreign Secretary (Dec.).
1853 Russell resigned as Foreign Secretary (but remained in Cabinet); Earl of Clarendon became Foreign Secretary (Feb.).
1855 Resignation of Russell (Jan.).
   Resignations of Gladstone, Herbert and Graham (Feb.).
   Labouchere became Colonial Secretary (Oct.).
1861 Sir George Grey became Home Secretary.
1864 Edward Cardwell became Colonial Secretary.
1867 Resignations of the Earl of Carnarvon, General Peel and Viscount Cranborne (Mar.).
   Gathorne Hardy became Home Secretary (May).
1870 W.E. Forster (Education) entered Cabinet; Lord Granville became Foreign Secretary (July); John Bright resigned as President of the Board of Trade (Dec.).

1873   Robert Lowe succeeded Bruce as Home Secretary.
        Gladstone combined Chancellorship of the Exchequer with his
        post as Prime Minister.
1876   Benjamin Disraeli took additional post of Lord Privy Seal,
        entering the Lords as Earl of Beaconsfield.
1878   Lord Salisbury succeeded Lord Derby as Foreign Secretary.
1882   Childers succeeded Gladstone as Chancellor of the Exchequer
        (Dec.). Kimberley went to India Office, Lord Derby became
        Colonial Secretary.
1886   W.H. Smith became Chief Secretary for Ireland (Jan.). Resigna-
        tion of Joseph Chamberlain and George Trevelyan (Apr.).
1887   George Goschen succeeded Randolph Churchill as Chancellor
        of the Exchequer (Jan.). Lord Salisbury became Foreign
        Secretary (Jan.). G.W. Balfour appointed Chief Secretary for
        Ireland (Mar.).
1900   Lord Lansdowne succeeded Lord Salisbury at Foreign Office
        (Oct.). C.T. Ritchie succeeded Ridley as Home Secretary.
1903   Resignation of Joseph Chamberlain; Alfred Lyttelton became
        Colonial Secretary (Sept.). Austen Chamberlain became Chan-
        cellor of the Exchequer.
1905   Walter Long succeeded George Wyndham as Chief Secretary
        for Ireland.
1907   Birrell succeeded Bryce as Chief Secretary for Ireland.
1908   Sir Henry Fowler (created Viscount Wolverhampton) became
        Lord President of the Council (Sept.).
1910   Winston Churchill succeeded Herbert Gladstone as Home Sec-
        retary (Feb.); Sydney Buxton went to Board of Trade.
1911   Winston Churchill became First Lord of the Admiralty; Reginald
        McKenna became Home Secretary (Oct.).
1912   Haldane became Lord Chancellor (June); Seely became Sec-
        retary for War.
1914   John Burns succeeded Buxton as President of the Board of
        Trade (Feb.). Asquith combined War Office with Premiership
        (Mar.). Resignations of Lord Morley and John Burns on out-
        break of war (Aug.). Asquith gave up War Office, Lord Kitchener
        became Secretary for War.

House of Commons

Parliamentary reform

Prior to the 1832 Reform Act, politics in Britain was dominated by a narrow, landed elite, reflected in the structure of Parliament. The House of Lords was composed of the hereditary peerage, while the Commons was composed of 431 borough and 122 county members. Only a twentieth of the adult population could vote and qualifications varied widely. Some decayed towns had only a handful of electors, but were still represented by two MPs. Others, such as Westminster, had thousands of electors on a wide franchise. Many large manufacturing towns, such as Birmingham and Manchester, were unrepresented. All English counties sent two members to Parliament, irrespective of size. Electoral politics were often corrupt, with widespread bribery and huge election costs for the candidates. Many 'pocket' boroughs remained virtually nominated seats. In 1820 144 peers controlled 300 MPs. Cornwall was notorious for 'rotten boroughs' with many under Crown influence and small numbers of voters. 'Connections' of patronage and influence under noble patrons were the dominant political groupings for much of the period. The Act of Union with Ireland in 1800 brought 100 Irish MPs to the Commons.

The first step towards parliamentary reform occurred with the 1832 Reform Act. Though this Act made only fractional extensions to the franchise, and only removed some of the worst of the abuses of the old rotten boroughs, it was important in that it marked the first change in the old system. Some 143 seats were disfranchised, including the more notorious rotten boroughs, and the new manufacturing areas were represented for the first time. Thus representation in Cornwall was much reduced, while in Lancashire it was greatly increased.

Far more important in the path to parliamentary democracy were the Reform Acts of 1867 and 1884, together with the 1872 Ballot Act. After 1867, with the 'leap in the dark', the proportion of adults able to vote rose to 16 per cent. Further extension of the franchise occurred, to the rural labourers in 1884, and to universal adult male suffrage in 1918.

The franchise (prior to 1832)

England and Wales: In the counties the voting qualification was the possession of freehold property valued for the land tax at 40 shillings per annum – the 40s freeholder. In the boroughs various qualifications applied. The main types were:

1. Scot and lot: right of voting vested in inhabitant householders paying poor rate.
2. Householder or 'potwalloper': right of voting vested in all inhabitant householders not receiving alms or poor relief.
3. Burgage: voting rights attached to property in the borough.
4. Corporation: right of voting confined to the corporation.
5. Freeman: right of voting rested in the freemen of the borough.
6. Freeholder: right of voting lay with the freeholders.

English boroughs

Electors	SL	H	B	C	FM	FH	Total
Over 5,000	1	1	–	–	5	–	7
1,001–5,000	6	2	–	–	24	4	36
601–1,000	7	5	–	–	9	1	22
301–600	10	1	–	–	13	–	24
101–300	8	5	10	1	11	1	36
51–100	4	–	10	2	5	–	21
50 or fewer	2	–	15	26	13	–	56
Total	38	14	35	29	80	6	202

Note: SL–Scot and lot; H–Householder; B–Burgage; C–Corporation; FM–Freeman; FH–Freeholder.

Scotland: In the Scottish counties the franchise belonged to freeholders possessing land valued at 40s 'of old extent' or to owners of land rated at £400 Scots (*c.* £35 sterling). In Sutherland the vote also extended to tenants of the Earl of Sutherland. The Scottish boroughs, or burghs, were combined in groups for the purpose of electing MPs by a process of indirect election. Voting was vested in the small burgh councils.

The composition of the House of Commons in 1815

Constituencies	MPs
English boroughs	
196 boroughs each returning 2 members	392
5 boroughs each returning 1 member	5

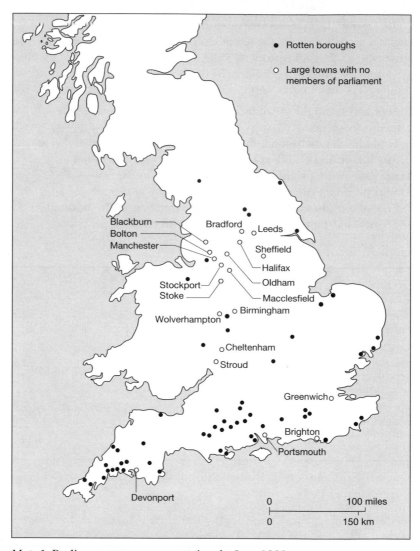

• Rotten boroughs

o Large towns with no
  members of parliament

Blackburn
Bolton
Manchester
Bradford
Leeds
Sheffield
Halifax
Stockport
Stoke
Oldham
Macclesfield
Wolverhampton
Birmingham
Cheltenham
Stroud
Greenwich
Brighton
Portsmouth
Devonport

| 0 | | 100 miles |
| 0 | | 150 km |

Map 1: Parliamentary representation before 1832
Source: C. Cook and J. Stevenson, *Longman Atlas of Modern British History* (1978), p. 162.

2 boroughs (City of London and Weymouth)
each returning 4 members   8

English counties
40 counties each returning 2 members   80

English universities
2 universities each returning 2 members   4

Welsh boroughs
5 boroughs each returning 1 member   5
7 groups of boroughs each returning 1 member   7

Welsh counties
12 counties each returning 1 member   12

Scottish burghs
15 burghs each returning 1 member   15

Scottish counties
27 counties each returning 1 member   27
6 counties, grouped in pairs, 1 of each pair
alternately returning 1 member   3

Total constituencies 314   *Total MPs* 558

As a result of the Act of Union in 1800, 100 extra members representing
Ireland were added to the existing members of the House of Commons.

The Reform Crisis: background to events

1812   London Hampden Club founded to promote cause of parlia-
        mentary reform.
1816   Cobbett produced first cheap edition of the *Political Register*,
        disseminating reform ideas among the poorer classes. Spa Fields
        meetings in London addressed by Henry Hunt; petition for
        reform.
1817   Convention of reformers in London. Burdett's motion for reform
        defeated in the House of Commons.
1818   Sir Robert Heron's motion for triennial parliaments defeated
        in the House of Commons. Burdett's motions for annual parlia-
        ments, manhood suffrage, secret ballot and equal electoral dis-
        tricts defeated by 106 votes to nil.
1819   Reform meetings at Birmingham, Stockport and Manchester.
        Meeting at St Peter's Fields (Peterloo) broken up by magistrates
        and troops. Henry Hunt arrested. Widespread protests.

1821   Seats of Grampound transferred to Yorkshire. Lord Durham's
        Bill advocating triennial parliaments, equal electoral districts
        and ratepayer franchise defeated.
1822   Lord John Russell's motion to redistribute 100 members from
        the smallest boroughs defeated. County meetings organised by
        leading Whigs to promote cause of reform.
1826   Further reform proposals by Russell defeated in the House of
        Commons.
1827   Bill to redistribute seats of Penryn to Manchester and Birming-
        ham defeated by the House of Lords.
For a detailed chronology of 1828–32 see p. 5.

The Reform Act of 1832

1. Disfranchisement clauses
  (a) 56 nomination or rotten boroughs returning 111 members of
      parliament lost representation.
  (b) 30 boroughs with less than 4,000 inhabitants lost 1 member of
      parliament each.
  (c) Weymouth and Melcombe Regis gave up 2 of their 4 members.
      143 seats made available for redistribution.

2. Enfranchisement
  (a) 65 seats awarded to the counties.
  (b) 44 seats distributed to 22 large towns, including Birmingham,
      Manchester, Leeds, Sheffield and the new London metropolitan
      districts.
  (c) 21 smaller towns given 1 member each.
  (d) Scotland awarded 8 extra seats.
  (c) Ireland given 5 extra seats.

3. Franchise qualifications
  (a) Borough franchise regularised, right of voting vested in all house-
      holders paying a yearly rental of £10 and, subject to one-year
      residence qualification, £10 lodgers (if sharing a house and the
      landlord not in occupation).
  (b) In the counties, franchise granted to 40s freeholders; £10
      copyholders; £50 tenants; £10 long leaseholders; £50 medium
      leaseholders. Borough freeholders could vote in counties if their
      freehold was between 40s and £10, or if it was over £10 and
      occupied by a tenant.

New boroughs with two seats: Sunderland, Blackburn, Bolton, Oldham,
Halifax, Bradford, Leeds, Manchester, Sheffield, Macclesfield, Stoke,
Wolverhampton, Birmingham, Stroud, Marylebone, Tower Hamlets, Green-
wich, Lambeth, Finsbury, Brighton, Devonport.

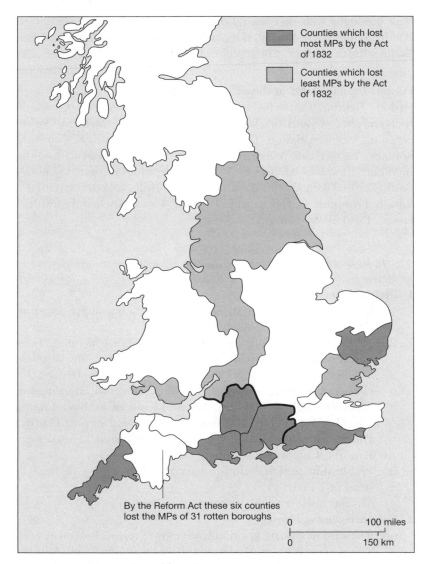

Counties which lost
most MPs by the Act
of 1832

Counties which lost
least MPs by the Act
of 1832

By the Reform Act these six counties
lost the MPs of 31 rotten boroughs

| 0 | | 100 miles |
| 0 | | 150 km |

Map 2: The Reform Act of 1832
Source: C. Cook and J. Stevenson, *Longman Atlas of Modern British History* (1978), p. 162.

New boroughs with one seat: Tynemouth, South Shields, Gateshead, Whitby, Whitehaven, Kendal, Bury, Salford, Ashton, Warrington, Walsall, Dudley, Kidderminster, Cheltenham, Frome, Chatham, Stockport.

Existing boroughs disfranchised: Appleby, Boroughbridge, Aldborough, Hedon, Newton, Castle Rising, Dunwich, Aldeburgh, Bishops Castle, Higham Ferrers, Orford, Brackley, Weobley, Wendover, Amersham, Queensborough, Wootton Bassett, Gatton, Bletchingley, Bedwyn, E. Grinstead, Romney, Ludgershall, Whitchurch, Haslemere, Winchelsea, Steyning, Bramber, Downton, Milbourne Port, Minehead, Newtown, Yarmouth, Corfe Castle, Okehampton, Bossiney, Camelford, Newport, Callington, Saltash, Plympton, St. Germans, E. Looe, W. Looe, Mitchell, Lostwithiel, Fowey, Tregony, St. Mawes.

The Reform Act of 1867 (and Scotland, 1868)

1. **Disfranchisement clauses**
   (a) 6 boroughs returning 2 members and 5 boroughs returning 1 member totally disfranchised.
   (b) 35 boroughs returning 2 members deprived of 1 member. These were: Andover; Bodmin; Bridgnorth; Bridport; Buckingham; Chichester; Chippenham; Cirencester; Cockermouth; Devizes; Dorchester; Evesham; Guildford; Harwich; Hertford; Huntingdon; Knaresborough; Leominster; Lewes; Lichfield; Ludlow; Lymington; Maldon; Malton, Marlborough; Marlow; Newport (I.o.W.); Poole; Richmond (Yorks.); Ripon; Stamford; Tavistock; Tewkesbury; Windsor; Chipping Wycombe.
   (c) Peeblesshire and Selkirkshire to return 1 member conjointly instead of 1 each.
   53 seats made available for redistribution.
2. **Enfranchisement clauses**
   (a) 9 new boroughs and London University to return 1 member each. These were: Burnley; Darlington; Dewsbury; Gravesend; Middlesbrough; Stalybridge; Stockton; The Hartlepools; Wednesbury.
   (b) 5 seats awarded to increase representation of Leeds, Liverpool, Birmingham, Manchester (from 2 seats to 3) and Salford (from 1 seat to 2).
   (c) Chelsea and Hackney each created 2-member seats.
   (d) 25 seats awarded to the English counties.
   (e) 1 extra seat awarded to Wales (Merthyr Tydfil became 2-member seat).
   (f) 5 additional seats awarded to Scottish burghs.
   (g) 3 extra seats awarded to Scottish counties.

3. Franchise qualifications

(a) Borough franchise extended to all householders paying rates and to lodgers paying a rental of £10, subject to a one-year residence qualification.

(b) County franchise extended to occupiers of property rated at £12 a year (£14 in Scotland) and to those with lands worth £5 a year.

The Reform and Redistribution Acts of 1884–85

1. Disfranchisement clauses

(a) 13 boroughs returning 2 members and 66 boroughs returning 1 member in England and Wales merged in the counties.

(b) 36 boroughs returning 2 members in England and Wales deprived of 1 member.

(c) Two 2-member boroughs, Macclesfield and Sandwich, disfranchised.

(d) 2 boroughs returning 1 member each in Scotland merged in the counties.

(e) 22 boroughs returning 1 member each in Ireland merged in the counties.

(f) 3 boroughs returning 2 members each in Ireland deprived of 1 member.

138 seats made available for redistribution.

2. Enfranchisement clauses

(a) London (including Croydon) to return 62 members instead of 22.

(b) 26 seats added to provincial English boroughs.

(c) 6 new provincial boroughs created in England and Wales returning 1 member each.

(d) 66 additional members allocated to English and Welsh counties.

(e) 7 seats added to Scottish counties.

(f) 7 seats added to Aberdeen, Edinburgh and Glasgow.

(g) 21 extra seats allocated to Irish counties.

(h) 4 seats allocated to Belfast and Dublin.

3. Franchise qualifications

The Representation of the People Act 1884 created a uniform franchise in both boroughs and counties of the United Kingdom on the basis of the 1867 borough franchise, to include:

(a) householders, subject to a one-year residential qualification and payment of rates;

(b) lodgers who occupied lodgings worth £10 a year, subject to a one-year residential qualification;

(c) an occupation franchise for those with lands or tenements worth £10 a year.

Representation of major towns after 1885

After 1885 the following towns returned more than one member each. All other towns returned a single member each.

England

Four or more members:
London (61); Liverpool (9); Birmingham (7); Manchester (6); Sheffield (5); Leeds (5); Bristol (4).

Three members:
Bradford; Hull; Nottingham; Salford; Wolverhampton.

Two members:
Bath; Blackburn; Bolton; Brighton; Devonport; Derby; Halifax; Ipswich; Leicester; Newcastle; Northampton; Norwich; Oldham; Plymouth; Portsmouth; Preston; Southampton; Stockport; Sunderland; York.

Ireland
Belfast (4); Cork (2); Dublin (4).

Scotland
Aberdeen (2); Dundee (2); Edinburgh (4); Glasgow (7).

Wales
Merthyr Tydfil (2).

The changing membership of the House of Commons, 1832–85

1832–44	658	
1844–52	656	(Sudbury disfranchised in 1844)
1852–61	654	(St Albans disfranchised in 1852)
1861–65	656	(2 seats allocated to Birkenhead and Southern Lancashire in 1861)
1865–70	658	(2 seats allocated to Yorkshire West Riding in 1865)
1870–85	652	(disfranchisement of Beverley (2), Bridgwater (2), Cashel and Sligo, 6 seats in all)
1885	648	(disfranchisement of Macclesfield (2) and Sandwich (2))

By the 1885 Redistribution of Seats Act, the number of MPs was increased to 670, remaining at this level until the First World War.

House of Lords

Lord Chancellor (Speaker of the House of Lords)

For list of Lord Chancellors, see pp. 31–2.

Lord Chairmen of Committees

(*Deputy Speaker of the House of Lords; the Lord Chancellor is the Speaker*)
1814	Earl of Shaftesbury
1851	Lord Redesdale
1886	Duke of Buckingham and Chandos
1890	Earl of Morley
1905	Earl of Onslow
1911	Earl of Donoughmore

Note: For Party Leaders in the House of Lords, see p. 94 for Conservatives and p. 99 for Liberals.

Composition of the House of Lords 1830–1900

Year	Peers of royal blood	Dukes	Marquises	Earls	Viscounts	Barons	Archbishops & bishops	Irish representative prelates	Irish representative peers	Scottish representative peers	Total entitled to vote
1830	4	19	18	103 (1)	22	160	26	4	28	16	399
1837	3	21	19 (1)	112 (2)	19	193 (11)	26	4	28	16	421
1840	3	21	20 (1)	114 (3)	20	211 (7)	26	16	28	16	448
1845	3 (1)	20	20 (2)	115 (3)	21	200 (10)	26	4	28	16	434
1850	3 (1)	20 (1)	21 (3)	116 (2)	22 (1)	199 (5)	26	4	28	16	441
1855	3 (1)	20 (1)	21 (2)	112 (3)	22 (1)	196 (6)	26	4	28	16	433
1860	3 (1)	20 (2)	21 (2)	110 (5)	22 (1)	210 (5)	26	4	28	16	443
1865	3	20 (2)	19 (1)	109 (8)	21	207 (8)	26	4	28	16	434
1870	4	20	18	110 (4)	23	230 (9)	26	–	28	16	462
1875	5	21	18 (1)	111 (2)	24	244 (12)	26	–	28	16	478
1880	4	22 (1)	19 (1)	118 (3)	25 (1)	254 (6)	26	–	28	16	500
1885	5 (1)	22	20 (1)	119 (7)	28	277 (5)	26	–	28	16	526
1890	6 (1)	22	21 (1)	119 (3)	28 (1)	288 (6)	26	–	28	16	539
1895	6 (1)	22 (1)	22	121 (3)	29 (2)	308 (8)	26	–	28	16	561
1900	5 (1)	22	22 (1)	123 (1)	30 (4)	321 (7)	26	–	28	16	577

Note: Figures in brackets indicate minors.
Sources: Oliver & Boyd's *Edinburgh Almanac* for 1837 etc.; Royal Calendar, 1831 (for 1830 figures).

Chronology of key dates

1821	House of Lords defeated Bill to remove Catholic disabilities (Apr.).
1825	Roman Catholic Relief Bill rejected by Lords (May).
1828	Catholic Emancipation Bill passed Commons but defeated in Lords (May).
1829	Duke of Norfolk took his seat in the Lords (the first Roman Catholic under the Relief Bill).
1831	Lords rejected the Reform Bill (7 Oct.).
1832	Lords passed Reform Bill (4 June).
1856	Lords rejected attempt to introduce life peerages.
1858	Baron Rothschild first Jew admitted (26 July).
1868	Standing order abolished voting by proxy in Lords (31 Mar.).
1871	Act prohibited bankrupt peers from sitting or voting in Lords.
1872	Peers not permitted to vote in election of MPs (confirmed by case on appeal to Court of Common Pleas).
1876	Two life peers created (Lords Blackburn and Gordon) as Lords of Appeal in Ordinary.
1884	Conflict with Commons over Franchise Bill (July).
1886	Proposal to abolish hereditary principle defeated in Commons by 202–166 (5 Mar.).
1888	Second proposal to abolish hereditary principle defeated in Commons by 223–162 (9 Mar.).
1889	Proposal defeated again in Commons by 201–160 (May).
1890	Proposal further defeated by 201–139 (21 Mar.).
1893	Irish Home Rule Bill rejected by the Lords by 419–41 (Sept.).
1894	Conflict with Liberal Government over Employers' Liability Bill and Local Government Bill.
1895–1906	After fall of Liberal government, period of quiet in Lords' relations with Commons.
1906	Rosebery Committee Report recommended reform and reconstruction of House of Lords. No action taken on proposed reforms. Lords refused second reading for Licensing Bill by 272–96 (Nov.).
1909	Lords created crisis by rejecting second reading of Finance Bill (Lloyd George's People's Budget) by 370–75 on 30 Nov.
1911	Narrow vote in favour of Parliament Bill by 131–114 (10 Aug.). Under Parliament Act, all Bills certified by the Speaker of the House of Commons as Money Bills were to receive the Royal Assent one month after being sent to the House of Lords. In addition, any other Public Bill (except one for extending the life of a Parliament) passed by the

House of Commons in three successive sessions and rejected by the House of Lords, was nevertheless to receive the Royal Assent, provided that two years had elapsed between the second reading in the first session and the third reading in the third session of the House of Commons.

1913–14   Lords repeatedly rejected Government of Ireland Bill (Jan. and July), Disestablishment of Welsh Church Bill (Feb. and July) and Plural Voting Bill (July 1913 and July 1914).

Elections and party politics

The electorate

	Electorate (000)		Population (000)	
	England and Wales	UK	England and Wales	UK
1831	435	516	14,000	24,000
1833	700	813	14,000	24,000
1866	1,000	1,310	22,000	31,000
1868	2,000	2,500	22,000	31,000
1883	2,600	3,100	26,000	35,000
1885	4,400	5,600	27,000	36,000

Percentage of all adults (male and female) entitled to vote (approx.)

	(%)
1831	5
1833	7
1867	16
1884	$28\frac{1}{2}$
1918	74

Adult males able to vote

	England and Wales	Scotland	Ireland
1833	1 in 5	1 in 8	1 in 20
1869	1 in 3	1 in 3	1 in 6
1885	2 in 3	3 in 5	1 in 2

Legislation governing parliamentary representation and the conduct of elections, 1828–1918

1828   Polling limited in boroughs to 8 days. Several polling places to be provided where necessary.

1832   First Reform Act (for detailed franchise and redistribution provisions, see pp. 60–2). Time allowed for polling in each constituency reduced to 2 days (after 1853 reduced to 1 day in the boroughs); general elections still to take place over the course of a fortnight. Electoral register introduced.

1854   Corrupt Practices Prevention Act. Sponsored by Lord John Russell, the Act levied small fines for bribery, cheating and the use of undue influence and intimidation. The Act also contained another innovation: the election accounts. In future every candidate was to publish itemised accounts of his expenditure which an election auditor might inspect. However, the auditors possessed no powers of investigation, and they were unable therefore to prevent evasion of these terms of the Act.

1863   Office of election auditor replaced by that of returning officer.

1867   Representation of the People Act (for detailed franchise and redistribution provisions, see pp. 62–3).

1868   Parliamentary Elections Act transferred jurisdiction over disputed elections from selected committees of the House of Commons to the judges in the high court. Penalties for bribery strengthened.

1872   Ballot Act introduced voting by secret ballot and increased the number of polling places.

1878   The registration system in the English boroughs was reformed to improve the work of the overseers in compiling the original register, to minimise objections, and to assimilate the parliamentary and municipal electoral rolls. In some boroughs this reform did more to increase the electorate than the extension of the franchise had done in 1867.

1883   The Corrupt and Illegal Practices Act, 1883, was the first really effective measure against electoral corruption. The Act had two main objects: to lessen election expenditure and to make the penalties for corrupt practices much more severe. The first object was achieved by a list of maximum election expenses for various types of constituency. The number of clerks, messengers and committee rooms that might be employed was regulated on the same principle. More severe penalties were also introduced: all those found guilty by an election court of corrupt practices faced one year's imprisonment (with the option of hard labour) and a fine of £200; candidates found guilty of corrupt practices were to suffer perpetual exclusion from the constituency concerned, withdrawal of voting rights, and exclusion from the House of Commons and from all public and judicial offices for seven years.

1884   Representation of the People Act (for detailed provisions, see p. 63).

1885   Redistribution of Seats Act (for detailed provisions, see p. 63).

1918   Representation of the People Act. Vote given to all men over 21 and to women over 30 if they were ratepayers or wives of ratepayers.

General elections

Prior to 1832, the computation of election results is complicated by the vagueness of party lines, the number of uncontested elections and the presence of 'independent' candidates. All of these factors continued to operate to a greater or lesser degree after 1832, but the Reform Act of 1832 has generally been taken as the point from which an overall assessment of election results can be made in two-party terms.

The terms 'Conservative' (Tory) and 'Liberal' (Whig) represented for much of the nineteenth century only imprecise descriptions of political allegiance and cannot be regarded in the same way as the more definitive party labels of the twentieth century. For the complexity of political and party allegiance in the aftermath of the 1832 Reform Act, see N. Gash, *Reaction and Reconstruction in English Politics, 1832–52*, Oxford, 1965. The fullest reference source for election results in this period is F.W.S. Craig, *British Parliamentary Election Results, Volume 1: 1832–1885*, London, 1977.

Individual election results

1832   The election followed the extension of the franchise by the
         1832 Reform Act.

Seats

Conservatives (Tories)	179
Liberals (Whigs)	479
Total	658

Seats won by area

	Lib.	Con.
England:		
Counties	104	40
Boroughs & Univ.	244	83
Wales:		
Counties	6	9
Boroughs	10	4
Scotland:		
Counties	21	9
Burghs & Univ.	22	1
Ireland:		
Counties	45	19
Boroughs & Univ.	27	14
Totals:		
England	348	123
Wales	16	13
Scotland	43	10
Ireland	72	33
Total	479	179

1835   Melbourne refused to serve as Prime Minister without Lord
        Althorp (who in November 1834 was elevated to the House of
        Lords as 3rd Earl Spencer) to lead in the Commons. His only
        alternative suggestion to Althorp was Lord John Russell, whom
        the King would not accept. Consequently, Melbourne offered
        his resignation and William IV accepted it. Peel took office with
        a minority government. Eager to consolidate his party support
        and to show Conservative acceptance of the 1832 Reform Act,
        he decided to go to the country after three defeats in the House
        on the Irish Tithe Bill.

Seats

Conservatives	275
Liberals	383
Total	658

Seats won by area

	Lib.	Con.
England:		
Counties	74	70
Boroughs & Univ.	192	135
Wales:		
Counties	6	9
Boroughs	6	8
Scotland:		
Counties	16	14
Burghs & Univ.	22	1
Ireland:		
Counties	41	23
Boroughs & Univ.	26	15
Totals:		
England	266	205
Wales	12	17
Scotland	38	15
Ireland	67	38
Total	383	275

1837   By law Parliament had to dissolve within six months of the death of the monarch, in this case William IV.

Seats

Conservatives	309
Liberals	349
Total	658

Seats won by area

	Lib.	Con.
England:		
Counties	47	97
Boroughs & Univ.	185	142
Wales:		
Counties	3	12
Boroughs	8	6
Scotland:		
Counties	11	19
Burghs & Univ.	22	1
Ireland:		
Counties	44	20
Boroughs & Univ.	29	12
Totals:		
England	232	239
Wales	11	18
Scotland	33	20
Ireland	73	32
Total	349	309

1841   The Whig government, aware it was losing the confidence of the country, decided to go to the polls on what it hoped was a popular platform: vote by ballot and repeal of the Corn Laws.

Seats

Conservatives	368
Liberals	290
Total	658

Seats won by area

	Lib.	Con.
England:		
Counties	20	124
Boroughs & Univ.	167	160
Wales:		
Counties	3	12
Boroughs	7	7
Scotland:		
Counties	10	20
Burghs & Univ.	21	2
Ireland:		
Counties	39	25
Boroughs & Univ.	23	18
Totals:		
England	187	284
Wales	10	19
Scotland	31	22
Ireland	62	43
Total	290	368

1847   Peel resigned from office following the defeat of an Irish 'coercion' Bill, though a more significant factor in his departure was the opposition of the Tory Protectionists to his repeal of the Corn Laws in 1846.

Seats

Conservatives	327[1]
(Peelites and Protectionists)	
Liberals	329
Total	656[2]

Seats won by area

	Lib.	Con.
England:		
Counties	36	108
Boroughs & Univ.	186	139
Wales:		
Counties	3	12
Boroughs	7	7
Scotland:		
Counties	12	18
Burghs & Univ.	22	1
Ireland:		
Counties	37	27
Boroughs	26	15
Totals:		
England	222	247
Wales	10	19
Scotland	34	19
Ireland	63	42
Total	329	327

[1] Of the Conservatives about 225 were Protectionists and 100 were Peelites.

[2] In 1844 Sudbury was disfranchised for corruption, and thus the total number of MPs reduced from 658 to 656.

1852   Derby's insistence that the Conservative Party adhere to Protection weakened the position of the government. Following a powerful attack by Gladstone on Disraeli's Budget the government was defeated and resigned. Dissolution followed.

Seats

Conservatives (including Peelites)	331
Liberals	323
Total	654

Seats won by area

	Lib.	Con.
England:		
Counties	29	115
Boroughs & Univ.	187	136
Wales:		
Counties	4	11
Boroughs	7	7
Scotland:		
Counties	11	19
Burghs & Univ.	22	1
Ireland:		
Counties	39	25
Boroughs & Univ.	24	17
Totals:		
England	216	251
Wales	11	18
Scotland	33	20
Ireland	63	42
Total	323	331

1857   Dissolution following the defeat of Palmerston's government
        on a motion of censure of its Chinese policy.

Seats

Conservatives	281
Liberals (including Peelites)	373
Total	654

Seats won by area

	Lib.	Con.
England:		
Counties	50	94
Boroughs & Univ.	216	107
Wales:		
Counties	5	10
Boroughs	9	5
Scotland:		
Counties	15	15
Burghs & Univ.	23	0
Ireland:		
Counties	33	31
Boroughs & Univ.	22	19
Totals:		
England	266	201
Wales	14	15
Scotland	38	15
Ireland	55	50
Total	373	281

1859   Palmerston's government, weakened by the appointment of the disreputable Lord Clanricarde to the Cabinet in 1857, was defeated on the Conspiracy to Murder Bill, introduced in consequence of the Orsini bomb attempt on the life of Napoleon III.

Seats

Conservatives	307
Liberals	347
Total	654

Seats won by area

	Lib.	Con.
England:		
Counties	45	99
Boroughs & Univ.	202	121
Wales:		
Counties	5	10
Boroughs	9	5
Scotland:		
Counties	16	14
Burghs & Univ.	22	1
Ireland:		
Counties	28	36
Boroughs & Univ.	20	21
Totals:		
England	247	220
Wales	14	15
Scotland	38	15
Ireland	48	57
Total	347	307

1865   Parliament was reaching the end of its seven-year life and many
Liberals were anxious for an opportunity to state to the country
their opinion on the question of franchise reform. In view of
the unlikelihood of Palmerston, an opponent of reform, living
the length of another parliament, yet sensing that Palmerston's
personality might still prove an electoral asset, it was decided to
dissolve.

Seats[1]

Conservatives	298
Liberals	360
Total	658

Seats won by area

	Lib.	Con.
England:		
Counties	48	99
Boroughs & Univ.	198	126
Wales:		
Counties	6	9
Boroughs	12	2
Scotland:		
Counties	18	12
Burghs & Univ.	23	0
Ireland:		
Counties	32	32
Boroughs & Univ.	23	18
Totals:		
England	246	225
Wales	18	11
Scotland	41	12
Ireland	55	50
Total	360	298

[1] In 1861 additional seats were allotted as follows: 1 to S. Lancs, 1 to
Birkenhead and 2 to the West Riding of Yorks. The total number of
Members was thus increased from 654 to 658.

1868   Parliament dissolved following the considerable extension of the franchise by the 1867 Reform Act.

Seats

Conservatives	276
Liberals	382
Total	658

Seats won by area

	Lib.	Con.
England:		
Counties	45	127
Boroughs & Univ.	198	93
Wales:		
Counties	9	6
Boroughs	13	2
Scotland:		
Counties	24	8
Burghs & Univ.	28	0
Ireland:		
Counties	37	27
Boroughs & Univ.	28	13
Totals:		
England	243	220
Wales	22	8
Scotland	52	8
Ireland	65	40
Total	382	276

1871   After six years of office Gladstone sensed the growing unpopularity of the government in the country, and its increasing weakness in Parliament. This, coupled with internal party difficulties which eventually prompted him secretly to resign the leadership, led him to dissolve on the question of finance, hoping to save the government's position by the popularity of a budget surplus.

Seats

Conservatives	352
Liberals	242
Irish Nationalists	58
Total	652[1]

Seats won by area

	Lib.	Con.
England:		
Counties	27	145
Boroughs & Univ.	144	143
Wales:		
Counties	6	9
Boroughs	13	2
Scotland:		
Counties	17	15
Burghs & Univ.	23	5
Ireland:		
Counties	43	21
Boroughs & Univ.	27	12
Totals:		
England	171	288
Wales	19	11
Scotland	40	20
Ireland	70[2]	33
Total	300[2]	352

[1] The Reform Act of 1867 set the total number of MPs at 658. But in 1870 Beverley (2 seats), Bridgwater (2 seats), Sligo (1 seat) and Cashel (1 seat) were disfranchised. The 6 seats were not allotted elsewhere, thus reducing the total of Members to 652.

[2] Including Irish Nationalists.

1880   The Cabinet faced the difficulty of carrying a highly unpopular Water Bill, or dropping it with loss of face. Suddenly by-election results appeared to indicate a movement of public opinion in the Conservatives' favour and Disraeli dissolved Parliament.

Seats

Conservatives	238
Liberals	353
Irish Nationalists	61
Total	652

Seats won by area

	Lib.	Con.
England:		
Counties	54	118
Boroughs & Univ.	202	85
Wales:		
Counties	13	2
Boroughs	15	0
Scotland:		
Counties	26	6
Burghs & Univ.	27	1
Ireland:		
Counties	53	11
Boroughs & Univ.	24	15
Totals:		
England	256	203
Wales	28	2
Scotland	53	7
Ireland	77[1]	26
Total	414[1]	238

[1] Including Irish Nationalists.

1885   Despite the passage of the 1884 Reform Bill, the failures of the Liberal government at home and abroad, coupled with internal party divisions between Whigs, Moderates and Radicals, had weakened the administration. The Irish Nationalist MPs, annoyed at the attitude of the government towards Irish Home Rule, and tempted by the prospect of a Conservative government proving more sympathetic on the question, allied with the Conservatives to defeat the government on an increase in the beer and spirit duties. Gladstone resigned and the minority Conservative government which replaced him, as 'caretaker' government, soon called the dissolution.

Seats

Conservatives	250
Liberals	321
Irish Nationalists	86
Total	670

Seats won by area

	Lib.	Con.	Ind. Lib.	Scottish Crofter	Lab.	Irish Nat.	Total
England	233	214	4	–	4	1	456
Wales	29	4	–	–	1	–	34
Scotland	58	8	–	4	–	–	70
Ireland		16	–	–	–	85	101
Univ.	1	8	–	–	–	–	9
Total	321	250	4	4	5	86	670

1886   The Liberal Party split on the question of Home Rule.
        Gladstone's Home Rule Bill was defeated by a combination of
        Conservatives and Liberal Unionists and a dissolution followed.

Seats

Conservatives	316
Liberal Unionists	79
Liberals	190
Irish Nationalists	85
Total	670

Seats won by area

	Lib.	Lib. U.	Con.	Irish Nat.	Total
England	123	55	277	1	456
Wales	24	4	6	–	34
Scotland	43	17	10	–	70
Ireland	–	2	15	84	101
Univ.	–	1	8	–	9
Total	190	79	316	85	670

1892   Having fulfilled almost all his legislative commitments during a 6-year parliament, Salisbury advised the Queen to dissolve Parliament. He probably hoped that the timing of the election would marginally favour the Unionist forces, and would return a Liberal government with only a small majority and a weak parliamentary position.

Seats

Conservatives	268
Liberal Unionists	47
Liberals	270
Irish Nationalists	81
Others	4
Total	670

Seats won by area

	Lib.	Lib. U.	Con.	Lab.	Nat. Parnell	Nat.	Total
England	189	31	231	4	–	1	456
Wales	31	–	3	–	–	–	34
Scotland	50	11	9	–	–	–	70
Ireland	–	4	17	–	9	71	101
Univ.	–	1	8	–	–	–	9
Total	270	47	268	4	9	72	670

1895   A weak Liberal government, which had failed to carry many of
       its major legislative proposals, was defeated, probably willingly,
       on the Army Estimates and resigned. Lord Salisbury became
       Prime Minister and dissolved Parliament in order to gain the
       parliamentary strength the new Cabinet required.

Seats

Conservatives	341
Liberal Unionists	70
Liberals	177
Irish Nationalists	82
Total	670

Seats won by area

	Lib.	Lib. U.	Con.	Nat. Parnell	Nat.	Total
England	112	50	293	–	1	456
Wales	25	1	8	–	–	34
Scotland	39	14	17	–	–	70
Ireland	1	4	15	12	69	101
Univ.	–	1	8	–	–	9
Total	177	70	341	12	70	670

1900   Knowing the Liberal Party to be divided on the question of the
       South African War, Salisbury dissolved Parliament when the war
       turned in Britain's favour, thus taking advantage of the extreme
       patriotism it had engendered.

	Seats	Total vote	% share of total vote
Conservatives	334 }	1,797,444	51.1
Liberal Unionists	68 }		
Liberals	184	1,568,141	44.6
Irish Nationalists	82	90,076	2.5
Labour	2	63,304	1.8
Others	0	544	0.0
Total	670	3,519,509	100.0

Seats won by area

	Lib.	Lib. U.	Con.	Lib.-Lab.	Nat.	Total
England	123	45	287	–	1	456
Wales	26	–	6	2	–	34
Scotland	34	17	19	–	–	70
Ireland	1	3	16	–	81	101
Univ.	–	3	6	–	–	9
Total	184	68	334	2	82	670

1906   In 1905, with his party hopelessly divided on the tariff question, Balfour decided to resign. He hoped that the Liberals might split on the questions of Home Rule and the composition of a Liberal Cabinet, but Campbell-Bannerman succeeded in holding the party leadership and keeping his party together, and lost no time in going to the country to exploit the unpopularity and divisions of the Conservatives.

	Seats	Total vote	% share of total vote
Conservatives			
(*Free Trade and Tariff Reform*)	133 ⎫		
Liberal Unionists	24 ⎬	2,451,454	43.6
(*Free Trade and Tariff Reform*)			
Liberals	400	2,757,883	49.0
Irish Nationalists	83	35,031	0.6
Labour	30	329,748	5.9
Others	0	52,387	0.9
Total	670	5,626,503	100.0

Seats won by area

	Lib.	Con.	Lab.	Nat.
England	306	122	27	
Wales	33		1	
Scotland	58	10	2	
Ireland	3	16		82
Univs		9		

1910   January. The House of Lords having rejected Lloyd George's
        1909 'People's Budget', the government turned to the elector-
        ate for a mandate to force the Budget through the Lords.

	Seats	Total vote	% share of total vote
Conservatives	241 ⎫	3,127,887	46.9
Liberal Unionists	32 ⎭		
Liberals	275	2,880,581	43.2
Irish Nationalists	82	124,586	1.9
Labour	40	505,657	7.6
Others	0	28,693	0.4
Total	670	6,667,404	100.0

Seats won by area

	Lib.	Con.	Lab.	Nat.
England	188	234	33	1
Wales	27	2	5	
Scotland	59	9	2	
Ireland	1	19		81
Univs		9		

1910   December. Having failed to reach a compromise with the
        Unionists on the question of reform of the House of Lords,
        and under pressure from his Irish Nationalist and Labour allies
        to carry out its reform, Asquith sought a clear mandate from
        the electorate for reform. Given such a mandate, he had the
        King's assurance that enough new peers would be created to
        pass a Reform Bill.

	Seats	Total vote	% share of total vote
Conservatives	237 ⎫	2,420,566	46.3
Liberal Unionists	35 ⎭		
Liberals	272	2,295,888	43.9
Irish Nationalists	84	131,375	2.5
Labour	42	371,772	7.1
Others	0	8,768	0.2
Total	670	5,228,369	100.0

Seats won by area

	Lib.	Con.	Lab.	Nat.
England	187	234	34	1
Wales	26	3	5	
Scotland	58	9	3	
Ireland	1	17		83
Univs		9		

Uncontested seats (General elections)

Election	Total seats	Total	%
1832	658	189	28.7
1835	658	275	41.8
1837	658	236	35.9
1841	658	337	51.2
1847	656	367	55.9
1852	654	255	39.0
1857	654	328	50.2
1859	654	379	58.0
1865	658	303	46.0
1868	658	212	32.2
1874	652	187	28.7
1880	652	109	16.7
1885	670	43	6.4
1886	670	224	33.4
1892	670	63	9.4
1895	670	189	28.2
1900	670	243	36.3
1906	670	114	17.0
1910(Jan.)	670	75	11.2
1910(Dec.)	670	163	24.3

By-elections

Uncontested seats (By-elections)

From	Total	Uncontested	%
1832–35	58	23	39.7
1835–37	89	42	47.2
1837–41	105	57	54.3
1841–47	231	169	73.2
1847–52	172	99	57.6
1852–57	218	120	55.0
1857–59	90	66	73.3
1859–65	221	119	53.8
1865–68	141	96	68.1
1868–74	176	72	40.9
1874–80	193	70	36.3
1880–85	193	94	48.7
1885–86	38	23	60.5
1886–92	179	77	43.0
1892–95	103	50	48.5
1895–1900	113	34	30.1
1900–06	114	33	28.9
1906–10(Jan.)	100	32	32.0
1910(Jan.)–10(Dec.)	21	11	52.4
1910(Dec.)–18	247	132	53.4

Ministerial gains and losses at by-elections, 1868–1918

Administration		Losses	Gains	+/−
Gladstone	1868–74	30	6	−24
Disraeli	1874–80	15	10	−5
Gladstone	1880–85	25	6	−19
Gladstone	1886	2	–	−2
Salisbury	1886–92	22	2	−20
Gladstone/Rosebery	1892–95	9	4	−5
Salisbury	1895–1900	14	3	−11
Salisbury/Balfour	1900–05	26	2	−24
Campbell-Bannerman/Asquith	1906–10	18	–	−18
Asquith/Lloyd George	1910–18	16	4	−12

Note: Full details of the constituencies changing hands can be found in Chris Cook and Brendan Keith, *British Historical Facts, 1830–1900* (1975) and David Butler and Gareth Butler, *British Political Facts, 1900–1994* (1995).

Bribery

Boroughs disfranchised for corruption 1832–85

Borough	Date
Sudbury	29 July 1844
St. Albans	3 May 1852
Great Yarmouth	11 Nov. 1868
Lancaster	11 Nov. 1868
Reigate	11 Nov. 1868
Totnes	11 Nov. 1868
Beverley	4 July 1870
Bridgwater	4 July 1870
Cashel	1 Aug. 1870
Sligo	1 Aug. 1870
Macclesfield	25 June 1885
Sandwich	25 June 1885

Number of petitions succeeding on the ground of bribery, etc., 1832–1900

Year of general election	Number of petitions presented	Number successful
1832	23	6
1835	16	2
1837	47	4
1841	26	10
1847	24	14
1852	49	25
1857	19	5
1859	30	12
1865	61	13
1868	51	22
1874	22	10
1880	28	10
1885	8	3
1886	3	0
1892	12	5
1895	7	1

Source: C. O'Leary, *The Elimination of Corrupt Practices in British Elections, 1868–1911* (Oxford, 1962) App. 1.

Political parties

The emergence of the major parties

The period following the Reform Acts of 1832 and 1867 saw the birth of the two major parties that dominated Victorian politics. The Conservative Party became a coherent national party under the leadership of Disraeli. His great ministry (1874–1880) saw a major extension of party organisation. The main tenets of the Conservative creed grew up under him: an Anglican imperialist party of Church and squirearchy, strongest in the English counties but with much working-class support.

The Liberals reached their maturity under the leadership of Gladstone (whose first premiership began in 1868). The party, with a strong Nonconformist and business composition, still retained the loyalty of many old Whig families, (e.g. the Devonshires) until the split over Irish Home Rule in 1886. The party was strongest in the radical towns. The main principles of Gladstonian Liberalism were Free Trade, financial economy and political reform. A central party organisation, the National Liberal Federation, was established in 1877. The mid-Victorian Liberal Party was a combination of the old Whig landowners, the new industrialists (epitomised by the Manchester businessmen), lawyers and professional men with a sprinkling of Radicals.

The birth, in February 1900, of the Labour Representation Committee marked an important new development in the evolution of the modern British political system. The old two-party political monopoly of the Conservative and Liberal parties was challenged, although before the First World War the new Labour Party made only partial and spasmodic progress. These were the halcyon years of Liberalism, with the sweeping election landslide of 1906 and the creative genius of Lloyd George and Churchill between 1906 and 1914.

But though these years saw the triumph of Liberalism, many of the ideals and standards of the Gladstonian era were being increasingly challenged. The world of *laissez-faire* Liberalism was becoming increasingly irrelevant. The demands of social reform, whether pensions or sickness insurance, required the state itself to be a partner. Meanwhile, the needs of total war between 1914 and 1918 also transformed the powers of the state, as well as putting such severe strains on the Liberal Party that the party faced the interwar period in persistent decline.

Conservative Party

The origins of the Conservative Party have been variously traced to the seventeenth century, the era of party strife under Queen Anne, and the administration of Pitt the Younger. Other historians have preferred to date the decisive emergence of the Conservative Party from the resignation of Peel in 1846 or even from the Second Reform Act of 1867. Certainly the evolution of the Conservative Party represented no sharp break either in ideas or institutions with the older Tory Party. According to one authority the term 'Conservative Party' was first used in its modern political sense in an article in the *Quarterly Review* in January 1830 (R. Blake, *The Conservative Party from Peel to Churchill*, Eyre and Spottiswoode, 1970, pp. 6–7) and the use of the term 'Conservative' by individuals has been recorded earlier. By 1832 the phrase 'Conservative Party' was in common use by politicians and journalists to describe the personalities, ideas and institutions previously referred to as Tory, though the latter remained in use.

Leaders of the Conservative Party since 1834

House of Commons

Sir R. Peel	1834–July 1846
Lord G. Bentinck	July 1846–Dec. 1847
Lord Granby	Feb. 1848–Mar. 1848
no formal leaders	Mar. 1848–Feb. 1849
Triumvirate:	
B. Disraeli	
Ld Granby	Feb. 1849–Feb. 1852
J.C. Herries	
B. Disraeli	Feb. 1852–Aug. 1876
Sir S. Northcote	Aug. 1876–Jun. 1885
Sir M. Hicks Beach	Jun. 1885–Aug. 1886
Lord R. Churchill	Aug. 1886–Dec. 1886
W.H. Smith	Dec. 1886–Oct. 1891
A.J. Balfour	Oct. 1891–Nov. 1911
A. Bonar Law	Nov. 1911–

House of Lords

Duke of Wellington	1828–46
Lord Stanley (14th Earl of Derby, 1851)	1846–68
Earl of Malmesbury	1868–69
Lord Cairns	1869–70

Earl of Derby (15th)	elected leader 19 Feb. 1870 but declined to serve
Duke of Richmond	1870–76
Earl of Beaconsfield	1876–81
Marquis of Salisbury	1881–1902
Duke of Devonshire	1902–03
Marquis of Lansdowne	1903–16

The Conservative vote 1832–1910

Election	Candidates	Unopposed returns	MPs elected	Total votes	% of UK total
1832	350	66	175	241,277	29.4
1835	407	121	273	261,314	42.6
1837	485	121	314	379,811	48.3
1841	498	212	367	306,314	50.9
1847	421	212	324	205,481	42.2
1852	462	160	330	316,718	42.1
1857	351	148	264	239,712	33.1
1859	393	195	297	193,232	34.3
1865	407	143	288	346,116	39.8
1868	436	91	271	903,318	38.4
1874	507	125	350	1,091,622	43.9
1880	521	58	237	1,426,351	42.0
1885	602	10	249	2,020,927	43.5
1886	563	118	393	1,520,886	51.4
1892	606	40	313	2,159,150	47.0
1895	588	132	411	1,894,772	49.1
1900	569	163	402	1,767,958	50.3
1906	556	13	156	2,422,071	43.4
1910(Jan.)	594	19	272	3,104,407	46.8
1910(Dec.)	548	72	271	2,420,169	46.6

Chronology of key events

1832   175 Conservative MPs returned at general election; Carlton Club founded.

1834   Peel formed Cabinet and was thus recognised as party leader. Publication of Peel's 'Tamworth Manifesto', identifying the

Conservative Party as a party of moderate reform and attempting to extend the social composition of support for the party to the middle classes.

1834–5	Appearance of Conservative and Constitutional Associations.
1835	Peel's government left office after defeats on Irish Tithes Bill. Conservatives won 273 seats in general election.
1837	Conservatives won 313 seats and lost general election.
1839	Stanley and his Whig followers join Peel.
1841	Conservatives won general election with a majority of 78 (367 seats). Peel formed his second Cabinet.
1846	Party split on Peel's repeal of the Corn Laws. Peel retained most of the Cabinet, the Chief Whip Sir J. Young and Bonham, the party's election manager. The 'Protectionists' were led by Lord George Bentinck, supported by Stanley and Disraeli.
1847	A divided Conservative Party won 324 seats to the Liberals' 332. The party fund was used to support 'Peelite' candidates, of whom 89 were elected. Stanley now led the Protectionist Conservatives in the Lords; Bentinck led in the Commons.
1848	Death of Bentinck. Leadership of party in the Commons put into commission under a committee of Granby, J.C. Herries and Disraeli, but Disraeli was the effective leader.
1850	Death of Peel.
1852	Lord Derby (Stanley) formed a Cabinet (Feb.). It fell on Disraeli's Budget. In the general election 330 Conservatives were returned, but the Peelites joined a coalition government with the Liberals under Aberdeen (Dec.). Sir William Jolliffe made Chief Whip and Philip Rose, Disraeli's solicitor, made principal agent.
1855	Derby refused to form a government when Aberdeen's ministry fell.
1857	Conservatives won 264 seats in general election.
1858	Derby formed the 'Who? Who?' ministry (Feb.) (see p. 312).
1859	Derby resigned from office and Palmerston formed a Whig government. M. Spofforth succeeded Rose as principal agent.
1865	Conservatives lost general election (288 seats).
1866	Liberal government defeated on Reform Bill by an alliance of Whigs and Conservatives. Derby formed a government (June).
1867	Disraeli introduced a Reform Bill which considerably extended the franchise. It was passed. Conference of Conservative Working Men's Associations in London (Apr.). Inaugural meeting of the National Union of Conservative and Constitutional Associations (Nov.).
1868	Derby retired and was succeeded by Disraeli who formed a government (Feb.). M. Spofforth formed a Central Board to

organise for the election. Conservatives lost the Nov. election (276 seats).

1870   J.E. Gorst succeeded Spofforth as principal agent and set up a Conservative Central Office.

1871   Gorst and Keith-Falconer became honorary secretaries of the National Union.

1872   Disraeli's Crystal Palace speech at London conference of the National Union linked Conservative Party with the Empire and claimed the working class should support both.

1874   Conservatives won 350 seats and Disraeli formed a Cabinet. Gorst's engagement as party agent ended.

1877   W.B. Skene became principal Conservative agent. Gorst ceased to be secretary of National Union.

1880   Conservatives lost general election, winning only 236 seats. Skene resigned. Central Committee set up under chairmanship of W.H. Smith to enquire into state of party organisation. Gorst resumed position as principal agent (July). Rowland Winn became Chief Whip. Fourth Party ginger group of Lord Randolph Churchill, J.E. Gorst, A.J. Balfour and H. Drummond-Wolff emerged.

1881   Lord Beaconsfield (Disraeli) died. Party now led by Lord Salisbury in the Lords and Sir H. Stafford-Northcote in the Commons – a dual leadership.

1882   E. Stanhope became chairman of the Central Committee – Gorst resigned as principal agent.

1883   G.G.T. Bartley became principal agent. Lord Randolph Churchill attacked party leaders at a National Union Conference. Primrose League founded by Churchill and Drummond-Woff.

1884   Split in party organisation. National Union threatened with eviction from Conservative Central Office premises. July quarrel between Churchill and leaders resolved. Hicks-Beach elected chairman of National Union Council. Central Committee abolished. Primrose League officially recognised.

1885   Lord Salisbury invited to form a Cabinet. Is thus recognised as party leader. Conservatives won 249 seats in general election (a defeat). Captain R.W.E. Middleton became Principal Agent (the first time the title was used officially) and Akers-Douglas became Chief Whip.

1886   Salisbury's minority government fell on Jesse Collings's 'three acres and a cow' amendment to the Address. Liberal Party split on Home Rule. Conservatives and Liberal Unionists allied to defeat Home Rule Bill. Conservatives won election (317 seats). Salisbury PM, Churchill leader in Commons. In December Churchill resigned and a Liberal Unionist, Goschen, joined

Cabinet as Chancellor of the Exchequer. W.H. Smith became Leader of the House.

1891   Smith died, and A.J. Balfour became Leader of the House.

1892   Conservatives lost general election (268 seats).

1895   Conservatives won election (341 seats). Salisbury formed a government composed of Conservatives and Liberal Unionists.

1900   Conservatives won 'Khaki' election (334 seats). Salisbury formed another joint Conservative-Liberal Unionist government. Sir W.H. Walrond became Chief Whip.

1902   Salisbury retired and Balfour became PM. Liberal Unionist Duke of Devonshire led in the Lords. A. Acland Hood was Chief Whip.

1903   Party split on 'Tariff Reform' into Balfourites, Chamberlainites and Free Traders. Major Cabinet reconstruction. Lord Lansdowne (a Liberal Unionist) led the 'Unionists' in the Lords. Middleton retired as Principal Agent and was succeeded by L. Wells.

1905   Balfour resigned as PM.

1906   Conservatives defeated in general election, Unionist forces winning only 157 seats. Reorganisation of party begun, to give more strength to the regions. Percival Hughes succeeded A. Haig (appointed 1905) as Principal Agent.

1910   Party lost two general elections. Won 273 seats in Jan., 272 in Dec.

1911   Party again reorganised. Acland-Hood resigned as Chief Whip and was replaced by Balcarres; new office of Chairman of the Party Organisation was given to A. Steel-Maitland. Balfour resigned. Austen Chamberlain (a Liberal Unionist) and Walter Long entered leadership election, but withdrew in favour of Bonar Law. Lansdowne still led in the Lords.

1912   Formal amalgamation of Conservative and Liberal Unionist parties. J. Boraston became Principal Agent.

Liberal Party

As with the term 'Conservative', 'Liberal' only emerged gradually in the nineteenth century to describe one of the major groupings in British politics. The parliamentary Liberal Party was only formed in the late 1850s through a fusion of Whigs, 'Peelites' and radicals, but the term was used earlier to describe the opponents of the Conservatives. Historians have used both the terms 'Liberal' and 'Whig' for the period 1832–67. Thereafter 'Whig' is normally applied to the landed, upper-class element in the Liberal Party.

Leaders of the Liberal Party

House of Commons

Viscount Althorp	Mar. 1830–Nov. 1834
Lord J. Russell	Nov. 1834–Feb. 1855
Lord Palmerston	Feb. 1855–Oct. 1865
W.E. Gladstone	Oct. 1865–Feb. 1875
Lord Hartington	Feb. 1875–Apr. 1880
W.E. Gladstone	Apr. 1880–Mar. 1894
Sir W. Harcourt	Mar. 1894–Dec. 1898
Sir H. Campbell-Bannerman	Feb. 1899–Apr. 1908
H. Asquith	Apr. 1908–Oct. 1926

House of Lords

Earl Grey	1830–34
Viscount Melbourne	1834–42
Marquis of Lansdowne	1842–52
Earl of Aberdeen	1852–55
Earl Granville	1855–65
Earl Russell	1865–68
Earl Granville	1868–91
Earl of Kimberley	1891–94
Earl of Rosebery	1894–96
Earl of Kimberley	1897–1902
Earl Spencer	1902–05
Marquis of Crewe	1905–08
Viscount Grey	1908–23

The Liberal vote 1832–1910

Election	Candidates	Unopposed returns	MPs elected	Total votes	% of UK total
1832	636	109	441	554,700	66.7
1835	538	154	385	349,868	57.4
1837	506	115	344	417,826	51.7
1841	389	113	271	273,972	46.9
1847	393	137	293	259,310	53.9
1852	487	95	324	425,635	57.7
1857	506	176	377	464,120	65.1
1859	466	184	357	372,117	65.7
1865	515	160	370	508,456	60.2
1868	600	121	387	1,428,776	61.5
1874	489	52	242	1,281,330	52.7
1880	499	41	352	1,836,223	55.4
1885	572	14	319	2,199,998	47.4
1886	449	40	192	1,353,581	45.0
1892	532	13	272	2,088,019	45.1
1895	447	11	177	1,765,266	45.7
1900	402	22	183	1,572,323	45.0
1906	536	27	399	2,751,057	49.4
1910(Jan.)	511	1	274	2,866,157	43.5
1910(Dec.)	467	35	272	2,293,869	44.2

Chronology of key events

1832   Liberals won 483 seats. Grey became PM.
1834   Grey resigned when Althorp, leader in the Commons, refused to support the Irish Coercion Bill. Melbourne became PM, but resigned when Althorp was elevated to House of Lords.
1835   Liberals won 385 seats and Melbourne formed second Cabinet.
1836   Reform Club founded.
1837   Liberals won general election (345 seats).
1839   Melbourne resigned. Bedchamber crisis and Melbourne returned.
1841   Liberals lost general election (291 seats). Liberal government defeated in Commons and resigned.
1846   Break-up of Conservative ministry. Lord John Russell formed a Liberal Cabinet.

1847	Liberals won general election (332 seats). Lord John Russell PM.
1852	General election. Liberals won 324 seats. Whigs would no longer endure Russell's leadership and joined a coalition with the Peelites under Aberdeen.
1855	Aberdeen government fell over conduct of Crimean War. Palmerston became PM when Russell failed to form a government.
1857	Liberals (including Peelites) won 390 seats. Palmerston defeated in a motion of censure on his Chinese policy.
1859	Palmerston's government defeated on Conspiracy to Murder Bill. Palmerston won general election (357 seats). Willis' Rooms meeting where Whigs, Radicals and Peelites agreed to serve under Palmerston.
1860	Liberal Registration Association founded.
1865	Liberals won general election (370 seats). Palmerston died. Russell became PM.
1868	Liberals won general election (387 seats). Gladstone became PM.
1874	Liberals lost election (251 seats). Gladstone resigned leadership. Liberal Registration Association recognised and became known as Liberal Central Association.
1875	Meeting of Liberal MPs elected Hartington leader in the Commons.
1877	Foundation of the National Liberal Federation; first president was Joseph Chamberlain.
1880	Liberals won general election (353 seats). Hartington refused premiership and advised the Queen to make Gladstone PM, which she did.
1885	Government defeated on spirit duties and Gladstone resigned office. Liberals won general election (335 seats).
1886	Party split on Home Rule Bill. Liberal Unionists led by Chamberlain and Hartington helped Conservatives defeat the Bill. In general election Gladstonian Liberals badly beaten (191 seats). F. Schnadhorst became party agent (until 1892).
1887	National Liberal Club opened. Liberal Publication Department founded.
1891	'Newcastle Programme' adopted by conference, advocating extensive social reforms.
1892	Liberals won general election by a narrow majority (272 seats).
1894	Gladstone retired. Rosebery became PM. Harcourt led the party in the Commons.
1895	Liberals lost the general election (177 seats). Rosebery privately refused to work with Harcourt, and was titular leader only. Harcourt led the party in the Commons, Kimberley in the Lords.
1896	Rosebery formally resigned leadership.

1898   Harcourt resigned leadership of Liberal MPs.
1899   Campbell-Bannerman elected leader of Liberals in the Commons. Herbert Gladstone became Chief Whip. Party divided on question of South African War.
1900   Three-way split in party on motion of censure on Joseph Chamberlain, Colonial Secretary. Liberals lost general election (184 seats). Liberal Imperialists founded Liberal Imperialist Council under chairmanship of Sir Edward Grey.
1902   Foundation of Liberal League by the Liberal Imperialists, with Rosebery as president, Asquith, Fowler and Grey vice-presidents.
1903   Confidential electoral pact made with Labour Representation Committee, allowing a number of Labour candidates to stand unopposed by Liberals.
1905   Campbell-Bannerman became PM. Leading Liberal Imperialists joined government.
1906   Liberals won general election (400 seats).
1908   Death of Campbell-Bannerman. Asquith became PM.
1909   Lloyd George's Budget rejected by Lords.
1910   Liberals won 275 seats in Jan. general election and Asquith formed minority government. They won 271 seats in Dec. and Asquith was again PM.
1914   Outbreak of war. Morley, Burns and C.P. Trevelyan resigned from the government as Liberal pacifists.

Labour Party

The formation of the Labour Representation Committee in February 1900 is regarded as the 'birth' of the Labour Party. The actual title of Labour Party was not adopted until 1906. The numerous early attempts to secure representation in Parliament predate 1900 (such as the formation of the ILP in 1893). These early origins are set out below. It is important to remember that, from 1906 to 1914, the future success of the Labour Party was far from certain or secure.

Chronology

(1) The origins, 1867–1900
1867   Male working class enfranchised by Reform Act (see pp. 62–3).
1868   Establishment of the Trades Union Congress (see p. 159).
1869   Labour Representation League formed by trades unions and working class bodies in London.
1870   London Trades Council secretary George Odger defeated as Labour Representation League candidate at Southwark by-election.

1874   Two miners' leaders – Thomas Burt (Morpeth) and Alexander Macdonald (Stafford) – elected as Liberal MPs at general election.

1876   TUC Parliamentary Committee established Direct Labour Representation Association; members won council seats in Birmingham.

1879   TUC Parliamentary Committee issued first general election manifesto with nine demands, including legislation to provide for workmen's compensation, etc.

1880   Henry Broadhurst (Stoke on Trent) and Joseph Arch (Wilton) elected as working class Liberal MPs at general election.

1881   Democratic Federation formed (June) by the Marxist H.M. Hyndman with support of Eleanor Marx, William Morris and Harry Quelch.

1883   Democratic Federation renamed Social Democratic Federation (SDF) and began publishing journal *Justice*; TUC annual conference rejected motion to set up local and national funds to support working class MPs; Fabian Society founded.

1884   Socialist League broke away from SDF; bulk of trade unionists remained with SDF.

1885   TUC general election manifesto included demand for votes for women; ten trade unionists elected to Parliament as Liberal MPs.

1886   TUC established Labour Electoral Association, organised in nine areas, to which only *bona fide* working class bodies could affiliate.

1893   Birth of Independent Labour Party at Bradford (see p. 105).

1895   ILP fielded 28 candidates in general election. None was elected.

1898   West Ham became first British local authority with a majority of working class councillors.

1899   TUC annual conference voted by 546,000 votes to 434,000 to convene a special congress of 'all the co-operative, socialistic, trade union, and other working class organisations . . . to devise ways and means of securing the return of an increased number of Labour members to the next Parliament'.

(2) The formative years, 1900–14

1900   Labour Representation Committee (LRC) formed at two-day conference held at Memorial Hall, London (27 Feb.). Ramsay MacDonald secretary. LRC fielded 15 candidates at general election, two of whom – Richard Bell and Keir Hardie – were elected (Oct.).

1901   Social Democratic Federation (SDF) withdrew from the Labour Representation Committee (Aug.).

1902   Taff Vale decision undermined legal position of the trade unions (see p. 308).
        David Shackleton returned in Barnard Castle by-election (July).

1903   Electoral pact between MacDonald and Herbert Gladstone. Arthur Henderson and Will Crooks returned at by-elections. MPs elected with LRC support to be paid a maximum of £200 a year. Miners' Federation of Great Britain MPs began co-operation with LRC in the Commons.

1906   LRC fielded 50 candidates in general election; 29 elected (including J.R. Clynes, Will Crooks, Keir Hardie, Arthur Henderson, Ramsay MacDonald, Philip Snowden and Will Thorne). On their arrival in Parliament they assumed the title 'Labour Party'. Keir Hardie became chairman.

1907   Keir Hardie resigned as chairman and was succeeded by Ramsay MacDonald. Labour, the ILP, BSP and the Fabians agreed to Second International resolution on Militarism and International Conflicts to work to prevent the outbreak of war 'by whatever means seem[ed] to them most effective'.

1908   Parliamentary strength increased as Miners' Federation of Great Britain affiliated.

1909   Osborne judgement (see p. 161).

1910   Two general elections: 40 Labour MPs returned in the January election, 42 in December.
        Lloyd George's proposal to Ramsay MacDonald that he should join a coalition of moderate Liberals and Conservatives rejected after opposition from Arthur Henderson.

1911   MacDonald elected Parliamentary Labour Party (PLP) chairman. *Daily Herald* began publication.

1913   Trade Union Act partially reversed effect of Osborne judgement.

1914   Labour Party National Executive rejected Liberal offer of a new electoral pact, concessions on policy and a Cabinet seat for MacDonald in return for supporting a coalition government (Mar.). MacDonald resigned because the party would not oppose the War Estimates and Arthur Henderson became chairman of the parliamentary party (Aug.).

Other parties

Crofters' Party

This party represented the protest of Highland smallholders against the Liberal Party's neglect of their grievances. The 1884 Reform Act opened the way for them to channel their protest into electoral activity of an effective nature. In the Highlands they possessed their own organisation, and fought the 1885 election in alliance with the Highland Land League. 6 candidates stood (three closely associated with the League) and 5 were returned, for Caithness-shire, Ross-shire, Argyllshire, Wick Burghs and Inverness Burghs. In 1886 victories followed at north-west Lanarkshire and Sutherlandshire. At the 1892 general election the Crofters' candidates threw in their lot with Gladstone, and stood as Gladstonian Liberals.

Independent Labour Party

During the 1880s the idea of an independent party of labour proved slow to gain acceptance. Yet in 1892 Keir Hardie, one of its main advocates, and 3 other candidates, were returned as independent labour members at the general election. These successes were followed by the foundation of a national organisation, the Independent Labour Party (ILP), at Bradford in 1893.

In the 1895 election the ILP fielded 28 candidates but did not elect a single MP. Hardie lost his West Ham seat. In 1900 the ILP was one of the founding bodies of the Labour Representation Committee. Although affiliated to the Labour Party the ILP held its own conferences, sponsored its own candidates and maintained its own policies, even after the 1918 revision of the Labour Party Constitution.

Irish Nationalist Party

See p. 251 et seq.

Liberal Unionist Party

The Liberal Unionist Party was formed by those Liberals who left the party in opposition to Gladstone's 1886 Home Rule Bill. 93 Liberals voted against the Bill, 46 of them radical Unionists who followed Joseph Chamberlain, the rest Whig and moderate Liberal Unionists who followed the Marquis of Hartington. Both groups set up organisations to fight the 1886 election: Hartington founded the Liberal Unionist Association, Chamberlain the National Radical Union. An electoral agreement with the Conservatives secured the return of 77 Liberal Unionists, mainly Hartingtonians. In 1889 Chamberlain restyled his organisation the National Liberal Union and the two groups virtually amalgamated. In 1891 Hartington was elevated to the Lords as the Duke of Devonshire, and Chamberlain was elected leader of the Liberal Unionists in the Commons. In 1895 the Liberal Unionists took office in the Conservative government and the two parties became virtually fused. Separate organisations and funds were maintained until the two parties merged in 1912, but the merger was really a recognition of a *fait accompli*.

Estimates of Liberal Unionist strength

1886	77	1906	25
1892	45	1910 (Jan.)	32
1895	71	1910 (Dec.)	36
1900	68		

Peelites

In 1846 112 Tories voted with Peel for repeal of the Corn Laws, but 242 voted with Bentinck for Protection. Many of those who went into the lobby with Peel did so not out of love of Free Trade, but because of their personal loyalty to Peel and the desire to maintain him as Prime Minister. Among the followers of Peel were all but three of the Cabinet ministers, the Chief Whip, Sir J. Young, and Bonham, the party's election manager. Peel thus had the support of the most important elements in the Conservative Party. Accordingly, the party fund was used to finance Peelite candidates in the 1847 general election, and 89 of them were returned.

The Peelites constituted not only the intellectual leadership, the administratively able and the middle class of the Tory party, but also formed a body of centre opinion which overlapped with moderate Liberalism. Yet, up to his death in 1850 Peel failed to organise his followers in parliament. But in December 1852 they were able to join the coalition formed by the Peelite PM Aberdeen on favourable terms, being given half the Cabinet offices.

Sinn Fein

Gaelic for 'ourselves alone'. Irish nationalist party founded in 1902 by Arthur Griffiths (1872–1922) and formed into the Sinn Fein League in 1907–08 when it absorbed other nationalist groups. The group rose to prominence in the 1913–14 Home Rule crisis when many Sinn Feiners joined the Irish Volunteers and many Dublin workers joined the organisation. Sinn Fein members were involved in the Easter Rising in 1916 and one of the battalion commanders, Eamon de Valera (1882–1979), took over as leader in October 1917.

Socialist Labour Party

The Socialist Labour Party (SLP) developed out of the Scottish District of the Social Democratic Federation (see p. 306). It was established as a separate organisation in 1903, advocating a more militant class-conscious policy. From the first it expressed support for the ideas of the American Socialist, Daniel De Leon, and in 1906 it adopted a policy of Industrial

Unionism. During World War I the SLP became involved in the Shop Stewards and Workers' Committee Movement and in 1916–18 adopted a pro-Bolshevik policy.

Socialist Party of Great Britain

The Socialist Party of Great Britain (SPGB) was founded on 12 June 1904 with a provisional committee of 12 people in order to work for 'the establishment of a system of society based upon the common ownership and democratic control of the means and instruments for producing and distributing wealth by and in the interest of the whole community' (Declaration of Principles, 1904). Its founders broke away from the Social Democratic Federation 'to establish a genuine Socialist organisation'.

Machinery of government

Chronology of events

1836   Office of Treasurer of the Navy abolished. Duties assumed by Paymaster-General.

1839   Committee of the Privy Council on Education set up by Order in Council. Lord President became the responsible minister.

1851   Office of First Commissioner of Works and Public Building established.

1854   Secretary of State for War relieved of responsibility for colonial affairs. From 1855 to 1863 acted also as Secretary at War. Separate Secretary of State for the Colonies created.

1855   Board of Ordnance abolished.

1858   Government of India Act removed control of India from East India Company to the Crown. Ministerial responsibility for Indian affairs transferred from President of the Board of Control to Secretary of State for India in Council.

1863   Office of Secretary at War abolished.

1870   Major civil service reforms promulgated. Competitive entry examination for many departments (although not the Foreign Office).

1871   Office of President of the Local Government Board set up.

1885   Office of Secretary of State for Scotland created within government of United Kingdom. Not granted full powers of Secretaryship.

1889   Presidency of the Board of Agriculture created.

1911   Parliament Act (for details see p. 67).

SECTION TWO

Social and religious history

Population

The growth of Britain's population during the Industrial Revolution had been dramatic. It trebled in size between 1750 and 1850, after which it grew more steadily to 1914. Population growth was fastest in the industrial areas. By the early nineteenth century the birth rate was about a third higher in industrial areas than in rural ones because of earlier marriages. Despite high death rates, there was larger natural increase in industrial areas. Meanwhile migrants flowed into the industrial areas from the countryside, and from the poorer parts of Britain. By 1801 just over a fifth of the population lived in towns, increasing to over a half by 1861.

Urbanisation of the industrial areas led to the concentration of a large share of the population in a few conurbations, based on the capital and the coalfields. London was the biggest city in Western Europe by 1801. Its population had doubled in the eighteenth century to reach almost one million people. During the nineteenth century, it expanded rapidly to become the largest city in the world, with a population of 4.5 million by 1901.

Population growth 1801–1911

	Population (millions)			Rate of growth
	England and Wales	Scotland	Ireland	England and Wales annual average % increase
1801	8.9	1.6	5.2	1.10
1811	10.2	1.8	6.0	1.43
1821	12.0	2.1	6.8	1.81
1831	13.9	2.4	7.8	1.58
1841	15.9	2.6	8.2	1.43
1851	17.9	2.9	6.5	1.27
1861	20.1	3.1	5.8	1.19
1871	22.7	3.4	5.4	1.32
1881	26.0	3.7	5.2	1.44
1891	29.0	4.0	4.7	1.17
1901	32.5	4.5	4.5	1.22
1911	36.1	4.8	4.4	1.09

Source: B.R. Mitchell and P. Deane, *Abstract of British Historical Statistics* (1962) pp. 6–7.

Comparative population growth

	Annual average percentage increases	
	1800–50	1850–1910
England and Wales	1.8	1.6
Scotland	1.6	0.9
Ireland	0.6	0.6
France	0.7	0.2
Holland	0.8	1.5
Belgium	0.9	1.2
Norway	1.3	1.0

Source: N. Tranter, *Population since the Industrial Revolution: the case of England and Wales* (1973) p. 43.

Birth and death rates in England and Wales, 1841–1915 (per 000 population)

	Births	Deaths
1841–45	35.2	21.4
1846–50	34.8	23.3
1851–55	35.5	22.7
1856–60	35.5	21.8
1861–65	35.8	22.6
1866–70	35.7	22.4
1871–75	35.7	22.0
1876–80	35.4	20.8
1881–85	33.5	19.4
1886–90	31.4	18.9
1891–95	30.5	18.7
1896–1900	29.3	17.7
1901–5	28.2	16.1
1906–10	26.3	14.7
1911–15	23.6	14.3

Source: B.R. Mitchell and P. Deane, *Abstract of British Historical Statistics*, pp. 8–10, 29–30, 34–5, 36–7.

Birth and death rates in Scotland and Ireland, 1855–1914
(per 000 population)

	Scotland		Ireland	
	Births	Deaths	Births	Deaths
1855–59	33.8	20.4	–	–
1860–64	35.1	22.2	–	–
1865–69	35.1	21.8	26.4	17.0
1870–74	34.9	22.5	27.5	18.0
1875–79	35.1	21.2	25.8	18.9
1880–84	33.5	19.8	24.1	18.6
1885–89	31.9	18.7	23.1	18.1
1890–94	30.6	19.1	22.8	18.4
1895–99	30.1	18.1	23.4	17.9
1900–4	29.4	17.5	23.0	18.1
1905–9	28.1	16.3	23.4	17.2
1910–14	25.9	15.3	23.0	16.7

Source: B.R. Mitchell, *European Historical Statistics, 1750–1970* (1975),
pp. 110, 113, 117, 120, 122, 124.

Urbanisation

	% rural	% urban
1801	78	22
1851	50	50
1901	22	77

The largest towns (outside London)

1801		1861		1901	
1 Dublin	300,000	1 Liverpool	472,000	1 Glasgow	904,000
2 Edinburgh	83,000	2 Glasgow	443,000	2 Birmingham	760,000
3 Liverpool	82,000	3 Dublin	410,000	3 Liverpool	685,000
4 Glasgow	77,000	4 Manchester	399,000	4 Manchester	654,000
5 Manchester	75,000	5 Birmingham	351,000	5 Dublin	448,000
6 Birmingham	71,000	6 Leeds	207,000	6 Edinburgh	394,000

Growth of conurbations in late Victorian Britain

Area	Population 1871	Population 1901
Greater London	3,900,000	6,600,000
SE Lancashire	1,400,000	2,100,000
West Midlands	970,000	1,500,000
West Yorkshire	1,000,000	1,500,000
Merseyside	690,000	1,000,000
Tyneside	350,000	680,000

Emigration and immigration

In the period from 1815 to 1914, many millions emigrated. The outflow reached a peak in the years just prior to the First World War when at least 100,000 people left every year. A large share came from Ireland under the impact of the famine and poverty. About two-thirds of all emigrants went to the United States, which offered cheap land and the prospect of fortunes during the gold rushes in California (1849) and Alaska (1896).

Immigration also played an important part in developing the British economy and society. The first were the Irish, especially during the famine years (1846–49). European immigration of Jews and political refugees contributed greatly to British business and culture before 1914.

Number of emigrants, 1820–1919

1820–29	216,000	1870–79	1,653,000
1830–39	668,000	1880–89	2,568,000
1840–49	1,495,000	1890–99	1,792,000
1850–59	2,440,000	1900–09	2,613,000
1860–69	1,465,000	1910–19	2,483,000

Jewish population, 1890–1916

1891	101,000
1901	160,000
1905	227,000
1911	237,000
1916	257,000

Number of aliens from Europe in UK, 1881–1911

1881	118,000
1891	198,000
1901	248,000
1911	285,000

Education

A growing population and the development of industry created demands for education for the majority of the population, hitherto virtually uneducated. The Sunday School movement from 1785 and the 'monitorial system' from 1805 had some effect, but the Newcastle Report (1861) demonstrated their inadequacy. From 1833 the government made educational grants and began to take more control of education, leading in 1870 to Forster's Education Act which set up school boards and enforced minimum standards.

After 1870 the expenditure and control by the government on education increased. Later Acts raised the school leaving age, made attendance compulsory, and increased the number of free places in elementary and secondary schools. In this period, a major improvement in education for the middle classes took place with the reform of public schools. Started by Arnold at Rugby (1828–42) and Thring at Uppingham, the reforms spread. Many new schools were founded to provide an education for the emerging middle classes.

Education legislation and principal events

1814   British and Foreign School Society formed out of the Royal Lancastrian Society. No religious barriers were imposed and with the National Society it provided the basis on which the state system was to develop.

1828   The Revd Thomas Arnold became headmaster of Rugby and began the process of reform in the public schools by introducing the prefect system, the ideal of Christian duty and a more rigorous intellectual atmosphere. This influence spread to other schools through Vaughan at Harrow, Pears at Repton and Thring at Uppingham. Many public schools were founded from the 1830s on the new principles, providing education for the sons and daughters of the new middle classes.

1833   The Factory Act provided for the education of children working in textile factories. The first government grant, of £20,000, was made to education, shared between the British and Foreign Schools and the National Societies. A Committee of the

Privy Council on Education was set up in England and Wales, with the Lord President as head.

1839   The grant to the two educational societies was increased to £30,000 and government inspectors were appointed to supervise schools receiving the grant. Thereafter the subsidy was regularly increased.

1840   The Grammar School Act gave the Court of Chancery the power to alter the original statutes of the schools, thereby adapting them to meet new needs.

1844   Lord Shaftesbury organised 'Ragged Schools' for free education of the poorest children.

1858   The Newcastle Commission was appointed to survey the state of elementary education. One result of its recommendations was the establishment of the system of 'payment by results' in which the size of the government grant was dictated by the numbers of children in regular attendance and the number passing an annual examination in the three 'Rs' conducted by the school inspector.

1868   Public Schools Act. The Act regulated the administration of public schools and provided for the adaptation of their original charters to meet new circumstances.

1870   Education Act (Forster's). The first major Education Act. The existing 20,000 voluntary schools were given slightly increased grants. Where school places were insufficient, new school boards could be set up, or where the ratepayers demanded it, school boards could be rate-aided with powers to build schools and compel attendance. Board schools could provide religious instruction so long as it was not 'distinctive of any particular denomination'. School fees of a few pence each week were charged, but poorer parents could be excused payment. As a result of the Act voluntary schools and the new board schools constituted a dual system, each school's management committee dealing directly with Whitehall. Voluntary schools received no more rate aid and no more building grants.

1876   Education Act (Sandon's). The Act created school attendance committees for districts where there were no school boards and could compel attendance.

1880   Education Act. This made it compulsory for children to go to school between the ages of 5 and 10, when they could be exempted to work part-time in factories, if they had reached a certain educational standard.

1889   Education Act. County councils were empowered to levy a 1d rate for technical education. The Board of Education was set up.

1891   Assisted Education Act. This made available a capitation grant of 10s to all schools, enabling them to cease charging fees.

1891–5   From 1890 the system of payment by results was gradually dismantled and replaced by a system of block grants.

1893   Education (Blind and Deaf Children) Act. Made possible the establishment of special schools for the blind and deaf.

1902   Education Act (Balfour's). School boards were abolished and replaced by new local education authorities which were given the power to provide secondary education. In many cases new secondary schools were built and grants given to grammar schools.

1903   The Association to Promote the Higher Education of Working Men (from 1905 the Workers' Educational Association) founded by Albert Mansbridge. First branch opened in Reading in 1904.

1907   All secondary schools receiving grants from local education authorities to reserve 25 to 40 per cent of free places for children from elementary schools.

1918   Education Act (Fisher's), introduced by H.A.L. Fisher, President of the Board of Education. The Act raised the school-leaving age to 14 and abolished the remaining fees for elementary education in some schools.

Number of schools and children attending, 1819

	England	Wales	Scotland
Parochial schools			
Number	–	–	942
Children	–	–	54,161
Endowed schools			
Number	4,167	209	212
Children	165,433	7,625	10,177
Unendowed schools			
Number	14,282	572	2,479
Children	478,849	22,976	112,187
Sunday schools			
Number	5,162	301	807
Children	452,817	24,408	53,449

Source: *Parliamentary Papers*, 1820, XII, pp. 342–55.

P60
stats

Major public school foundations

Boys		Girls	
1841	Cheltenham	1850	North London Collegiate School
1843	Marlborough	1853	Cheltenham Ladies College
1847	Radley	1885	Roedean
1850	Bradfield		
1859	Wellington		
1862	Clifton		
	Haileybury		
1865	Malvern		

Expenditure on education in the United Kingdom, 1802–1910

	£million		£million
1802	0.06	1870	1.27
1820	0.10	1880	4.00
1830	0.10	1890	5.80
1840	0.17	1900	12.10
1850	0.37	1910	18.00
1860	1.27		

Sources: B.R. Mitchell and P. Deane, *Abstract of British Historical Statistics* (1962), pp. 396–9.

Average number of children at government-inspected day schools 1850–1900

1850	561	1880	3,625
1860	1,147	1890	4,720
1870	1,709	1900	5,770

Growth of the universities, 1815–1914

Chronology of university dates of foundation

1826	University College, London	1892	Reading
		1893	University of Wales
1829	Kings College, London	1895	London School of Economics
1831	Durham		
1851	Manchester	1900	Birmingham
1862	Southampton	1904	Leeds
1881	Liverpool	1905	Sheffield
1881	Nottingham	1908	Belfast

Social reform

Factory and industrial legislation

1819   Factory Act. Children under 9 years old prohibited from working in cotton mills; those over 9 restricted to a 12-hour day.

1831   Truck Act. The Act prohibited payment in goods and tokens. All workers other than domestic servants to be paid entirely in coin. Factory Act–no young people under 18 to work more than 12 hours a day.

1833   Factory Act (also known as Althorp's Act). The Act applied only to textile factories and limited the hours of work for children and youths. Children aged from 9 to 12 to work a maximum of 9 hours a day and no more than 48 hours a week. Youths from 13 to 18 to work a maximum of 12 hours a day and no more than 69 hours a week. The employment of children under 9 was prohibited, except in silk factories, and night work by workers under 18 was banned, except in lace factories. Children from 9 to 11 (later raised to 13) were to have 2 hours' compulsory education every day. The first four factory inspectors were appointed.

1842   Mines Act. This followed on a Royal Commission into mining conditions. The Act prohibited women and girls and boys under 10 years of age from being employed underground. Inspectors of mines were appointed.

1842   Factory Act. The Act applied to textile factories and laid down that women and youths and young girls between 13 and 18 were not to work more than 12 hours a day. Hours of work for children under 13 were reduced from 9 to 6½ hours a day with 3 hours' education. The age at which children could start work was lowered from 9 to 8.

1847   Factory Act. The Act restricted working hours for women and young persons in textile factories to 10 a day.

1850   Factory Act. The Act specified the hours within which women and young persons could work. They were allowed to work only between 6 a.m. and 6 p.m. with an hour's break for meals. They were not allowed to work after 2 p.m. on Saturdays. Although the Act effectively extended the permitted hours of work to

10½ per day, it was intended to imply limitations for men's hours by restricting the availability of assistance from women and young persons. This intention was circumvented by using child labour to do shift work alongside male workers.

1853   Factory Act. Intended to prevent the use of child labour for shift work, the Act laid down that children were to be employed only from 6 a.m. to 6 p.m. with 1½ hours for meals.

1864   Factory Acts (Extension) Act. Special regulations for health and safety were made for six 'dangerous' industries including match-making, cartridge-making and pottery. Existing Factory Acts were made to apply to these industries, extending their provisions for the first time beyond textile mills and mines.

1867   Factory Acts (Extension) Act. The Act extended all existing Factory Acts to places employing more than 50 people.

1874   Factory Act. The Act raised the minimum working age to 9. Women and young people were to work no more than 10 hours a day in the textile industry. Children up to 14 only to work for half a day.

1878   Factory and Workshops Act. Regulations made governing conditions in workshops.

1891   Factory and Workshops (Consolidation) Act. Safety and sanitary regulations extended. Minimum working age in factories raised to 11.

1901   Factory and Workshops Act. Minimum working age raised to 12.

1909   Trade Boards Act. Boards were set up to fix minimum wages in a number of sweated industries, such as tailoring, paper box-making, chain and lace-making.

Poverty and poor relief

Poverty remained a major social problem in Britain between 1815 and 1914. Population growth and industrialisation created problems by the end of the eighteenth century, especially in times of high food prices. The Speenhamland system supplemented wages from the parish poor rate when bread prices rose, but created heavier poor rates and discouraged farmers from paying realistic wages. The New Poor Law of 1834 reduced 'outdoor' relief and made workhouse conditions rather harsher so that only the most deserving would use them. Parishes were amalgamated into Poor Law Unions and the workhouse placed under guardians. Rural poverty remained an issue until the twentieth century and in the towns sickness, old age, and unemployment were only slowly alleviated by the provision by central government of social welfare benefits.

Several major social enquiries about 1900 showed that poverty remained a major problem. Charles Booth's survey, *The Life and Labour of*

the People in London, concluded that one person in three of the population lived below his basic 'poverty line'. Similar findings by Seebohm
Rowntree in York in 1902 led to a major effort towards social welfare.

The development of state welfare benefits began on a significant scale
under the Liberal governments of 1906–14. The Old Age Pensions Act
of 1908 marked a breakthrough in provision by the state for the elderly.
Between 1909 and 1911, sickness benefits, unemployment pay and labour
exchanges were set up to deal with the major crises of working life. The
money came from taxes on the rich levied by Lloyd George's 'People's
Budget' of 1909.

The Speenhamland system

The name of the system adopted by a resolution in 1795 of the Berkshire
magistrates at a meeting at Speenhamland near Newbury in May 1795
to supplement wages from poor rates on a sliding scale dictated by the
price of bread. Elements of the 'system' had been adopted informally as
a result of Gilbert's Act, and the practice now became widespread in the
agricultural counties of southern England. The system was later widely
criticised because it encouraged farmers to pay low wages and demoralised
the rural labourer.

Chronology of key events, 1815–1914

1819   Poor Relief Act (also known as Sturges Bourne Act). This enabled
        parishes to appoint a representative Poor Law Committee with
        voting powers determined by their contribution to the poor rates.
        The Act was an attempt to ensure that substantial property
        owners had an influential say in the conduct of poor relief.

1834   Poor Law Amendment Act. The Act followed from the *Report of
        the Royal Commission on the Poor Laws, 1834* which expressed
        widespread dissatisfaction with the administration, effects and
        growing cost of poor relief. The Act attempted to abolish 'out-
        door' relief for the able-bodied; relief was only to be granted to
        those who entered the workhouse after passing the 'workhouse
        test'. The workhouse regime was to be made as spartan as pos-
        sible to discourage all but the truly needy from applying for
        relief. Parishes were to be united into Unions and Union work-
        houses substituted for parish workhouses, to be run by elected
        boards of guardians. The Act also established three central Poor
        Law Commissioners to supervise the implementation of the Act.

1836   Registration of births, marriages and deaths made compulsory.

1842   *Enquiry into the Sanitary Conditions of the Labouring Population of
        Great Britain,* written by Edwin Chadwick, secretary to the Poor

Law Commissioners, revealed the totally inadequate drainage, sewerage and sanitation in the industrial areas.

1844   Poor Law Amendment Act. Owners and ratepayers were allowed votes for the election of guardians on a level with their assessment for poor rate. The Act also empowered mothers of illegitimate children to apply to the justices in petty sessions for a maintenance order against the father.

1845   Lunacy Act. Board of Commissioners set up to inspect asylums and other places where the mentally ill were kept.

1847   Poor Law Commission abolished following the abuses revealed in the Andover workhouse, replaced by a Poor Law Board responsible to a minister.

1848   Public Health Act allowed local boards of health to be set up and appoint medical officers of health.

1871   Local Government Board set up to supervise poor law and public health.

1872   Public Health Act. Appointment of medical officers of health made compulsory and sanitary authorities set up.

1875   Public Health Act. Local sanitary authorities given power to enforce sanitary regulations including drainage, sanitation and water supplies.

1906   Local authorities allowed to provide school meals.

1907   School medical examinations made compulsory and school medical services established.

1909   Old Age Pensions Act came into force, giving 5s per week pension to people over 70 years old with incomes less than £31 10s a year. Labour Exchanges set up to register vacant jobs and provide contact between employers and those requiring work.

1911   National Insurance Act. The Act provided insurance against sickness and unemployment to be paid for by contributions from the state, the employer and the employee. It covered those between 16 and 70 years old, but was limited to industries where unemployment was recurrent. Maternity grants introduced.

Expenditure on poor relief, 1800–85

Poor relief expenditure showed a great increase from 1750 to 1834, especially with the growth of the Speenhamland system. Expenditure dropped from £7 million to £4 million after 1834, but soon began to rise again, especially in periods of trade depression.

1800	£4,250,000	1850	£5,800,000
1812	£6,500,000	1875	£7,500,000
1825	£8,800,000	1885	£8,500,000

Health, life expectancy and hospitals

A medical revolution took place between 1815 and 1914. Although some improvements had taken place earlier (such as Jenner's use of vaccination in 1798), urgent action was needed in 1815. During the nineteenth century the insanitary towns of the Industrial Revolution were a prey to diseases caused by poor water supply, lack of sanitation, poor nutrition, and overcrowding. Serious cholera epidemics (1831–32, 1848, 1853, and 1865–66) alarmed the government and there was an investigation into public health led by Edwin Chadwick. As a result local medical officers were appointed and a number of Public Health Acts were passed which much reduced the incidence of disease. At the same time the use of anaesthetics by James Simpson after 1847 and the use of antiseptics by Joseph Lister from 1867 improved recovery rates from surgery. Voluntary hospitals were founded in London and other large cities before 1800, but with the Public Health Acts of the nineteenth century local authorities also began to put up hospitals.

The medical professions began to emerge in their modern form in the nineteenth century. The medical schools were regulated and proper examinations introduced. In the Crimean War (1854–56) Florence Nightingale showed the value of efficient nursing and in 1860 the first nursing school was set up in London.

Chronology

(See also chronology on Housing and environment, p. 125.)

1831–32 First major cholera epidemic stimulated sanitary improvements.

1840 Select Committee on the Health of Towns exposed slum conditions.

1842 Chadwick's Report on the Sanitary Condition of the Labouring Poor.

1847 First Medical Officer of Health in Liverpool.
James Simpson discovered chloroform anaesthetic.

1848 Health of Towns Act established central Board of Health and local boards. Further cholera epidemic.

1853 Further cholera epidemic.

1854 Value of efficient nursing demonstrated by Florence Nightingale and Mary Seacole.

1860 First training school for nurses at St Thomas's Hospital.

1865–66 Further cholera outbreak.

1867 Lister developed antiseptic techniques.

1868 Invention of thermometer.

1875 Public Health Act.

1891	Public Health (London) Act provided for limited control of pollution.
1897	Discovery of x-rays by Röntgen.
1907	School Health Board established.
1911	National Insurance Act.
1912	Presence of vitamins identified in food.
1919	Ministry of Health founded.

Life expectancy at birth

1871	42 years
1901	48 years
1911	53 years

The scourge of tuberculosis – deaths (by decade)

1851–60	65,900	1891–1900	61,600
1861–70	69,300	1901–10	56,500
1871–80	69,700	1911–20	51,400
1881–90	66,600		

Hospital foundations

1816	Royal Ear Hospital (London)
1816	Royal Westminster Ophthalmic Hospital
1816	Royal Waterloo Hospital for Children and Women
1818	West London Infirmary (Charing Cross Hospital)
1828	University College Hospital, London
1828	Royal Free Hospital (London)
1829	Manchester Hospital for Children
1832	Sheffield Royal Infirmary
1835	St Mark's Hospital for Cancer
1838	Royal National Orthopaedic Hospital
1838	Metropolitan Ear, Nose and Throat Hospital
1847	Samaritan Free Hospital for Women
1848	Victoria Park Hospital for Diseases of the Heart and Lungs
1854	Royal Hospital for Incurables
1855	Poplar Hospital for Accidents
1857	Royal Eye Hospital, London
1857	National Hospital for Diseases of the Heart
1858	Royal Dental Hospital, London
1859	National Hospital for Paralysis and Epilepsy
1861	National Dental Hospital
1867	Queen's Hospital for Children
1873	National Temperance Hospital
1887	London Skin Hospital

Housing and environment

Introduction

One of the most persistent social problems of the period 1815–1914 was housing. Population growth and rapid urbanisation created great physical difficulties in providing decent and healthy conditions. Though the housing stock grew considerably to cope with population growth, many of the early houses built were squalid, back-to-back houses built in regular courts and streets, sharing common closets and water supplies.

Slum clearance was started in many major cities by the middle of the nineteenth century. The Artisans' Dwelling Act (1875) gave local authorities power to clear slums and the Public Health Act (1875) laid down minimum conditions for construction, sewerage, drainage, and water supply.

Industrialisation had also created new towns where industry demanded the concentration of population. Communications centres for both canals and railways were important examples of new town development, such as Stourport and Crewe, Swindon and Rugby. Towns such as Barrow-in-Furness, Birkenhead and Middlesbrough experienced mushroom growth. At the same time there were schemes for model towns and 'garden cities'. Examples of these were Port Sunlight (started in 1887 by Lord Leverhulme), Bourneville and Letchworth. These formed the basis for town planning schemes developed in the twentieth century, following the Town Planning Act of 1910.

Chronology of key dates

1840   Select Committee on the Health of Towns exposed slum conditions in many industrial towns.

1842   Chadwick's Report on the Sanitary Condition of the Labouring Poor.

1848   Health of Towns Act set up central Board of Health and local boards.

1851   Labouring Classes Lodging Houses Act permitted local authorities to appoint commissioners to erect or purchase lodging houses for the working classes. Little used.

1853–6   Smoke Abatement Acts for the metropolitan area.

1866   Sanitary Act empowered local authorities to act against smoke nuisances.

1868   Artisans' and Labourers' Dwellings Act (also known as Torrens' Act) gave local authorities powers to compel owners to demolish or repair insanitary houses.

1875   Artisans' and Labourers' Dwellings Improvement Act gave local authorities powers of compulsory purchase of areas 'unfit for human habitation'.
          Public Health Act included smoke abatement section.

1881   Smoke Abatement Committee formed.
1885   Royal Commission on the Housing of the Working Classes revealed the poor state of housing in London and other major cities. The Commission recommended the appointment of additional sanitary inspectors, the rating of derelict land and government loans to build working-class housing.
1887   Work begun on Port Sunlight.
1890   Housing of the Working Classes Act granted local councils further powers to close insanitary houses and to build council houses using money from the local rates.
1891   Public Health (London) Act provided for limited control of smoke pollution.
1899   Coal Smoke Abatement Society formed.
1909   Housing Acts.

Number of houses at census, 1851–1911

1851	3,700,000	1891	6,960,000
1861	4,190,000	1901	7,990,000
1871	4,790,000	1911	8,940,000
1881	6,290,000		

Source: C. Cook and J. Stevenson, *Longman Atlas of Modern British History: a Visual Guide to British Society and Politics* (1978).

Women and society

Background note: The publication in 1792 of Mary Wollstonecraft's *Vindication of the Rights of Women* presented the first clear statement of the need for political and civil equality for women.

The status of women

Chronology of key events, 1815–1914

1839   Custody of Infants Act gave mothers of 'unblemished character' access to their children in the event of separation or divorce.

1847   Queens College for Women opened.

1848   Women admitted to London University.

1849   Bedford College opened.

1850   North London Collegiate Day School for girls established by Frances Buss.

1854   Cheltenham Ladies' College founded.
Florence Nightingale nursed Crimean War-wounded in Scutari.

1857   Matrimonial Causes Act set up divorce courts. Women obtained limited access to divorce, though, unlike men, only for a specific cause other than adultery. Rights of access to children after divorce extended. Women given right to their property after a legal separation or a protection order given as a result of husband's desertion.

1858   *Englishwoman's Journal* launched to debate issues of women's work, legal rights, suffrage and education. Founding spirits were Barbara Leigh Smith (1827–91) and Bessie Rayner Parkes (1829–1925).
Dorothea Beale became headmistress of Cheltenham Ladies College.

1859   Society for Promoting the Employment of Women founded. Followed by establishment of the Victoria Press (a women's printshop run by Emily Faithfull) and a Ladies' Institute (at 19, Langham Place, London).
First woman to be entered on the Medical Register (Elizabeth Blackwell).

1863   Girls of 16 allowed to sit the Cambridge Local Examination.
Royal Commission established to examine girls' schools.

1864   First of Contagious Diseases Acts passed.

1865   Petitions organised by the 'Ladies of Langham Place' for a Women's Suffrage Bill (the 'Langham Place Petition').

1866   Second Contagious Diseases Act.

Barbara Bodichon formed first Women's Suffrage Committee.

1867   John Stuart Mill published speech on *Admission of Women to Electoral Franchise*; followed by *The Subjection of Women* (1869).

1869   Vote in local elections given to women ratepayers.

1870   Married Women's Property Act allowed women to retain £200 of their own earnings. Education Act provided elementary education for girls as well as boys.

1871   Newnham College, Cambridge, founded.

1872   London School of Medicine for Women opened. Hitchin College (later Girton College) moved to Cambridge.

Girls' Public Day School Trust formed.

1873   Custody of Infants Act extended access to children to all women in the event of separation or divorce.

1876   Medical schools opened to women.

1877   Married Women's Property Act provisions extended to Scotland.

1878   Association for the Education of Women in Oxford (AEW) formed. Women admitted to University of London.

1879   Opening of Lady Margaret Hall and Somerville College, Oxford.

1882   Married Women's Property Act allowed women to own and administer their property.

1884   Married Women's Property Act made a woman no longer a 'chattel' but an independent and separate person.

1886   Guardianship of Infants Act. Women could be made sole guardian of children if husband died.

Foundation of St Hugh's and St Hilda's Colleges, Oxford.

Repeal of the Contagious Diseases Acts (of 1864, 1866 and 1869).

1888   Match girls' strike (see p. 160).

1894   Local Government Act. Women eligible to vote for parochial councils.

1897   Foundation of National Union of Women's Suffrage Societies under the presidency of Mrs Millicent Fawcett.

1901   Emmeline Pankhurst elected to Manchester School Board.

1903   Women's Social and Political Union (WSPU) founded by Emmeline Pankhurst in Manchester with slogan 'Deeds not Words'.

1905   Arrest of Christabel Pankhurst and Annie Kenney after first militant incidents.

1906   WSPU fields candidates in general election.

1907   3,000 WSPU branches formed; Hyde Park demonstration attracted 250,000; *Votes for Women* sold 40,000 copies weekly. First women's parliament met at Caxton Hall. Breakaway Women's Freedom League formed.

1909   First hunger strike in protest at treatment of suffragettes in prison (by Marjorie Wallace Dunlop in July). Force-feeding of suffragettes in prison began (Sept.).

1910   Formation of a Conciliation Committee to draft a Women's Suffrage Bill (3 subsequently drafted, but all failed). WSPU truce inaugurated brief period of peaceful protests. 'Black Friday' riot outside House of Commons; 120 women arrested (18 Nov.). WSPU renewed truce.

1911   Numerous peaceful protests; 60,000 women marched on Women's Coronation Procession (17 June). Widespread window-smashing marked outbreak of militant tactics (Nov.) which included firing and bombing of houses and churches.

1912   WSPU headquarters raided (5 Mar.). Arrest of Pethick-Lawrences (sentenced to imprisonment). Nationwide hunger strike by suffragette prisoners. New paper, the *Suffragette*, launched. Militancy at a new peak.

1913   Passing of Prisoners' Temporary Discharge for Ill-Health Act (known as the Cat and Mouse Act) (April). Hunger strikers released only to be rearrested. WSPU Lincoln's Inn House raided (April). Death of Emily Wilding Davison in protest at the Derby race at Epsom (June). Force-feeding reintroduced (Oct.). Bomb attack on Holloway Gaol (Dec.).

1914   Sylvia Pankhurst expelled from WSPU. Suffragette attacks reached a climax. Painting at National Gallery slashed by Mary Richardson (Mar.). Suffragette campaign halted by outbreak of war (4 Aug.).

1918   Women partially enfranchised by Representation of the People Act (Feb.). Certain women over 30 years of age received the vote. Women eligible to become Members of Parliament. Countess Markiewicz elected to Commons, but did not take her seat.

1919   Passing of Sex Disqualification Removal Act. Lady Astor first woman to sit in the Commons.

Suffrage and anti-suffrage societies, 1865–1918

The women's suffrage movement gave birth to an extraordinary variety of organisations, and brought into political activity a large number of women of all classes. Two organisations, the National Union of Women's Suffrage Societies (NUWSS) and the Women's Social and Political Union (WSPU) were the most important in the decade before 1914, representing the constitutionalists and the militants respectively. A number of other organisations pursued their own campaigns, however, either under the umbrella of the NUWSS or as breakaways from the WSPU. Names of organisations changed rapidly. The list below gives the major groupings.

Central Society for Women's Suffrage

Created in 1900 from a reunion of earlier bodies. It was the successor body of a series of women's suffrage organisations dating back to the 1860s. The Women's Suffrage Petition Committee, founded in late 1865, became the Women's Suffrage Provisional Committee in the autumn of 1866, the Women's Society for Obtaining Political Rights for Women in July 1867, and the London National Society for Women's Suffrage a month later. In 1871 this split, one faction retaining the old name, and another becoming known as the Central Committee of the National Society for Women's Suffrage, which became the name of the reunited society in 1877. This split again in 1888, over the question of political affiliation, into the Central Committee of the National Society for Women's Suffrage (Central and East of England Society for Women's Suffrage, 1897) and the Central National Society for Women's Suffrage (Central and Western Society for Women's Suffrage, 1897). These were reunited in 1900 as the Central Society for Women's Suffrage, known as the London Society for Women's Suffrage from 1907.

National League for Opposing Women's Suffrage

The Women's National Anti-Suffrage League was founded in 1908, largely through the inspiration of Mrs Humphrey Ward, and under the presidency of the Countess of Jersey. In July 1910 the Men's League for Opposing Women's Suffrage was founded, with the Earl of Cromer as president. The two Leagues amalgamated in January 1911 as the National League for Opposing Women's Suffrage. Lord Cromer became president, succeeded in 1912 by Lord Curzon and Lord Weardale. The League was dissolved in 1918. There was also a Scottish Women's National Anti-Suffrage League, which the Duchess of Montrose founded in 1910.

National Union of Women's Suffrage Societies

Established in 1897 as a federation of all the suffrage groups then existing, some of which dated back to 1867. Mrs Fawcett was the president, and throughout the suffrage campaign the NUWSS remained the chief constitutional organisation. Its members were referred to as 'suffragists'. After the Representation of the People Act was passed in 1918 the name was changed to National Union of Societies for Equal Citizenship, later the National Council for Equal Citizenship. In 1946 this was incorporated into the National Women Citizens' Association.

Votes for Women Fellowship

Founded in 1912 by the Pethick-Lawrences as a breakaway from the WSPU.

Women's Freedom League

Founded in 1907 as a breakaway from the Women's Social and Political Union by, among others, Mrs Despard, Edith How-Martyn and Teresa Billington-Greig.

Women's Social and Political Union

The WSPU (founded in Manchester in 1903 by Emmeline Pankhurst) was the chief militant suffrage society, and remained so despite various splits and the establishment of new organisations: the Women's Freedom League, 1907; the Votes for Women Fellowship, founded by the Pethick-Lawrences, 1912; and the East London Federation of the Suffragettes, founded by Sylvia Pankhurst in 1913, which in February 1916 became the Workers' Suffrage Federation.

Women's Tax Resistance League

The League was established in 1909, growing out of the Women's Freedom League, and extending its tactic of organising tax resistance as a weapon in the suffrage campaign.

Workers' Socialist Federation

The East London Federation of the Suffragettes was established in 1913 by Sylvia Pankhurst as a breakaway from the Women's Social and Political Union. In 1916 it became the Workers' Suffrage Federation, and in 1918 the Workers' Socialist Federation.

Workers' Suffrage Federation

See Workers' Socialist Federation.

The regulation of sexuality, 1815–1914

Note: Throughout this period homosexuality remained a crime, punishable by death until 1861.

1861   Homosexual act of sodomy no longer a capital offence.

1869   Term 'homosexuality' invented (entering the general vocabulary in the 1880s).

1883   Publication of *A Problem in Greek Ethics* by John Addington Symonds (1840–93) increased awareness of homosexuality in classical world.

1885   Labouchere amendment to Criminal Law Amendment Act made 'gross indecency' between men illegal, whether in public or private.

1889   Cleveland Street scandal exposed male brothel.

1895   Trial of Oscar Wilde (1854–1900) attracted great public interest. Wilde prosecuted under 1885 Labouchere amendment (see above).

1897   *Sexual Inversion* published by Havelock Ellis (1859–1939). The term became popularised.

1908   Publication of *The Intermediate Sex* by Edward Carpenter (1844–1929).

Press

By 1800 there was a flourishing provincial and national press, the latter using the mail-coach system to cover the country. Increased production came with the development of steam printing, used on *The Times* by 1814, but newspapers bore a heavy stamp duty until 1855, restricting their readership largely to the upper and middle classes. Cheaper newspapers became possible after 1855 and improved public education led to the birth of mass circulation papers such as Alfred Harmsworth's *Daily Mail*, started in 1896. The number of newspapers grew most rapidly in the late nineteenth and the first part of the twentieth century.

Chronology of major developments in the press

1814   Steam presses used to print *The Times*.
1815   Newspaper stamp duty became 4d per copy.
1816   Cobbett's 2d *Political Register* ('Tuppenny Trash') published.
1817   John Black became editor of the *Morning Chronicle*. *Reformist Register* published.
1820   Imprisonment of Richard Carlile of *The Republican*.
        Thwaites Wright became editor of the *Morning Herald*.
1821   *Manchester Guardian* first published: John Edward Taylor proprietor, Jeremiah Garnett editor.
1822   W. Mudford became editor of *The Courier*.
        Sunday Times first appeared, with D.W. Harvey MP as editor/proprietor. Liberal in politics before 1845.
1827   *The Standard* founded, with Dr Giffard as editor.
        Applegarth-Cowper four-cylinder press able to print 5,000 copies per hour of *The Times*.
        Thomas Barnes appointed editor of *The Times* (until 1841).
1837   Newspaper tax reduced from 4d to 1d; Isaac Pitman's simplified shorthand introduced.
        Invention of electric telegraph greatly facilitated collection of news.
1843   *News of the World* founded as Sunday newspaper.
1850   Circulation of *The Times* reached 34,000.
1851   First news agency, Reuters, formed in London.

1855   Repeal of Stamp Duty on newspapers permitted cheap press.
1860   Circulation of *Reynold's News* reached 350,000.
1870   Education Act provided basis of mass reading public.
1881   George Newnes produced *Tit-Bits* magazine for mass audience.
1896   *Daily Mail* founded by Alfred Harmsworth, later Lord Northcliffe
        (1865–1922); first mass circulation newspaper, priced at ½d.
1900   *Daily Express* started by Arthur Pearson (1866–1921).
1901   Circulation of *Daily Mail* passed one million.
1904   *Daily Mirror* refounded as ½d illustrated newspaper, the first to
        make regular use of halftone photographs.
1908   Harmsworth acquired *The Times.*
1914   Press censorship introduced under Defence of the Realm Act of
        August 1914 and strengthened in subsequent amendments.

The rise of the English provincial press after 1815

1815   *Carlisle Patriot*
1821   *Brighton Gazette*
        Manchester Guardian
1824   *Manchester Courier*
1827   *Brighton Guardian*
1828   *Western Times* (Exeter)
1832   *Halifax Guardian*
        Newcastle Journal
1834   *Bradford Observer*
1836   *Doncaster Chronicle*
1850   *Huddersfield Weekly Chronicle*
1851   *Huddersfield Weekly Examiner*
1852   *Hull Daily News*
1853   *Halifax Courier*
1855   *Midland Free Press* (Leicester)
        Liverpool Daily Post
        Sheffield Daily Telegraph
1857   *Birmingham Daily Post*
1858   *Western Daily Press* (Bristol)
1859   *Bristol Observer*
1860   *Western Daily Mercury* (Plymouth)
        Western Morning News (Plymouth)
1867   *Leeds Evening Express*
1868   *Bradford Daily Telegraph*
        Sussex Daily News (Brighton)
1869   *Northern Echo* (Darlington)
1870   *Eastern Daily Press* (Norwich)
1872   *Leeds Daily News*
        Leicester Daily Post

1874	*East Anglian Daily Times* (Ipswich)
	Leicester Daily Mercury
1877	*Bath Daily Chronicle*
1879	*Derby Daily Telegraph*
	Worcester Daily Times
1880	*Northampton Daily Chronicle*
1884	*Bradford Citizen*
	Derby Express

Law and order

Riots and public order

Riots and disturbances were a common feature of nineteenth-century life. By 1815, political and economic riots were becoming more common and were widespread during the post-war period. The most important were the Luddite outbreaks in the North and Midlands. The causes included high prices, depressed trade, and reactions to the use of labour-saving machinery. Large numbers of soldiers were required to control the Luddites and many were brought to trial and executed before the riots subsided.

In 1830–32, the 'Captain Swing' riots took place, caused by low wages and unemployment amongst the agricultural labourers (see p. 290). In 1839, trade depression and disappointment with the Reform Bill of 1832 (p. 60) led to agitation for the Six Points of the Charter, the principal demand of which was for universal suffrage.

1815
Mar. Riots in London against passing of the Corn Laws.
Disturbances amongst Tyneside keelmen during labour dispute.
Farm machinery broken at Gosbeck, Suffolk.
July–Aug. Further machine-breaking disturbances in Suffolk.
Oct. Disturbances at Hull, Sunderland and South Shields during seamen's strike.
Nov. Disturbances amongst Bilston colliers following a wage cut.

1816
Feb. Machine-breaking at Huddersfield.
Apr.–June Food riots, machine-breaking and arson in Norfolk, Suffolk, Cambridgeshire and Essex. Most serious disturbances at Bridport, Norwich, Downham Market, Littleport, Brandon and Ely.
July–Aug. Food riots at Frome, Stockport, Bolton, Coventry, Hinckley and Birmingham.
Oct. Disturbances in South Wales during strikes amongst colliers and ironworkers.
Nov.–Dec. Food riots at Carlisle, Huddersfield, Oldham, Sheffield and Dundee.

Dec. Spa Fields riots in London when the followers of Thomas Spence attempted to seize the Tower and the Bank of England.

1817
Jan. Attack upon the Prince Regent's coach on return from the state opening of Parliament.
Disturbances amongst South Wales iron-workers.
Feb. Food riots at Amlwch and Tremadoc in Wales.
Mar. Food riot at Maryport. Strikes and food riots at Radstock.
March of the 'Blanketeers' set off from Manchester.
Broken up near Stockport. Further disturbances in South Wales.
June Pentrich 'rising' in Derbyshire led by Jeremiah Brandreth.
Huddersfield 'rising'. Minor skirmishes.

1818
July–Aug. Disturbances during strike of Manchester cotton spinners.
Aug. Riots at Stockport during strike of power-loom weavers.
Squatters' riots at Rhydoldog in Carnarvonshire.
Nov. Food riots amongst colliers at Whitehaven.

1819
July Orange riots in Liverpool.
Aug. Peterloo 'Massacre' (16th).
Reform disturbance at Macclesfield and Stockport.
Oct. Disturbances during keelmen's strike at North Shields.

1820
Feb. Cato Street conspiracy uncovered.
Mar. Election riot at Banbury.
Disturbances at South Shields amongst seamen.
Anti-clearance disturbances at Culrain, Gruids and Achness in Ross-shire and Sutherland.
Mar.–Apr. Disturbances amongst wool-croppers near Huddersfield and Barnsley 'rising'.
Apr. 'Battle of Bonnymuir' near Glasgow between weavers and troops.
June Demonstrations in London in support of Queen Caroline.
Nov. Widespread demonstrations in support of Queen Caroline.

1821
Jan. Disturbances in Shropshire during colliers' strike.
Mar. Anti-clearance disturbance at Gruids, Scotland.
Aug. Riots in London during funeral of Queen Caroline.

1822
May Disturbances during colliers' strike in South Wales. Riots in Frome and Warminster over use of the guy-shuttle.

July Disturbances amongst Norwich weavers over a wage reduction.
Oct.–Nov. Disturbances during keelmen's strike on the Tyne.

1824
Aug. Houses demolished by squatters at Fishguard.

1825
Aug. Disturbances during seamen's strike at Sunderland.

1826
Apr.–May Power-looms broken at Accrington, Blackburn, Bury, Chaddeston, Rawtenstall, Long Holme, Edenfield, Summerseat and Manchester. Also attacks on power-looms by Bradford worsted weavers.

1829
May Attacks on weaving factories and provision shops in Manchester.
June–July Food disturbances in Bolton, Wigan and Preston.

1830
Apr. Beginning of 'Captain Swing' disturbances in southern counties of England (see p. 290).
Nov. Reform disturbances in London.
Dec. Disturbances in the Ruabon area as a result of a strike amongst the North Wales colliers.

1839
July 'Bull Ring' riots in Birmingham. Pro-Chartist demonstrations.
Nov. Newport 'rising' led by John Frost suppressed.

1840
Chartist 'rising' in Dewsbury and Sheffield.

1842
July–Aug. 'Plug-plot' riots and Chartist general strike in the North and Potteries.

1848
Apr. Chartist demonstration at Kennington Common (10th).

1852
Stockport riots between Catholics and Protestants; two Catholic churches sacked.

1855
'Sunday trading' riots in Hyde Park, London, against Act prohibiting trading on Sundays.

1862
'Garibaldi' riots in Hyde Park, London between Irish and Italians.

1866
July Reform demonstration broke down Hyde Park railings.
Oct. Sheffield 'outrages': attacks upon non-union labour by Sheffield cutlers.

1867
May Reform League demonstration at Hyde Park in defiance of Home Secretary's ban.
Sept. Fenian rescue of prisoners in Manchester.
Dec. Gunpowder attack by Fenians on Clerkenwell Prison.

1868
'Murphy' riots in Ashton and Stalybridge; attacks on Irish Catholics provoked by anti-Catholic lecturer, William Murphy.

1886
Feb. 'Black Monday'; unemployed riots in West End of London, following meeting of Social Democratic Federation in Trafalgar Square (8th)

1887
Nov. 'Bloody Sunday'; meeting of Social Democratic Federation in Trafalgar Square broken up by police and troops (13th).

1893
Two people killed during clashes between troops and strikers at Acton Hall Colliery, near Featherstone.

1909
Serious sectarian riots in Liverpool.

The police

In 1815, the concept of a professional police force had not yet developed nationally. Professional policing started in London in the late eighteenth century when Fielding set up the Bow Street Runners. In 1792 seven more police offices were opened in London with a few dozen professional constables and the growing problem of crime led to the establishment of the Metropolitan Police in 1829. This replaced the confusion of authorities with a single force for all of London except the City of London, which retained a separate force. Police forces then spread through the country to other large towns and into the rural areas, where they had an important influence in reducing crime, especially after 1856 when county and borough forces were made obligatory and placed under the supervision of Her Majesty's Inspectors of Constabulary.

Growth of police numbers in England and Wales

1856	15,000
1870	26,000
1880	31,000
1890	38,000
1901	43,000
1911	51,000

Source: C. Cook and J. Stevenson, *Longman Atlas of Modern British History: a Visual Guide to British Society and Politics* (1978).

Chronology of developments in the police

1829   Metropolitan Police Act set up a paid, uniformed police force for the metropolitan area excluding the City of London, under the authority of two commissioners and the Home Secretary. It was the first modern police force. The first London police had been set up under the Middlesex Justices' Act of 1792.

1833   Lighting and Watching Act permitted any town with a population of over 5,000 to appoint paid watchmen.

1835   Municipal Corporations Act required each of the 178 boroughs to appoint a watch committee and to set up a force of constables.

1839   County Police Act permitting justices to set up a paid county police force. In 1840 authorisation given to amalgamate borough and county forces where desired.

1842   Plain clothes detective force established in London.

1856   County and Borough Police Act compelled all counties and boroughs to establish and maintain a police force. Three Inspectors of Constabulary appointed to assess their efficiency and report to parliament; forces certified as efficient to qualify for an exchequer grant towards the cost of the force. Boroughs of under 5,000 people, maintaining their own forces, not to be eligible for a grant.

1866   Maximum pay of constables raised to 23s 4d (and to 29s 6d in 1876), reflecting their increasing efficiency and status.

1877   Municipal Corporations (New Charters) Act prohibited newly incorporated boroughs of under 20,000 inhabitants from setting up police forces.

1878   CID established.
1884   Establishment of Special Branch to deal with offences involving the security of the state.
1885   Number of 'inefficient' police forces fell to 25 (down from 120 in 1857).
1888   Local Government Act abolished police forces run by boroughs with a population of less than 10,000. Control of the county police forces transferred to standing joint committees of county councillors and justices. Metropolitan Police headquarters moved to New Scotland Yard.
1890   Pensions introduced for long-serving police. Number of 'inefficient' police forces fell to zero.

Reform of the courts

The development of the police was paralleled by moves to reform the antiquated justice system then prevalent. Court and civil law reform became major themes.

Chronology of major developments

1813   Stipendiary magistrates appointed in Manchester.
1830   Abolition of certain sinecures by Lord Brougham as Chancellor.
1836   Liverpool appointed stipendiary magistrates (followed by Birmingham, 1856, and Leeds, 1859). Reform allowed prisoners accused of serious crimes to have counsel to represent them.
1844   Abolition of imprisonment for debts under £20.
1846   System of county courts established to allow cheaper settlement of small debts.
1861   Imprisonment for debt finally ended.
1873   Major reform of courts. A single High Court established, replacing 7 existing courts.
1879   Appointment of Director of Public Prosecutions (DPP) to arrange prosecution of serious criminal cases.

Prisons and penal reform

Long-term imprisonment was virtually unknown in Britain before the middle of the nineteenth century, except for debt. Most criminals were either executed or transported. Early penal reformers such as John Howard and Elizabeth Fry wanted to reduce capital punishment for minor offences and make long-term imprisonment an opportunity for moral reformation. The major reduction of capital statutes was carried out under Sir Robert Peel's Home Secretaryship after 1822. Transportation was finally abolished in 1853. New prisons were built to house prisoners, often using prison methods borrowed from the United States, such as the 'silent' and 'solitary' systems, while capital punishment was reserved for a small number of major offences. This system basically remained the same into the twentieth century.

Chronology of events

1818	Establishment of House of Commons committee to report on capital offences.
1822	Peel appointed Home Secretary.
1823	Prisons Act began reform of prison system. Five Acts passed by Parliament, abolishing death penalty for over 100 offences.
1824	Prison Discipline Act. Together with the 1823 Prisons Act, this established rules for prisons and ordered JPs to inspect them (although this was widely ignored).
1832	Abolition of death penalty for house-breaking, horse-stealing, sheep-stealing and coining false money.
1835	Appointment of Home Office Inspectors to visit prisons.
1837	Number of capital offences further reduced.
1839	New South Wales refused to accept transported convicts (now sent to Van Diemen's Land).
1842	Pentonville prison built.
1847	Theft charges against children under 14 to be dealt with by magistrates (who could discharge them even if found guilty).
1850	Age limit of 1847 Act raised to 16.
1853	End of transportation to Van Diemen's Land (transported convicts now sent to Western Australia).
1854–57	Establishment of reformatory schools for juvenile offenders.
1861	Capital offences reduced to four. Death penalty for attempted murder abolished.
1867	Final end of transportation.

Crime and punishment

The gradual development of more effective police forces, new penal policies, and an improvement in living standards helped to reduce the number of crimes in proportion to the total population from the middle of the nineteenth century. Growth of population and the increasing efficiency of the police and legal system led to a rise in the number of both serious and minor offences brought before the courts in the period up to 1914.

However, during the nineteenth century prison sentences were gradually made less severe as part of a general process of humane reform of the penal system. Sentences became shorter, fines were used more and transportation for life was ended.

The changing prison population, 1880–1910

1880	28,700
1890	18,300
1900	17,500
1910	22,000

Committals for indictable offences in England and Wales, 1805–56

	Total		Total		Total		Total
1805	4,605	1818	13,567	1831	19,647	1844	26,542
1806	4,346	1819	14,254	1832	20,829	1845	24,303
1807	4,446	1820	13,710	1833	20,072	1846	25,107
1808	4,735	1821	13,115	1834	20,168	1847	28,833
1809	5,330	1822	12,241	1835	20,731	1848	30,349
1810	5,146	1823	12,263	1836	20,984	1849	27,816
1811	5,337	1824	13,698	1837	23,612	1850	26,813
1812	6,576	1825	14,437	1838	23,094	1851	27,960
1813	7,164	1826	16,164	1839	24,443	1852	27,510
1814	6,390	1827	17,921	1840	27,187	1853	27,057
1815	7,818	1828	16,564	1841	27,760	1854	29,359
1816	9,091	1829	18,675	1842	31,309	1855	25,972
1817	13,932	1830	18,107	1843	29,591	1856	19,437

Note: The judicial statistics were altered and extended in 1857 to contain new categories of information.
Source: *British Parliamentary Papers*.

Crimes known to the police, 1857–1900

	England and Wales	Scotland
1857	91,671	–
1865	92,522	–
1870	90,532	118,105
1875	82,316	123,169
1880	98,440	122,656
1885	86,905	114,865
1890	81,773	136,505
1895	81,323	134,357
1900	77,934	33,492

Note: Figures relate to indictable, generally more serious, offences, reported to or discovered by the police. Figures for Scotland up to 1895 also include minor, non-indictable, offences.

Transportation

Transportation became increasingly common in the late eighteenth century as a substitute for capital punishment, but was gradually replaced by long-term imprisonment in the United Kingdom after 1840. As a result, the numbers of those transported gradually declined, falling to almost negligible proportions after 1853, until it was finally ended in 1867.

Numbers transported to Australia, 1815–53

5-year period	Maximum		Minimum	
1815–19	1818	3,350	1815	1,093
1820–24	1820	3,989	1824	1,887
1825–29	1829	4,797	1826	2,178
1830–34	1833	6,871	1832	4,522
1835–39	1835	6,077	1839	3,711
1840–44	1842	5,528	1841	3,489
1845–49	1845	3,632	1848	1,634
1850–53	1850	3,204	1853	1,569

Source: G.L. Shaw, *Convicts and the Colonies* (1966), pp. 361–8.

The abolition of capital offences

The abolition of a multitude of capital offences was one of the major features of the first three decades of the nineteenth century. In 1800 there were about 200 capital offences on the statute book. The first of the eighteenth-century capital statutes to be repealed, as a result of Romilly's campaign, came with the 1808 Larceny Act, which abolished the death sentence for larceny from the person, and broadened the definition of the offence. The Stealing from Bleaching Grounds Act, 1811 and the Stealing of Linen Act, 1811, repealed two obsolete capital statutes.

Key Acts concerning the death penalty

1820   Stealing in Shops Act raised the minimum amount stolen in shops which would constitute a capital offence from 5s to £15.

1823   Judgement of Death Act gave discretion to the judge to abstain from pronouncing the death sentence on a person convicted of any crime except murder, if the judge felt the offender was fit to be recommended for the King's mercy.

A separate Act abolished the death penalty for: (a) larceny of property to the value of 40s on ships on navigable rivers; (b) larceny of property to the value of 40s in shops.

1827–28   Series of measures known as 'Peel's Acts', essentially consoli-
          dating statutes, codifying the statute law. Under these Acts
          the 'benefit of clergy' was abolished, and the death penalty
          restricted to those felonies from which 'benefit of clergy'
          had previously been excluded, or which new statutes would
          expressly specify should be capital. The punishment for non-
          capital felonies was to be transportation or imprisonment. At
          the same time, the Larceny Act was abolished.

1830   Forgery Act. This consolidated the law relating to forgery. It
          abolished the death sentence for a number of offences, but
          retained it for 42 kinds of forgery.

1832   Forgery Act. Repealed the 1830 Act and now abolished the
          death sentence for all forgery offences, except forgery of wills
          and of powers of attorney for the transfer of government
          stock.

Local government

In 1815, local government had hardly changed over the preceding centuries. However, during the nineteenth century, it was gradually rationalised. Modern local government was initiated with the Municipal Reform Act of 1835. These reforms began an era of active local government and 'civic pride', under such leaders as Joseph Chamberlain in Birmingham. Further major developments in local government came with the creation of county councils, county borough councils (1888), and urban district, rural district and parish councils (1894). Meanwhile, wider powers were given to local authorities under the Public Health Act 1875, the Education Act 1902 and the Housing Act 1909.

1818   Vestries Act (also known as Sturges Bourne Act) established a system of voting according to landownership in electing parish officers.

1831   Vestries Act (also known as Hobhouse Act) provided for the election of members of parish vestries and a secret ballot if requested by five ratepayers. One-third of elected representatives to retire each year.

1835   Municipal Reform Act. All members of town councils to be elected by the ratepayers, and town councils to publish their accounts. Local government was placed in the hands of the mayor, aldermen and council, elected by the burgesses or resident ratepayers – freemen having no rights as burgesses but holding the parliamentary franchise. Franchise in local elections extended to all males over 21 who had been owners or tenants of property for two and a half years and had paid rates. Towns with over 6,000 population were divided into wards for voting. Property qualifications introduced, restricting election of town councillors to property owners.
        Highways Act abolished old statute labour and permitted a highway rate to be levied.

1850   Public Libraries Act (see p. 185).

1855   Public Libraries Act (see p. 185).

1855   Metropolis Management Act. The Act set up the Metropolitan Board of Works as the main authority for London.

1862   Highways Act provided for compulsory uniting of parishes into highway authorities if deemed appropriate.

1869   Vote in local elections granted to women ratepayers.

1875   Public Health Act.

1888   Local Government Act. Administration of counties, including levying of rates, maintenance of roads, bridges, lunatic asylums and poor relief transferred to county councils elected by ratepayers.

1889   Establishment of London County Council (LCC).

1892   Public Libraries Act – major step forward in development of libraries (see p. 185).

1894   Local Government Act created rural and urban district councils. All county and parliamentary electors given the vote in local elections. Civil functions of parish vestries were transferred to new parish councils and parish meetings. Women eligible to vote for parish councils.

1899   Local Government Act converted the London vestries into borough councils.

1902   Education Act (see p. 117).

1907   Women enabled to become councillors under provisions of Qualification for Women (County and Borough Councils) Act.

1909   Housing Act.

Occupations and social structure

As a result of the Industrial Revolution, Britain's social structure changed from one with a small middle class of professional men and merchants, becoming more complex.

With a larger middle class of manufacturers, businessmen and professionals and a large industrial workforce of artisans and factory workers, Patrick Colquhoun's estimate of the social structure about 1815 shows the growth of workmen and artisans with the Industrial Revolution, and the growing complexity of the 'middle' and professional classes.

Royalty and nobility	3,000
Baronets, knights and squires	50,000
Upper clergy, merchants and bankers, upper civil servants and lawyers	40,000
Independent gentry	150,000
Upper doctors and other professionals	20,000
Army and navy officers	70,000
Lesser clergy	75,000
Upper freeholders	300,000
Ship owners, lesser merchants, shipbuilders, engineers and builders	200,000
Lesser professionals, civil servants and dissenting ministers	250,000
Innkeepers	375,000
Shopkeepers and hawkers	600,000
Master craftsmen and manufacturers	450,000
Lesser freeholders	900,000
Farmers	1,300,000
Teachers, actors, clerks and shopmen	320,000
Artisans and other skilled workers	4,500,000
Agricultural labourers, miners, workers and road and canal seamen	3,500,000
Personal and household servants	1,300,000
Sailors and soldiers	800,000
Paupers, vagrants, prisoners and lunatics	1,900,000

behalf of the government, Wilberforce suggested that the
apply to *all* combinations and this was supported by Pitt. The
ed for summary prosecution before a single magistrate on
ce of one or more witnesses. Workmen could be sentenced
onths in gaol or two months in a House of Correction with
ur for: (a) combining to improve conditions or raise wages;
cing others to leave work; (c) refusing to work with others;
ding meetings with the purpose of improving wages and condi-
persuading others to attend such a meeting or raise money for
eeting; (e) contributing to the expenses of anyone tried under
(f) holding money for a combination and refusing to answer
ns about it.

nation Act 1800

ions to the 1799 Combination Act complained about the vague-
f its language; the use of summary jurisdiction; the possibility of
oyer-magistrates trying their own workmen; the compulsion to
er questions about money possibly held for a combination, thereby
minating oneself or else face automatic sentence under the Act.
ions for total repeal led by the Whig, Sheridan, were resisted by Pitt
claimed that provisions for summary prosecution of combinations
e essential. The Combination Act of 1800, therefore, retained the
ncipal features of the 1799 Act, but modified some of its features,
tably: (a) two magistrates instead of one to try cases; (b) employer-
gistrates prohibited from trying cases of men in their own trade;
an arbitration provision was introduced; (d) masters were prohibited
m combining to reduce wages, increase hours or worsen conditions.

mbination Act 1824

rovisions

Previous statutes relating to combinations, including Act of 1800,
almost entirely repealed.
Combinations – (a) to get, increase or fix wages; (b) to lessen or alter
hours; (c) to reduce amount of work; (d) to induce another to depart
from employment before end of time for which hired, or (e) to quit
or return his work before end of time for which hired, or (f) to
refuse to enter into employment; or (g) to regulate production or
management methods – not to be liable to indictment or prosecution
for conspiracy or other crime under common or statute law.
A similar provision applied to combinations of masters.
Violence to persons or property, or threats or intimidation, which
achieved purposes 2(a) to (g), made an offence, whether committed
by an individual or by a combination; penalty was imprisonment and
being 'kept to hard labour' for up to two months.

Principal occupation groups in Britain in 1851 in order of size

	Male	*Female*
Total population	10,224,000	10,736,000
Population of 10 years old and upwards	7,616,000	8,155,000
Agriculture: farmer, grazier, labourer, servant	1,563,000	227,000
Domestic service (excluding farm service)	134,000	905,000
Cotton worker, every kind, with printer, dyer	255,000	272,000
Building craftsman: carpenter, bricklayer, mason, plasterer, plumber, etc.	442,000	1,000
Labourer (unspecified)	367,000	9,000
Milliner, dressmaker, seamstress (seamster)	494	340,000
Wool-worker, every kind, with carpet-weaver	171,000	113,000
Shoemaker	243,000	31,000
Coal-miner	216,000	3,000
Tailor	135,000	18,000
Washerwoman		145,000
Seaman (merchant), pilot	144,000	
Silk worker	53,000	80,000
Blacksmith	112,000	592
Linen, flax-worker	47,000	56,000
Carter, carman, coachman, postboy, cabman, busman, etc.	83,000	1,000
Ironworker, founder, moulder	79,000	590
Railway driver, etc. porter, etc. labourer, platelayer	65,000	54
Hosiery worker	35,000	30,000
Lace worker	10,000	54,000
Machine, boiler-maker	63,000	647
Baker	56,000	7,000
Copper, tin, lead-miner	53,000	7,000
Charwoman		55,000
Commercial clerk	44,000	19
Fisherman	37,000	1,000
Miller	37,000	562
Earthenware worker	25,000	11,000
Sawyer	35,000	23
Shipwright, boat-builder, block- and mast-maker	32,000	28
Straw-plait worker	4,000	28,000

	Male	Female
Wheelwright	30,000	106
Glover	4,500	25,000
Nailer	19,000	10,000
Iron-miner	27,000	910
Tanner, currier, fellmonger	25,000	276
Printer	22,000	222

Source: Compiled from figures collected in 1851 census, *Parliamentary Papers*, LXXXVIII, 1852–3.

Trade unionism a[nd the] Labour movement

Attempts at modern trade unionism only began to ga[in ground after] the repeal of the repressive Combination Acts of 1799– [1800. Though] in 1825 new legislation hindered their effective operation, [attempts] were made (notably in Robert Owen's Grand National Conso[lidated Trade] Union) to found a general Trade Union covering all workers. [The] formation of the Amalgamated Society of Engineers marked [the rise of] 'model unionism'. The extension of the vote to the urban wo[rkers] in 1867 was rapidly followed by the first Trades' Union Congre[ss] and the vital 1871 and 1875 Trades' Disputes Acts. A new deve[lopment] came with the successful dock strike of 1889, marking the rise [of 'new] unionism'; the era of union organisation for the mass of unskilled w[orkers.] Though challenged by adverse legal judgments such as the Taff Va[le case] of 1901, by the First World War trade unionism had established it[self as] a powerful force. Special problems obstructed the rise of agricu[ltural] trade unionism. Joseph Arch's Agricultural Labourers' Union achie[ved a] rapid rise to 150,000 members by 1872, but by 1888 it had collaps[ed.]

The Combination Acts

Repeal of the Combination Acts

Movement for reform headed by Francis Place, master tailor of [Charing] Cross, former journeyman breeches-maker. Joseph Hume, rad[ical MP,] led the movement within Parliament. In February 1824 Hu[me moved] resolutions in the House of Commons for a Committee to c[onsider] laws on the emigration of artisans, the exportation of mac[hinery and] combinations of workmen. As a result the Combination Act [of 1824 was] passed, virtually repealing all the provisions of the 1800 Ac[t.]

Combination Act 1799

Passed as a result of petition of master millwrights of Lon[don] to outlaw combinations in the trade. Although combina[tions of] men could already be prosecuted as conspiracies and for [restraint] in common law, the petition sought an Act similar to [the fifty or] so Acts passed during the eighteenth century to provi[de summary] prosecution (i.e. before a magistrate) of combinatio[ns]

Principal occupation groups in Britain in 1851 in order of size

	Male	*Female*
Total population	10,224,000	10,736,000
Population of 10 years old and upwards	7,616,000	8,155,000
Agriculture: farmer, grazier, labourer, servant	1,563,000	227,000
Domestic service (excluding farm service)	134,000	905,000
Cotton worker, every kind, with printer, dyer	255,000	272,000
Building craftsman: carpenter, bricklayer, mason, plasterer, plumber, etc.	442,000	1,000
Labourer (unspecified)	367,000	9,000
Milliner, dressmaker, seamstress (seamster)	494	340,000
Wool-worker, every kind, with carpet-weaver	171,000	113,000
Shoemaker	243,000	31,000
Coal-miner	216,000	3,000
Tailor	135,000	18,000
Washerwoman		145,000
Seaman (merchant), pilot	144,000	
Silk worker	53,000	80,000
Blacksmith	112,000	592
Linen, flax-worker	47,000	56,000
Carter, carman, coachman, postboy, cabman, busman, etc.	83,000	1,000
Ironworker, founder, moulder	79,000	590
Railway driver, etc. porter, etc. labourer, platelayer	65,000	54
Hosiery worker	35,000	30,000
Lace worker	10,000	54,000
Machine, boiler-maker	63,000	647
Baker	56,000	7,000
Copper, tin, lead-miner	53,000	7,000
Charwoman		55,000
Commercial clerk	44,000	19
Fisherman	37,000	1,000
Miller	37,000	562
Earthenware worker	25,000	11,000
Sawyer	35,000	23
Shipwright, boat-builder, block- and mast-maker	32,000	28
Straw-plait worker	4,000	28,000

	Male	Female
Wheelwright	30,000	106
Glover	4,500	25,000
Nailer	19,000	10,000
Iron-miner	27,000	910
Tanner, currier, fellmonger	25,000	276
Printer	22,000	222

Source: Compiled from figures collected in 1851 census, *Parliamentary Papers*, LXXXVIII, 1852–3.

Trade unionism and the Labour movement

Attempts at modern trade unionism only began to gain ground after the repeal of the repressive Combination Acts of 1799–1800. Although in 1825 new legislation hindered their effective operation, many attempts were made (notably in Robert Owen's Grand National Consolidated Trade Union) to found a general Trade Union covering all workers. In 1851 the formation of the Amalgamated Society of Engineers marked the birth of 'model unionism'. The extension of the vote to the urban working class in 1867 was rapidly followed by the first Trades' Union Congress (1868) and the vital 1871 and 1875 Trades' Disputes Acts. A new development came with the successful dock strike of 1889, marking the rise of 'new unionism'; the era of union organisation for the mass of unskilled workers. Though challenged by adverse legal judgments such as the Taff Vale case of 1901, by the First World War trade unionism had established itself as a powerful force. Special problems obstructed the rise of agricultural trade unionism. Joseph Arch's Agricultural Labourers' Union achieved a rapid rise to 150,000 members by 1872, but by 1888 it had collapsed.

The Combination Acts

Repeal of the Combination Acts

Movement for reform headed by Francis Place, master tailor of Charing Cross, former journeyman breeches-maker. Joseph Hume, radical MP, led the movement within Parliament. In February 1824 Hume moved resolutions in the House of Commons for a Committee to consider the laws on the emigration of artisans, the exportation of machinery and combinations of workmen. As a result the Combination Act of 1824 was passed, virtually repealing all the provisions of the 1800 Act.

Combination Act 1799

Passed as a result of petition of master millwrights of London for a Bill to outlaw combinations in the trade. Although combinations of workmen could already be prosecuted as conspiracies and for other offences in common law, the petition sought an Act similar to another 40 or so Acts passed during the eighteenth century to provide for summary prosecution (i.e. before a magistrate) of combinations in particular trades. On behalf of the government, Wilberforce suggested that the Act should apply to *all* combinations and this was supported by Pitt. The Act provided for summary prosecution before a single magistrate on the evidence of one or more witnesses. Workmen could be sentenced to three months in gaol or two months in a House of Correction with hard labour for: (a) combining to improve conditions or raise wages; (b) inducing others to leave work; (c) refusing to work with others; (d) attending meetings with the purpose of improving wages and conditions or persuading others to attend such a meeting or raise money for such a meeting; (e) contributing to the expenses of anyone tried under the Act; (f) holding money for a combination and refusing to answer questions about it.

Combination Act 1800

Objections to the 1799 Combination Act complained about the vagueness of its language; the use of summary jurisdiction; the possibility of employer-magistrates trying their own workmen; the compulsion to answer questions about money possibly held for a combination, thereby incriminating oneself or else face automatic sentence under the Act. Petitions for total repeal led by the Whig, Sheridan, were resisted by Pitt who claimed that provisions for summary prosecution of combinations were essential. The Combination Act of 1800, therefore, retained the principal features of the 1799 Act, but modified some of its features, notably: (a) two magistrates instead of one to try cases; (b) employer-magistrates prohibited from trying cases of men in their own trade; (c) an arbitration provision was introduced; (d) masters were prohibited from combining to reduce wages, increase hours or worsen conditions.

Combination Act 1824

Provisions

1. Previous statutes relating to combinations, including Act of 1800, almost entirely repealed.
2. Combinations – (a) to get, increase or fix wages; (b) to lessen or alter hours; (c) to reduce amount of work; (d) to induce another to depart from employment before end of time for which hired, or (e) to quit or return his work before end of time for which hired, or (f) to refuse to enter into employment; or (g) to regulate production or management methods – not to be liable to indictment or prosecution for conspiracy or other crime under common or statute law.
    A similar provision applied to combinations of masters.
3. Violence to persons or property, or threats or intimidation, which achieved purposes 2(a) to (g), made an offence, whether committed by an individual or by a combination; penalty was imprisonment and being 'kept to hard labour' for up to two months.

4. Administration by summary trial before two magistrates; master, or fathers or sons of masters, engaged in any trade or manufacture being excluded from administering this law.

Combination Act 1825

Parliamentary Committee set up to inquire into working of 1824 Act. Chaired by Wallace, Master of the Mint; Hume also on Committee, and he with Place managed to reduce severity of 1825 Act. Trade union committees set up all over country to agitate against re-enactment of Combination Laws.

Provisions

1. Combination Act of 1824 repealed.
2. Act exempted from prosecution only those combinations of workmen or masters which met together solely to agree what wages or hours of employment to require or demand. Combinations for any other objects unlawful. The effect of this provision was to allow collective bargaining only over wages and hours; strikes or lock-outs to alter *these* terms not in practice regarded as unlawful, though the Act did not confer a *right* to strike or lock-out (no such provision being known to English law until the Industrial Relations Act of 1971).
3. A series of offences introduced, each punishable by imprisonment with or without hard labour for up to three months: the use of
   (a) *violence*, construed by judges to mean the infliction of bodily harm or any act of injury to property, with the intention to coerce another;
   (b) *threats*, construed as creating fear in a person's mind that some evil might befall him, with a coercive result;
   (c) *intimidation*, i.e. fear created by actions rather than words (as in b) with the effect of coercing another;
   (d) *molestation*, vaguely meaning interference with another – e.g. as by picketing; and
   (e) *obstruction*, e.g. of right of free passage into or out of work, along a highway, etc. Also applied to picketing, in order to force someone to
      (i)   leave his employment;
      (ii) refuse to take employment;
      (iii) join a club or association;
      (iv) contribute to a fund;
      (v)   obey rules, for example, of a combination;
      (vi) change his method of manufacture; or
      (vii) limit the number of his apprentices, and so on.

The overall effect of the statute was to enforce a narrow definition of the lawful activities of a trade union, confining these to peaceful collective bargaining over wages and hours only. Combination to negotiate outside these limits was liable at law not only as contravening the terms of the statute, but as criminal conspiracy at common law 'in restraint of trade'. In addition, many of the methods which a union might employ in furtherance of its objectives were liable to prosecution as intimidation, etc., crimes which were exceedingly ill-defined.

Chartism

The movement

Chartism was one of the most significant movements for political and social reform in Victorian Britain. Taking its name from the People's Charter, between 1838 and 1858 it gradually became an expression of working class unrest against the Poor Law, economic conditions and the difficulty of developing effective Trade Unions. In July 1839 Thomas Attwood, MP for Birmingham and head of the Birmingham Political Union, failed to persuade Parliament to accept a petition with 1,200,000 signatures. A division then arose between the three leaders: Lovett, a moderate; O'Brien, who saw the Charter as the means to bring about a social revolution; and O'Connor, who in 1842 renounced the original Charter and pursued instead a Utopian concept of agricultural social reform.

A proposed general strike never materialised though there were sporadic outbreaks of violence such as that at Newport in 1839. A second petition, with 3,000,000 signatures, was rejected by Parliament in May 1842 and for a time the movement seemed near to collapse. However, in April 1848 O'Connor managed to revive interest, threatening a mass procession to Parliament to deliver a third petition. When the government began assembling troops to resist the demonstration it was called off and though vestiges of the movement survived until 1858 it was of no further political importance. Its main significance was the proof that the working classes could be organised on a massive scale.

1836
Apr. Foundation of Association of Working Men to procure a Cheap and Honest Press.
May Newspaper duty reduced to 1d.
June Foundation of London Working Men's Association (LWMA).

1837
Jan. Foundation of East London Democratic Association.
May Birmingham Political Union revived; committee of LWMA and radical MPs prepared the Charter.
Nov. *Northern Star* issued for first time (at 4½d) at Leeds.

1838

May People's Charter published, London. National Petition published, Birmingham.

June Foundation of Great Northern Union, Leeds by Feargus O'Connor. Foundation of Northern Political Union, Newcastle.

Dec. The first arrest: Revd. J.R. Stephens for addressing open-air meeting in Hyde.

1839

Feb. General Convention of the Industrious Classes opened (4th) at British Hotel, Charing Cross.

Mar. Major-General Sir C. Napier took command of Northern District (until Sept. 1841).

May Convention moved to Birmingham; divisions appeared between 'Physical' and 'Moral' Force Chartists. Several moderate delegates left.

June Chartist petition with 1,280,000 signatures presented to Parliament (14th); rejected (12 July) by 235 votes to 46.

July Bull Ring riots, leading to the Birmingham, Bolton and Manchester Police Acts (repealed 1842).

Sept. Convention dissolved (after failure of Sacred Month.)

Nov. Newport rising, to free Vincent. John Frost and other participants arrested, tried and transported.

1840

Jan. Abortive 'risings' in Dewsbury and Sheffield.

July National Charter Association (NCA) founded (Manchester). Lovett released (imprisoned since July 1839).

1841

Apr. Foundation by Lovett of the National Association of the United Kingdom for Promoting the Political and Social Improvement of the People.

Aug. General election. O'Connor released (imprisoned since March 1840).

1842

Apr. First Complete Suffrage Union Conference at Birmingham. NCA Convention (London) (12th).

May Second National Petition rejected by Parliament.

Aug. Plug riots. Trough of trade cycle, meaning wage cuts and unemployment.

Dec. Collapse of Second Complete Suffrage Union Conference (Birmingham).

1843
Sept. Chartist Convention at Birmingham accepted Land Plan.

1844
Aug. O'Connor–Cobden debate, Northampton.

1845
Sept. Agricultural Co-operative Society founded. Foundation of the Society of Fraternal Democrats.

1846
June Repeal of the Corn Laws.

1847
May Ten Hours Act. O'Connorville, first land settlement opened.

1848
Feb. French Revolution. Publication of *Communist Manifesto.*
Apr. Chartist Convention, London. Kennington Common meeting. O'Connor presented the National Petition (10th); it was rejected.
May National Assembly. Arrests of Chartist leaders in North.
June Clashes between police and Chartists in East End of London.
Aug. Abortive risings at Ashton, Dukinfield, Stalybridge and Oldham.

1849
Dec. Chartist Delegate Conference.

1850
Jan. Foundation of the National Reform League (Bronterre O'Brien).
Mar. National Charter League (O'Connorite).
Aug. Chartist Land Company dissolved by Act of Parliament.

1851
Jan. O'Connorite Convention (Manchester).
Mar. London Conference adopted wide programme.

1852
Jan. Harney bought *Northern Star,* which became the *Star of Freedom.* Ernest Jones and Harney quarrelled: O'Connor insane.

1854
Mar. Labour parliament, Manchester (Jones).

1858
Feb. Last Chartist Convention.

Chronology of trade union history

Early trade unionism: 1815–51

1815   Seamen's strike in northeastern ports. Compromise settlement reached with shipowners.

1816   Strikes against lay-offs and wage reductions in iron-working districts. Renewed machine-breaking in textile districts.

1817   March of the 'blanketeers' (distressed Lancashire weavers) from Manchester for relief and parliamentary reform broken up by troops.

1818   Weavers' and spinners' strikes in Lancashire and attempts to form a 'General Union of the Trades'. Metropolitan Trades Committee sets up early general union, the 'Philanthropic Hercules'.

1819   Keelmen's strike on Tyneside.

1820   Scottish weavers strike, and clashes with troops.

1821   Strikes and riots in Shropshire iron districts.

1824   Campaign for repeal of the Combination Laws managed by Francis Place and Joseph Hume, MP (see p. 151). The 1824 Act led to a rapid increase in trade union activity with extensive strikes, including some violence. This resulted in a new Act, the Combination Act of 1825.

1825   Combination Act passed (see p. 153).
        Trades Newspaper founded by John Gast and others.

1829   General Union of Spinners formed by John Doherty in Manchester. Also launched Union of Trades.

1830   Union of Trades changed name to National Association for the Protection of Labour and formed branches in cotton districts, Midlands and Potteries. Strike of Northumberland and Durham Colliers' Union under leadership of Thomas Hepburn. Strike broken by eviction of colliers from their houses.

1831   Collapse of spinners' union after strikes early in the year; Doherty founded *Voice of the People* journal.

1832   Industrial unrest in South Wales. Merthyr occupied by miners. Exchange of goods made by cooperative production facilitated by National Equitable Labour Exchange. National Association for the Protection of Labour collapsed. Operative Builders' Union formed as federation of building unions; executive was Grand Committee, appointed by Grand Lodge of 'Builders' Parliament' which met twice a year. Involved in a series of strikes and lockouts to change contract system of labour. William Benbow's *Grand National Holiday and Congress of the Productive Classes* suggested the idea of a general strike.

1833   Widespread 'turn-outs' of workmen led to moves for general unions. Owenite Grand National Moral Union of the Productive Classes formed in October at conference of delegates from Co-operative and Trade Societies 'to establish for the productive classes a complete dominion over the fruits of their own industry'. In November Robert Owen and John Fielden established the Society for Promoting National Regeneration with the intention of securing an eight-hour day by means of a limited general strike on 1 March 1834.

1834   On 13 February conference of trade union delegates in London decided to consolidate all trade unions in a single body with Central Committee and district lodges, The Grand National Consolidated Trades' Union (GNCTU) of Great Britain and Ireland. It had up to 16,000 fee-paying members, mainly in London and provincial skilled trades, but gained little support from several important groups, such as builders, potters, cotton spinners and Yorkshire cloth workers. Widespread strike movement by GNCTU defeated by lock-outs and internal divisions.

Owen became Grand Master of reconstituted union known as British and Foreign Consolidated Association of Industry, Humanity and Knowledge, but most unions had seceded from the body and it was virtually defunct by the end of 1834.

In March 1834 six labourers (the 'Tolpuddle Martyrs') convicted and sentenced to transportation for seven years for administering illegal oaths in connection with the Agricultural Labourers' Friendly Society at Tolpuddle, Dorset. Widespread protests all over the country, including a peaceful demonstration of 40,000–50,000 in London. The men were eventually pardoned and allowed to return to England.

1837   Leader of the Cotton Spinners' Association deported after he had been charged with conspiracy over the murder of a 'blackleg' in Glasgow.

1842   Strikes of coal-miners and other workers merge into General Strike for the Charter. Widespread stoppage of work enforced over much of northern England by drawing plugs from engine boilers, hence called the 'Plug-plot' riots.

1844   Miners' Association strike in the Northeast and Yorkshire. Strike defeated after four months in a spate of mass evictions and use of strike-breakers.

1851   Amalgamated Society of Engineers founded, the beginning of 'New Model Unionism'. Initial membership 12,000, rising to 33,000 in 1868 and 71,000 in 1891.

New Model Unionism, 1851–88

1853   Amalgamated Association of Operative Cotton Spinners formed.

1854   Imported Irish labour used to defeat Preston cotton spinners' strike.

1855   Society benefit funds protected by Friendly Societies Act.

1858   Formation of National Miners' Association by Alexander Mac-Donald, and of Glasgow Trades Council. Nine-week strike in the Staffordshire collieries.

1859   Peaceful picketing allowed by Molestation of Workmen Act. Building workers' strike in London and intimidation in the Manchester building trade.

1860   London Trades Council and Amalgamated Society of Carpenters and Joiners formed. Coal Mines Regulation Act abolished truck payment and regulated conditions of employment.

1864   First national conference of trade union delegates.

1865   Reform League formed to win enfranchisement for the working class.

1866   'Sheffield Outrages' (October); attacks on non-union cutlery-workers by fellow workmen. As a result, Royal Commission on Trade Unions established. *Hornby* v. *Close* case: decision against trade union trying to recoup funds from a defaulting local treasurer raised doubts over the degree of protection for funds given by Friendly Societies Act of 1855. Short-lived United Kingdom Alliance of Organised Trades formed.

1867   Master and Servant Act amended to limit prosecution of strikers for breach of contract, but unions remained dissatisfied because criminal action still possible for 'aggravated cases'. The 'Junta' – Applegarth, Allan, Coulson, Odger and Guile – masterminded trade union case for Royal Commission, with Frederic Harrison as their nominee. Report of Royal Commission recommended legalisation of trade unions.

1868   First Trades Union Congress (TUC) at Manchester; 34 delegates with no formal organisation.

1869   Second TUC at Birmingham; 40 delegates representing 250,000 members.

1871   Trade Union Act and Criminal Law Amendment Act; gave unions legal recognition and right to protect their funds, although picketing was made illegal in any form. The TUC established its Parliamentary Committee and the Amalgamated Society of Railway Servants was formed. 'Nine Hours' strike by engineers in the Northeast secured shorter hours.

1872   National Agricultural Union formed by Joseph Arch. Soon had 10,000 members and a weekly journal, *Labourers' Chronicle*, which reached a circulation of 30,000.

1874   Trade unionists Alexander MacDonald and Thomas Burt elected as MPs for Stafford and Morpeth respectively. Royal Commission on Labour laws set up.

1875   Conspiracy and Protection of Property Act allowed peaceful picketing and eliminated conspiracy from trades disputes unless they were illegal. Employers and Workmen Act limited penalty in breach of contract to civil damages. Henry Broadhurst became secretary of the TUC.

1878   Nine-week strike of cotton weavers in Lancashire; disturbances at Preston and Blackburn.

1880   Employers' Liability Act. Re-emergence of socialist influence in next few years.

1886   National Federation of Labour formed on Tyneside.

1887   Attack launched on Broadhurst at TUC, Keir Hardie accusing him of not properly serving the movement by collaborating with the employers.

1888   H.H. Champion's *Labour Elector* launched, advocating the establishment of an Independent Labour Party. Strike of the women match-makers of Bryant & May in London. The start of 'New Unionism'.

The new unionism

1889   In March, Will Thorn began to organise gas workers, who successfully fought to reduce hours from 12 to 8 per day. In August, the London dockers' strike saw the dockers winning 6d per hour, and was followed by the establishment of the Dock, Wharf, Riverside and General Labourers Union under Ben Tillett. Miners Federation of Great Britain (MFGB) formed.

1890   Formation of Shipping Federation, the employers' response to New Unionism.

1892   Keir Hardie carried motion for a labour representation fund at TUC, although little progress was made.

1893   Independent Labour Party set up and National Free Labour Association established. Two people killed after clashes between strikers and soldiers at Ackton Hall Colliery, near Featherstone.

1894   Change in Standing Orders of TUC; representation now related to the number of members affiliated to TUC.

1896   *Lyons* v. *Wilkins* case; injunction against Amalgamated Trade Society of Fancy Leather Workers prevented them from picketing Lyons' premises. Employers Federation of Engineering Associations formed.

1897–98   July 1897–January 1898, national lock-out in engineering industry ends in success for employers. Scottish TUC formed.

1898	Employers' Parliamentary Council formed to counter effects of TUC Parliamentary Committee.
1899	Formation of General Federation of Trade Unions to control a fund for mutual support in the event of strikes.
1900	Labour Representation Committee (LRC) formed, following Scottish Workers Parliamentary Election Committee.
1901	Taff Vale case. A strike against the Taff Vale Railway Co., sanctioned by the Amalgamated Society of Railway Servants (ASRS), was opposed legally by Ammon Beasley, the company manager, on the strength of the *Lyons* v. *Wilkins* case. The legal case continued after the strike had ended, with the Law Lords under Lord Halsbury granting the injunction against the ASRS to stop picketing, and making the funds of the union liable for damages amounting to £23,000.
1905	'Caxton Hall Concordat' – mutual support by LRC and Parliamentary Committee of TUC for members standing for parliamentary election.
1906	Twenty-six Labour MPs elected in January general election, following secret agreement between Ramsay MacDonald, secretary of the LRC and Herbert Gladstone, Liberal Whip, aimed at securing trade union and working-class representation. Parliamentary Labour Party formed. Trades Disputes Act freed trade unions from liability for damages by strike, reversing Taff Vale judgment.
1907	ASRS threatened national railway strike, but government intervention secured agreement.
1908	Strike of Amalgamated Engineers in Northeast ended in defeat after seven months.
1909	Miners Federation formally affiliated to Labour Party. Trade Boards set up by Winston Churchill to fix wages in industries liable to cheap labour. Osborne judgment: judgment against ASRS prevented the trade unions from using their funds for political purposes.
1910	Ten months' strike by miners in South Wales, accompanied by rioting and the despatch of troops. Tom Mann published *Industrial Syndicalist* and then joined with Tillett and Havelock Wilson to form the National Transport Workers' Federation.
1911	Strikes of dockers and seamen joined in August by railway unions, but settled after two days by Lloyd George's intervention. Two men killed by troops during clashes in Liverpool.
1912	February: miners' national strike for minimum wage, which continued until April. District minimum wages achieved. May: London dock strike collapsed after use of blackleg labour to break the strike.

1913   Trade Union Act: reversed the Osborne judgment, allowing the unions to use their funds for political purposes under certain circumstances. Eight-month strike of Irish Transport Union. National Union of Railwaymen formed by amalgamation of ASRS and other railway unions. ASLEF and Clerk's Union remained independent.

1914   Attempt to organise 'Triple Alliance' of miners, railwaymen and transport workers. Not able to organise properly before outbreak of First World War. Strike truce declared shortly after outbreak of the war by TUC.

Trades Union Congress

Date	Place of meeting	Number of delegates	Number of members represented
1868	Manchester	34	118,367
1869	Birmingham	48	250,000
1871	London	50	289,430
1872	Nottingham	77	255,710
1873	Leeds	132	730,074
1874	Sheffield	169	1,191,922
1875	Liverpool	151	818,032
1875	Glasgow	139	539,823
1876	Newcastle	140	557,823
1877	Leicester	141	691,089
1878	Bristol	136	623,957
1879	Edinburgh	115	541,892
1880	Dublin	120	494,222
1881	London	157	463,899
1882	Manchester	153	509,307
1883	Nottingham	163	471,651
1884	Aberdeen	142	598,033
1885	Southport	141	580,976
1886	Hull	143	633,088
1887	Swansea	156	674,034
1888	Bradford	165	816,944
1889	Dundee	211	885,055
1890	Liverpool	457	1,470,191
1891	Newcastle	552	1,302,855
1892	Glasgow	495	1,219,934
1893	Belfast	380	900,000
1894	Norwich	378	1,100,000

Trades Union Congress (*Cont.*)

Date	Place of meeting	Number of delegates	Number of members represented
1895	Cardiff	330	1,000,000
1896	Edinburgh	343	1,076,000
1897	Birmingham	381	1,093,191
1898	Bristol	406	1,184,241
1899	Plymouth	384	1,200,000
1900	Huddersfield	386	1,250,000
1901	Swansea	407	1,200,000
1902	London	485	1,400,000
1903	Leicester	460	1,500,000
1904	Leeds	453	1,423,000
1905	Hanley	457	1,541,000
1906	Liverpool	491	1,555,000
1907	Bath	521	1,700,000
1908	Nottingham	522	1,777,000
1909	Ipswich	598	1,705,000
1910	Sheffield	505	1,648,000
1911	Newcastle	523	1,662,000
1912	Newport	495	2,002,000
1913	Manchester	560	2,232,000

Growth of trade union membership

1869	250,000	1900	2,022,000
1889	679,000	1905	1,997,000
1890	871,000	1910	2,565,000
1895	1,504,000	1914	4,145,000

Analysis of trade union membership, 1888

Metals, engineering and shipbuilding	190,000
Mining and quarrying	150,000
Textiles	200,000
Building	90,000
Transport	60,000
Clothing	40,000
Printing and paper	30,000
Woodworking and furnishing	20,000
Agriculture and fishing	10,000
Others	40,000

Fluctuations in industrial militancy, 1893–1914

	Number of stoppages beginning in year	Aggregate duration in working days of stoppages in progress in year
1893	599	30,440,000
1894	903	9,510,000
1895	728	5,700,000
1896	906	3,560,000
1897	848	10,330,000
1898	695	15,260,000
1899	710	2,500,000
1900	633	3,090,000
1901	631	4,130,000
1902	432	3,440,000
1903	380	2,320,000
1904	346	1,460,000
1905	349	2,370,000
1906	479	3,020,000
1907	585	2,150,000
1908	389	10,790,000
1909	422	2,690,000
1910	521	9,870,000
1911	872	10,160,000
1912	834	40,890,000
1913	1,459	9,800,000
1914	972	9,880,000

The co-operative movement

Background

Co-operativism was an important early form of socialism. It was strong in
Britain after 1837. In 1844 the modern pattern of co-operativism, run
on business lines and created by workmen, emerged at Rochdale. In
1863 the Co-operative Wholesale Society was founded in Manchester
to become one of the world's largest trading organisations. In 1917 the
co-ops founded their own political party, closely associated with the
Labour Party. The Scottish C.W.S, founded in 1868, collaborated with its
English counterpart but was distinct from it.

Chronology of main events

1832	Owenite Co-operative Congress in Manchester.
1844	Rochdale Society of Equitable Pioneers established.
1852	First Industrial and Provident Society Act passed.
1853	Society for Promotion of Industrial and Provident Societies formed. Co-operative League founded.
1860	Pitman's *Co-operator* first published.
1863	First Scottish National conference. *Scottish Co-operator* first published. C.W.S. founded, Manchester.
1867	Co-operative Insurance Company established.
1868	Scottish C.W.S. founded, Glasgow.
1869	First Co-operative Congress, London.
1870	Central Board elected.
1871	*Co-operative News* first published.
1873	Edward Vansittart Neale became first General Secretary.
1875	First Constitution of Co-operative Union.
1881	Parliamentary Committee set up.
1882	Co-operative Productive Federation formed.
1883	Co-operative Permanent Building Society founded.
1885	Union's first Education Committee formed.
1886	Emile de Boyve (France) proposed international co-operative organisation at Plymouth Congress.
1889	Co-operative Union registered.
1892	J.C. Gray appointed General Secretary.
1894	Irish Agricultural Organisation Society established, Dublin.
1895	International Co-operative Alliance founded, London.
1897	Irish Agricultural Wholesale Society established, Dublin.
1898	Union's Central Education Committee set up.
1900	Parliamentary Committee became Joint Parliamentary Committee.
1901	Argicultural Organisation Society, England established.

Main co-operative groups

Co-operative Union Ltd: Set up as the national federation of the consumer co-operative societies in the British Isles. It was established after the Co-operative Congress of 1869 when a Central Board for co-operatives was set up. This became the Co-operative Union in 1889.

Co-operative Women's Guild: Founded in 1883 as the Women's League for the Spread of Co-operation. It then became the Women's Co-operative Guild. The Guild's importance in co-operative activities lay in its organisation of women and its breaking of the male monopoly of co-operative organisation in its early days. Its main area of activities was that of consumer affairs.

International Co-operative Alliance: Founded by the International Co-operative Congress held in London in 1895 as a worldwide confederation of co-operative organisations of all types. The Alliance acted as a forum for exchange of information, promoted mutual trading and financial relations between co-operative organisations, and generally represented the co-operative movement internationally.

National Co-operative Men's Guild: Founded in 1911 to provide a forum for men co-operators to discuss co-operative matters and problems. It became the League of Co-operators in 1962.

Royal Arsenal Co-operative Society Ltd: Founded as the Royal Arsenal Supply Association in 1868 and registered under its present name in 1873. Its Political Purposes Committee was first established in 1921.

Scottish Co-operative Women's Guild: The first branch was formed under the auspices of Kinning Park Co-operative Society in 1890. The national organisation was formed in 1892.

Religion

The Church of England

There had been comparative stagnation in the Church of England in the eighteenth century. Little had been done to meet the needs of an expanding industrial population. Eventually this position changed after 1815. Anglicanism revived with grants for church building in 1818 and 1824, so that over 4,500 churches were built or rebuilt by 1875. Abuses were reformed by the Ecclesiastical Commissioners after 1840. Even so the 1851 Religious Census revealed that only half the population went to church and only half of these were Anglicans. The late nineteenth century saw church-going remaining high in the countryside but declining in urban areas. The scientific discoveries of the nineteenth century had done a great deal to undermine fundamental religious attitudes by questioning the authority of the Bible, especially Darwin's *The Origin of Species* (1859). Church building failed to keep pace with population growth and movement. After the First World War religious adherence was obviously on the decline.

Nonconformity

Methodism grew rapidly from the mid-eighteenth century, especially in places where Anglicanism was weak, such as mining and industrial areas. By the early nineteenth century Methodism had separated from the Church of England and was the largest Nonconformist church. By 1815, the Methodists had over 200,000 members. Other dissenters, especially the Baptists and Congregationalists, grew in numbers in many areas. The Roman Catholics showed increased membership mainly due to Irish immigration.

Major events in nineteenth-century church history – England

1815   Bryanites or 'Bible Christians' separated from Methodists.
1816   Motion for Catholic relief defeated in the Lords.

1817   Military and Naval Officers' Oath Bill opened all ranks in the Army and Navy to Catholics.

1818   Church Building Society founded. At its instigation Parliament granted £1 million for church building and appointed a Commission to superintend its distribution.

1820   Revd Darby left Church of England and founded Plymouth Brethren, teaching a rigid Calvinism and the priesthood of all believers.

1826   Rose preached at Cambridge on duties of the clergy and founded modern High Churchmanship.

1828   Repeal of Test and Corporation Acts, hence admitting Nonconformists to Parliament. Church Building Act passed.

1829   Catholic Emancipation passed; Catholics permitted to sit in Parliament.

1831   Formation of Congregational Union of England and Wales.

1832   Palmer's *Origines Liturgicae* prepared the way for the Oxford Movement and Rose founded *British Magazine* for defence of High Church principles. Church Inquiry: Commissioners appointed.

1833   Keble's Assize Sermon on 'National Apostasy' denounced suppression of 10 Irish bishoprics and was later declared by Newman to have inaugurated the Oxford Movement. *Tracts for the Times* began to appear. Nonconformists allowed to celebrate marriages in their chapels.

1834   Lords defeated admission of Nonconformists to university degrees. Wesleyan Methodist Association founded.

1835   Wiseman returned to England to lecture on the beliefs and system of Catholicism. Pusey joined the High Church movement.

1836   Tithes paid in kind commuted into a rent charge to vary with the price of corn. Ecclesiastical Commissioners incorporated. Newman's *Prophetical Office of the Church* defined the theory of the Oxford Movement. Church Pastoral Aid Society founded. Solemnisation of Marriages Act permitted licences to be issued for marriage in register offices and Nonconformist chapels.

1837   Additional Curates Society founded to provide extra clergy.

1838   Pluralities Act and Acts for building and enlarging churches passed. Froude's *Remains*, edited by Newman and Keble, condemned the Reformation.

1840   New Church Discipline Act.

1841   Tait and three other Oxford tutors issued protest against *Tract 90*, in which Newman explained the Thirty-nine Articles in a Catholic sense. Newman censured and persuaded to end the *Tracts*. Miall founded *The Nonconformist*.

1842   Gedney case. Privy Council confirmed that baptism by Wesleyan Methodists was valid by ecclesiastical and civil law.

1843   Newman resigned as vicar of St Mary's Oxford. Pusey forbidden to preach for two years. New Parishes Act. 'Disruption' in Scotland and formation of Free Church of Scotland.

1844   Ward's *Ideal of a Christian Church* condemned by Oxford authorities. Nonconformists founded Liberation Society.

1845   Ward joined the Roman Catholic Church; Newman followed. Pusey and Marriott led the Anglo-Catholic Party.

1846   The Evangelical Alliance formed to oppose Romanism, Puseyism and rationalism.

1847   United Presbyterian Church of Scotland formed. Church of England diocese of Manchester created.

1848   Gorham controversy over baptism represented further conflict between evangelicals and High Church school.

1849   Wesleyan Methodist Reformers formed after 'Fly-sheets' controversy led to expulsion from main body.

1850   Roman Catholic bishops in the United Kingdom after 300 years. One province, under Cardinal Wiseman (1802–65), Archbishop of Westminster, with suffragans at Beverley, Birmingham, Clifton, Hexham, Liverpool, Newport and Menevia, Northampton, Nottingham, Plymouth, Salford, Shrewsbury and Southwark. The Ecclesiastical Titles Act, the result of anti-papal agitation, forbade Roman Catholic bishops to take any ecclesiastical title already appropriated to the Church of England. The Act was never enforced and was repealed in 1867. Beginning of 'papal aggression' scare in England. No-popery riots at Exeter, etc.

1851   Census of church attendance revealed that only half the population regularly attended Sunday worship. Archdeacon Henry Edward Manning (1808–92) joined Church of Rome (cardinal 1875). First diocesan synod of clergy held by Bishop Phillpotts of Exeter.

1852   Convocation recommenced (at Canterbury).

1854   Act for extending licences of dissenting places of worship.

1857   Divorce obtainable in court, not by private Act of Parliament. Wesleyan Methodist Association joined with Wesleyan Reformers as United Methodist Free Churches.

1859   Darwin published the *Origin of Species by Natural Selection*, starting controversy about the literal truth of the Bible.

1860   At meeting of British Association in Oxford, Bishop Wilberforce attacked and Huxley defended Darwin's theory of evolution. English Church Union founded to organise High Church movement. *Essays and Reviews* published and aroused considerable controversy over their 'broad church' views, attaching little importance to nicety of dogma but stressing Christian virtues. Act for opening grammar schools to Dissenters.

1861   Convocation condemned *Essays and Reviews.*

1862   *The Pentateuch,* by Dr Colenso, Bishop of Natal, asserted that the Bible contains 'unhistorical parts'. Condemned by convocation and excommunicated.

1863   Bishop of London's fund for remedying spiritual destitution founded.

1864   Newman published his spiritual autobiography, *Apologia pro Vita Sua.*

1865   'General' William Booth assumed leadership of a Christian Mission for the 'evangelisation of the very lowest classes', later called the Salvation Army. Church Association formed to oppose ritualism. Manning appointed Catholic Archbishop of Westminster.

1866   Pope condemned efforts to promote Anglican and Catholic reunion. Act for removing religious oaths for public offices.

1868   Compulsory church rates abolished by Gladstone. Irish Church Disestablishment Bill introduced by Gladstone.

1869   Irish Church Disestablishment passed, effective from 1 January 1871.

1870   Forster's Education Act doubled state grant to Church of England and Roman Catholic schools. It also introduced board schools, paid for by rates, in which any catechism or formulary distinctive of any denomination was forbidden (Cowper-Temple clause).

1871   Universities Tests Act. No declaration or oath to be made at matriculation or taking of degree. Motion for disestablishment of English Church obtained 96 votes. Synod of Lincoln held by Bishop Wordsworth.

1874   Gladstone's pamphlets on Vaticanism declared papal decree of 1870 inconsistent with civil allegiance.

1875   Leys School, Cambridge, founded by Wesleyan Methodists.

1876   Presbyterian Church of England formed.

1877   Methodist Conference admitted laity. Creation of Anglican dioceses of Truro and St Albans.

1878   General William Booth formally constituted as superintendent of Salvation Army with control over funds and property and the power to nominate successor. Catholic hierarchy restored in Scotland (see p. 176). Catholic diocese of Beverley divided into Leeds and Middlesbrough. Lay representatives at Methodist Conference.

1880   Burial Laws Amendment Act allowed Nonconformists to inter dead with services of their own sect in parish churchyard.

1881   Ecumenical conference in London of British, colonial and American Methodists. Revised version of the New Testament appeared.

1882   General Booth set forth his principles in the *Contemporary Review*, upholding the gospel, opposing sectarianism and requiring implicit obedience from his 'soldiers', aiming at the reformation of 'drunkards and other reprobates'. Anglican diocese of Newcastle created. Roman Catholic diocese of Portsmouth carved from Southwark; Menevia separated from Newport.

1883   Tothill prison site, Westminster, bought for Roman Catholic cathedral.

1884   Anglican diocese of Southwell created.

1888   *Lux Mundi*, a collection of essays, defined the position of the new Oxford Movement. Anglican diocese of Wakefield established.

1889   Mansfield Congregational College, Oxford, founded.

1890   General Booth published *In Darkest England, and The Way Out*, an exposé of destitution and poverty among the 'submerged tenth'. Bishop of Lincoln prosecuted in the Archbishop's Court for High Church practices.

1891   General Baptist Church and the Particular Baptist Church (Calvinist) united in Baptist Union. Church's *History of the Oxford Movement* published.

1892   National Council of the Evangelical Free Churches formed. Conference held at Grindelwald discussed reunion of Established Church and Nonconformist bodies.

1894   Informal discussions began about Catholic and Anglican reunion. Bill for disestablishment of Anglican Church in Wales failed to reach second reading in Parliament.

1895   Construction of Catholic Cathedral at Westminster begun.

1896   Pope condemned Anglican Orders and attempt at reconciliation came to an end. Free Church Federation established.

1898   Benefices Act forbade the public sale of advowsons and increased the power of bishops. Renewed attacks by Low Church Anglicans upon the ritualist party. Marriage Act allowed authorised person, usually resident minister, to replace registrar in dissenting chapel registered for marriages.

1899   Protestant agitation continued and archbishops pronounced against use of incense and processional lights. Balfour declared in favour of a Catholic university in Ireland.

1900   Union of Free Church of Scotland and United Presbyterian Church of Scotland.

1904–5   Great Welsh revival. Large increases in membership of Nonconformist churches.

1905   Anglican dioceses of Southwark and Birmingham created.

1906   Royal Commission appointed to consider Welsh Disestablishment.

1907   United Methodist Church formed from several existing separate
Methodist churches.

1911   Three provinces created in Roman Catholic Church: Archi-
episcopal Westminster (with Northampton, Nottingham, Ports-
mouth, Southwark); Archiepiscopal Birmingham (with Clifton,
Newport, Plymouth, Shrewsbury, Menevia); Archiepiscopal
Liverpool (with Hexham and Newcastle, Leeds, Middlesbrough,
Salford). Women representatives at Methodist Conference.

1914   Disestablishment of the Anglican Church in Wales. New Anglican
bishoprics of St Edmundsbury and Ipswich, Chelmsford and
Sheffield.

Church attendances in major cities in 1882 (% of total population)

Sheffield	23	Southampton	38
Nottingham	24	Hull	41
Liverpool	26	Portsmouth	41
Bristol	31	Bath	52

The Church of England: clergy and Easter Day communicants, 1831–1911

	Clergy	Easter Day communicants (000s)
1831	14,933	605
1841	15,730	755
1851	16,194	875
1861	17,966	995
1871	19,411	1,110
1881	20,341	1,225
1891	22,753	1,490
1901	23,670	1,945
1911	23,193	2,293

Source: A.D. Gilbert, Religion and Society in Industrial England:
Church, Chapel and Social Change, 1740–1914 (1976), p. 28.

The 1851 Religious Census of England and Wales

	Persons present at church on census Sunday	% of total population	% 'at church' on census Sunday
Church of England	2,971,268	17	47
Nonconformist	3,110,782	17	49
Roman Catholic	249,389	1	4
Other	24,793	0.1	0.4
Total	6,356,222	35	100

Note: The government's Census of Religious Worship was a unique attempt to enumerate religious attendance in the nineteenth century. It was based on a return of all those attending places of worship for morning, afternoon or evening services on a given Sunday in 1851. *Source*: G. Best, *Mid-Victorian Britain, 1851–75* (1971), p. 179.

The Church of England: number of churches and chapels

1831	11,900	1871	15,500
1841	12,700	1881	16,300
1851	14,000	1891	16,900
1861	14,700	1901	17,400

The Church of England: declining share of marriages performed in church

	Roman Catholic (%)	Other Christian (%)	Civil (%)	Church of England (%)
1844	2	5	3	91
1854	5	6	5	84
1864	5	9	8	78
1874	4	11	11	75
1884	4	12	13	71
1894	4	12	15	69
1904	4	13	18	64

Nonconformist church membership in England, 1838–1900

	Congregationalists (000s)	Baptists (000s)	Presbyterians (000s)
1838	127	100	10
1850	165	140	15
1880	190	200	56
1900	257	239	78

Source: A.D. Gilbert, *Religion and Society in Industrial England: Church, Chapel and Social Change, 1740–1914* (1976), p. 37.

Methodist membership in England and Wales, 1816–1914

1816	189,777	1866	547,613
1819	194,670	1871	570,936
1821	215,466	1876	610,846
1826	267,652	1881	630,575
1831	288,182	1886	676,542
1836	364,641	1891	690,022
1841	435,591	1896	702,411
1846	452,238	1901	732,668
1851	490,000	1906	800,234
1856	443,493	1911	783,723
1861	513,628	1914	777,886

Source: A.D. Gilbert, *Religion and Society in Industrial England: Church, Chapel and Social Change, 1740–1914* (1976), p. 31; A.H. Halsey (ed.), *Trends in British Society since 1900* (1972), p. 433.

The Roman Catholic Church, 1840–1911

	Estimated Catholic population	Churches and chapels	Actual mass attendants
1840	700,000	469	371,500
1851	900,000	597	482,000
1891	1,357,000	1,387	726,000
1911	1,710,000	1,773	915,000

Major events in nineteenth-century church history – Ireland

1829   Catholic Emancipation (see p. 248).

1845   Maynooth College for the education of Roman Catholic priests, which had been constituted without controversy with a parliamentary grant in 1795, now incorporated and endowed after a battle in Parliament. Similar controversy preceded the foundation of Queen's Colleges at Cork, Belfast and Galway, where no religious test was to be applied.

1846–47   Potato famine (see p. 303).

1868   Gladstone's moves to disestablish Irish church, supported by House of Commons but defeated in the Lords, resulted in the fall of Disraeli ministry.

1869   Gladstone's Liberal ministry disestablished Irish church. Act vested all ecclesiastical property in commissioners. No bishop to sit in House of Lords. Compensation for holders of benefices, Protestant Nonconformist ministers in receipt of grant from Regium Donum. Surplus of funds to be used for the relief of suffering. Under its new constitution the Church of Ireland had a General Synod (House of Bishops, House of Representatives with 208 clergy and 416 laymen, elected triennially by dioceses).

1873   Gladstone's Irish University Bill, to create single Irish university, denounced by Irish Protestants, Roman Catholics and English Nonconformists. Defeated by 3 votes, Gladstone resigned. Disraeli refused office. After a week Gladstone resumed office.

1881   Parnell's Land League supported by most priests.

1882   £2,000,000 of Irish Church Fund used to pay arrears of rent which tenants could not pay.

1888   Papal decree forbidding boycotting. Forty Irish Roman Catholic Members of Parliament passed resolution that the Vatican had no right to interfere with the Irish people in the management of their political affairs.

1890   Parnell divorce case. Gladstone was forced by Nonconformist supporters to make Parnell's retirement a condition of continued association of Liberals with Irish National Party. Priests refused to accept Parnell, a Protestant, as still being leader; Parnell's supporters refused to accept his resignation.

1899   Belfast Cathedral started; north transept still to be built.

1912   Ulster Protestants opposed Home Rule and threatened armed resistance to an Irish legislature.

Religious affiliations in nineteenth-century Ireland

	1834		1881	
	000s	%	000s	%
Roman Catholic	6,436	81	3,952	77
Anglican	853	11	636	12
Presbyterian	643	7	486	9
Others	40	1	86	2

Source: figures compiled from R. Dudley Edwards, *An Atlas of Irish History* (1973), p. 127, and G. Best, *Mid-Victorian Britain, 1851–75* (1971), p. 193.

Religious affiliations in Irish provinces in 1861

	Roman Catholics (%)	All Protestants (%)
Ulster	50.5	49.47
Leinster	85.9	14.01
Munster	93.8	6.07
Connaught	94.84	5.13

Source: R. Dudley Edwards, *An Atlas of Irish History* (1973), p. 129.

Major events in nineteenth-century church history – Scotland

1829   Catholic Emancipation (see p. 248).

1843   Third of established Church of Scotland, led by evangelical Thomas Chalmers (1780–1847), broke away because of lay patronage to form Free Church of Scotland.
Evangelical Union formed by those who left United Secession Church and by ministers from Congregational Union.

1845   New poor law transferred relief from kirk sessions to parish councils.

1847   United Secession Church and Relief Synod merged to form United Presbyterian Church.

1875   Patronage Act reversed.

1878   The Roman Catholic hierarchy was restored. The Roman Catholic Church then claimed between 200,000 and 300,000 adherents in Scotland.

1900   United Presbyterian Church and Free Church of Scotland merged to form United Free Church of Scotland. Small group of Free Church of Scotland remained outside merger, to be known as Wee Frees.

1921   Church of Scotland Act gave the United Presbyterian Church complete autonomy and character of a national church.

Church membership in Scotland, 1831–1901

	Episcopal Church (000s)	Presbyterian Church of Scotland (000s)	Free Church (000s)	United Presbyterian Church (000s)	Wesleyan Methodist (000s)	Baptist (000s)
1831	–	–	–	–	4	–
1841	–	–	–	–	4	–
1851	14	–	199	–	4	–
1861	–	–	243	154	4	–
1871	–	436	–	163	5	9
1881	–	528	312	175	5	10
1891	36	600	337	185	7	12
1901	47	662	288	194	8	17

Source: C. Cook and B. Keith, *British Historical Facts, 1830–1900* (1975), pp. 222–30.

Major events in nineteenth-century church history – Wales

1818–21   Revival movement at Bedd Gelert, Carnarvonshire, led by Richard Williams.

1826   Calvinistic Methodist Church obtained legal existence as corporate body. Confession of Faith, attached to constitutional deed, put church in doctrinal straitjacket.

Advocates of disestablishment claimed Nonconformist proportion of population as high as 13 to 1.

1829   Catholic Emancipation. Mass petition to Parliament protesting against Act.

1859–61   Revival movement led by Humphrey Jones.

1870   Gladstone appointed Welsh-speaking Welshman, Dr Joshua Hughes, to see of St Asaph, thus encouraging recovery of Church of England in Wales. First Welsh-speaking bishop since reign of Queen Anne.

1870s	Political demands for disestablishment by Nonconformists became more bitter and movement grew in power.
1881	Welsh Sunday Closing Act (first parliamentary Act to give Wales separate treatment) reflected strength of Nonconformity.
1885	Disestablishment now a regular election issue
1886	Resolution in favour of disestablishment tabled in Commons (similar resolutions in 1889, 1891). Outbreak of tithe riots.
1895	Bill to disestablish the Anglican Church in Wales defeated.
1904	Revival movement led by Evan Roberts in South Wales. Backed by Nonconformist resentment of the Education Act and Liberal attacks on Licensing Act ('Beer and the Bible').
1905	Liberal government of Campbell-Bannerman appointed commission to study position of church in Wales.
1909	Second Bill to disestablish the Anglican Church in Wales defeated in Lords.
1914	Act to disestablish and disendow Welsh church. Owing to First World War Act did not operate until 1920.
1922	Constitution for disestablished church: 6 dioceses instead of previous 4 – Brecon and Monmouth added to Llandaff, St Asaph, St David's, Bangor.

Nonconformist church membership in Wales, 1815–1900

	Congregationalist (000s)	Baptist (000s)	Presbyterians (000s)
1815	23	–	–
1838	43	25	110
1851	60	35	–
1870	–	60	245
1880	116	80	275
1890	130	91	288
1900	150	107	324

Source: C. Cook and B. Keith, *British Historical Facts, 1830–1900* (1975), pp. 226–9.

Missionary societies

The background

Most of the major missionary societies had been founded by 1815. The SPCK had been founded back in 1698, the USPG in 1701. Other major early foundations were the Baptist Missionary Society (founded 1792 as the Particular Society for Propagating the Gospel Among the Heathen), the British and Foreign Bible Society (1804); the Church Missionary Society (1799); the London Missionary Society (1795) and the Edinburgh Missionary Society (1796).

Dates of foundation of selected missionary societies, 1815–1914

1824	Church of Scotland Foreign Missions Committee
1834	Female Education Society
1836	Colonial Missionary Society
1841	Jerusalem and the East Mission
1843	Loochow Naval Mission
1844	Patagonian Missionary Society (after 1852 the South American Missionary Society)
1847	Presbyterian Church of England Foreign Missions Committee
1848	Melanesian Mission
1853	Anglo-Continental Society (became Anglican and Foreign Church Society in 1904)
1858	Christian Vernacular Education Society for India
1859	Universities Mission to Central Africa
1865	China Inland Mission
1867	Baptist Zenana Mission
1868	Friends Foreign Mission Association (Quaker)
1877	Cambridge Mission to Delhi
	School and Tract Book Society (for China)
1878	Livingstone Inland Mission
1880	Church of England Zenana Missionary Society
1889	Cape General Mission (became the South African General Mission in 1894)
1895	Africa Inland Mission
1900	United Free Church of Scotland Foreign Mission
1910	Conference of British Missionary Societies formed following the World Missionary Conference in Edinburgh
1912	Conference for World Mission

Philanthropy

Dates of foundation of major philanthropic and charitable organisations

(See above for missionary societies.)

1818	Church Building Society
1823	Anti-Slavery Society
1824	Royal National Lifeboat Institution
	Royal Society for the Prevention of Cruelty to Animals
1830	Liverpool Night Asylum for the Houseless

1839   London Society for Teaching the Blind to Read
1841   Metropolitan Association for the Improvement of the Dwellings
        of the Industrious Classes
1844   Ragged School Union
c.1844 Society for Improving the Condition of the Labouring Classes
c.1851 Alleged Lunatics Friend Society
1852   General Society for the Improvement of Dwellings of the Work-
        ing Classes
1856   Association for Promoting the General Welfare of the Blind
1857   Discharged Prisoners Aid Society
1859   Metropolitan Drinking Fountain and Cattle Trough Association
c.1860 Association for the Christian and Domestic Improvement of
        Young Women
1860   Society for the Relief of Distress
1862   Peabody Trust
1863   Liverpool Central Relief Society
c.1863 Improved Industrial Dwellings Company
1864   Destitute Children's Dinner Society
1866   Barnardo's Homes
1867   Edinburgh Society for Improving the Condition of the Poor
1869   Charity Organisation Society
1884   London Society for the Prevention of Cruelty to Children (later
        National Society)
        East End Dwellings Company
1891   City Parochial Foundation (London)

The Jewish community

1840   First reform group in London established at the West London
        Synagogue.
1845   Jews admitted to office in the municipalities. Beginning of
        removal of Jewish disabilities.
1846   Jews placed on same footing as Protestant dissenters concern-
        ing schools.
1847   Election of Lionel Nathan Rothschild for City of London:
        unable to take his seat.
1858   Alteration of form of parliamentary oath allowed Jews to sit in
        Parliament. Lionel Nathan Rothschild took seat in Commons
        (first Jew to do so).
1871   Foundation of Anglo-Jewish Association.
1885   Nathaniel Meyer Rothschild became first Jew to sit in House of
        Lords when he was created a Baron.
1898   Zionist Federation of Great Britain formed (16 March), inspired
        by World Zionist Federation of Dr Theodore Herzl.

Temperance

Chronology

1830   Beerhouse Act heralded 'free trade in beer'.
1831   British and Foreign Temperance Society formed (29 June).
1834   Parliamentary Select Committee on Intemperance reported.
1839   Sunday morning closing of public-houses in London. This reform was achieved by a clause in the Metropolitan Police Act.
1842–8 Sunday morning closing extended throughout England.
1843   National Temperance Society formed.
1851   London Temperance League formed.
1853   United Kingdom Alliance formed.
1855   United Kingdom Band of Hope formed (1 June).
1856   National Temperance League established.
1860   New wine licence (='grocer's licence') created by Gladstone.
1862   Permissive Bill Resolution first moved in Commons by Wilfrid Lawson
1869   Wine and Beerhouse Act: 'Free Trade in Beer' ended. Convocation of Canterbury Report on Intemperance presented.
1871   National Union for suppression of intemperance formed.
1872   Licensing Act.
1873   Church of England Temperance Society formed.
1874   Licensing Act, amending the Act of 1872.
1876   British Women's Temperance Society formed (April).
1879   London Temperance Hospital opened.
1880   Local Option resolution carried, for the first time, in the House of Commons.
1890   'Direct Popular Veto' included in the Newcastle Programme.
1891   House of Lords judgment in *Sharp* v. *Wakefield*.
1893   Sir William Harcourt introduced Local Veto Bill in the Commons. The Bill made no progress.
1895   Local Veto Bill reintroduced. The Bill made no progress.
1896   First Royal Commission on Licensing Laws appointed.
1899   Report of the Royal Commission on Licensing Laws presented.
1904   Temperance opposition aroused by 1904 Licensing Act.
1905   Bill to prohibit sale of liquor on Sunday defeated in Commons (114 to 108). Temperance Legislation League formed.

Christian Socialism

Christian Socialism (unkindly dubbed 'muscular Christianity' by its detractors) was a movement which began in the mid-nineteenth century with the object of emphasising the social principles found in the New Testament. It sought to establish industrial co-operatives. To further the education of the poorer classes it founded the Working Men's College in 1854. The movement's leaders were John Malcolm Forbes Ludlow (1821–1911), Charles Kingsley (1819–75), F.D. Maurice (1805–72), and Thomas Hughes (1822–96) whose novel *Tom Brown's Schooldays* displays many of the tenets of the movement.

Organisations of Christian Socialists included:

1. Christian Social Union

Formed in 1889 by Scott Holland, Charles Gore and Bishop B.F. Westcott. Rooted in the Oxford Movement, the 'sacramental Socialists' owed much to F.D. Maurice as also to non-religious stimuli. However, they had a firm theological foundation for their cause, drawing on the Bible and the tradition and doctrines of the Church to affirm that one is a Socialist by the very fact that one is a Christian. By the late 1890s the radical spirit of the CSU had already waned, the organisation appeared narrow and, though not disbanded until the 1920s, the Union was superseded by the League (see below).

2. Church Socialist League

Founded in 1906 as a result of discontent among Christian Socialists with the Guild of St Matthew and the Christian Social Union (above). Its platform was more clearly Socialist than any other Christian organisation of the period. Its policy was sympathetic to Guild Socialism. See also Labour Church Movement (p. 297).

Leisure

The rise of organised sport

Prior to the Victorian period, leisure time had usually been spent at or near home by both rich and poor. The age of mass holidays came with the development of the railways in the nineteenth century. The growing urban population was able to take cheap, rapid excursions to seaside resorts which sprang up on all parts of the coast. The first excursion by train was arranged by Thomas Cook in 1841 (from Leicester to Lough-borough). A further stimulus to holidays came with the 1871 Bank Holidays Act. Many of the largest holiday resorts grew rapidly in the period after the coming of the railways. Southend and Bournemouth came within easy range for visitors from the Home Counties and London. Blackpool became the main holiday resort for the industrial areas of Lancashire and Yorkshire.

Perhaps the greatest transformation of leisure time was in the rise of organised sport. It was only towards the end of the nineteenth century that mass spectator sport was organised on a national basis. This was shown most obviously by the growth of football.

Association football

From being a purely local activity football became a nationally organised game with a Football Association with professional players. The FA Cup, started in 1871, soon drew huge attendances for its Cup Finals. By 1914 the game had become an established part of urban life.

Key dates

1848	The first rules drawn up at Cambridge University.
1862	Notts. County founded first professional football club.
1863	Football Association founded.
1867	Queen's Park, the oldest Scottish club, founded.
1871	FA Cup inaugurated.
1872	First official international, between Scotland and England.
1873	Scottish FA formed.
1876	FA of Wales formed. The first international between Scotland and Wales.

1879   First international between England and Wales.
1880   Irish FA formed and the start of the Irish Cup.
1882   Formation of Football League with 12 clubs.
1885   Professionalism became legal in England.
1888   Football League formed.
1890   Irish and Scottish Leagues formed.
1892   Division Two of Football League formed.
1893   Professionalism adopted in Scotland.
1898   Players' Union first formed.

Dates of foundation of selected football clubs

Club	Year	Club	Year
Arsenal	1866	Liverpool	1892
Aston Villa	1874	Manchester City	1880
Birmingham City	1875	Manchester United	1885
Blackburn Rovers	1874	Middlesbrough	1876
Blackpool	1887	Millwall	1885
Bolton Wanderers	1874	Newcastle United	1882
Bristol City	1895	Norwich City	1905
Burnley	1881	Nottingham Forest	1865
Cardiff City	1899	Plymouth Argyle	1886
Carlisle United	1903	Portsmouth	1898
Charlton Athletic	1906	Preston North End	1880
Chelsea	1905	Queens Park Rangers	1885
Coventry City	1883	Rotherham	1884
Crystal Palace	1905	Sheffield United	1889
Derby County	1884	Sheffield Wednesday	1866
Everton	1878	Southampton	1885
Fulham	1880	Stoke City	1863
Huddersfield Town	1908	Sunderland	1879
Hull City	1904	Tottenham Hotspur	1882
Ipswich Town	1880	West Bromwich Albion	1879
Leeds United	1904	West Ham United	1900
Leicester	1884	Wolverhampton Wanderers	1877

Other sporting landmarks

1823   Rugby   Webb Ellis began rugby at Rugby School.
1860   Golf   First professional golf tournament at Prestwick.
1861   Cricket   First foreign tour (to Australia) by English
                    cricketers.
1861   Hockey   Blackheath Hockey Club formed.
1864   Athletics   First modern athletics match at Oxford
                    (Oxford *v* Cambridge).

1866	Boxing	Boxing reorganised by Queensbury Rules.
1869	Swimming	London Swimming Association formed.
1871	Rugby	Rugby Football Union founded.
1873	Cricket	Formation of County Championship.
1875	Swimming	English Channel swum by Captain Webb.
1876	Cricket	First Test Match: England v Australia.
1877	Tennis	Wimbledon Lawn Tennis Championship begun.
1895	Rugby	Secession of 22 Northern Rugby League clubs.
1896	Olympics	Birth of modern Olympics.
1908	Olympics	Olympic Games held in London.

Illiteracy and reading

Before the spread of compulsory elementary education from the end of the nineteenth century, illiteracy was a major social problem. The early Sunday Schools concentrated on teaching reading and writing but even by 1839 42% of the population was still illiterate (25% women, 17% men). Self-help efforts by working men in the mid-nineteenth century and the growth of education gradually reduced the problem so that by the First World War illiteracy had effectively been eliminated except for a small minority. Reading habits were stimulated by the growth of circulating libraries from the end of the eighteenth century, and especially the development of rate-assisted free libraries in most cities and towns from 1850.

Chronology of key dates

1850   Boroughs with population above 10,000 given powers to establish public libraries. Expenditure limited to ½d in the £ rate. No power to purchase books.

1854   Provisions of 1850 Act extended to Scotland.

1855   Increase of permitted expenditure (to 1d in the £ rate) under the Public Libraries Act.

1872   Free Guildhall Library opened, London (5 Nov).

1877   Library Association (for librarians) established (2 Oct).

1879   Metropolitan Free Library Association formed (4 Apr).

1887   Number of free libraries established totalled 133.

1892   Public Libraries Act. A landmark piece of legislation. All local government units (except county councils) permitted to become library authorities.

1902   Large endowments by Andrew Carnegie for libraries.

1919   Public Libraries Act removed limits on expenditure.

Theatre and music hall

By the mid-nineteenth century the respectable Victorian theatre was almost entirely an upper-class entertainment, while the lower classes went to the music halls. By the Edwardian period the music halls were one of the principal forms of popular entertainment and many performers became national figures. In the serious theatre the period before 1914 saw a revival of drama, with writers such as George Bernard Shaw.

Chronology of key dates

1843   Theatre Act allowed theatres to serve food and drink. Led to rise of music halls.

1848   First music hall (Surrey Music Hall) opened.

1878   Safety laws forced smaller halls to close.

1904   Beginning of variety theatre with opening of London Coliseum.

1912   First command performance.

SECTION THREE

Economic history

The national economy

Chronology of economic events

1815   Corn Law permitted import of foreign corn only when price of
        wheat reached 80s a quarter (Mar.).
1816   Bank failures precipitated by economic crisis.
1817   Lace machines destroyed in first outbreak of Luddite violence
        (see p. 299) (Feb.).
1819   Peel's Act (July) pledged return to gold standard by 1823.
1821   Bank of England resumed cash payments; early return to gold
        standard (May).
1822   Modification of Navigation Acts (June).
1823   Entry of Huskisson into Cabinet as reforming President of the
        Board of Trade (Jan.).
1824   Combination Law reform (June) (see p. 152).
1825   First steam railway opened (Stockton–Darlington) (Sept.).
1828   St Katharine's Dock, London, opened.
1830   Death of Huskisson at opening of the Liverpool and Manches-
        ter Railway (Sept.).
1833   Bank Act passed, making Bank of England notes legal tender.
        Usury Laws attenuated (Aug.).
1835   Brunel signed contract for the *Great Eastern*.
1836   Specie Circular in the U.S.A., curtailing boom and precipitating
        British crisis of 1837 (July).
1837   Chartered Companies Act. Letters patent could be granted to
        some limited liability companies. Beginning of Victorian com-
        pany legislation.
1838   Establishment of the Anti-Corn Law League (Sept.).
1842   Reintroduction of income tax at 7d in £ recommended by Peel
        in Budget speech. Tariff on 700 articles to be abolished, also
        (Mar.).
1844   Conversion of National Debt, from $3\frac{1}{2}\%$ to $3\frac{1}{4}\%$ and then 3%,
        set in hand by Goulburn's third Budget (Apr.).
        Bank Charter Act. Separation of Bank of England's function
        into Banking and Issuing Depts. Fiduciary Issue limited to £14m
        (July).

Railway Regulation Act. Gladstone's 'parliamentary' train. Treasury option to purchase railways at 25 years' profits. Beginning of interventionist railway legislation (Aug.).

1845   Lord John Russell's 'Edinburgh Letter' in favour of Corn Law Repeal. Whigs as a whole moving towards same position (Nov.).

1846   House of Lords passed Corn Law Repeal, following Irish famine (Jun.).

1847   Bank Charter Act suspended by 'Open Letter' from Treasury. Crisis, following prosperity of 1844–7.

1848   John Stuart Mill's *Principles of Political Economy* (Apr.).

1849   Repeal of Navigation Laws (June).

1851   Official opening of Great Exhibition (May).

1852   First congress of Co-operative Societies in London. Industrial and Provident Societies Act.

1853   Gladstone presented first Budget. Retention of income tax, lowering level of exemption, extension to Ireland. Tariffs on 123 articles abolished (18 Apr.).

1854   End of Usury Act (10 Aug.).

1855   Stamp tax on newspapers abolished (15 June).

1856   Bessemer process of steelmaking proposed to British Association (13 Aug.).

1857   Bank Charter Act suspended by 'Open Letter' from Treasury (12 Nov.).

1860   Supplementary Convention, completing Cobden–Chevalier Treaty, signed. Highpoint of free trade (16 Nov.).

1861   Gladstone's Budget abolished the paper duties (15 Apr.). Post Office Savings Banks opened (16 Sept.).

1862   Act for Incorporation, Regulation and Winding-Up of Trading Companies and other Associations. Climax of mid-Victorian company legislation (7 Aug.).

1865   Commercial Treaty between Britain and *Zollverein*.

1866   'Black Friday', after Overend and Gurney crash. Crisis, with Bank Rate staying at 10% for longest period in British history (11 May).

1871   Legalisation of trade unions (see p. 159).

1872   Anglo-French Commercial Treaty.

1873   Bank Rate at 9% for 13 days to meet shortage of cash through commercial failures (Nov.).

1878   City of Glasgow Bank crash (2 Oct.). Scotland badly affected, with many bankruptcies.

1879   Gilchrist-Thomas steel process. Harbinger of Britain's decline from supremacy in heavy industries. Henry George's *Progress and Poverty* published. British Chamber of Commerce established in Paris (12 July).

1880   Employers' Liability Bill (7 Sept.).
1882   First meeting of London Chamber of Commerce (25 Jan.).
1886   Trafalgar Square riots. Protest against unemployment (8 Feb.).
1888   Forthcoming conversion of the National Debt explained to House
        of Commons by Goschen. Saving of £1.4m from Apr. 1889, and
        of £2.8m from Apr. 1903 (9 Mar.).
1889   London dockers' strike (see p. 160).
1890   Rumours of imminent Barings failure circulated in City. Bank
        of England organised rescue operation (8 Nov.).
1894   Harcourt's reform of Death Duties in his second Budget
        (16 Apr.).
1896   Beginning of period of gold abundance, with discoveries in
        South Africa and Alaska.
1897   Workmen's Compensation Act.
1900   Taff Vale strike in South Wales.
1902   London Colonial Conference favoured Imperial Preference over
        Free Trade.
1906   Trade Disputes Act legalised picketing.
1908   Old Age Pensions Bill.
1909   Peoples Budget (for details, see p. 302).
1910   First 'job centres' opened.
1911   Passing of National Insurance Act.

National income and expenditure

Growth of national income per head, 1800–1921 (current prices)

1800	£18	1871	£47
1822	£21	1901	£76
1841	£26	1921	£82
1861	£42		

National Income, 1855–1915 (at factor cost)

	Total (£m)		Total (£m)
1855	636	1890	1,385
1860	694	1895	1,447
1865	822	1900	1,750
1870	936	1905	1,776
1875	1,113	1910	1,984
1880	1,076	1915	2,591
1885	1,115		

Source: B.R. Mitchell and P. Deane, *Abstract of British Historical Statistics*,
Cambridge (1962), pp. 367–8.

1. Government expenditure

On the eve of the Napoleonic Wars the government spent about £18 million annually, mainly on the armed forces and public administration. Though wars usually increased public expenditure, the normal peacetime expenditure of the government remained low until the end of the nineteenth century. The 1871 budget totalled £67 million, representing only about 10% of the gross national product. This was mainly spent on the armed forces and the civil service.

For most of the nineteenth century it was considered appropriate for governments to spend as little money as possible. Wars were seen as a necessary evil in their effect on expenditure and income: both in terms of debt and taxes. By the middle of the nineteenth century *laissez-faire* doctrines reinforced the demand for 'peace, retrenchment, and reform' and under Gladstone, the Liberal Party campaigned for the minimum expenditure by the government, reduction in taxes, and non-interference by government in private enterprise and local activities. By 1914 the cost of armaments had soared with the expansion of the Empire and the growing rivalry of the Great Powers in Europe. Under the Lloyd George budgets of 1909–11 the government also assumed responsibility for expenditure on a wide range of social services, including health insurance, pensions, education, and unemployment benefit.

2. Growth of government income

Growth in government expenditure was balanced by increases in taxation and government debts. Until the 1840s most revenues came from indirect taxes, mainly customs and excise. The demand for 'free trade' led to a reduction in customs and the development of direct taxation, such as income tax, introduced by Peel in 1842. Nonetheless, in 1871 customs and excise still provided two-thirds of government revenue and income tax only one-tenth. To finance increased social services and armaments, the Liberal government before 1914 raised the level of income tax and increased estate or 'death' duty on inherited wealth. These taxes were further increased in the First World War.

Banking, finance and investment

The growth of early banking

To meet the needs of economic growth many banks had been founded in the eighteenth century; by 1800 there were over 70 banks in London and 400 private country banks. These were small and restricted by law from competition with the Bank of England, leaving them vulnerable during financial crises, such as that of 1816.

After 1826 the system was strengthened by allowing joint stock banks and note issues outside a 65-mile radius of London; after 1833 they were permitted within this area. These steps created a national system which provided the capital for further investment. Henceforth the banking system developed rapidly during the years up to 1914. The Bank of England gradually acquired greater responsibility for the whole financial system of the country and curtailed its functions as a private bank. From 1890 it handled foreign exchanges and held the country's gold reserves. It also dictated the general rate of interest through the Bank Rate and supported other banks in times of crisis.

Smaller banks amalgamated during the nineteenth century and by 1914 only 40 were left. By 1914 London was the centre of the international money market.

Gold and silver coinage provided the mainstay of the currency until 1821 when a gold standard was adopted by which notes could be redeemed in fixed values of gold. Gold sovereigns still circulated until the First World War.

Key dates

1694   Modern banking began with foundation of Bank of England (and in 1695 Bank of Scotland).
1816   Financial crisis caused bank failures.
1826   Number of country banks totalled 554.
1833   Bank Act (made Bank of England notes legal tender).
1844   Bank Charter Act. Note issue and central banking functions of the Bank of England regularised.
1855   Limited Liability Act limited responsibility of investors in the event of bankruptcy of the company.
1857   Collapse of over 130 banks.

1861   Post Office Savings Bank opened.
1890   Bank of England became responsible for foreign exchange and
        gold reserves.
1894   Estate, or 'death', duties introduced.

Savings bank deposits, 1820–1920 (£m)

1820	3.5	1880	80.0
1830	14.6	1890	115.0
1840	23.5	1900	191.0
1850	29.0	1910	232.0
1860	42.0	1920	356.0
1870	53.0		

Source: C. Cook and J. Stevenson, *Longman Atlas of Modern British History: a Visual Guide to British Society and Politics* (1978).

Bank clearings (London and provinces), 1868–1918 (£m)

1868	3,400	1898	8,600
1878	4,900	1908	12,700
1888	6,900	1918	22,900

Bank of England notes in circulation, 1760–1920

1770	5,200	1850	20,300
1780	7,376	1860	20,600
1790	10,737	1870	26,300
1800	15,946	1880	25,400
1810	22,907	1890	25,300
1820	23,892	1900	28,300
1830	20,758	1910	31,600
1840	16,773	1920	102,700

Capital and investment

Investment both at home and overseas played an important part in the growth of the British economy. The modern Stock Exchange was founded in 1773 and enabled financiers and industrialists to raise money for future investment. With the development of the economy the number of loans raised steadily increased. An important development was the rise of insurance companies to protect fixed assets and people. Amongst the most important was Lloyd's marine insurance, founded in 1692.

The expansion of industry required increased capital. Safeguards for investors (as with the Limited Liability Act of 1855) helped the process of raising money. New capital issues on the London money market grew rapidly.

New capital issues on London money market (£m)

1870	92	1900	166
1880	122	1910	267
1890	143	1920	368

'Consols'

The yield on 'consols' provided a barometer for the performance of the British economy and the general wellbeing of the nation by showing the state of confidence in government stock.

Yield on consols (%)

1816	5.0	1876	3.2
1826	3.8	1886	3.0
1836	3.4	1896	2.5
1846	3.1	1906	2.8
1856	3.2	1916	4.3
1866	3.4		

Overseas investment

After 1870, when profits from domestic investment declined, an increasing amount of capital was invested abroad and increased the balance of overseas credit. Overseas investment played a vital part in British prosperity between 1800 and 1914, by which time over £4,000 million had been invested. This provided an enormous gain to the British economy by providing lucrative profits, much of which was used to finance imports. Investment was usually in government bonds, taken out in services and capital goods, such as docks, harbours and banks. Over a third of all investment was in railways and British investment funded railway development in many parts of Asia, Africa and Latin America. Little of the investment went to the new colonies.

Statistics

Foreign investment, 1860–1914 (as a percentage of gross national product)

1860–64	2.3	1890–94	4.1
1865–69	3.7	1895–99	2.4
1870–74	5.7	1900–04	2.0
1875–79	2.1	1905–09	5.8
1880–84	4.1	1910–14	7.8
1885–89	5.7		

Earnings from foreign investment, 1820–1910 (£m)

1820	2.5	1870	35.0
1830	4.0	1880	57.0
1840	7.1	1890	94.0
1850	9.5	1900	105.0
1860	19.0	1910	170.0

Agriculture

Chronology of key events

1822   Board of Agriculture (established 1793) wound up. Invention of rotary digging machine.

1833   Foundation of Royal Jersey Agricultural and Horticultural Society.

1834   Sentence of seven years' transportation imposed on Tolpuddle Martyrs (see p. 309). Pardoned in 1837.

1835   Arrival of first shipment of Peruvian guano, one of the earliest imported fertilisers.

1836   First use of combine harvesters in United States.

1838   Foundation of English Agricultural Society (became Royal Agricultural Society).

1842   Farmers' Club formed. Superphosphate patented.

1843   Rothamsted experimental station founded. Introduction of clay drainage pipes aided under-draining.

1845   Royal Agricultural College at Cirencester founded.

1849–53   One of worst agricultural crises of the century (exacerbated by bad harvests in 1848, 1850, 1852 and 1853).

1851   Introduction of reaping machine.

1872   Peak acreage of tillage (9.6m acres). Declined to 6.5m by 1913. National Agricultural Labourers' Union established.

1878   Foundation of English Jersey Cattle Society.

1879   Introduction of mechanical separators for milk (followed by gradual use of milking machines in 1880s).

1882   Discovery of the bacillus of bovine TB.

1886   Measures to control anthrax introduced.

1889   Establishment of new Board of Agriculture.

1907   Establishment of the National Cattle Breeders' Association.

1908   Formation of Lincolnshire Farmers Union (rapidly developed into National Farmers Union).

1909   Establishment of British Friesian Cattle Society.

1910   Introduction of King Edward potato variety.

1921   Ministry of Agriculture created from Board of Agriculture.

The Corn Laws

These regulations, controlling the import and export of grain to and from Britain became of major political importance in the early nineteenth century.

In 1815 a Corn Law was passed prohibiting the import of corn until the domestic price had risen to 80s a quarter. This measure failed to stabilise prices: dealers kept corn off the market to force prices up above 80s, then flooded the market with imported grain, causing price slumps. Furthermore, the high cost of bread, staple of the popular diet, meant that less was spent on other agricultural produce, causing an agrarian recession. In 1828 a sliding scale was introduced, by which high duties replaced total prohibition, the duties on imports being lowered as home prices rose. Again speculators stored imported corn until the duty fell to its lowest point, and then flooded the market at the point where domestic prices were highest.

Because the Corn Laws protected the interests of the landed class, they drew the opposition of the emerging industrial middle class and in 1839 the Anti-Corn Law League was founded, soon gathering working class support. A series of bad harvests up to 1842 and a trade depression between 1839 and 1843 swelled the League's ranks; in 1842 Sir Robert Peel, the Prime Minister, reduced the duty on corn. However, it was the failure of the Irish potato crop in 1845 and the outbreak of widespread famine in Ireland that persuaded Peel and Parliament of the need to repeal the Corn Laws. In 1846 the duty was very greatly reduced and in January 1847 it was suspended until March 1848. After 1848 duty was fixed at one shilling a quarter. It was finally abolished in 1869.

The Great Depression

The 'Great Depression' represented a heavy fall in agricultural prices because of foreign imports and bad harvests. By the 1870s the opening of new wheat lands in Russia, North America and the colonies, the development of transcontinental railway systems, and rapid, cheap ocean transport led to a flood of cheap grain on to the British market, followed by a rapid decline in wheat prices and farm rents. Imported wheat and meat began to make up a large percentage of the food eaten in the country. Under the impact of the depression there was a change in the pattern of British agriculture, away from wheat and cereals towards mixed farming, with greater emphasis on pasture. Many labourers were forced off the land, the number dropping from over a million in 1871 to 600,000 in 1901.

Statistics

Price of wheat (shillings per quarter) 1870–1904

1870–74	55s 0d	1890–94	29s 8d
1875–79	47s 8d	1895–1900	27s 10d
1880–84	42s 5d	1901–04	27s 4d
1885–89	31s 7d		

The corn trade: imports of wheat and flour (annual average per decade)

	Imports (000s of cwt)		Imports (000s of cwt)
1810–19	2,617	1870–79	50,406
1820–29	1,631	1880–89	70,282
1830–39	3,743	1890–99	85,890
1840–49	10,676	1900–09	102,551
1850–59	19,326	1910–19	104,502
1860–69	33,692		

Source: B.R. Mitchell and P. Deane, *Abstract of British Historical Statistics,* Cambridge (1962), pp. 94–5, 97–9.

Fall in farm rents, 1870–1914 (shillings per acre average)

1870–74	28	1895–99	21
1875–79	30	1900–04	20
1880–84	26	1905–09	21
1885–89	23	1910–14	21
1890–94	22		

Imports of wheat from USA (000s of cwt)

1860	6,497	1885	24,273
1865	1,178	1890	17,201
1870	12,372	1895	27,084
1875	23,523	1900	32,588
1880	36,191		

Free trade and protection

Chronology of key events

1815   Corn Law passed prohibiting import of wheat into Britain until price of wheat on the domestic market reached 80s. per quarter. Passed in order to protect the interests of British farmers who had invested heavily in agricultural production during the Napoleonic Wars, the Act aroused considerable opposition from commercial interests led by the Anti-Corn Law League after 1838.

1822–25 Revision of mercantilist Navigation Acts begun by Thomas Wallace, Vice-President of the Board of Trade, and continued by William Huskisson as Secretary to the Board of Trade. Obsolete penalties on Dutch shipping were removed; restrictions on shipping of other European nations considerably eased; but imperial trade was still reserved to British or colonial shipping.

1823   Huskisson obtained Reciprocity of Duties Act in order to permit reduction of duties with individual countries on a reciprocal basis. By 1830 such treaties concluded with most European states.

1824–25 Huskisson reduced tariffs on imports and exports to an average of 20% (maximum of 30%). Over 1,000 Customs Acts repealed and remaining tariffs codified.

1826   Consolidated tariff brought into operation for the whole of the United Kingdom.

1828   'Sliding scale' introduced to modify operation of Corn Law of 1815. High duties on imports now only payable when domestic price of corn low, and progressively reduced as price rose. Though a step towards free trade in line with the other commercial legislation of the 1820s, it failed to satisfy manufacturers and consumers.

1842–45 Sir Robert Peel reduced or abolished duties on a wide range of raw materials, food and manufactured goods.

1846   Repeal of the Corn Laws. Free trade in corn established apart from minor registration dues (removed in 1869).

1853	Gladstone halved duties on fruit and dairy produce and cotton yarn.
1860	Gladstone abolished all duties on fruit, dairy produce, and on all manufactured goods. Free Trade treaty signed with France.
1865	Death of apostle of free trade, Richard Cobden (2 Apr.).
1873	Inauguration in London of new Free Trade League.
1902	'Fiscal Inquiry' Blue Book issued by Board of Trade (16 Sept.). Cabinet crisis resulted in resignation of Chamberlain, Ritchie, etc. (Sept.).
1903	Chamberlain's speech at Birmingham advocating imperial preference (15 May). Tariff Reform League formed (21 July). Free Trade Union set up in response. Resignation of Duke of Devonshire (6 Oct.).
1904	First meeting of Chamberlain's Tariff Commission (15 Jan.). Inaugural meeting of Unionist Free Trade Club under Duke of Devonshire.
1910	Constitutional Free Trade Association formed.

Key trade statistics

During the nineteenth century, industrial products such as iron and cotton began to dominate the trading pattern. Trade expanded rapidly after the end of the Napoleonic Wars with the growth of industrial production and the end of trade restrictions in force during the wars, such as the Continental System and the Orders in Council. Expanding markets provided the key to further industrial expansion and a growing standard of living at home. Under the stimulus of free trade opinion all restrictions were lifted from trade, so that it was able to leap in volume after 1850, thus stimulating further economic development.

The revival of trade: 1800–49 (annual average per decade in £m). Figures are for Great Britain

	Imports	Exports	Re-exports
1800–09	28.7	25.4	12.2
1810–19	31.6	35.0	11.7
1820–29	38.3	46.1	10.0
1830–39	52.0	76.0	11.6
1840–49	79.4	124.5	17.0

Imports and exports, 1860–1919 (annual averages per decade in £m)

	Imports	Exports
1860–69	260.9	159.7
1870–79	360.6	218.1
1880–89	393.6	230.3
1890–99	435.8	237.1
1900–09	570.4	333.3
1910–19	937.5	504.6

Source: C. Cook and J. Stevenson, *Longman Atlas of Modern British History: a Visual Guide to British Society and Politics* (1978).

Principal components of British imports, 1800–29 (% of total value)

	Corn	Other foods	Textile raw materials	Other raw materials	Other
1800–09	5	42	19	6	28
1810–19	5	41	26	8	20
1820–29	3	35	33	10	19

Source: B.R. Mitchell and P. Deane, *Abstract of British Historical Statistics*, Cambridge (1962), pp. 285–9.

Principal components of British imports, 1860–1919 (% of total value)

	Foodstuffs	Textile raw materials	Other raw materials	Manufactured goods	Other
1860–69	30	30	16	2	22
1870–79	30	35	12	2	21
1880–89	35	27	12	3	23
1890–99	35	21	12	4	28
1900–09	32	19	14	6	29
1910–19	31	19	16	6	28

Source: B.R. Mitchell and P. Deane, *Abstract of British Historical Statistics*, Cambridge (1962), pp. 298–301.

Principal components of British exports, 1800–30
(% of total value)

	Cotton	Woollen goods	Iron and steel	Other materials	Other
1800–09	39	24	5	4	28
1810–19	53	16	4	3	24
1820–29	62	12	4	2	20

Source: B.R. Mitchell and P. Deane, *Abstract of British Historical Statistics*, Cambridge (1962), pp. 293–5.

Principal components of British exports, 1830–1919
(% of total value)

	Cottons	Other textiles	Iron and steel	Machinery	Coal	Vehicles
1830–39	48	24	11	1	1	–
1840–49	45	25	15	1	2	–
1850–59	36	24	18	2	2	–
1860–69	36	26	15	3	3	–
1870–79	33	22	16	4	4	–
1880–89	32	17	15	5	5	–
1890–99	28	16	14	7	7	–
1900–09	26	12	14	7	10	3
1910–19	25	15	12	5	10	2

Source: B.R. Mitchell and P. Deane, *Abstract of British Historical Statistics*, Cambridge (1962), pp. 302–6.

Geographical distribution of British trade (% of total value)

	1800	1850	1900
South America	18	16	8
Africa	15	3	3
North America	1½	15	25
Asia	12	12	12
Europe	35	33	44
Others	18½	21	8

Source: B.R. Mitchell and P. Deane, *Abstract of British Historical Statistics*, Cambridge (1962), pp. 312–26.

The balance of payments of the United Kingdom,
1816–1913 (annual averages in £m, all figures rounded)

	Balance of visible trade	Balance of invisible trade	Net balance
1816–20	−11	+18	+7
1821–25	−8	+18	+10
1826–30	−15	+17	+3
1831–35	−13	+19	+6
1836–40	−23	+26	+3
1841–45	−19	+25	+6
1846–50	−26	+30	+5
1851–55	−33	+41	+8
1856–60	−34	+60	+26
1861–65	−59	+81	+22
1866–70	−65	+106	+41
1871–75	−64	+139	+75
1876–80	−124	+149	+25
1881–85	−99	+161	+61
1886–90	−89	+177	+88
1891–95	−134	+186	+52
1896–1900	−159	+199	+40
1901–05	−177	+226	+49
1906–10	−144	+290	+146
1911–13	−140	+346	+206

Living standards: prices and wages

The standard of living has generated enormous debate among historians. The question of the general quality of life involves consideration of such matters as housing, working conditions, education, leisure and the like. Many of these are difficult to estimate with precision and reliable evidence is lacking even on wages and prices. As a result generalisation is difficult for the nineteenth century. Conditions varied from area to area, with occupation and class, and also at different periods. It is clear that up to the mid-nineteenth century there were marked fluctuations in prices, with which wages might not have kept pace, leading to deterioration of living standards. During the latter part of the century, however, falling prices and rising wages combined to raise living standards.

Prices

The Rousseaux price index, 1815–1913
(Index of total agricultural and principal industrial products; average of 1865 and 1885 = 100)

Year	Index	Year	Index	Year	Index	Year	Index
1815	164	1832	109	1850	95	1868	115
1816	144	1833	107	1851	91	1869	107
1817	161	1834	112	1852	94		
1818	160	1835	112	1853	112	1870	110
1819	147	1836	123	1854	125	1871	115
		1837	118	1855	125	1872	128
1820	132	1838	119	1856	124	1873	127
1821	121	1839	130	1857	127	1874	121
1822	116			1858	111	1875	117
1823	120	1840	128	1859	115	1876	115
1824	122	1841	121			1877	110
1825	133	1842	111	1860	120	1878	101
1826	117	1843	105	1861	115	1879	98
1827	117	1844	108	1862	120		
1828	112	1845	110	1863	121	1880	102
1829	110	1846	109	1864	119	1881	99
		1847	115	1865	117	1882	101
1830	109	1848	100	1866	120	1883	101
1831	112	1849	95	1867	118	1884	95

1885	88	1892	82	1900	91	1908	87
1886	83	1893	82	1901	86	1909	91
1887	81	1894	74	1902	86		
1888	84	1895	72	1903	86	1910	97
1889	84	1896	73	1904	83	1911	102
		1897	74	1905	86	1912	104
1890	87	1898	78	1906	93	1913	106
1891	86	1899	84	1907	97		

Source: B.R. Mitchell and P. Deane, *Abstract of British Historical Statistics*, Cambridge (1962), pp. 471–3.

Average price of wheat, 1815–1914 (by calendar year; per imperial quarter)

	s.	d.		s.	d.		s.	d.		s.	d.
1815	65	7	1840	66	4	1865	41	10	1890	31	11
1816	78	6	1841	64	4	1866	49	11	1891	37	0
1817	96	11	1842	57	3	1867	64	5	1892	30	3
1818	86	3	1843	50	1	1868	63	9	1893	26	4
1819	74	6	1844	51	3	1869	48	2	1894	22	10
1820	67	10	1845	50	10	1870	46	11	1895	23	1
1821	56	1	1846	54	8	1871	56	8	1896	26	2
1822	44	7	1847	69	9	1872	57	0	1897	30	2
1823	53	4	1848	50	6	1873	58	8	1898	34	0
1824	63	11	1849	44	3	1874	55	9	1899	25	8
1825	68	6	1850	40	3	1875	45	2	1900	26	11
1826	58	8	1851	38	6	1876	46	2	1901	26	9
1827	58	6	1852	40	9	1877	56	9	1902	28	1
1828	60	5	1853	53	3	1878	46	5	1903	26	9
1829	66	3	1854	72	5	1879	43	10	1904	28	4
1830	64	3	1855	74	8	1880	44	4	1905	29	8
1831	66	4	1856	69	2	1881	45	4	1906	28	3
1832	58	8	1857	56	4	1882	45	1	1907	30	7
1833	52	11	1858	44	2	1883	41	7	1908	32	0
1834	46	2	1859	43	9	1884	35	8	1909	36	11
1835	39	4	1860	53	3	1885	32	10	1910	31	8
1836	48	6	1861	55	4	1886	31	0	1911	31	8
1837	55	10	1862	55	5	1887	32	6	1912	34	9
1838	64	7	1863	44	9	1888	31	10	1913	31	8
1839	70	8	1864	40	2	1889	29	9	1914	34	11

Source: B.R. Mitchell and P. Deane, *Abstract of British Historical Statistics*, Cambridge (1962), pp. 487–9.

Wages

'Real' wage levels were determined in this period by three main factors: 'money' wages or wage rates, price levels and regularity of employment. The course of both 'real' and 'money' wages was often complex, with major variations for different periods, regions, and groups of workers. Skilled workers tended to fare best, though many were displaced by machinery in the later stages of industrialisation. Towards the end of the nineteenth century, falling prices created a rise in real incomes for almost all groups in regular employment.

Money wages in Great Britain, 1816–60 (1840 = 100)

1816	117	1845	98
1820	110	1850	100
1824	105	1855	117
1831	101	1860	115
1840	100		

Source: P. Deane and W.A. Cole, *British Economic Growth, 1688–1959*, Cambridge (1969), p. 23.

Money wages and real wages in the United Kingdom, 1850–1906 (1850 = 100)

	Money wages	Real wages
1850	100	100
1855	116	94
1860	114	105
1866	132	117
1871	137	125
1874	155	136
1877	152	132
1880	147	132
1883	150	142
1886	148	142
1891	162	166
1896	162	177
1900	179	184
1906	181	194

Source: P. Deane and W.A. Cole, *British Economic Growth, 1688–1959*, Cambridge (1969), p. 25.

Unemployment

With industrialisation the level of employment in Britain became subject to fluctuations both in domestic and overseas trade. Cyclical trade depressions occurred, causing unemployment; the most severe came in 1816–19, 1829–32, and 1842. The fluctuations were less severe in the mid-Victorian period, but after 1870, foreign competition and low profits led to periodic heavy unemployment. No official statistics exist, but the following list gives at least a guide to the years of heaviest unemployment.

Percentages unemployed in certain trade unions – 1851–1914

Year	%	Year	%
1851	3.9	1883	2.6
1852	6.0	1884	8.1
1853	1.7	1885	9.3
1854	2.9	1886	10.2
1855	5.4	1887	7.6
1856	4.7	1888	4.9
1857	6.0	1889	2.1
1858	11.9	1890	2.1
1859	3.8	1891	3.5
1860	1.9	1892	6.3
1861	5.2	1893	7.5
1862	8.4	1894	6.9
1863	6.0	1895	5.8
1864	2.7	1896	3.3
1865	2.1	1897	3.3
1866	3.3	1898	2.8
1867	7.4	1899	2.0
1868	7.9	1900	2.5
1869	6.7	1901	3.3
1870	3.9	1902	4.0
1871	1.6	1903	4.7
1872	0.9	1904	6.0
1873	1.2	1905	5.0
1874	1.7	1906	3.6
1875	2.4	1907	3.7
1876	3.7	1908	7.8
1877	4.7	1909	7.7
1878	6.8	1910	4.7
1879	11.4	1911	3.0
1880	5.5	1912	3.2
1881	3.5	1913	2.1
1882	2.3	1914	3.3

Industries

Coal

Coal became one of the great industries of the period, most particularly after 1850. The number of men employed rose fourfold between 1851 and 1913. South Wales became the most important coalfield by 1914 with its good quality coal for export. Population grew, coal-exporting ports developed, and collieries spread along the valleys. Coal output peaked just before the First World War. Coal exports greatly increased from 1850 to 1913, when 98 million tons out of 287 million produced were exported, a tenth of all UK exports.

Key statistics

Labour employed in mines

1860	307,000
1880	504,000
1900	820,000

Source: C. Cook and J. Stevenson, *Longman Atlas of Modern British History: a Visual Guide to British Society and Politics* (1978).

Coal output

	Tons (000,000)	% exported		Tons (000,000)	% exported
1800	11.0	2.0	1860	80.0	9.2
1816	15.9	2.5	1865	98.2	9.3
1820	17.4	1.4	1870	110.4	13.4
1825	21.9	1.4	1875	131.9	13.5
1830	22.4	2.2	1880	146.8	16.3
1835	27.7	2.7	1885	159.4	19.3
1840	33.7	4.8	1890	181.6	21.3
1845	45.9	5.5	1895	189.7	22.6
1850	49.4	6.8	1900	225.2	25.9
1855	61.5	8.1			

Source: B.R. Mitchell and P. Deane, *Abstract of British Historical Statistics*, Cambridge (1962), pp. 115–19, 120–1.

Steel

Steel became a major industry after 1860 when several new processes became available to produce steel cheaply, quickly, and in large quantities. Bessemer's Converter (1856) was followed by Siemens's 'open hearth' (1869), both of which used hot gases to produce the steel. In 1879 the Thomas-Gilchrist process was developed to use phosphoric ores. As a result of these developments steel could be used more extensively. Steel began to be used for railway lines (from 1864), larger and stronger bridges (such as the Forth Bridge, 1890), machinery, engineering tools and armaments. By the end of the nineteenth century steel-hulled ships and steel-framed buildings were being developed. Production of steel grew rapidly, though it did not outstrip iron until after 1918.

Britain dominated world steel output in the nineteenth century until the Thomas-Gilchrist process allowed the USA and Germany to use their extensive deposits of phosphoric ores. By 1900 both had overtaken British production. British steel exports rose dramatically in the late nineteenth century.

Key statistics

Steel production, 1870–1920 (000 tons)

1870	300	1900	5,000
1880	1,250	1910	6,500
1890	3,500	1920	9,000

Source: C. Cook and J. Stevenson, *Longman Atlas of Modern British History: a Visual Guide to British Society and Politics* (1978).

Steel exports (000 tons)

1870	620
1900	950
1925	2,000

Iron production (000 tons)

1820	450
1850	2,000
1875	6,500
1900	9,000

Textiles

Numbers employed in factories (000)

1835	219	1847	316
1838	259	1850	331

1856	379	1885	504
1861	452	1890	529
1867	401	1895	539
1870	450	1901	523
1874	480	1904	523
1878	483	1907	577

Cotton production and exports (annual average per decade)

	Raw cotton (retained imports, 000 lb)	Exports of piece goods (000 yd)
1810–19	96,000	227,000
1820–29	173,000	320,000
1830–39	302,000	553,000
1840–49	550,000	978,000
1850–59	795,000	1,855,000
1860–69	803,000	2,375,000
1870–79	1,244,000	3,573,000
1880–89	1,473,000	4,575,000
1890–99	1,556,000	5,057,000

Shipbuilding

The shipbuilding industry underwent remarkable expansion in the nineteenth century. The development of iron ships from the 1860s, steam power, and larger tonnages, concentrated the industry in places with access to coal, iron and steel, and engineering skills, such as the Clyde, Tyne, Mersey, Barrow and Belfast. By 1914 shipbuilding was a major industry in which Britain dominated the world.

Key statistics

Ships built and registered in the United Kingdom, 1820–1913 (000 tons)

1820	66.7	1880	403.8
1830	75.5	1890	652.0
1840	211.3	1900	739.0
1850	133.7	1910	601.0
1860	212.0	1913	975.2
1870	342.7		

Source: B.R. Mitchell and P. Deane, *Abstract of British Historical Statistics*, Cambridge (1962), pp. 221–2.

Transport

Ports and shipping

During the nineteenth century the two most important developments were the development of iron or steel vessels and the replacement of sail by steam power. Iron or iron-clad vessels became accepted by the middle of the nineteenth century, after the *Great Britain* had proved its durability. Steam could not compete at first with fast 'clipper' ships such as the *Cutty Sark*, due to fuel costs. Though the first steam crossing of the Atlantic was in 1838, it was not until the development of screw propulsion (1843), the compound expansion engine (1854) and the turbine engine (1894) that steam eclipsed sail.

The period saw tremendous growth and expansion in the major docks. London remained the pre-eminent port in the country throughout, but new ports, such as Cardiff, Glasgow, Hull and Liverpool grew to serve the manufacturing centres. By 1880 London and Liverpool were dominant.

Chronology of key events

1828	Opening of St Katharine's Dock (London).
1838	*Sirius* and *Great Western* crossed Atlantic, America–Liverpool, in 15 days.
1840	Cunard Line founded.
1843	*Great Britain* crossed Atlantic in two weeks.
1854	Advent of compound expansion engine.
1858	*Great Eastern* launched.
1869	Opening of Suez Canal.
1894	Steam turbine invented by Parsons.
1907	Launching of *Mauritania*.
1913	Launching of *Lusitania*.

Growth of London Docks, 1789–1914

1789	Brunswick Dock, Blackwall Dock
1802	West India Dock
1803	London Dock
1806	East India Dock
1807	Surrey Commercial Dock

1828   St Katharine's Dock
1855   Victoria Dock
1868   Millwall Dock
1880   Royal Victoria Dock and Albert Dock
1886   Tilbury Dock
1914   King George V Dock

Shipping registered in the United Kingdom 1790–1920

	(000 tons)		*(000 tons)*
1790	1,383	1860	4,659
1800	1,699	1870	5,691
1810	2,211	1880	6,575
1820	2,439	1890	7,979
1830	2,202	1900	11,514
1840	2,768	1910	16,768
1850	3,565	1920	18,111

Source: B.R. Mitchell and P. Deane, *Abstract of British Historical Statistics*, Cambridge (1962), pp. 217–19.

Tonnage cleared by major ports, 1880 (000 tons)

London	12,900	Newport	2,400
Liverpool	10,300	South Shields	1,900
Cardiff	8,000	Southampton	1,700
Newcastle	5,200	Sunderland	1,600
Hull	3,400	Middlesbrough	1,200
Glasgow	2,500	Grimsby	1,200

Source: C. Cook and J. Stevenson, *Longman Atlas of Modern British History*, London (1978), p. 54.

Railways

After the opening of the first railway between Stockton and Darlington in 1825, railway growth was rapid.

Following the Liverpool–Manchester Railway of 1830, the London–Birmingham Railway, completed in 1838, was the first trunk route to link London with the provinces. Between 1844 and 1846 occurred the first railway boom in which private companies built many new lines. By 1850 Wales, Scotland, the North, Midlands, East Anglia, the West Country, and the south coast were linked to London. Over 3,000 miles of track had been laid and railway construction took a large share of both labour supply, the 'navvies', and of capital. Railway contractors such as Brassey and Hudson made fortunes.

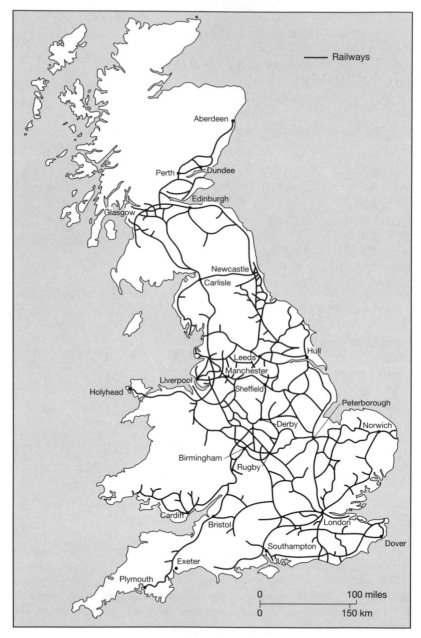

Map 3. The railway network in 1852
Source: Charles More, *The Industrial Age: Economy and Society in Britain,
1750–1995* (Second Edn, 1997), p. 419.

Chronology of key developments

1825	Opening of Stockton and Darlington Railway.
1830	Canterbury and Whitstable line opened.
1832	Opening of Leicester and Swannington Railway.
1834	Opening of Leeds and Selby Railway.
1838	Completion of London–Birmingham trunk route. Euston opened. Great Western Railway opened (from Paddington to Maidenhead, 4 June). Dundee and Arbroath Railway opened (6 Oct.).
1839	First section of Midland Counties Railway opened (from Derby to Nottingham). London and Croydon Railway opened (5 June). Birmingham and Derby Railway opened (Aug.).
1840	London and Southampton Railway opened (11 May). Midland Counties Railway reached Leicester (4 May) and Rugby (30 June).
1841	Great Western Railway completed London–Bristol route (30 June).
1842	Railway Clearing House set up.
1844	Midland Railway created by amalgamations.
1845–47	Peak of 'railway mania'.
1848	Opening of Caledonian Railway from Carlisle to Edinburgh and Glasgow (15 Feb.).
1850	Completion of 'East Coast Route' from London to Edinburgh and Glasgow (7 Aug.).
1854	North Eastern Railway founded.
1855	First special postal train begun by Great Western Railway.
1862	Amalgamations created Great Eastern Railway.
1863	First underground railway in London (the Metropolitan Railway from Bishop's Road to Farringdon Street) opened (10 Jan.).
1876	Completion of Settle and Carlisle line.
1878	First Tay Bridge opened (1 June).
1879	Tay Bridge disaster (28 Dec.).
1885	Opening of the Severn Tunnel.
1887	New Tay Bridge opened.
1889	Regulation of Railways Act passed (30 Aug.). Enforced the block system, interlocking of signals, etc.
1890	Forth Bridge opened (4 Mar.). Opening of first electric underground railway (City and South London Railway) (18 Dec.).
1892	Last broad gauge trains withdrawn.
1893	Opening of first section of the elevated Liverpool Overhead Railway (6 Mar.).
1899	Opening of Marylebone, last London terminus to be built.

1903   Conversion of Mersey Railway to electrification (3 May).
1904   Further electrification schemes: North East Railway completed
        first section of Tyneside electrification (29 Mar.). Liverpool–
        Southport line electrified by the Lancashire and Yorkshire
        Railway (Apr.).
1905   Electrification completed of 'Inner Circle' on London
        underground.

Railway mileage and passengers carried in the United Kingdom, 1845–1900

	Miles open	Passengers carried (m.)		Miles open	Passengers carried (m.)
1845	2,441	30.4	1875	14,510	490.1
1850	6,084	67.4	1880	15,563	596.6
1855	7,293	111.4	1885	16,594	678.1
1860	9,069	153.5	1890	17,281	796.3
1865	11,451	238.7	1895	18,001	903.5
1870	13,562	322.2	1900	18,680	1,114.6

Source: B.R. Mitchell and P. Deane, *Abstract of British Historical Statistics*, Cambridge (1962), pp. 225–7.

SECTION FOUR

Foreign affairs, defence and the Empire

The armed forces

Office holders

For Secretaries of State for War and Colonies, see p. 36; for Secretaries of State for War after 1855, see p. 37; for First Lords of the Admiralty, see p. 36.

Commanders-in-Chief

1811	Duke of York	1852	Viscount Hardinge
1827	Duke of Wellington	1856	Duke of Cambridge
1828	Viscount Hill	1895.	Viscount Wolseley
1842	Duke of Wellington	1900	Earl Roberts

In 1904 Sir N. Lyttleton was appointed Chief of the General Staff, to be succeeded in 1908 by Sir W. Nicholson. His title became Chief of the Imperial General Staff in 1909. Nicholson was succeeded by French in 1912.

Major military legislation and administrative reforms

1832	All naval business consolidated under the Board of Admiralty.
1837	Lord Howick's Commission advocated the centralisation of the civil business of the Army in the hands of the Secretary at War.
1847	Life service in the Army abolished; replaced by a minimum term of 10 years.
1852	Militia Act reorganised militia and placed it under the control of the Secretary at War.
1853	Continuous Service Act reorganised naval service with fixed terms of enlistment.
1854–55	Secretary of State for War took overall control of the armed forces, though discipline and command of the Army reserved to the Commander-in-Chief at the Horse Guards. Board of Ordnance abolished and duties of Secretary at War combined with Secretary of State for War.
1856	Staff college set up at Sandhurst.
1858	Creation of the Indian Army. Army of the East India Company transferred to the control of the Crown.

1859   Volunteer force created to protect against threat of French invasion.

1860   Sir James Graham's Committee on Military Organisation declared that the Commander-in-Chief was subordinate to the Secretary of State, and recommended that the Horse Guards and the War Office should be under the same roof.

1862   Fixed terms of enlistment made compulsory in the Navy. House of Commons' resolution in favour of self-governing colonies undertaking their own defence. By 1870 colonial garrisons (excluding India) were under 24,000 men, as against nearly 50,000 in 1858.

1867   Army of Reserve Act planned formation of a trained reserve of 80,000 men.

1868   Edward Cardwell became Secretary for War and began period of reform.

1870   War Office Act. Following the recommendations of Lord Northbrook's Committee, the Horse Guards moved to the same building as the War Office, which was organised into three departments: Military under the Commander-in-Chief; Supply under the Surveyor-General; and Finance under the Financial Secretary. The Secretary of State was confirmed in his responsibility for Army business as a whole. Army Enlistment Act fixed terms of enlistment at 12 years, part on active service, part with the reserve.

1871   Purchase of commissions abolished. Flogging suspended in the Navy in peacetime.

1872   Cardwell reorganised regimental structure on basis of linked battalions, one to serve abroad, one to remain at home. Regiments to have local attachment for recruiting.

1879   Flogging in Navy suspended in wartime.

1881   Flogging abolished in the Army. Regular and militia battalions of the Army amalgamated into territorial regiments with local designation and depot.

1902   Committee of Imperial Defence created.

1904   Office of Commander-in-Chief abolished; Army Council established and General Staff created.

1906   Richard Haldane became Secretary for War and began series of 'Haldane reforms'.

1907   British Expeditionary Force created for commitment to the Continent in the event of European war. Territorial Reserve Forces Act abolished militia and volunteers and replaced them with Territorial regiments organised by county associations.

1914–15   Kitchener's 'New Army' raised from volunteers.

Growth of defence spending

Expenditure on the armed forces grew substantially in the period up to 1914 with the growth of Empire and rivalry with European powers.

Expenditure on the armed forces

1802	£37,000,000	1880	£25,000,000
1814	£72,000,000	1900	£70,000,000
1830	£15,000,000	1921	£292,000,000
1856	£47,000,000		

Size of the Army and Navy

	Army	Navy		Army	Navy
1815	204,386	85,384	1870	113,221	61,000
1820	92,586	23,000	1880	131,859	58,800
1830	88,848	29,000	1890	153,483	68,800
1850	99,128	39,000	1900	430,000	114,880
1855	223,224	70,000	1914*	733,514	147,667

* January

Source: C. Cook and B. Keith, *British Historical Facts 1830–1900*, London (1975), p. 185.

British wars and campaigns, 1815–1914

Third Maratha War (India) 1817

Attacks by Marathas and bands of marauding robbers called Pindaris. On 21 December 1817 Sir Thomas Hyslop crushed the army of Maratha leader, Holkar, at Mahidput. In 1818, Lord Rawdon-Hastings hunted down the Pindaris; the ruler of the Marathas, the Peshwa, surrendered on 2 June.

Wars with Burma 1824–26, 1852–53, 1885–92

The threat of a Burmese invasion of India led to a British declaration of war on 5 March 1824. An expedition under Sir Archibald Campbell imposed the treaty of Yandabo on 24 February 1826. An appeal for protection by British merchants at Rangoon in 1852 resulted in a further expedition which captured Rangoon. South Burma was annexed in December 1852. In 1885, as a result of King Thibaw's confiscation of the property of the Bombay-Burma Company, a British amphibious force invaded Burma and on 1 January 1886 it was annexed as a province of the Indian Empire. Guerrilla warfare continued until 1892.

Battle of Navarino 1827

By the treaty of London signed on 6 July 1827 France, Russia and England threatened action in support of the Greeks who were fighting for their independence from the Ottoman Empire, unless the Turks agreed to an armistice. On 8 September 1827 the Egyptian fleet landed fresh troops at Navarino to suppress the Greek rebellion. On 20 October the Egyptian – Turkish fleet was destroyed by the action of British, French and Russian squadrons. Russia subsequently declared war on Turkey on 26 April 1828, and Greek independence was recognised by the treaty of London of 7 May 1832.

Kaffir Wars 1834–35, 1877–78

In December 1834 the Kaffirs invaded British territory. They were driven back, and in April 1835 a punitive expedition was mounted against them. This was the sixth in a series of wars with the Kaffirs; the ninth and last took place 1877–78.

Wars with China 1839–42, 1856–60

The 'Opium War' of 1839–42 originated in drastic action taken by the Chinese against British merchants in an attempt to curb the opium trade. An expedition under Sir Hugh Gough captured Canton on 24 May 1841. Shanghai was captured on 19 June 1842, and peace was concluded by the treaty of Nanking on 29 August 1842. Chinese seizure of the British ship, the *Arrow*, at Canton in October 1856 led to renewed fighting. Canton was taken and the Taku forts near Tientsin were silenced. The treaty of Tientsin was signed on 26 June 1858. However, in 1859 a naval force under Admiral James Hope was repulsed at the Taku forts on the way to obtain ratification of the treaty. A British and French expedition led by Sir Hope Grant captured the Taku forts and occupied Peking on 9 October 1860. The treaty of Peking, ending the war, was signed on 24 October 1860.

Afghan Wars 1839–42, 1878–81

Fears regarding the threat to India posed by Russian activity in Afghanistan led to a British invasion which captured Kabul on 7 August 1839. Following an uprising, General Elphinstone's force was massacred at Gardamak on 13 January 1842, while attempting to withdraw. Parts of Kabul were destroyed by a punitive expedition in September 1842, but the country was then evacuated. A further British invasion was mounted in 1878. A British force was defeated at Maiwand on 27 July 1880, but Sir

Frederick Roberts relieved Kandahar on 1 September. A pro-British government was established and the evacuation of Afghanistan completed by April 1881.

Conquest of Sind (India), 1843

Following friction between the rulers of Sind and the British, the British Residency in the capital, Hyderabad, was attacked. Sir Charles Napier marched to its relief, defeated the enemy at Miari on 17 February 1843 and proceeded to conquer the territory. He summed up his campaign in a one-word message to the Governor-General: 'Peccavi' ('I have sinned').

Maori Wars 1843–48, 1860–70

The Maoris' resentment of encroachment by British settlers in New Zealand led to periods of guerrilla warfare. The uprisings were suppressed by a combination of the local militia, helped by troops from Britain and Australia, and diplomacy.

Sikh Wars 1845–46, 1848–49

On 11 December 1845 a Sikh army crossed the Sutlej into British Indian territory. Sir Hugh Gough beat off an attack at Mudki on 18 December, and then defeated the Sikhs at the battle of Ferozeshah on 21–22 December. Further defeats were inflicted by the British at Aliwal (29 January 1846) and Sobraon (10 February 1846), and by the treaty of Lahore, signed on 11 March 1846, the Punjab became a British protectorate. A mutiny at Multan on 20 April 1848 sparked off a Sikh uprising. Gough invaded the Punjab and fought inconclusive battles at Ramnagar (22 November 1848) and Chilianwala (13 January 1849), before finally defeating the Sikhs at Gujerat on 21 February 1849. The Punjab was subsequently annexed.

Crimean War 1854–55

Turkey declared war on Russia on 23 September 1853. The Turkish fleet was destroyed at Sinope on 30 November 1853, and a Franco-British fleet entered the Black Sea to protect the Turkish coast. France and Britain declared war on Russia on 28 March 1854. In September 1854 an allied force landed on the Crimean Peninsula and besieged Sebastopol. Major battles fought were Alma (20 September), Balaclava (25 October) and Inkerman (5 November). The French capture of the Malakoff strongpoint on 8 September 1855 led to the Russian evacuation of

Sebastopol. The Russians accepted a preliminary peace on 1 February 1856 and the treaty of Paris was signed in March 1856. British losses were 4,600 killed and 13,000 wounded, a further 17,500 died of disease.

Persian War 1856–57

On 1 November 1856 Britain declared war on Persia, which had occupied Herat in Afghanistan. Sir James Outram led an invasion of Persia, and by a peace treaty signed in March 1857 the Shah agreed to evacuate Afghanistan.

Indian Mutiny 1857–58

The mutiny broke out at Meerut on 10 May 1857. From there the mutineers marched on Delhi and seized the city. The mutiny spread rapidly and the British were besieged at Cawnpore and Lucknow. At Cawnpore they surrendered on 26 June to Nana Sahib, who then massacred his prisoners. In September 1857 the British recaptured Delhi. Sir Henry Havelock reached Lucknow, but was himself besieged there until relieved in November by Sir Colin Campbell, who evacuated the defenders. Lucknow was finally recaptured in March 1858. In Central India Sir Hugh Rose defeated Tantia Topi at Gwalior on 19 June 1858. Peace was proclaimed on 8 July 1858.

Abyssinian War 1867–68

An expedition of British and Indian troops led by Sir Robert Napier was sent to rescue diplomats and Europeans held by King Theodore of Abyssinia in his capital, Magdala. Theodore's army was defeated at Arogee and he committed suicide on 10 April 1868. Magdala was stormed and the hostages rescued on 13 April.

Ashanti Campaign 1873–74

After initial fighting, Sir Garnet Wolseley, the administrator and Commander-in-Chief on the Gold Coast, mounted an expedition against Kumasi, the capital of the Ashanti, who were threatening British settlements. Kumasi fell in February 1874 and peace was imposed. Further expeditions took place against the Ashanti in 1896 and 1900, the latter leading to the annexation of the territory.

Zulu War 1878–79

The Zulus under Chief Cetewayo ignored a British demand on 11 December 1878 for the establishment of a British protectorate over Zululand.

Lord Chelmsford invaded Zululand on 11 January 1879, but part of his army was annihilated at Isandhlwana on 22 January. The defence of Rorke's Drift during the following night saved Natal from being over-run. After the arrival of reinforcements, Chelmsford defeated Cetewayo in the battle of Ulundi on 4 July 1879.

First South African (Boer) War 1880–81

Great Britain annexed the Transvaal Boer Republic in 1877. In December 1880 the Boers proclaimed their independence. General Sir George Colley, leading British troops from Natal, was defeated and killed at Majuba Hill on 27 February 1881. The British government decided on withdrawal. An armistice was signed on 6 March 1881, and peace made by the Convention of Pretoria on 5 April 1881. The Boers were granted their independence under British suzerainty.

Egyptian War 1882

A nationalist uprising led by Colonel Arabi against the growth of European influence in Egypt resulted in June 1882 in the deaths of many Europeans in riots in Alexandria. As a result British forces bombarded and occupied Alexandria and Colonel Arabi's revolt was crushed at the battle of Tel-el-Kebir on 13 September 1882.

The Sudan 1884–85, 1896–99

In October 1883 an Egyptian army led by Colonel Hicks was defeated at El Obeid by the Sudanese forces of the Mahdi. In January 1884 General Gordon was sent to Khartoum to bring back the Egyptian garrison, but he remained and was cut off. A relief expedition under Sir Garnet Wolseley arrived on 28 January 1885, two days after Khartoum had fallen and Gordon had been killed. The British government undertook the reconquest of the Sudan in 1896. The Sudanese were defeated on 2 September 1898 at the battle of Omdurman, and on 19 January 1899 an Anglo-Egyptian condominium was established over the Sudan.

Boxer Rising 1900

The 'Boxers' was a popular term for members of the Society of Harmonious Fists, a secret organisation opposed to European commercial interests in China at the turn of the twentieth century, which had the tacit approval of the Chinese authorities and the Dowager Empress. Its members attacked Christians and workers on European-controlled railways, prompting the European states to take steps to protect their nationals.

British troops were fired upon at Taku. In an uprising on 19 June 1900, the European legations were besieged and the German minister assaulted. A six-nation expeditionary force, including Japanese and US troops, landed at Tientsin on 14 July and stormed Peking on 14 August, forcing the Empress and Dowager Empress to flee. A peace agreement, the Boxer Protocol, was signed by China and 12 nations on 7 September 1901.

Boer War 1899–1902

The strained relations between the British Empire and the independent Boer republics of Transvaal and Orange Free State reached crisis point over the political rights of foreigners (Uitlanders) in Transvaal. In October 1899 a Boer ultimatum to Britain to withdraw border reinforcements was ignored, and the Boers launched offensives into Natal and Cape Colony. Ladysmith, Kimberley and Mafeking were all besieged, and three successive defeats at Stormberg, Magersfontein and Colenso during 'Black Week' (10–15 December 1899) forced the British on to the defensive. British attempts to relieve Ladysmith ended in defeat at Spion Kop and Vaal Krantz. The arrival of Lord Roberts and Lord Kitchener galvanised the British to victory at Paardeberg in February 1900 and relief of all three besieged towns. The Boer capitals of Bloemfontein and Pretoria were captured by June, ending all formal conflict. Boer resistance continued for 18 months with guerrilla attacks on British positions. Kitchener responded by burning Boer farms and incarcerating Boer women and children in concentration camps, where over 20,000 died. Boer leaders eventually capitulated at Vereeniging on 31 May 1902, ending the biggest and most expensive war for Britain between Waterloo and the First World War. British casualties were 5,774 killed and 22,829 wounded; the Boers lost an estimated 4,000 killed.

Expedition to Tibet 1903–04

A British expedition led by Colonel Younghusband invaded Tibet to force the Dalai Lama to enter into negotiations about the frontier with India. After fierce fighting, Younghusband reached Lhasa on 3 August 1904, and a treaty was signed on 7 September.

Treaties, alliances and conventions

Chronology of major treaties

1815
25 Mar. Treaty of alliance with Austria, Prussia and Russia against Napoleon signed at Vienna, each power engaging to furnish 180,000 men.
9 June Act of the Congress of Vienna signed by Britain, Austria, France, Portugal, Prussia, Russia and Sweden.
20 Nov. Treaty of peace with France signed at Paris.

1827
6 July Treaty with France and Russia for pacification of Greece signed at London.

1830
3 Feb. Protocol signed with France and Russia concerning Greek independence.

1831
20 Jan. Protocol of conference regarding the separation of Belgium and The Netherlands signed by Britain, Austria, France, Prussia and Russia.

1832
7 May Convention regarding the sovereignty of Greece signed by Britain, France, Russia and Bavaria.

1833
22 Mar. Supplementary Convention regarding the traffic in slaves, signed by Britain and France.

1834
22 Apr. Treaty of Quadruple Alliance with France, Spain and Portugal for the pacification of the Iberian Peninsula.
5 Sept. Agreement with Russia to respect the integrity and independence of Persia.

1839
19 Apr. Treaty between Britain, Austria, France, Prussia, Russia and Belgium regarding Belgium and The Netherlands.

1840
7 Feb. Treaty with Saxe-Coburg-Gotha for the marriage of Victoria to Prince Albert.
15 July Convention between Britain, Austria, Prussia, Russia and Turkey for the pacification of the Levant.

1841
13 July Convention between Austria, France, Prussia, Russia and Turkey regarding the Dardanelles.
20 Dec. Treaty for the suppression of the African slave trade signed by Britain, Austria, France, Prussia and Russia.

1842
28 Aug. Treaty of Nanking between Britain and China ending the Opium War; Hong Kong was ceded to Britain and the five treaty ports were opened to foreign trade.

1846
15 June Treaty with the United States settling the Oregon boundary with Canada.

1847
5–6 Apr. Agreement with China concerning entrance of British subjects to Canton, trade at Honan, etc.

1854
2 Dec. Treaty of alliance with Austria and France.

1855
21 Nov. Treaty with France and Sweden and Norway regarding the integrity of the United Kingdoms of Sweden and Norway.

1856
30 Mar. Peace of Paris ending the Crimean War signed by Britain, Austria, France, Prussia, Russia, Sardinia and Turkey.
15 Apr. Treaty between Britain, Austria and France guaranteeing the independence and integrity of the Ottoman Empire.

1860
23 Jan. Treaty of Commerce with France.

1863
16 July Treaty for the Redemption of the Scheldt Toll.

1864
22 Aug. Geneva Convention regarding the amelioration of the condition of the wounded in armies in the field.
Treaty concerning reunion of the Ionian Islands to Greece.

1868
International Telegraph Convention.

1871
13 Mar. Treaty concerning the navigation of the Black Sea and the Danube between Britain, Austria, France, Germany, Italy, Russia and Turkey.
8 May Treaty between Britain and the United States regarding the amicable settlement of disputes.

1878
13 July Treaty arising out of the Congress of Berlin signed by Britain, Austria-Hungary, France, Germany, Italy, Russia and Turkey for the settlement of Balkan problems.
14 Aug. Agreement between Britain and Turkey regarding British government of Cyprus.
1 June Convention for the formation of a Universal Postal Union.

1880
31 Mar. Agreement with France, Germany, Austria-Hungary and Italy concerning the Egyptian Debt.

1881
18 Sept. Final Act for the settlement of the frontier between Greece and Turkey agreed between Britain, Austria-Hungary, France, Germany, Italy and Russia.

1883
13 Feb. International agreement on the navigation of the Danube.

1885
26 Feb. General Act of the 15-nation conference at Berlin regarding affairs of Central Africa.
17 Mar. Declaration regarding Egyptian finances and the free navigation of the Suez Canal by Britain, Austria-Hungary, France, Germany, Italy and Russia.
29 Apr. Agreement between Britain and Germany regarding spheres of action in Africa.
10 Sept. Protocol between Britain and Russia regarding the Afghan frontier.

1888
29 Oct. Convention respecting the free navigation of the Suez Canal.

1889
14 June Final Act of the conference on the affairs of Samoa.

1890
17 Mar. Convention with China relating to Sikkim and Tibet.
14 June Agreement with Zanzibar placing Zanzibar under the protection of Britain.
1 July Agreement between Britain and Germany regarding Zanzibar, Heligoland and spheres of influence in Africa.
5 Aug. Declarations exchanged with France respecting territories in Africa.

1891
26 June Agreement with France regarding spheres of influence in Africa.
4 July Final protocol signed of the Universal Postal Convention.

1893
8 July Protocol with Germany respecting the delimitation of the Anglo-German boundary in East Equatorial Africa.
12 July Arrangements with France fixing boundary between British and French possessions on the Gold Coast.
31 July Protocol with France respecting territories in the region of the Upper Mekong.
12 Nov. Agreement with Afghanistan respecting frontier between India and Afghanistan.
15 Nov. Agreement with Germany respecting boundaries in Africa.

1894
5 May Protocol between Britain and Italy regarding spheres of influence in eastern Africa.

1897
18 Sept. Convention with France concerning Tunis.

1898
14 June Convention with France concerning spheres of influence east and west of the Niger.
Convention signed with China over Wei-hai-wei base.
30 Aug. Convention with Germany regarding Portuguese Africa and Timor.

1899

29 July International conventions for the peaceful settlement of international disputes; for adapting to maritime warfare the principles of the Geneva Convention; and with respect to the laws and customs of war by land.

Sept.–Dec. Exchange of notes with the United States accepting the commercial policy of the 'open door' in China.

7 Nov.–2 Dec. Conventions with Germany and the United States relating to Samoa.

1900

16 Oct. Agreement with Germany regarding China. Both parties agreed to restrain foreign territorial aggression in China and maintain the 'open door' for trade.

1902

30 Jan. Anglo-Japanese Alliance signed. Concluded initially for five years, both powers recognised the special interests of each other in China, and Japan's interests in Korea. Agreement to remain neutral in the event of war with a third power, or provide assistance in the event of war with two other powers. Renewed in August 1905 and modified to provide for mutual support in the event of attack by another power.

1904

8 Apr. Anglo-French *Entente* (*Entente Cordiale*) signed. Although no formal military alliance was arranged, there was an unwritten understanding of mutual assistance if required. Agreed that Egypt and Morocco should be under British and French influence respectively. Disputes over Newfoundland, Madagascar and Siam settled.

1907

31 Aug. Anglo-Russian *Entente* signed. Settled outstanding differences over Afghanistan, Tibet and Persia, paving the way for Russia to side with Britain and France against Germany in 1914.

1914

3 Sept. Triple *Entente* signed between Britain, France and Russia agreeing not to make a separate peace with Germany.

Britain, the alliance system and the origins of the First World War, 1894–1914

1894

Jan. France and Russia signed defensive alliance.

1896

Jan. 'Kruger telegram' incident. William II sent a telegram of congratulation to President Kruger of the Boer Republic on the failure of the Jameson raid on the Transvaal. Widely interpreted in Britain as an antagonistic act.

1898

Mar.–Apr. Breakdown of Anglo-German negotiations for agreement to resist Russian expansion in the Far East.

Sept. Confrontation between British forces under Kitchener and French expeditionary force under Marchand at Fashoda in the Sudan. After a period of great tension between the two countries, a compromise was reached allowing the French to withdraw.

1899

Mar. Anglo-French agreement over their spheres of influence in Africa. France was excluded from the Nile Valley but was allowed to consolidate its position in north, west and Saharan Africa. First German Naval Law passed.

May–July The Hague Peace Conference failed to achieve agreement on disarmament.

Oct. Outbreak of Boer War increased British diplomatic isolation.

1900

June Second German Naval Law.

1901

Mar.–May Breakdown of Franco-German negotiations for an alliance.

1902

Jan. Great Britain and Japan signed defensive alliance.

1904

Apr. *Entente Cordiale.* Great Britain and France signed agreement on colonial disputes.

1905

Feb.–July First Morocco crisis. William II intervened in Moroccan affairs, a French area of influence. Germany failed to obtain international support but France agreed to an international conference.

1906

Jan.–Apr. Algeçiras conference provided peaceful settlement of the Moroccan crisis, but increased German isolation. During the crisis France and Britain held military talks, including a commitment for a British expeditionary force to be sent to the continent.

Feb. Great Britain launched the *Dreadnought*, the first all big-gun battleship, rendering existing naval vessels obsolete and intensifying the naval race with Germany.

1907

June–Oct. Germany rejected any scheme for disarmament at the second Hague Peace Conference.

July Triple Alliance renewed for six years.

Aug. Britain and Russia signed a convention; Britain, France and Russia known as the Triple Entente.

1908

Oct. Austria-Hungary annexed Bosnia-Herzegovina: Russia backed down from intervention. William II's comments in an interview in the *Daily Telegraph* increased Anglo-German antagonism.

1909

Jan. Agreement made for international exploitation of Moroccan mines.

Feb. France and Germany signed an agreement recognising France's political rights in Morocco in return for economic equality.

1911

1 July Second Morocco crisis. German gunboat, the *Panther*, arrived in Agadir.

4 July Germany warned of Great Britain's concern for Moroccan question.

July–Nov. Talks between France and Germany resulted in end of crisis. Germany recognised the French protectorate in Morocco (11 Oct), while France signed agreement to pay compensation to Germany (4 Nov).

28 Sept. Italy sent ultimatum to the Ottoman Empire not to resist troops sent to Tripoli in Libya.

29 Sept. Italy declared war on the Ottoman Empire; Italian forces bombarded Tripoli and made landings.

5 Nov. Italian Prime Minister declared Tripoli annexed.

1912

Feb. Haldane mission to Germany failed to end naval race.

Mar. Germany published Third Naval Law.

18 Apr. Italian fleet bombarded Turkish forts in the Dardanelles.

Sept. Serbia, Montenegro, Greece and Bulgaria formed Balkan League against the Ottoman Empire.

6 Oct. Great Powers backed French proposals to avert Balkan War.

8 Oct. Montenegro declared war on the Ottoman Empire.

12 Oct. The Ottoman Empire refused to undertake reforms in its Balkan territories proposed by Great Powers.

17 Oct. The Ottoman Empire declared war on Bulgaria and Serbia.

18 Oct. Italy and the Ottoman Empire signed peace treaty at Lausanne, leaving Tripoli and Cyrenaica under Italian suzerainty.

24 Oct. Turks suffered defeats by Bulgarians at Kirk-Kilisse and by the Serbs at Kumanovo.

9 Nov. Greeks took Salonica.

3 Dec. Armistice between the Ottoman Empire, Bulgaria, Serbia and Montenegro. Russia and Austria-Hungary mobilised.

1913

6 Jan. Peace conference between the Ottoman Empire and Balkan states suspended.

Mar. Greeks took Janina; Adrianople surrendered to Bulgarians.

15 Apr. Turks and Bulgarians ceased fighting.

22 Apr. Austria-Hungary moved forces to near Montenegrin border.

30 May Preliminaries of peace signed between Balkan states and the Ottoman Empire.

31 May Serbs and Greeks signed secret military convention against Bulgaria.

June Germany made fiscal provisions to double the strength of her army.

30 June Fighting broke out between Bulgaria and her former allies.

10 Aug. Balkan states signed Treaty of Bucharest.

30 Sept. Treaty of Constantinople between the Ottoman Empire and Bulgaria ended Second Balkan War.

1914

15 June Anglo-German agreement on Baghdad Railway and Mesopotamia.

28 June Archduke Francis Ferdinand assassinated by Slav extremists at Sarajevo.

23 July Austria-Hungary sent Serbian government a ten-point ultimatum demanding firm steps to suppress anti-Austrian activities by Slav extremists and (clause 6) participation of Austrian delegates in official enquiry into the assassination.

24 July Russian government declared it would defend Serbia against Austro-Hungarian attack.

25 July Serbia made conciliatory reply to Austrian ultimatum, but would not accept clause 6 as contrary to the constitution. Austria-Hungary found the reply unsatisfactory and mobilized against Serbia.

26 July Grey's proposal of an international conference to settle the Austro-Serbian dispute rejected by Austria-Hungary and Germany. Austrian forces mobilised on Russian frontier.

28 July Austria-Hungary declared war on Serbia.

30 July Russia began general mobilisation.

31 July Germany demanded that Russia cease mobilisation.

1 Aug. Germany declared war on Russia; France mobilised. Italy declared her neutrality. German-Turkish treaty signed.

2 Aug. Germany occupied Luxembourg and sent ultimatum to Belgium demanding passage for her troops. Russians invaded East Prussia.

3 Aug. Germany declared war on France and began invasion of Belgium. British ultimatum to Germany.

4 Aug. Germany declared war on Belgium: Britain declared war on Germany.

5 Aug. Austria-Hungary declared war on Russia.

10 Aug. France declared war on Austria-Hungary.

12 Aug. Britain declared war on Austria-Hungary.

The empire

The expansion of the British Empire

Territories added to the Empire: 1802–1914

Aden	Colony (1839) and adjacent protectorate
Ascension	Admiralty-administered territory (1815)
Australia	First settled 1788; 6 self-governing colonies (1855 and later)
Basutoland	Protectorate (1871); colony (1884)
Bechuanaland	Protectorate (1885)
British Guiana	Ceded colony (1814)
British Honduras	First settled 1638; colony (separated from Jamaica 1884)
British North Borneo	Protectorate (1893)
British Solomon Islands	Protectorate (1893)
British Somaliland	Protectorate (1887)
Brunei	Protectorate (1888)
Burma	Indian province (1852)
Canada	Ceded colonies from 1714 onwards; self-governing Federation (1867)
Cape of Good Hope	Ceded colony (1814)
Cayman, Turks and Caicos Islands	Ceded (1670). Dependencies of Jamaica (1848)
Ceylon	Ceded colony (1802)
Christmas Island	Annexed (1888)
Cocos-Keeling Islands	Annexed (1857)
Cook Islands	Protectorate (1888)
Cyprus	British-administered territory (1878)
East African Protectorate	Protectorate (1895)
Egypt	Occupied by British since 1882
Falkland Islands	Colony (1833)
Fiji	Colony (1874)
Gambia	Colony (1843) and adjacent protectorate (1888)
Gilbert and Ellice Islands	Protectorate (1892)

Gold Coast	Settlement began 1750; colony (1821 and 1874)
Hong Kong	Ceded colony (1843)
India	Settlement began 1601; Indian Empire (1876)
Labuan	Colony (1848) governed by North Borneo Company (1890)
Lagos	Colony (1861)
Leeward Isles	Colonies federated (1871)
Malay States	9 Protectorates, 4 of which were federated
Maldive Islands	Protectorate (1887)
Malta	Ceded colony (1814)
Mauritius	Ceded colony (1814)
Natal	Colony (1843)
New Zealand	Self-governing colony (1854)
Newfoundland	Settlement began 1623; self-governing colony (1855)
Nigeria	Protectorates (1900); colony of Lagos joined Southern Nigeria, 1906
Northern Rhodesia	Chartered Company Territory (1889)
Nyasaland	Protectorate (1891)
Orange Free State	Colony (1902); province of Union of South Africa, 1910
Papua	Protectorate (1884); colony (1888), administered by Australia after 1906
Pitcairn	Settled 1790; colony (1898)
St Helena	Administered by East India Co. (1833)
St Lucia	Ceded Colony (1814)
Sarawak	Protectorate (1888)
Sierra Leone	Colony (1808) and adjacent protectorate (1896)
Singapore	Under Indian government (1824); part of Straits Settlements (1867)
Southern Rhodesia	Chartered Company (1889)
Straits Settlements (Singapore, Penang, Malacca)	Colonies (1867)
Sudan	Condominium with Egypt (1899)
Swaziland	Protectorate (1903)
Tonga	Protectorate (1900)
Transvaal	Annexed (1902); province of Union of South Africa, 1910
Trinidad and Tobago	Ceded (1802 and 1814); colony (combined 1889)

Tristan da Cunha	British settlement (1815)
Uganda	Protectorate (1894)
Windward Isles	Colonies (1763 and 1814, federated in 1885)
Zanzibar	Protected state (1890)

Chronology of imperial developments

1814   Following defeat of Napoleon, Britain acquired St Lucia, Malta, Mauritius, British Guiana, Seychelles, Windward Islands and Cape of Good Hope as recognised colonies.

1815   Britain established protectorate over Ionian Islands. Ascension Island occupied.

1816   Java restored to Dutch rule.

1817   Third Maratha War destroyed Maratha power. Possessions in Guiana and Senegal restored to France.

1818   Rajputana States came under British protection.

1819   East India Company founded Singapore.

1821   Amalgamation of North West Company and Hudson's Bay Company. Royal African Company dissolved and its possessions taken over by British Crown.

1823   New South Wales became a Crown colony.

1824   Burmese War (see p. 221). Singapore ceded to Britain.

1826   Penang, Malacca and Singapore joined to form Straits Settlements.

1827   Western Australia explored by Captain Stirling.

1830   Edward Gibbon Wakefield formed the Colonisation Society.

1833   East India Company ceased to trade; Governor-General of Bengal became Governor-General of India. Indian Legislative Council established. Slavery abolished in the British Empire. Falkland Islands annexed.

1834   South Australia Act authorised the establishment of a colony.

1835   Great Trek of Boer colonists from the Cape.

1837   Aborigines Protection Society founded. New Zealand Association begun by Wakefield. Rebellion of Papineau and Mackenzie in Canada.

1838   Earl of Durham became Governor-General of Canada. Apprenticeship system in West Indies abolished.

1839   Aden annexed. First Afghan War (see p. 222). First China 'Opium' War (see p. 222). Republic of Natal founded. Durham Report published. It suggested process of granting greater autonomy to colonies.

1840   Canada Act reunited Upper and Lower Canada in a single administration and legislature. New Zealand annexed: treaty of

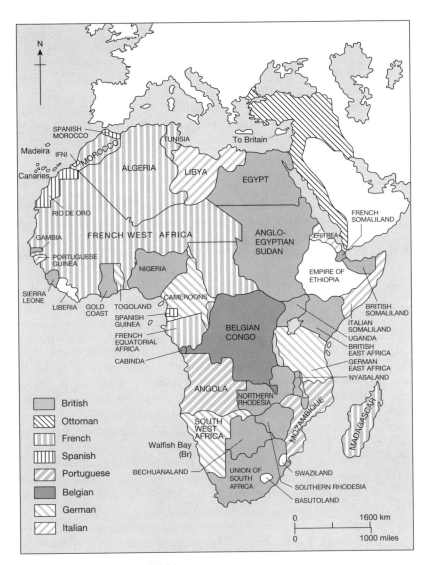

Map 4. The partition of Africa

Waitangi aimed to protect Maoris by forbidding private sale and purchase of land. Transportation to New South Wales discontinued.

1841   James Brooke appointed Rajah of Sarawak. Retreat from Kabul.

1842   Treaty of Nanking ended the war with China (see p. 222). Hong Kong ceded to Britain, and five treaty ports (Amoy, Canton, Foochow, Ningpo and Shanghai) opened to British trade. Ashburton treaty settled the Maine boundary. Representative government established in New South Wales. Conquest of Burma and Assam began.

1843   Maori Wars began. Sind conquered. Natal annexed.

1845   First Sikh War (see p. 223).

1846   Oregon treaty fixed the boundary of Canada at the 49th Parallel. Earl Grey's Act established two provinces in New Zealand, each with executive and legislative councils under the Governor.

1847   Elgin became Governor-General of a united Canada. Governor of Cape Colony became High Commissioner for South Africa.

1848   Orange Free State became a Crown colony. Second Sikh War: Punjab annexed. Nova Scotia became the first colony with a responsible ministry.

1849   Navigation Acts repealed.

1851   Australian gold rush. Victoria became a separate colony.

1852   Rangoon annexed in Second Burmese War (see p. 221). By the Sand River Convention, Britain abandoned attempts to control the Boer trekkers. Responsible government attained in New Zealand.

1853   Cape Colony gained representative government.

1854   Bloemfontein Convention: Orange Free State gained self-rule. Separate Colonial Office established.

1855   New South Wales, Victoria and Newfoundland granted responsible government.

1856   Oudh annexed. War with China renewed. South Australia and Tasmania gained responsible government.

1857   Indian Mutiny began in Meerut in May, quickly spreading across northern India (see p. 224). When the revolt was quelled the Crown assumed direct control of India. A Secretary of State for India was established with a Council of India to advise him. The East India Company's rule was abolished.

1858   Treaty of Tientsin secured, when Anglo-French forces defeated the Chinese. China repudiated the treaty in 1859. British Columbia became a Crown colony.

1859   Queensland became a separate colony with responsible government. Sir George Grey, Governor of Cape Colony, proposed a plan for South African federation.

1860   Britain attained full Free Trade. Maori Wars recurred when the New Zealand Company broke the treaty of Waitangi (see p. 223).

1861   Lagos annexed. India Councils Act. Parliamentary committee
        agreed territories enjoying responsible government should make
        a greater contribution to their own defence.

1864   Quebec Conference laid the foundation for the Dominion of
        Canada.

1865   Colonial Laws Validity Act: colonial legislatures could pass laws
        contrary to the common law of England, but not contrary to
        Acts of the imperial parliament applying to the colony. Gover-
        nor Eyre suppressed Morant rising in Jamaica.

1867   British North America Act created the Dominion of Canada as
        a self-governing federation of four provinces. Straits Settlements
        became a Crown colony.

1869   Suez Canal opened. Hudson's Bay Company ceded its terri-
        torial rights to the Dominion of Canada. Rebellion led by Louis
        Riel in Canada.

1870   Manitoba admitted to Dominion of Canada.

1871   British Columbia joined the Dominion of Canada. Griqualand
        West annexed (diamond fields discovered there). Protectorate
        proclaimed in Basutoland. Dutch ceded Gold Coast forts to
        Britain.

1872   Responsible government implemented in Cape Colony.

1873   Ashanti War (see p. 224). Prince Edward Island joined the
        Dominion of Canada.

1874   Fiji Islands annexed. Treaties with chiefs of Perak and Selangor
        by which British Residents were to give advice to the Malay
        rulers.

1875   Suez Canal shares purchased giving United Kingdom a majority
        holding. Lord Carnarvon launched plan for South African
        Confederation.

1876   Victoria created Empress of India. Lord Lytton became Viceroy.

1877   Transvaal annexed.

1878   Cyprus occupied under the treaty of Berlin. Dual control estab-
        lished in Egypt (Britain and France). Walvis Bay, South Africa,
        annexed. Second Afghan War began.

1879   British Resident at Kabul murdered. Peace restored when
        Afghanistan independence was recognised, 1880. Zulu War;
        British defeated at Isandhlwana, victorious at Ulundi (see p. 224).

1880   First Boer War began (see p. 225).

1881   British defeated at Majuba Hill. Convention of Pretoria recog-
        nised the Transvaal as an independent republic subject to the
        suzerainty of the Queen. Revolt of the Mahdi in the Sudan (see
        p. 225).

1882   British North Borneo Company chartered. Four territories
        organised from the Canadian prairies. Alberta, Athabasca,

Assiniboine and Saskatchewan. Revolt of Arabi Pasha, defeated at Tel-el-kebir (see p. 225). Britain occupied Egypt and assumed control of Egyptian finances.

1883   British force under Hicks Pasha defeated in the Sudan. Sir Evelyn Baring (Lord Cromer) appointed British agent and Consul-General in Egypt. Sir J.R. Seeley's *Expansion of England* published.

1884   Imperial Federation League founded. Transvaal recognised as the South African Republic, when Britain abandoned her suzerainty. Berlin Conference opened. It established ground rules for partition of Africa. Britain took possession of remainder of New Guinea after German annexations.

1885   Death of General Gordon at Khartoum. Crisis in Penjdeh, the disputed boundary area between Afghanistan and Russian Turkestan. Indian National Congress founded. Upper Burma invaded (see p. 221). Protectorate established in Bechuanaland. Federation of the Windward Islands.

1886   Royal Niger Company chartered for trade and government. Anglo-German treaties partition East Africa and the Pacific. Gold discovered in the Transvaal; Johannesburg founded. Annexation of Burma.

1887   First Colonial Conference. Protectorate proclaimed in British Somaliland.

1888   Imperial British East Africa Company chartered. Zululand annexed. Protectorates in Matabeleland, British North Borneo and Sarawak

1889   British South Africa Company chartered; began colonisation in what became Rhodesia. Federation of Australia proposed by Sir Henry Parkes at Tenterfield.

1890   Anglo-German treaties concerning East Africa. Rhodes became Prime Minister of Cape Colony. Responsible government in Western Australia.

1891   Anglo-Portuguese colonial treaty recognised British protectorate in Nyasaland.

1892   India Councils Act introduced first Indian members to the Viceroy's legislative council. Gold discovered in Western Australia.

1893   Responsible government in Natal. Durand Line fixed the frontier between Afghanistan and British India.

1894   L.S. Jameson appointed administrator of Southern Rhodesia. Protectorate established in Uganda.

1895   Joseph Chamberlain appointed Colonial Secretary. British East Africa protectorate established. Jameson led an unsuccessful raid into the Transvaal.

1896   Kitchener advanced into the Sudan. Second Ashanti War: the monarchy was abolished and a protectorate established.

1897   Milner became High Commissioner of the Cape. Second Colonial Conference on Queen's Diamond Jubilee. Royal Commission on the West Indies. Convention at Adelaide to prepare terms for Australian Federation.

1898   Niger convention with France. Wei-hai-wei leased. Confrontation with France at Fashoda on Upper Nile. Anglo-Egyptian condominium proclaimed over the Sudan after the defeat of the Mahdi at Omdurman. Curzon appointed Viceroy of India.

1899   Anglo-French agreement concerning the Nile Valley. Royal Niger Company lost its powers to the Crown. Second Boer War began. Britain defeated at Magersfontein, Stormberg and Colenso.

1900   Ladysmith, Kimberley and Mafeking relieved. Boxer Rising in China. First Pan-African Congress in London. Cook Islands annexed. Protectorate established in Tobago.

1901   Commonwealth of Australia established. North West Frontier Province created.

1902   Peace of Vereeniging: Transvaal and Orange Free State annexed. Colonial Conference decided to meet again every four years.

1904   Anglo-French *entente*: acceptance of mutual spheres of influence in Africa.

1905   Partition of Bengal alienated Hindu nationalists. Alberta and Saskatchewan created as provinces of Canada.

1906   Transvaal gained responsible government. All-India Muslim League formed: British promised Muslims separate electorates.

1907   Australia and New Zealand gained Dominion status. Imperial Conference: Dominions division established in the Colonial Office. Orange Free State gained responsible government. Gorst became British agent in Egypt and increased the powers of provincial councils.

1909   Morley–Minto constitutional reforms in India. India Councils Act.

1910   Union of South Africa formed.

1911   Coronation Durbar: Indian capital transferred from Calcutta to Delhi; division of Bengal abandoned.

1914   Protectorate proclaimed in Egypt. Cyprus annexed. Northern and Southern Nigeria protectorates joined together. France and Britain conquered German colonies except German East Africa.

British India

Chronology of events

1819   Elphinstone became Governor of Bombay (until 1827). Occupation of Singapore.

1820   Munro became Governor of Madras.

1822	Regulation XXII (on Land Settlement).
1824–26	First Burma War. Annexation of Arakan and Tenasserim (see p. 221).
1827	Siege of Bharatpur.
1828	Governor-Generalship of Lord William Bentinck began (ended 1835).
1829	*Brahmo Samaj* founded.
	Suppression of *thagi* began.
1831	Administration of Mysore taken over.
	Journey of Burnes up the Indus.
	Meeting of Bentinck with Ranjit at Rupar.
1833	Under the Charter Act, East India Company's trade abolished.
	Regulation IX (Land Settlement).
1834	Annexation of Coorg.
	Peshawar taken by Ranjit.
1835	Metcalfe lifted press restrictions.
	Macaulay's Minute: Education Minute.
	English the Court language.
1836	Auckland became Governor-General (until 1842).
1837	Burnes mission to Kabul.
	Severe famine began in northern India.
1838	Tripartite Treaty.
1839	Death of Ranjit Singh.
	Outbreak of First Afghan War (see p. 222).
	Ended in 1842.
1842	Lord Ellenborough became Governor-General.
	Reoccupation of parts of Afghanistan.
1843	War against the Baluchi Ameers of Sind leading to the annexation of the country by Sir Charles Napier. The Baluchis were defeated at Miani (17 Feb.) and the capital Hyderabad occupied (see p. 223).
1844	Lord Hardinge became Governor-General.
	Defeat of Gwalior Army.
1845	Sikh army crossed the Sutlej into British territory (11 Dec.).
	Start of First Sikh War (see p. 223).
1848	Lord Dalhousie became Governor-General.
	Second Sikh War.
1849	Sikhs defeated at Gujerat (21 Feb.); Sikh army surrendered (14 Mar.); annexation of the Punjab (7 Apr.).
1852	Annexation of Pegu and Rangoon in Second Burma War.
1853	Renewal of Charter of East India Company.
	Competition introduced for Indian Civil Service.
	Annexation of Nagpur. Cession of Berar by Nizam.
	First railway opened. Telegraph link from Calcutta to Agra.

1854	Sir Charles Woods' Despatch on Education. Beginning of rise of jute industry.

1854   Sir Charles Woods' Despatch on Education.
        Beginning of rise of jute industry.
1857   Indian troops at Meerut rioted (10 May); outbreak of the Indian mutiny (see also p. 224). Siege of Cawnpore began (7 June); British surrender to Nana Sahib (26 June). Lucknow besieged by the mutineers (20 June); Delhi retaken by British troops (14–20 Sept.). General Havelock relieved Lucknow (25 Sept.) but was in turn besieged there (17 Nov.); Sir Colin Campbell relieved Lucknow a second time and evacuated it.
1858   Lucknow finally recaptured (11–19 Mar.). Sir Hugh Rose stormed Jhansi (3 Apr.) and defeated Tantia Topi at Kalpi on 22 May. Peace proclaimed (8 July). India came under the Crown.
1859–60 Financial reforms of James Wilson. Bengal hit by indigo disputes.
1861   Indian Councils Act and High Courts Act. Indian Penal Code introduced.
1862   Lord Elgin appointed Governor-General.
1863   Death of Dost Muhammad. The Ambela campaign.
1864   Sir John Lawrence appointed Governor-General.
1865   Orissa hit by famine.
1868   Amir Sher Ali received subsidies. Punjab and Oudh Tenancy Acts.
1869   Lord Mayo appointed Viceroy.
1872   Lord Northbrook appointed Viceroy.
1873   Khiva in Central Asia occupied by Russia.
1875   Founding of Aligarh College.
1876   Proclamation of Queen Victoria as Empress of India.
        Lord Lytton appointed Viceroy. Occupation of Quetta.
        Famine in south India (until 1878).
1878   Second Afghan War (see p. 222).
1879   Fresh expedition to Afghanistan reached Kabul (Oct.); new ruler installed. British brigade sent from Kandahar to assist him defeated at Maiwand. Sir Frederick Roberts marched an army 300 miles to relieve Kandahar.
        Cotton duties abolished. Vernacular Press Act.
1880   Appointment of Lord Ripon as Viceroy. Famine Commission Report.
1881   Evacuation of Afghanistan completed (Apr.). The rendition of Mysore. Passing of first Factory Act.
1882   Hunter Educational Commission.
1883–4 Local Government Acts. Start of Ilbert Bill controversy.
1884   Appointment of Lord Dufferin as Viceroy.
        Russian advance in Central Asia continued with taking of Merv.

1885	The Penjdeh incident (confrontation with Russians). Outbreak of Third Burma War (see p. 221). Foundation of Indian National Congress. Passing of Bengal Tenancy Act.
1886	Annexation of Upper Burma. Death of Shri Ram Khrishna.
1887	Opening of Tata's Nagpur cotton mill.
1888	Lord Lansdowne appointed Viceroy.
1891	Passing of second Factory Act and Age of Consent Act.
1892	Indian Councils Act.
1894	Lord Elgin became Viceroy.
1895	Expedition against Chitral.
1898	Curzon appointed Viceroy.
1901	North West Frontier Province created.
1905	Partition of Bengal alienated Hindu nationalists.
1906	All-India Muslim League formed.
1909	Morley–Minto Constitutional Reforms. India Councils Act.
1911	Coronation Durbar. Indian capital transferred to Delhi from Calcutta. Partition of Bengal abandoned.

Office holders

President of the Board of Control

June	1816	George Canning
Jan.	1821	Charles Bathurst
Feb.	1822	Charles Watkins William Wynn
July	1828	Viscount Melville
Sept.	1828	Lord Ellenborough
Dec.	1830	Charles Grant
Dec.	1834	Lord Ellenborough
Apr.	1835	Sir John Hobhouse
Sept.	1841	Lord Ellenborough
Oct.	1841	Lord Fitzgerald
May	1843	Earl of Ripon
July	1846	Sir John Hobhouse
Feb.	1852	Fox Maule
Feb.	1852	John Charles Herries
Dec.	1852	Sir Charles Wood
Mar.	1855	Robert Vernon Smith
Mar.	1858	Earl of Ellenborough
June	1858	Lord Stanley

Note: The office was abolished by the 1858 Government of India Act and its functions transferred to the Secretary of State for India.

Secretary of State for India

Sept.	1858	Lord Stanley
June	1859	Sir Charles Wood
Feb.	1866	Earl de Grey & Ripon
July	1866	Viscount Cranborne
Mar.	1867	Sir Stafford Northcote
Dec.	1868	Duke of Argyll
Feb.	1874	Marquis of Salisbury
Apr.	1878	Viscount Cranbrook
Apr.	1880	Marquis of Hartington
Dec.	1882	Earl of Kimberley
June	1885	Lord Randolph Churchill
Feb.	1886	Earl of Kimberley
Aug.	1886	Viscount Cross
Aug.	1892	Earl of Kimberley
Mar.	1894	Henry Hartley Fowler
July	1895	Lord George Hamilton
Oct.	1903	William St John Brodrick
Dec.	1905	John Morley
Nov.	1910	Earl of Crewe
Mar.	1911	Viscount Morley
May	1911	Earl of Crewe

Ireland

Ireland since the Act of Union

On 1 August 1800 the Act of Union received the Royal Assent. It established the 'United Kingdom of Great Britain and Ireland'. Its main provisions included: succession of the Crown to be governed by the same provisions as the union with Scotland; Irish parliament abolished; 32 Irish peers (28 temporal, 4 spiritual) to sit in the House of Lords and 100 members (64 county, 35 borough and 1 university) in the House of Commons. The churches were united, but the financial systems remained distinct. Ireland was to provide 2/17 of United Kingdom expenditure.

The following chronology of major events in Ireland is divided into four sub-sections:

1. Catholic Emancipation
2. Ireland, 1832–73
3. The nationalist movement
4. Ulster unionism

Catholic Emancipation

The issue of Catholic Emancipation (or relief) was one of the great political divides of the early part of this period. It involved freeing Catholics from disabilities which prevented them from holding office, voting or serving in Parliament. Unlike Protestant Dissenters, Catholics had received no freedom of worship under the 1689 Toleration Act. Though in practice they did receive a degree of toleration, they were formally excluded from ministerial and administrative office, commissions in the armed services and from universities under a series of acts known collectively as the Penal Laws.

From 1807, when Sydney Smith, Canon of St Paul's, took up the Protestant Dissenters' cause, agitation grew for the repeal of the Test and Corporation Acts of Charles II. In 1828 they were repealed and the remaining discriminatory legislation against Catholics was shown to be an anachronism. There were only 60,000 Catholics in England but the majority of the Irish population was Catholic and was beginning to refuse to accept the Protestant ascendancy.

In May 1823, Daniel O'Connell (1775–1847) revived an old Catholic association which raised a rent of 1d a month from the Irish Catholic community. Its aim was to promote Protestant MPs sworn to Emancipation. The Association was suppressed in 1829. Events then moved swiftly (see chronology below).

1808   Grattan's motion for Catholic Emancipation defeated in the Commons by 281 votes to 128.

1810   Catholic Committee set up to campaign for Catholic Emancipation. Reconstituted in 1811 as the Catholic Board.

1812   Motion to consider Catholic claims passed by 225 votes to 106.

1813   Emancipation Bill defeated in committee.

1814   Catholic Board dissolved by government order.

1817   Irish and British exchequers united because of increase of Irish national debt. Partial failure of potato crop.

1819   Catholic Emancipation Bill defeated in the Commons.

1821   Catholic Emancipation defeated in the House of Lords.

1823   Catholic Association founded by O'Connell to campaign for political and other rights.

1824   Catholic Association opened to associate members at 1d per week, the 'Catholic rent.'

1825   O'Connell unsuccessfully prosecuted for incitement to rebellion. Catholic Association suppressed but refounded under new name. Sir Francis Burdett introduced relief bill, allied to raising county franchise from 40s to £10 and payment of Catholic clergy from public funds. Rejected in the House of Lords.

1826   Catholic Association secured return of members pledged to Emancipation in Louth, Monaghan, Waterford, and Westmeath.

1828   Election of O'Connell for Co. Clare.

1829   Catholic Emancipation Act (10 Geo. IV, c.7). Roman Catholics made eligible for all offices of state except Regent, Lord Lieutenant, and Lord Chancellor. No oath of supremacy required to sit in either house of Parliament. Catholic Association and similar organisations suppressed. £10 franchise replaced 40s franchise in counties.

1830   Beginning of anti-tithe campaign.

1832   Irish Reform Act received Royal Assent (7 Aug.).

Ireland 1832–73

1832   Irish Reform Act received Royal Assent, 7 Aug.

1833   Irish Church Temporalities Act suppressed 10 sees and reduced the revenues of the rest. Surplus revenues to be administered for purely ecclesiastical purposes.

1836	Recurrence of potato famine.
1838	Tithe Act removed a popular source of grievances.
1840	Irish Municipal Corporations Act enfranchised £10 house-holders, abolished 58 corporations, established 10 new ones, and overhauled municipal administration. 'Young Ireland' Party formed.
1842	*The Nation* magazine founded by group of 'Young Ireland' journalists to promote nationalism.
1843	O'Connell began programme of mass meetings to promote repeal of the union at Trim (16 Mar.), but forced to cancel monster meeting at Clontarf (Oct.) when government declared it illegal. O'Connell arrested, tried for sedition and conspiracy and sentenced to a year's imprisonment and a fine, but judgment reversed in the House of Lords.
1845	Grant to Irish Catholic college at Maynooth increased in spite of bitter opposition in Parliament. Irish National Education Board formed.
1845–50	Great famine due to successive failures of potato crop as a result of blight. Irish population fell from 8,178,124 in 1841 to 6,552,386 in 1851 as a result of deaths and emigration.
1847	'Young Ireland' set up the Irish Confederation under William Smith O'Brien. O'Connell's death at Genoa, 15 May. 39 repealers returned in the general election. John Mitchell began publication of *United Irishman* newspaper, promoting radical agrarian reform.
1848	Arrest of Mitchell, 13 May; 'Young Ireland' rising in Tipperary easily suppressed and leaders transported (July). Encumbered Estates Act passed.
1849	Serious affray between Catholics and Protestants at Dolly's Brae.
1850	Establishment of Queen's University, Belfast. Irish Franchise Act increased voters from 61,000 to 165,000.
1851	First meeting of Catholic Defence Association.
1852	Warrenstown Tenant Right demonstration.
1853	Income tax extended to Ireland.
1858	Fenian Brotherhood started by John O'Mahoney and James Stephens, directed at achieving nationhood 'soon or never'.
1862	Catholic University College founded in Dublin.
1867	Failure of Fenian insurrection.
1868	Election of Gladstone as Prime Minister.
1869	Disestablishment and Disendowment of the Irish Church. From January 1871 the Church of Ireland was disestablished; all property except churches in use was vested in a body of commissioners for Irish Church temporalities. Compensation set

at £16 million, half of the capital of confiscated property, the remainder to be used for public benefit.

1870   Land Act designed to protect the tenant. The Ulster custom was established by law where it already existed; elsewhere greater compensation was to be given for improvements and for disturbance. Agrarian disorder continued. Home Government Association formed by Irish Protestant Conservative lawyer, Isaac Butt. In 1873 re-formed as Home Rule League.

The nationalist movement

In November 1873 the Home Rule League was founded in Dublin with the object of winning self-government for Ireland. The League put forward candidates at the general election of 1874, and 59 Home Rulers were returned for Irish constituencies. But only two of these seats were in Ulster. Almost immediately after the election the Home Rule members met in Dublin, and adopted resolutions constituting themselves 'a separate and distinct party in the House of Commons', appointed an Executive Council, secretaries and whips, and agreed upon motions to be introduced. Thus, there was at Westminster after 1874 an Irish party stronger in numbers and in organisation, and with a clearer and more comprehensive policy, than any Irish party which had preceded it there. I. Butt was party leader, but the most active members were J.G. Biggar (who initiated in 1875 the policy of 'obstruction') and C.S. Parnell.

When Butt died in 1879 W. Shaw was elected chairman of the party. In the general election of 1880, 61 Home Rule candidates were returned, many of whom owed their success to Parnell's backing. And when the newly elected members met to elect a party chairman, Parnell defeated the rather colourless Shaw by 23 votes to 18. The result led to a split in the party: most of those who had voted against Parnell refused to serve under him. The dissidents did not, however, form a new party of their own; and the only effective Home Rule party was that led by Parnell. The strength of the Parnellites rose during the life of the parliament to about 40. In 1885 the Home Rulers won 86 seats, and 85 in the following year. Parnell's divorce case in 1890 split the party. 45 nationalists demanded his resignation as party leader; 26 continued to support him. Parnell's death in 1891 did not reunite the party. At the general election of 1892 only 9 Parnellites were returned, and 71 anti-Parnellites. The former were led by J. Redmond, the anti-Parnellites by J. McCarthy. In 1895 there were 12 Parnellites and 70 anti-Parnellites. Only in 1900 did the Irish nationalists reunite, under the leadership of Redmond. 82 Nationalists were returned in 1900, 83 in 1906. In 1910 they found themselves again holding the balance between Liberals and Conservatives, having over 80 seats, and pressed Asquith to remove the House of Lords' veto, thus opening the way for a Home Rule Bill to pass.

1872   Six Home Rulers in Parliament committed themselves to land reform and denominational education.

1873   Home Rule League founded in Dublin.

1874   Home Rule League led by Isaac Butt won 59 seats in general election and initiated policy of 'obstruction'.

1879   Death of Isaac Butt; Land League formed by Michael Davitt (Parnell as president), for fair rents to be fixed by arbitration, fixity of tenure while rent was paid and freedom of the tenant to sell his right of occupancy (the Three Fs).

1880   Parnell became the new leader of the 61 Home Rulers returned in the general election. 'Boycotts' organised against those who offended against the Land League's code. Troops used to harvest crops on Lord Erne's land managed by Captain C.C. Boycott, who gave his name to the tactic used against him.

1881   New Coercion Act passed in March. But in April Gladstone introduced a new Land Act conceding many of the basic demands of the Land League. Its reception was hostile and in October Parnell was imprisoned in Kilmainham Gaol, and was not released until April 1882. A 'No Rent' movement was launched in protest at the imprisonment.

1882   By the so-called 'Kilmainham treaty' Parnell promised to use his influence to end crime and disorder, while the government promised a new policy of conciliation. Spencer became new Viceroy and Lord Frederick Cavendish, Chief Secretary. On 6 May, Cavendish and T.H. Burke, the Under-Secretary, were murdered in Phoenix Park by 'the Invincibles'; New Crimes Bill introduced. National League founded by Parnell, closely linked to Irish parliamentary party.

1884   Franchise Act gave the counties (outside Ulster) to the Home Rulers.

1885   Redistribution Act. Number of Irish MPs unchanged despite the fall in population. Ashbourne's Act: provided the advance to the tenant of the whole sum needed to buy his land, to be repaid over 49 years at 4 per cent. In three years the £5 million grant was exhausted. 85 Home Rulers returned for Irish seats in the general election. They held the balance in the House of Commons and chose to support Gladstone because of a press rumour that he was in favour of Home Rule. Home Rule Bill defeated in Commons, 343–313 (93 Liberals voted against).

1886	General election: 85 Home Rulers returned, but in England Home Rule was heavily rejected. National League organised a plan of campaign by tenants against landlords.
1887	Parnell accused of complicity in agrarian outrages in letter in *The Times*; cleared by committee of enquiry, who discovered the forgery.
1890	Parnell cited in Mrs O'Shea's divorce, which made continued alliance with the Liberals impossible. The Home Rulers split, 26 supporting Parnell, the majority disavowing him.
1891	Death of Parnell (October). Chief Secretary Balfour encouraged land purchase; £30 million made available. Congested Districts Board set up to assist poorest areas.
1893	Second Home Rule Bill; this would continue Irish representation at Westminster. Defeated in House of Lords. Gaelic League founded.
1898	William O'Brien put new life into the Home Rule movement with the United Ireland League, begun in Connaught with a policy of agrarian reform. Doctrine of 'Sinn Fein' ('ourselves alone') preached by *United Irishman*, a weekly paper published in Dublin by A. Griffith. James Connolly founded the Irish Socialist Republican Party.
1900	Irish Nationalists reunited under Redmond; 82 returned in general election.
1902	Sinn Fein founded by Arthur Griffith.
1903	'Wyndham's Act' went far to making sale of estates universal; £100 million made available for land purchase by tenants.
1904	Negotiations between government and Irish Nationalists for a scheme for devolution.
1906	83 Irish Nationalists returned at the general election. Bill to introduce devolution rejected by Redmond, but no alternative offered by government.
1907	Augustine Birrell became Chief Secretary. Sinn Fein League organised for 'the re-establishment of the independence of Ireland'.
1908	Sinn Fein contested North Leitrim by-election; violence, but Redmond won. Universities' Act founded Queen's University, Belfast, and National University of Ireland.
1909	Birrell Act to encourage land purchase eased financial clauses of Wyndham's Act.
1910	At the January general election, 70 followers of Redmond and 11 independent Irish Nationalists returned.
1912	Liberal government introduced a Home Rule Bill for the whole of Ireland.
1913	Home Rule Bill defeated in the House of Lords, but awaited automatic implementation under provisions of Parliament Act;

idea of excluding Ulster from its provisions raised by Liberal government. Citizen Army, later known as the 'Irish Volunteers', formed in the South.

1914   Asquith persuaded Redmond to accept exclusion of Ulster from operation of Home Rule for 6 years, but Carson rejected compromise. 'Mutiny' at the Curragh (headquarters of the British army in Ireland) following rumours of unwillingness of army officers to coerce the Ulster Protestants. Gun-running into Ulster and Dublin armed the two 'volunteer' forces. Conference at Buckingham Palace in July failed to reach agreement on Ulster's exclusion from Home Rule. Outbreak of First World War deferred implementation of Home Rule.

Ulster unionism

1892   June: Duke of Abercorn declared in Belfast: 'We will not have Home Rule.'
1893   Edward Saunderson, MP for North Armagh, helped establish the Ulster Defence Union.
1905   Ulster Unionist Council established; a large representative body with a permanent executive committee.
1910   Sir Edward Carson led the Ulster Unionists in opposition to plans for Home Rule.
1911   Carson declared in Belfast: 'We will yet defeat the most nefarious conspiracy that has ever been hatched against a free people.' Unionist Council prepared plans to take over civil administration in Ulster in event of Home Rule.
1912   Bonar Law, the Conservative leader, espoused Unionist cause 'as the cause of the Empire'. At Blenheim supported plans for Ulster resistance. Ulster Volunteers formed as a military force to resist Home Rule. Ulster's 'Solemn League and Covenant' signed by over 200,000 Protestants.

SECTION FIVE

Biographies

Aberdeen, 4th Earl of, George Hamilton-Gordon (1784–1860): Hamilton-Gordon became Earl of Aberdeen in 1801. From 1806 to 1814 he was a Scottish representative peer, and served as ambassador extraordinary at Vienna in 1813. In 1814 he represented Britain in the negotiation of the treaty of Paris. Later that year he was created a peer of the United Kingdom. He held office as Chancellor of the Duchy of Lancaster, Jan.–June 1828, as Foreign Secretary, 1828–30, as Secretary for War and the Colonies, 1834–35 and as Foreign Secretary again, 1841–46. After 1846 he was leader of the Peelite faction in the House of Lords. Between 1852 and 1855 he presided as Prime Minister over a coalition of Whigs and Peelites. In 1855 he resigned when Roebuck's motion for a committee of enquiry into the conduct of the Crimean War was carried.

Albert, Prince Consort (1819–61): Born 26 Aug. 1819, 2nd son of Ernest, Duke of Saxe-Coburg-Gotha, married Queen Victoria 10 Feb. 1840; proposed parliamentary annuity of £50,000, reduced to £30,000; Privy Councillor, 1840; naturalised Englishman, 1840; Regent, in event of Queen's death, 1840; Chairman, Royal Commission on Fine Arts, 1841–61; President, Royal Society of Arts, 1843; elected Chancellor of Cambridge University, 1847; purchased Osborne (1845) and Balmoral (1848); President, Royal Commission on Great Exhibition, 1849–51; created Prince Consort by Letters Patent 25 June 1857; died at Windsor 14 Dec. 1861; buried finally at Frogmore.

Applegarth, Robert (1833–1925): Secretary of Amalgamated Society of Carpenters and Joiners (1862), and dominating figure in London Trades Council which advocated industrial conciliation and arbitration of disputes; he and four other union leaders assumed title 'Conference of Amalgamated Trades' in attempt to influence 1867 Royal Commission into unionism; cautious attitude of 'Junta' leaders helped disarm criticism of unionism.

Arch, Joseph (1826–1919): Liberal MP 1885–86, 1892–1902; pioneer of agricultural trade unionism, forming first agricultural labourers' union, 1872; puritan and Primitive Methodist lay preacher.

Asquith, Herbert Henry, 1st Earl of Oxford and Asquith (1852–1928): Asquith was Liberal MP for East Fife, 1886–1918 and for Paisley, 1920–24. In 1925 he was created Earl of Oxford and Asquith. He was Home Secretary, 1892–95, Chancellor of the Exchequer, 1905–08 and Prime Minister 1908–16. During 1914 he was also Secretary for War. He resigned the premiership in 1916 and became leader of the opposition. In 1926 he resigned the leadership of the Liberal Party when it failed to endorse his censuring of Lloyd George for refusing to attend a shadow cabinet. Asquith's term as PM was a troubled one, embracing the budget, House of Lords and Ulster crises, suffragette militancy and the outbreak of the First World War.

Attwood, Thomas (1783–1856): MP for Birmingham from 1832. Birmingham banker and currency reformer. Led campaign in Birmingham against the Orders in Council in 1812. In Dec. 1829 set up the Birmingham Political Union (BPU), to press for parliamentary and currency reform. Campaigned against the New Poor Law and revived BPU in 1837 to campaign on behalf of currency reform and the People's Charter. Delegate to Chartist convention of 1839.

Bagehot, Walter (1826–77): Journalist and writer. Editor of *The Economist*. Lasting fame as author of *The English Constitution* (on the workings of the political system). Also wrote *Lombard Street* (on the workings of the City of London).

Balfour, Arthur James, 1st Earl of Balfour (1848–1930): Balfour was Conservative MP for Hertford, 1874–85, for Manchester East, 1885–1906, and for the City of London, 1906–22. He was created an earl in 1922. Balfour served as parliamentary private secretary to his uncle, Lord Salisbury, 1878–80. In 1885 he was President of the Local Government Board and in 1886 was Secretary for Scotland. He was Chief Secretary for Ireland, 1887–91, and Leader of the Commons and First Lord of the Treasury, 1891–92 and 1895–1902. He became Prime Minister in 1902, resigning in 1905. He resigned the leadership of the Conservative Party in 1911. In 1914 he was made a member of the Committee of Imperial Defence and attended meetings of the War Cabinet, 1914–15. He served as First Lord of the Admiralty, 1915–16 and as Foreign Secretary, 1916–19. He was Lord President of the Council, 1919–22 and 1925–29. A well-connected Conservative, Balfour proved a highly intelligent and able administrator in most offices. But as PM and party leader he gave an impression of indecision and indifference on the question of Tariff Reform which split the party. After the Liberal government's reform of the House of Lords, accusations of ineffectuality and nepotism helped persuade Balfour to resign the leadership.

Baring, Sir Francis: See Northbrook, 1st Lord.

Barnett, Dame Henrietta Octavia (1851–1936): Social reformer. Hon. Secretary, State Children's Aid Association. Founder and President of London Pupil Teachers' Association. Vice-President, National Association for the Welfare of the Feeble-Minded. Founder of Hampstead Garden Trust, 1903, and a prominent supporter of the Garden City ideal. Lecturer on Housing, Poor Law and Social Subjects.

Barnett, Samuel Augustus (1844–1913): Social reformer and churchman. Vicar of St Jude's, Whitechapel. Founded Charity Organisation Society, 1869. A founder and Warden of Toynbee Hall, 1884–1906. President of Toynbee Hall, 1906–13. Canon of Westminster from 1906.

Bathurst, 3rd Earl, Henry Bathurst (1762–1834): Cabinet minister who first held office in 1783. Served under Lord Liverpool as Secretary for War and the Colonies, 1812–27. He was Lord President of the Council from 1828 to 1830.

Bax, Ernest Belfort (1854–1926): Socialist writer and theorist. A founder member of the Social Democratic Federation, 1881; and of the Socialist League, 1885. Co-editor (with William Morris) of the League's paper, *Commonweal*. Later associated again with the SDF and editor for a time of *Justice*. Author of works on socialism.

Beaconsfield, 1st Earl of: See Disraeli.

Bentham, Jeremy (1748–1832): Utilitarian theorist and philanthropist. Author of *Introduction to the Principles of Morals and Legislation* (1788), *Fragment on Government* (1776) and *Parliamentary Reform in the Form of a Catechism* (1817). After concentrating initially on penal reform and schemes for a model prison, he turned to advocacy of parliamentary reform on the basis of utilitarian principles. Associate of James Mill, Samuel Romilly, Francis Place and Sir Francis Burdett amongst others.

Besant, Annie (1847–1933): Social reformer. Leader of the theosophy school of philosophy. A prominent figure in India's struggle for independence from Britain. Besant lectured widely on a number of social issues, including planned parenthood and labour reform. In 1888, she helped organise a strike at a London match factory, one of the first successful strikes by unskilled workers. In 1894, Besant moved to India, where she continued her work in theosophy and began supporting Indian educational reform. In 1898, she opened the Central Hindu College at Benares, India. In the early 1900s, she became involved in the independence movement and, in 1916, founded the Indian Home Rule League.

Bexley, Baron (1766–1851): Politician and cabinet minister. As Nicholas Vansittart he was Liverpool's long-time Chancellor of the Exchequer (1812–23). Created Baron Bexley in 1823. Chancellor of the Duchy of Lancaster, 1830–38.

Billington-Greig, Teresa (1877–1964): Feminist. Advocate of women's suffrage and founder of the Women's Freedom League in 1907.

Birkbeck, George (1776–1841): Proponent of evening classes for adult education. Founder, in 1824, of the London Mechanics Institute. Birkbeck College is named after him.

Blatchford, Robert Peel Glanville (1851–1943): Socialist populariser and journalist. Founder and editor from 1891 of *The Clarion*, a popular socialist journal. Author of *Merrie England, Britain for the British* and other socialist tracts and novels. A supporter of the British Socialist Party, 1911. Supported British involvement in World War I.

Booth, Charles (1840–1916): Shipowner and social investigator. Privy Councillor 1904; member of Royal Commission on Poor Law, 1905–09; contributed greatly to knowledge of social problems and statistical methodology in 17-volume *Life and Labour of The People in London* (1891–1903); advocate of old-age pensions for all.

Booth, William (1829–1912): Founder and first General of Salvation Army, which began as Christian mission intended to evangelise and serve London poor; originally ordained minister of Methodist New Connexion, 1852; resigned 1861 to become itinerant evangelist and social worker; particularly interested in problems of alcoholics and released prisoners. His son, William Bramwell Booth (1856–1929) was Chief of Staff of the Salvation Army, 1880–1912 and General, 1912–29.

Bright, John (1811–89): Radical MP 1840; Liberal MP 1843–89; President of Board of Trade, 1868–70; Chancellor of Duchy of Lancaster, 1873–74 and 1880–82; first entered politics in 1840s and became associated with Cobden (*q.v.*) in leading Anti-Corn Law League; ardent supporter of Free Trade; supported admission of Jews to House of Commons, 1858, and campaign leading to 1867 Reform Act; opposed Crimean War, Irish Home Rule and Gladstone government's Egyptian venture of 1882.

Brougham, Henry Peter, 1st Baron Brougham and Vaux (1778–1868): Politician, barrister and writer. Founder of *Edinburgh Review*, 1802; associated himself with cause of Queen Caroline in 1820; helped found London University in 1828; Lord Chancellor, 1830–34; as Lord Chancellor, introduced rational reforms in legal system and supervised passage of 1832 Reform Bill through Lords; gave his name to the carriage henceforth known as 'brougham'.

Brunel, Isambard Kingdom (1806–59): Outstanding Victorian engineer. He was chief engineer of the Great Western Railway. Famous for his great ships, e.g. *Great Western, Great Britain*, and *Great Eastern*. Well known as an entrepreneur.

Buller, Sir Redvers Henry (1839–1908): Army commander. Entered Army 1858. Served in the Chinese War of 1860, the expedition to put down the Red River rebellion in Canada (1870), the Ashanti War of 1873, the Kaffir War of 1878, the Zulu War, winning the V.C., the Egyptian War (1882) and the Sudan expedition (1884–85). Commander at Aldershot, 1898, and Commander-in-Chief in South Africa, 1899–1900.

Burdett, Sir Francis (1770–1844): Radical politician. MP for Boroughbridge 1796–1802, Middlesex 1802–04, 1805–06, Westminster 1807–37, North Wiltshire 1837–44. Leader of 'Westminster radicals' from 1807 and proposer of reform measures in 1809, 1817 and 1818. Imprisoned in Tower in 1810 for a libel on the House of Commons and for protests over Peterloo in 1821. Disagreements with more radical reformers led Burdett to play a less prominent part in reform activities after 1832.

Butler, Josephine Elizabeth (1828–1906): Social reformer and moral campaigner. Involved in movements for the higher education of women, for rights for married women, and against the Contagious Diseases Acts. Secretary, Ladies' National Association for the Repeal of the Contagious Diseases Acts, 1869–85. Campaigned against White Slave traffic; advocate of social purity. Author of numerous tracts and books.

Campbell, Sir Colin: See Clyde, Lord.

Campbell-Bannerman, Sir Henry (1836–1908): Liberal MP for Stirling Burghs, 1868–1908. He was Financial Secretary to the War Office, 1871–74 and 1880–82. He was Financial Secretary to the Admiralty 1882–84 and Chief Secretary for Ireland 1884–85. He served as Secretary for War in 1886 and 1892–95. He led the Liberal Party in the Commons 1899–1908, and was Prime Minister, 1905–08, when he retired through ill-health. Campbell-Bannerman was the last Liberal PM to win office with a Liberal majority, and succeeded in uniting a party previously divided on imperial questions.

Canning, George (1770–1827): MP for Newport, 1794–96 and 1806–07, for Wendover, 1796–1802, for Tralee, 1802–06, for Hastings, 1807–12, for Liverpool 1812–22, for Warwick 1823–26, for Newport 1826–27 and for Seaford in 1827. He held the offices of Under-Secretary for Foreign Affairs, 1796–99, President of the India Board, 1799–1800, Paymaster-General, 1800–01, Treasurer of the Navy, 1804–06, Foreign Secretary, 1807–09 and 1822–27 and President of the India Board, 1816–21. He became Prime Minister and Chancellor of the Exchequer in 1827, shortly before his death. Better known for his liberal views on foreign policy, Canning was also able to hold together a Tory–Whig coalition in 1827. After his death the government was unable to continue for long.

Cardigan, 7th Earl of (James Thomas Brudenell) (1797–1868): Entered Army, 1824. Lieutenant-Colonel of the 15th Hussars, 1832. Forced to resign this command, 1834. Purchased command of the 11th Light Dragoons, 1836. In 1854 he was appointed commander of the Light Cavalry Brigade in the Crimea under his brother-in-law, the Earl of Lucan. On 24 Oct. 1854 he led the charge of the Light Brigade at the battle of Balaclava. Inspector-General of Cavalry, 1855–60.

Cardwell, Edward (1813–86): Conservative MP 1842–46; Peelite and Liberal MP 1847–74; President of Board of Trade, 1852–55; Secretary for Ireland, 1859–61; Secretary for Colonies, 1864–66; Secretary for War, 1868–74. Prepared ground for colonial military campaigns during imperialist period by expansion and modernisation of Army to meet challenge of Prussian unification and militarisation.

Carpenter, Edward (1844–1929): Socialist author and publicist. Promoter of women's rights and sex reform. Author of *Civilisation: its Cause and Cure, Towards Democracy, Love's Coming of Age, The Intermediate Sex*, etc.

Carson, Sir Edward (1854–1935): Unionist MP, Dublin University, 1892–1918; Belfast, 1918–21. Appointed Solicitor-General, 1900–05. Leader of the anti-Home Rule movement. Founded the Ulster Volunteer Force in 1913. Attorney-General, 1915–16; First Lord of Admiralty, 1916–17.

Castlereagh, Viscount, Robert Stewart, 2nd Marquis of Londonderry (1769–1822): Secretary for Ireland, 1798–1801; Secretary for War and Colonies, 1805–06, 1807–09; Foreign Secretary, 1812–22. Advocate of union of Britain and Ireland; resigned when George III vetoed Catholic Emancipation; quarrel with Canning led to duel and resignation of both men in 1809; very influential at Congress of Vienna in implementing ideas regarding European balance of power, but rapidly disillusioned with functioning of Congress System. Committed suicide, 1822.

Chamberlain, Joseph (1836–1914): Politician. Mayor of Birmingham, 1873–75; MP for Birmingham, 1876–1910 first as a Liberal, later as a Unionist; President of Board of Trade, 1880–85; Colonial Secretary, 1895–1903. Unitarian and reformer who pioneered slum clearance in Birmingham; broke away from Gladstone to form Liberal Unionists in 1886 in opposition to Irish Home Rule; joined Salisbury's Conservative–Unionist government, and as Colonial Secretary became great exponent of tariff reform and imperial federation.

Chamberlain, Sir (Joseph) Austen (1863–1937): Conservative politician. Unionist MP for Worcestershire East, 1892–1914; Birmingham West from

1914; Chancellor of the Exchequer, 1903–05, 1919–21; Secretary of State for India, 1915–17; Lord Privy Seal, 1921–22, when also Conservative leader; Foreign Secretary, 1925–29; First Lord of Admiralty, 1931. Son of Joseph Chamberlain (*q.v.*) whose parliamentary seat he took over in 1914. Won Nobel Peace Prize for prominence in discussions leading to Locarno treaties of 1925.

Champion, Henry Hyde (1859–1928): Socialist propagandist. First secretary, Social Democratic Federation. Parliamentary candidate, Independent Labour Party. Assistant editor, *Nineteenth Century.* Emigrated to Australia, 1893.

Chelmsford, 2nd Lord, Frederic Augustus Thesiger (1827–1905): Entered Rifle Brigade, 1844. Served in the Crimea and the Indian Mutiny. Deputy Adjutant-General in the Abyssinian expedition; Adjutant-General in the East Indies, 1869–74. Commanded troops in the Kaffir War of 1878, and in the Zulu War. After the initial disaster at Isandhlwana, he defeated Cetewayo at Ulundi in July 1879. Lieutenant of the Tower of London, 1884–89.

Childers, Hugh Culling Eardley (1827–96): Liberal politician. MP for Pontefract, 1860–85 and for South Edinburgh, 1886–92. His posts included First Lord of the Admiralty, 1868–71 and Chancellor of the Duchy of Lancaster, 1872–73. In Gladstone's later administration he was Secretary for War, 1880–82, Chancellor of the Exchequer, 1882–85 and Home Secretary in 1886.

Churchill, Lord Randolph Henry Spencer (1849–94): Conservative MP 1874–94; Secretary for India, 1885–86; Leader of the House and Chancellor of the Exchequer 1886; during 1880s, became leader of Tory Democracy, which sought a core of working-class support by maintaining Disraeli's policy of social reform; resigned from government in response to increased expenditure, thus prematurely ending his political career.

Churchill, Sir Winston Leonard Spencer (1874–1965): Churchill entered Parliament as Conservative MP for Oldham in 1900. In 1904 he became a Liberal in protest at the Conservative policy on Tariff Reform, but remained member for Oldham until 1906. He was Liberal MP for Manchester North West, 1906–08 and for Dundee, 1908–22. Prior to 1914 Churchill held office as Under-Secretary for the Colonial Office 1906–08, President of the Board of Trade, 1908–10, Home Secretary, 1910–11, First Lord of the Admiralty, 1911–15. His subsequent career, particularly as wartime leader during the Second World War, made him one of the great statesmen of the twentieth century.

Clarendon, Earl of, George William Frederick Villiers (1800–70): Succeeded his uncle as 4th Earl, 1838. Long career in politics including President of the Board of Trade, 1846–47, Lord Lieutenant of Ireland, 1847–52 and Chancellor of the Duchy of Lancaster, 1864–65. He was Foreign Secretary on three occasions 1853–58, 1865–66 and 1868–70.

Clyde, Lord, Sir Colin Campbell (1792–1863): Army commander. Commander of the Highland Brigade in the Crimea, 1854. On the outbreak of the Indian Mutiny he was appointed Commander-in-Chief in India. For his services there he was raised to the peerage, 1858. Field-Marshal, 1862.

Cobbett, William (1762–1835): MP for Oldham 1832–35. Radical journalist. Started political career as loyalist writer, but moved into opposition after the resumption of war with France in 1803 and espoused the cause of parliamentary reform. Imprisoned for two years in 1810 for his protests over the flogging of a soldier, he took refuge in America, 1817–19. As author of the *Political Register* and several influential pamphlets, he was especially noted for his attacks on 'Old Corruption'. His writings on rural life, especially *Rural Rides* (1830), contained a bitter attack on agricultural change and the pauperisation of the rural labourer.

Cobden, Richard (1804–65): Liberal MP 1841–65; active after 1835 as pamphleteer, chiefly concerned with issues of free trade and disarmament; together with Bright (*q.v.*) led Anti-Corn Law League; responsible for commercial treaty with France in 1860, reducing tariffs; helped maintain relations between Lincoln and Palmerston administrations during American Civil War.

Colley, Sir George Pomeroy (1835–81): Army commander. Entered Army, 1852. Served in China in 1860, and managed the transport services in the Ashanti War of 1873. Secretary to the Viceroy of India, 1876. Chief of Staff in the Zulu War. Appointed Governor and Commander-in-Chief of Natal in 1880. Commanded in the first war against the Boers, and was killed at the battle of Majuba Hill on 27 Feb. 1881.

Coote, William Alexander (1842–1919): Social morality crusader. Secretary, National Vigilance Association, 1885–1919. Organiser of numerous National Committees for the Suppression of the White Slave Trade throughout the world.

Davies, (Sarah) Emily (1830–1921): Promoter of Higher Education for Women. Hon. Secretary, Girton College, Cambridge.

Davitt, Michael (1846–1906): Irish nationalist leader. Son of an Irish Roman Catholic peasant; joined the Fenians in 1865; founded Land League, 1879; Irish Nationalist MP 1892–93, 1895–99; endured several spells of imprisonment. Supporter of democratic nationalism, land nationalisation and anti-clericalism.

Derby, 14th Earl of, Edward George Geoffrey Smith Stanley (1799–1869): Stanley was Whig MP for Stockbridge, 1820–26, for Preston, 1826–30, for Windsor, 1831–32 and for Lancashire North, 1832–44. In 1844 he was elevated to the House of Lords as Lord Stanley of Bickerstaffe. Stanley served as Under-Secretary to the Colonial Office, 1827–28, Chief Secretary for Ireland 1830–33 and Colonial Secretary, 1833–34. In 1834 he resigned office in protest at the proposed lay appropriation of surplus Irish Church revenue. He served in Peel's government as Colonial Secretary, 1841–45. In 1845 he resigned in protest at proposals to repeal the Corn Laws. He became Prime Minister of Conservative governments 1852, 1858–59 and 1866–68. The major aim of Stanley and his colleagues in repeatedly agreeing to form minority governments was to establish the Conservative Party as a credible governing force. It was probably the desire to achieve this which prompted his 1866–68 government to extend the franchise.

Derby, 15th Earl of, Edward Henry Stanley (1826–93): Conservative (then later a Liberal) politician. His early ministerial posts included Colonial Secretary, 1858 and Secretary for India, 1858–59. Declined the Greek Crown, 1863. Foreign Secretary, 1866–68, 1874–78. Resigned over Eastern Question, 1878. Left Conservative Party, 1879. Liberal Colonial Secretary, 1882–85. Leader of Liberal Unionists in the Lords, 1886–91.

Devonshire, Duke of, Spencer Compton Cavendish, Marquis of Hartington (1833–1908): Liberal, later Liberal Unionist, leader and defender of free trade. His numerous posts included Chief Secretary for Ireland, 1870–74, Leader of the Liberal Party in the Commons, 1875–80, Secretary for India, 1880–82 and Secretary for War, 1882–85. He was successively Liberal Unionist leader in the Commons (1886–91) and the Lords (1891–95). He was Lord President of the Council, 1895–1903, until he resigned over the free trade issue.

Dickens, Charles (1812–70): One of the greatest Victorian novelists. Also a journalist, his writings exposed many of the evils of Victorian society (e.g. the corruption of the legal system in *Bleak House*, the abuses of the Poor Law and private education).

Disraeli, Benjamin, 1st Earl of Beaconsfield (1805–81): Disraeli was Conservative MP for Maidstone, 1837–41, for Shrewsbury, 1841–47 and for Buckinghamshire, 1847–76. He served as Leader of the Commons and Chancellor of the Exchequer in 1852, in 1858–59 and 1866–68. He was Prime Minister in 1868 and again 1874–80, also holding the office of Lord Privy Seal, 1876–78. Disraeli was created Earl of Beaconsfield in 1876. He led the Conservative Party until shortly before his death in 1881. Disraeli was a leading Conservative opponent of repeal of the Corn Laws. In 1867 he was responsible for a large extension of the franchise and as Conservative Prime Minister sought to emphasise Tory interest in social reform and the benefits of the Empire to the working class. As a novelist he dramatised the themes of his Toryism, in particular attacking the existence of 'two Englands'.

Edward VII: See p. 27.

Ellis, (Henry) Havelock (1859–1939): Psychologist and man of letters. Author of numerous works on sex psychology, marriage, men and women, art, literature, philosophy, travel. Editor, Contemporary Science series of books. A founder member of the Fellowship of the New Life, 1883. Member of the Committee, Eugenics Education Society. Hon. President, World Congress for Sexual Reform.

Fawcett, Dame Millicent (1847–1929): Leader of Women's Suffrage campaign. President, National Union of Women's Suffrage Societies, 1897–1918. Leader of Ladies' Commission of Inquiry into Boer War concentration camps.

Fisher, 1st Baron, John Arbuthnot Fisher (1841–1920): Naval leader. Fisher joined the Navy in 1854 and served in the Crimean War. He had great energy and enthusiasm for new developments in naval warfare. As Commander-in-Chief in the Mediterranean, 1899–1902, he introduced new techniques in training and tactics, and as First Sea Lord, 1904–10, he pushed through the creation of a British battlefleet of big-gun ships. The first, the *Dreadnought*, with 10 12-inch guns, was launched in 1906. He retired in 1910, but returned as First Sea Lord in October 1914 when Battenberg resigned. Fisher resigned in 1915 after clashes with Churchill, the First Lord of the Admiralty, over the wisdom of the Dardanelles expedition.

Forster, William Edward (1818–96): Liberal politician. Elected MP for Bradford, 1861–86. His government posts included Vice-President of the Privy Council Committee on Education (1868–74) (with a seat in Cabinet) and Chief Secretary for Ireland, 1880–82. He resigned in 1882 over Gladstone's 'weak' Irish policy and opposed Home Rule in 1886.

Fry, Elizabeth (1780–1845): Social reformer and Quaker; visit to Newgate prison prompted her to become a champion of prison reform, especially regarding the treatment of women prisoners. Her activities were largely directed towards improving prison conditions in order to 'reform' prisoners. She became a European authority on prison reform.

Galton, Sir Francis (1822–1911): Scientist; founder of study of eugenics. Secretary, British Association, 1863–68. President, Anthropological Institute, 1885–88. Author of studies on biology and heredity.

George, David Lloyd, 1st Earl Lloyd George of Dwyfor (1863–1945): Lloyd George was Liberal MP for Caernarvon Boroughs, 1890–1945. He served as President of the Board of Trade, 1905–08, Chancellor of the Exchequer, 1908–15, Minister of Munitions, 1915–16, Secretary for War, 1916 and was Prime Minister, 1916–22. He led the Liberal Party, 1926–31. In 1945 he was created Earl Lloyd George. As Chancellor Lloyd George proved a radical social reformer, and as Minister of Munitions and wartime PM an efficient and dynamic administrator and leader. Seeking to thwart the ambitions of socialists and the Labour Party, he was often a keen advocate of Liberal–Conservative fusion or coalition, and it was Conservative backbench unrest at such a possibility that caused them to rebel against his government in 1922. His decision to oust Asquith from the premiership in 1916, and then to continue the wartime coalition after 1918, also did irreparable harm to the Liberal Party.

George IV: See p. 26.

Gladstone, William Ewart (1809–98): Gladstone was Conservative MP for Newark, 1832–46, then Peelite MP for Oxford University, 1847–65, and subsequently Liberal MP for a variety of seats, 1865–95. In a long ministerial career he held office as President of the Board of Trade, 1843–45, Colonial Secretary, 1845–46, Chancellor of the Exchequer on four different occasions (1852–55, 1859–66, 1873–74, 1880–82), and Prime Minister also on four occasions (1868–74, 1880–85, 1886, 1892–94). He resigned office in 1845 over the Maynooth Grant. In 1894 he resigned over the Estimates. He was the towering figure of Victorian Liberalism, with a passionate commitment to Irish Home Rule in his later years.

Glasier, John Bruce (1859–1920): Socialist publicist. Chairman, Independent Labour Party, 1900. Editor, *Labour Leader*.

Goderich, 1st Viscount: See Ripon, Earl of.

Goldie, Sir George Dashwood Taubman (1846–1925): Imperialist. Known as the 'founder of Nigeria'. Attended Berlin Conference, 1884–85, as an expert on the Niger question. Served Royal Commission on the South African War, 1902–03. He was subsequently President of the National Defence Association.

Gordon, Charles George (1833–85): Military leader. Gordon joined the Royal Engineers in 1852, and took part in the Crimean War and the capture of Peking in 1860. He took command of the Chinese forces, the 'Ever Victorious Army', which crushed the Taiping Rebellion, earning him the nickname of 'Chinese' Gordon. He then entered the service of the Khedive of Egypt and administered the Sudan, 1877–80. As a devout evangelical Christian, one of his main concerns was the suppression of the slave trade. In 1884 he accepted the commission to organise the evacuation of the Sudan in the face of the rebellion led by the Mahdi. However, he remained in Khartoum. A relief expedition was sent too late, and Gordon was killed when Khartoum fell to the Mahdi's forces on 26 Jan. 1885. In England the Prime Minister, Gladstone, the 'Grand Old Man', was renamed the 'MOG' ('Murderer of Gordon').

Goschen, Viscount, George Joachim Goschen (1832–1907): Liberal (later Liberal Unionist and Conservative) politician. Held office as President of the Poor Law Board, 1868–71 and First Lord of the Admiralty, 1871–74. Became a Liberal Unionist, 1886. Served as Chancellor of the Exchequer, 1887–92 and then First Lord of the Admiralty, 1895–1900.

Gough, Sir Hugh, 1st Viscount Gough (1779–1869): Army commander. Entered Army 1793. By 1815 he had served at the Cape, the West Indies and in the Peninsula. Commanded the troops in China who captured the Canton forts in 1841. Commander-in-Chief in India, 1843. Successfully commanded in the First Sikh War, and was finally victorious in the Second Sikh War before the arrival of Sir Charles Napier, sent to replace him after the heavy losses of the initial battles. Field-Marshal, 1862.

Goulburn, Henry (1784–1856): Tory politician. Served as Chief Secretary for Ireland, 1821–27, Chancellor of the Exchequer, 1828–30 and Home Secretary, 1834–35. Unsuccessfully contested Speakership in 1839. Chancellor of the Exchequer, 1841–46.

Graham, Sir James Robert George (1792–1861): MP from 1818, first at Hull, then St Ives and Carlisle; First Lord of the Admiralty, 1830; Home Secretary 1841–46; First Lord of the Admiralty, 1852; Canningite in 1820s, Graham joined Grey 1830–34 when he and Stanley seceded from the Whigs on the question of Irish Church Reform; as Peelite Home Secretary was responsible for public order during Chartist disturbances.

Grant, Sir James Hope (1808–75): Army commander. Entered Army 1826. Served in China, 1840–42, and distinguished himself in the First and Second Sikh Wars. Took part in the Indian Mutiny, and successfully commanded in China, 1860. Commander-in-Chief at Madras, 1862–63. Quartermaster-General at the Horse Guards, 1865. Commander at Aldershot, 1870.

Granville, Earl, Granville George Leveson-Gower (1815–91): leading figure in Liberal hierarchy. Served on several occasions as Foreign Secretary (1851–52, 1870–74, 1880–85) and as Colonial Secretary (1868–70, 1886). Liberal leader in the Lords after 1855.

Grey, 2nd Earl, Charles Grey, Viscount Howick (1764–1845): Grey was MP for Northumberland, 1786–1807, for Appleby in 1807. He was styled Viscount Howick in 1806 on his father's elevation in the peerage and succeeded as 2nd Earl Grey in 1807. He held office as First Lord of the Admiralty in 1806, and as Foreign Secretary 1806–07. He was Prime Minister, 1830–34. Grey was a conservative Whig, and although he accepted the need for franchise reform, and was PM when the 1832 Reform Bill was passed, he saw the 1832 Act as a final concession to popular opinion and not as the start of a continuous process of reform.

Grey, 1st Viscount, Sir Edward Grey (1862–1933): Liberal MP, Berwick-on-Tweed, 1885–1916; Foreign Secretary, 1905–16. His support of Britain's obligation to help Belgium in 1914 took Britain into the First World War; believed in international arbitration, used successfully in Balkan Wars; later a champion of the League of Nations.

Grey, Maria Georgina Shirreff (1816–1906): Educationalist and author. Promoter of women's education. Initiated Girls' Public Day School Company, 1872, which had 25 schools by 1929. Founded Maria Grey Training College for Women Teachers, 1878.

Harcourt, Sir William George Granville Venables Vernon (1827–1904): Liberal MP for Derby then West Monmouthshire, 1868–1904; Home Secretary, 1880–85; Chancellor of the Exchequer, 1886 and 1892–95; Liberal leader in the House of Commons, 1894–98; influential parliamentarian; introduced single graduated estate duty in 1894.

Hardie, James Keir (1856–1915): Labour leader. Independent Labour MP for West Ham, 1892–95; Chairman ILP, 1893–1900, 1913–15; Labour MP for Merthyr Tydfil, 1900–15; chairman, Labour Party, 1906, coal-miner who became foremost British socialist, establishing Scottish Labour Party in 1888 and helping to establish the ILP in 1893; crucial influence in shaping political history of British Labour movement, and directing it into independence of existing major parties.

Harrison, Frederic (1831–1923): Author and positivist. Member of Royal Commission on Trade Unions, 1867–69. Secretary, Royal Commission for Digesting the Law, 1867–70. Professor of Jurisprudence and International Law to Inns of Court, 1879–89. Alderman, London County Council, 1889–93. President of English Positivist Committee, 1880–1905.

Hartington, Marquis of: See Devonshire, Duke of.

Havelock, Sir Henry (1795–1857): Army commander. Entered Army 1815. Served in First Burmese War, First Afghan War, the Gwalior Campaign (1843) and the First Sikh War. Commanded a division in Persia in 1857. Distinguished service in the Indian Mutiny: in command of a mobile column he relieved Lucknow. Died of dysentery 24 Nov. 1857.

Hicks Beach, Sir Michael Edward (1837–1916): Conservative politician. Numerous high public offices, including Chief Secretary for Ireland, 1874–78 (with seat in the Cabinet in 1876), Colonial Secretary, 1878–80, Chancellor of the Exchequer and Leader of the Commons, 1885–86. Subsequently served as Chief Secretary for Ireland, 1886–87 (when he resigned, but remained as a Cabinet Minister without Portfolio), President of the Board of Trade, 1888–92 and Chancellor of the Exchequer, 1895–1902. Created Viscount (later Earl) St Aldwyn.

Hill, Octavia (1838–1912): Philanthropist, housing reformer, member of Commons Preservation Society and co-founder of the National Trust. Served as Member of the Royal Commission on the Poor Law, 1905.

Holyoake, George Jacob (1817–1906): Leading co-operator and secularist. Editor of the *Reasoner*, 1846–66. Author of histories of the Co-operative Movement, and of works on secularism.

Howard, Sir Ebenezer (1850–1928): Town planner. Founded the Garden City Association, 1899. Director of First Garden City Ltd and Welwyn Garden City Ltd. A pioneer of environmental housing.

Howell, George (1833–1910): Trade union leader and radical politician. Elected Liberal MP for Bethnal Green North-East, 1885–95.

Hudson, George (1800–71): Railway promoter and speculator. Known as the 'Railway King'. A moving force behind the spate of railway amalgamations which created the Midland Railway, etc. He lost much of his fortune in the railway panic of 1847–48.

Hunt, George Ward (1825–77): Conservative politician. MP for Northamptonshire North, 1857–77. He served as Financial Secretary to the Treasury, 1866–68, Chancellor of the Exchequer for a brief period in 1868 and First Lord of the Admiralty, 1874–77.

Hunt, Henry (1773–1835): MP for Preston, 1830–32. A wealthy gentleman-farmer who rose to prominence as a Radical candidate for Bristol in 1812. The leading radical orator of the post-1815 period and main speaker at St Peter's Fields in Aug. 1819 for which he was sentenced to 30 months in Ilchester gaol. Continued to support manhood suffrage until his death in 1835.

Huskisson, William (1770–1830): MP for Morpeth, 1796–1802; for Liskeard, 1802–07; Hawick, 1807–12; Chichester, 1812–23; Liverpool, 1823–30; President of Board of Trade, 1823–27; Secretary for War and Colonies, 1827–28; Tory reformer and protégé of Pitt, who continued Pitt's work of fiscal reform; resigned as Secretary for War following clash with Wellington; killed by locomotive while attending opening of Liverpool and Manchester Railway.

Hyndman, Henry Mayers (1842–1921): British Marxist; author of *England for All*, 1881, and many other works of socialist propaganda; founder of Social Democratic Federation; important influence on many early socialists; failed to recognise the importance of trade unions and working-class liberals as potential supporters of working-class political party.

Iddlesleigh, Earl of: See Northcote, Sir Stafford.

Jameson, Sir Leander Starr (1853–1917): Imperialist and businessman. President of the British South African Company. Served as member of South African Legislature, 1910–12. Famous as architect of failed Jameson Raid (see p. 297).

Jenkinson, Robert Banks: See Liverpool, Earl of.

Johnston, Sir Harry Hamilton (1858–1927): Explorer and colonial administrator. Commissioner and Consul-General, British Central Africa Protectorate, 1891. Consul-General, Regency of Tunis, 1897–99. Special Commissioner, Commander-in-Chief and Consul General, Uganda Protectorate, 1899–1901. Author of works on the empire, racial questions etc.

Jones, Ernest (1819–69): Advocate of socialist ideas. Son of a wealthy cavalry officer who became a barrister. Joined O'Connorite Chartists in 1846. Stood as Chartist candidate for Parliament. Imprisoned in 1848 for advocating 'physical force'; he wrote *Chartist Songs*, 1846, and edited the *People's Paper*, 1852–58.

Keble, John (1792–1866): Anglican theologian. Professor of Poetry at Oxford, 1831; became leading member of Oxford Movement following sermon in 1833 against proposed suppression of 10 Irish bishoprics; contributed to *Tracts for the Times*; friend and adviser of Newman (*q.v.*) and later worked closely with Pusey (*q.v.*) to keep High Church movement attached to Church of England; Keble College, Oxford, was founded in his memory.

Kenney, Annie (1879–1953): Pioneer advocate of women's suffrage. A millworker from the age of 10. Loyal lieutenant of Christabel Pankhurst. She gave up politics after 1918.

Kingsley, Charles (1819–79): Advocate of Christian socialism. Served as Chaplain to Queen Victoria. Best known for such popular novels as *Westward Ho!* and *The Water Babies*.

Kirk, Sir John (1832–1922): Naturalist and administrator. Fellow of the Royal Society. Chief Officer of Livingstone's expedition to Africa, 1853–64. H.M. Agent and Consul-General, Zanzibar, 1886. Special Commissioner to Niger, 1895. Foreign Secretary, Royal Geographical Society.

Kitchener, 1st Earl, Horatio Herbert Kitchener (1850–1916): Military leader. Kitchener joined the Royal Engineers in 1870. He served in the Sudan and Egypt, 1882–85, and was Governor-General of East Sudan, 1886–88. As Commander-in-Chief ('Sirdar') of the Anglo-Egyptian Army in the 1890s he undertook the reconquest of the Sudan, defeating the dervishes at Omdurman on 2 Sept. 1898. In the Boer War he acted as Chief of Staff to Roberts until Nov. 1900. On becoming Commander-in-Chief in South Africa he broke the resistance of the Boers by the use of blockhouses and concentration camps. As Commander-in-Chief in India, 1902–09 he quarrelled over control of the Indian Army with the Viceroy, Lord Curzon, who resigned in 1905. Kitchener was British Agent and Consul-General in Egypt, 1911–14, then on 5 Aug. 1914 he was appointed War Minister. He had enormous success in raising new volunteer armies for the Western Front, but the habits of military command did not fit him to work well with his political colleagues. He was drowned on a mission to Russia on 5 June 1916, when the cruiser *HMS Hampshire* struck a mine off the Orkney Islands.

Lamb, William: See Melbourne, Viscount.

Lancaster, Joseph (1778–1838): Pioneer educationalist. Famous as leading advocate of the 'monitorial system' whereby selected pupils relayed class instruction to the rest of the pupils.

Law, Andrew Bonar (1858–1923): Conservative politician. Law was Conservative MP for Glasgow Blackfriars, 1900–06, for Dulwich, 1906–10, for Bootle, 1911–18, for Glasgow Central, 1918–23. He was parliamentary secretary to the Board of Trade, 1902–05. In 1911 he became leader of the Conservative Party. He took office in the wartime coalition as Colonial Secretary, 1915–16, and Chancellor of the Exchequer, 1916–18. In the post-war coalition he was Lord Privy Seal and Leader of the House of Commons, 1919–21. In 1921 he resigned. In 1922 he became leader of the Conservative Party again, following the revolt of the Conservative backbenchers, and Prime Minister. He retired in 1923 and died the same year. The main significance of Law's premiership was that it proved the Conservatives could form a government without the Liberal Lloyd George being necessary to lead them.

Lee, Henry William (1865–1932): Socialist propagandist. Secretary, Social Democratic Federation, 1885–1911 and then British Socialist Party, 1911–13. Helped found pro-war National Socialist Party, 1916. Editor, *Justice*, after 1913.

Lewis, Sir George Cornwall (1806–63): Whig politician. Editor, *Edinburgh Review*, 1852–55. Subsequently held important Cabinet office as Chancellor of the Exchequer, 1855–58, Home Secretary, 1859–61 and Secretary for War, 1861–63.

Liverpool, 2nd Earl of, Robert Banks Jenkinson (1770–1828): Jenkinson was MP for Appleby, 1790–96, and for Rye, 1796–1803. In 1803 he became Baron Hawkesbury. He was Master of the Mint, 1799–1801, Foreign Secretary 1801–04, Home Secretary, 1804–06 and 1807–09. He succeeded as 2nd Earl of Liverpool in 1808. From 1809 to 1812 he held the office of Secretary for War and the Colonies, and became First Lord of the Treasury (and Prime Minister) in 1812, a post he held until 1827. Liverpool's ministry was perhaps more impressive than that of the more famous Pitt, and was based both on Liverpool's own political skill and on the collective talents of his ministers.

Livingstone, David (1813–73): Scottish emplorer of Africa. Discoverer of the Zambesi river's course, the Victoria Falls and Lake Nyasa (now Lake Malawi). He campaigned against the Arab-led slave trade. At one time presumed lost, he was found by Stanley on 10 Nov. 1871.

Lloyd George, David: See George.

Lowe, Robert (1811–92): Liberal politician. A *Times* leader writer after 1850. Vice-President of the Privy Council Committee on Education, 1859–64. A leader of the Adullamites against the Reform Bill in 1865. Subsequently served under Gladstone as Chancellor of the Exchequer, 1868–73 and Home Secretary, 1873–74. Created Viscount Sherbrooke, 1880.

Ludlow, John Malcolm (1821–1911): Social reformer and Christian Socialist. Secretary to Royal Commission on Friendly and Benefit Building Societies, 1870–74. Chief Registrar of Friendly Societies, 1874–91. Editor of *Politics for the People, Christian Socialist*, etc.

McCarthy, Justin (1830–1912): Irish novelist, journalist and politician. Journalist in Ireland from 1848. Editor, *Morning Star*, 1864–68. Leader writer on *Daily News* from 1871. MP. Chairman, Irish Parliamentary Party, 1890–96. Author of various works of fiction and history.

MacDonald, James Ramsay (1866–1937): Labour politician. MacDonald was one of the most important figures in the evolution of the Labour Party. He was secretary of the Labour Representation Committee and the Labour Party, 1900–12, treasurer of the party 1912–24 and Chairman, 1911–14. He was Chairman of the Independent Labour Party, 1906–09, and of the Parliamentary Labour Party in 1922. He was first elected to Parliament for Leicester in 1906 (losing his seat in 1918 after his pacifist stance in World War I). After 1918 he was first adulated as Labour's Prime Minister and then reviled for his betrayal of the party in 1931.

Malmesbury, Earl, James Howard Harris (1807–89): Tory politician. He served as Foreign Secretary, 1852 and 1858–59. He was subsequently Lord Privy Seal, 1866–68, 1874–76 and also Conservative leader in the Lords, Feb.–Dec. 1868.

Mann, Tom (1856–1941): Trade union leader and socialist propagandist. Miner and artisan who came to London from Birmingham, and joined trade union movement in 1881; joined Hyndman's (*q.v.*) Social Democratic Federation in 1885, and supported the movement to establish eight-hour working day; involved in dockworkers' strike, 1889. A leader of the militant industrial struggles before the First World War, he became general secretary of the Amalgamated Society of Engineers, 1918–21, and a leading member of the Communist Party.

Manning, Henry Edward (1808–92): Religious leader, an evangelical who swung to Tractarian side in 1840s and became one of leaders of the

Oxford Movement after Newman's (*q.v.*) secession in 1845; received into Roman Catholic Church in 1851 and reordained. Roman Catholic archbishop of Westminster from 1865, he became a cardinal; gave support to doctrine of Papal Infallibility at Vatican Council (1869–70); prominent in social work of all kinds and in 1889 successfully mediated in London dock strike.

Martineau, Harriet (1802–76): Philanthropist. Author of *Illustrations of Political Economy*, 1832, moral tales designed to explain workings of economic laws, and of *Forest and Game Law Tales* and the novel *Deerbrook*; visited USA 1834–36 and became advocate of abolition of slavery; *Positive Philosophy*, 1853, was a popularisation and condensation of Comte's philosophy.

Mason, Charlotte Maria Shaw (1842–1923): Educationalist. Founded the Parents' National Education Union, 1887, the Ambleside House of Education, and the Parents' Union School, 1891.

Mayhew, Henry (1812–87): Pioneer of systematic social investigation; in 1849–50, published 76 letters about London poor (*London Labour and the London Poor*) as part of *Morning Chronicle*'s nationwide survey of poverty; republished 1861–62, but then discontinued following reaction to vigour of its attack on political economy of day; joint first editor of *Punch*, 1841.

Melbourne, 2nd Viscount, William Lamb (1779–1848): Politician. Lamb was Whig MP for Leominster in 1806, for Portarlington, 1807–12, for Northampton, 1816–19 and for Hertfordshire, 1819–29. In 1829 he became Viscount Melbourne. He held office as Secretary for Ireland, 1827–28 and Home Secretary, 1830–40. Melbourne was Prime Minister in 1834 and again, 1835–41. A Whig, and disliked as such by the King, Melbourne's outdated view of the constitution helped result (in 1834) in his being the last PM to be dismissed by the monarch. Between 1835 and 1841 Melbourne proved reluctant to respond to the Chartist and Anti-Corn Law movements.

Mill, John Stuart (1806–73): Liberal MP for Westminster, 1865–68; influenced by Bentham (*q.v.*) and utilitarian philosophy of James Mill, became leading philosopher of nineteenth-century liberalism; advocate of equal rights for women and respect for minorities; author of *On Liberty*, 1859; humanist who saw need for state intervention to prevent abuses of *laissez-faire*; later regarded himself as socialist.

Monteagle, Baron: See Spring-Rice, Thomas.

Morley, Viscount, John Morley (1838–1923): Liberal politician. Editor of *Pall Mall Gazette*, 1880–83. A long career in government included posts as Chief Secretary for Ireland, 1886, 1892–95; Secretary of State for India, 1905–10 and Lord President of the Council. He resigned in protest at the declaration of war in August 1914.

Morris, William (1834–96): Idealist socialist, poet, painter, designer; founder of Arts and Crafts movement; established close association between art and political beliefs; involved in creation of Socialist League, 1884, and Hammersmith Socialist Society, 1890; lasting artistic influence, and a major influence on later socialists.

Naoroji, Dadabhai (1825–1917): Indian political leader. Prime Minister of Baroda, 1874. Liberal MP for Finsbury Central, 1892–95 (first Indian Member of Parliament). President, Indian National Congress (1886, 1893, 1906). President, London Indian Society.

Napier of Magdala, Lord, Robert Cornelius Napier (1810–90): Army commander. Despatched as second-in-command of the Central India force under Sir Hugh Rose, 1858. Commanded a division in the Chinese War of 1860. Returning to India in 1861, he was given command of the Bombay Army in 1865, and of the expedition to Abyssinia in 1867, for which he was created Baron Napier of Magdala. Commander-in-Chief in India, 1870–76. Governor of Gibraltar, 1876–82. Constable of the Tower of London, 1887–90.

Newman, John Henry (1801–90): Theologian. Brought up in Church of England under evangelical influence, in 1833 he became leading spirit of the Oxford Movement; he wrote 24 *Tracts for the Times* between 1833 and 1841; he believed the Church of England should hold an intermediate position between Romanism and Protestantism; he withdrew from Oxford following controversy over interpretation of the Thirty-nine Articles in 1841, and was received into the Roman Catholic Church in 1845; he became a cardinal and had considerable influence on the revival of Catholicism in England.

Nightingale, Florence (1820–1910): Pioneer of the modern profession of nursing who achieved fame in the Crimean War. Reforms in the nursing profession followed her work.

Northbrook, Lord, Sir Francis Thornhill Baring (1796–1866): Whig politician. MP for Portsmouth, 1826–65. Junior Treasury appointments in 1830s. Chancellor of the Exchequer, 1839–41. First Lord of the Admiralty, 1849–52.

Northcote, Sir Stafford Henry (1818–87): Conservative politician. Served as President of the Board of Trade, 1866–67. Chairman, Hudson's Bay Company, 1869–74. Chancellor of the Exchequer under Disraeli, 1874–80 and also Leader of the House of Commons. Created Earl of Iddesleigh, 1885. Served as Foreign Secretary, 1886–87.

O'Brien, James Bronterre (1805–64): Irish radical and advocate of land nationalisation and extension to workers of credit based on it; member of Working Men's Association; Chartist who advocated violence, but after 1839 stressed need for middle-class support and thereafter advised moderation.

O'Connell, Daniel (1775–1847): Irish nationalist; known as 'The Liberator'. Born in County Kerry, he founded the Catholic Association in 1823 as a mass movement to campaign for Catholic Emancipation. Elected for County Clare in 1828, but as a Catholic not allowed to take his seat. His efforts helped to secure the passing of the Roman Catholic Relief Act, 1829. Subsequently, took seat as MP for County Clare, 1830, and for Waterford, 1832. Organised mass meetings in 1842 and 1843 to secure repeal of the 1800 Act of Union. His cancellation of the Clontarf meeting in October 1843 discredited him with many Irish extremists. He died at Genoa.

O'Connor, Feargus (1794–1885): Chartist leader. MP for Cork, 1832–35; MP for Nottingham from 1847; leading Chartist who owned and edited Chartist periodical *Northern Star* and dominated militant northern section of movement; organised Chartist demonstration, 1848.

Owen, Robert (1771–1858): Utopian socialist propagandist. Scottish millowner who attempted at New Lanark to create model factory employing no young children, educating older children and limiting adult hours; used term 'socialist' to describe experiment; *New View of Society*, 1813, expounded value of cooperative ideal; unsuccessful in attempt to establish socialistic community in USA, 1825–29; help found Grand National Consolidated Trades Union, 1834.

Palmerston, 3rd Viscount, Henry John Temple (1784–1865): Temple was Tory MP for Newport, 1807–11, for Cambridge University, 1811–31, Whig member for Bletchingly, 1831–32, for Hampshire South, 1832–34, and for Tiverton, 1835–65. Temple succeeded as Viscount Palmerston in 1802. He was a Lord of the Admiralty, 1807–09. In 1809 he declined the Chancellorship of the Exchequer and became Secretary for War, 1809–28. He was Foreign Secretary, 1830–34, 1835–41, 1846–51, and

Home Secretary, 1852–55. He was Prime Minister 1855–58 and 1859–65. Palmerston captured the imagination of mid-Victorian Britain by his aggressive nationalism, and his popularity was such that he was returned as Prime Minister in 1859 despite his known hostility to the growing demand for electoral reform.

Pankhurst, Christabel (1881–1958): Proponent of women's suffrage. A founder and leader of the Women's Social and Political Union (see p. 131). In later years, a religious propagandist. Daughter of Emmeline Pankhurst (see below).

Pankhurst, Emmeline (1858–1928): Feminist leader. Joint founder and leader after 1898 of Women's Franchise League, and with daughter Christabel of more militant Women's Social and Political Union, 1903; talks with Prime Minister in 1906 led to disillusionment with Liberals and resort to more violent tactics; engaged in arson and hunger strikes while imprisoned; encouraged women to join armed forces and work in industry during First World War.

Parnell, Charles Stewart (1846–91): Irish nationalist leader. Son of Anglican gentry family, educated at Cambridge. Nationalist MP for Co. Meath, 1875–80, Cork, 1880–91, leading Irish Nationalist Party in Parliament from 1878. Led agitation for Home Rule, skilfully co-ordinating political bargaining at Westminster with more radical movements in Ireland. Career ruined when cited in O'Shea divorce case of 1890.

Passfield, 1st Baron: See Webb.

Peel, Sir Robert, 2nd Baronet (1788–1850): Conservative politician. Peel was Tory MP for Cashel, 1809–17, for Oxford University, 1817–28, for Westbury, 1829, and for Tamworth, 1830–50. He was Under-Secretary at the Colonial Office, 1810–12, Chief Secretary for Ireland, 1812–18, Home Secretary, 1822–27 and 1828–30, Leader of the Commons, 1828–30 and Prime Minister and Chancellor of the Exchequer, 1834–35. He again became Prime Minister in 1841, resigning in 1845, but resuming office when the Whigs could not form a government. He retained the premiership until 1846. Peel is best remembered for his financial reforms and for his endeavours to prove that Conservatism was compatible with cautious reform. His repeal of the Corn Duties in 1846 split his party and left him at the head of a band of Free Trade 'Peelites' until his death in a riding accident in 1850.

Potter, George (1832–93): Trade union leader. He was a carpenter prominent in London builders' strike of 1859; he ran an influential labour paper in London, *Beehive*, to encourage strikes in provinces; and was an aggressive unionist who saw the vote as a necessity for members to secure legislation safeguarding union funds and protecting rights; in the summer of 1864 he organised Conference of Trades; as president of London Working Men's Association, opened Trade Union Congress in 1868.

Pusey, Edward Bouverie (1800–82): Regius Professor of Hebrew and Canon of Christ Church, Oxford; leading member of Oxford Movement; became leader following Newman's withdrawal, 1841; assisted in establishment of first Anglican sisterhood; sermon on absolution in 1846 led to practice of private confession in Anglican Church.

Raglan, Lord, Fitzroy James Henry Somerset (1788–1855): Army career. Military Secretary to Wellington, 1811–14 and again 1818–52. On Wellington's death in 1852 he was appointed Master-General of the Ordnance. In 1854 he went to the Crimea as Commander-in-Chief of the British expeditionary force. His leadership was heavily criticised, especially with the failure of the Allied attack on Sebastopol in June 1855.

Redmond, John Edward (1856–1918): Irish nationalist leader. Son of an Irish Catholic gentry family, he was Irish Nationalist MP for New Ross, 1881–85; N. Wexford, 1885–91, Waterford, 1891–1918, and leader of reunited Nationalist Party from 1900. Worked for Home Rule by constitutional means up to Easter rising of 1916, but the rise of Sinn Fein made his approach seem redundant.

Rhodes, Cecil John (1853–1902): Champion of the British imperial cause in southern Africa. Went to Africa in 1870 where he earned a fortune from diamond-mining. Founded De Beers Company in 1880 at Kimberley and acquired interests in the Transvaal gold-fields. In 1887 founded the British South Africa Company to develop the region north of the Transvaal, later known as Rhodesia, and in 1890 mounted an expedition which established a settlement in Salisbury and secured the rest of the country. Made premier of Cape Colony in 1890, but was forced to resign in 1896 because of his connection with the Jameson raid. He left most of his fortune to Oxford University.

Ripon, 1st Earl of, Frederick John Robinson, 1st Viscount Goderich (1782–1859): Robinson was MP for Carlow Borough, 1806–07, and for Ripon, 1807–27. In 1827 he was created 1st Viscount Goderich. In 1833 he was created Earl of Ripon. Robinson was President of the Board of Trade and Treasurer of the Navy, 1818–23, Chancellor of the Exchequer, 1823–27, Secretary for War and Colonies, Apr.–Aug. 1827 and 1830–33.

He served as Prime Minister, Aug. 1827–Jan. 1828, as Lord Privy Seal, Apr. 1833–May 1834, as President of the Board of Trade, 1841–43 and as President of the Board of Control, 1843–46. Goderich was asked to serve as Prime Minister following the death of his friend, Canning. He proved unable to control his ministry and resigned following the refusal of Huskisson and Herries to serve together.

Roberts, 1st Earl, Frederick Sleigh Roberts (1832–1914): Military leader. The son of a general, Roberts was born in India and joined the Bengal Artillery in 1851. He won the Victoria Cross during the Indian Mutiny, in Jan. 1858. As commander of the Punjab Frontier Force, he defeated the Afghans and imposed the treaty of Gardamak in May 1879. After a British force had been defeated by the Afghans at Maiwand, Roberts became a national hero by marching his army 300 miles in 22 days to relieve Kandahar on 1 Sept. 1880. He was Commander-in-Chief in India, 1885–93 and in Ireland, 1895–99. After the initial British disasters in the Boer War, Roberts was sent to command in South Africa. He returned to England in 1901 to be Commander-in-Chief (until 1904). His last years were devoted to advocating conscription through the National Service League. He died on 14 Nov. 1914 after contracting pneumonia during a visit to Indian troops in France.

Robinson, Frederick: See Ripon, Earl of.

Rosebery, 5th Earl of, Archibald Philip Primrose, 1st Earl of Midlothian (1847–1929): Created earl in 1868, Rosebery held first the office of Under-Secretary to the Home Office, 1881–83. In 1885 he became First Commissioner of Works and later in the year Lord Privy Seal. He served as Foreign Secretary in 1886 and 1892–94. He was Prime Minister and Lord President of the Council, 1894–95. In 1889 and 1890 and again in 1892 he was chairman of the London County Council. After internal party squabbles he resigned the leadership of the Liberal Party in 1896. An exceptionally gifted individual, Rosebery proved a surprisingly inept premier, and through hesitancy and indecision failed to return to office after resigning the party leadership.

Russell, 1st Earl, Lord John Russell (1792–1878): Liberal politician. Russell was MP for Huntingdonshire, 1820–26, for Bandon Bridge, 1826–30, for Tavistock in 1831, for Devon, 1831–32, for Devon South, 1832–35, for Stroud, 1835–41 and for the City of London, 1841–61. In 1861 he was created Earl Russell. He was Postmaster-General, 1830–34, obtaining a seat in the Cabinet in 1831, Home Secretary, 1835–39 and Colonial Secretary, 1839–41. He served as Prime Minister, 1846–52. After resigning the premiership he held office as Foreign Secretary,

1852–53, Minister without Portfolio, 1853–54, Lord President of the Council, 1854–55, Colonial Secretary, 1855; and Foreign Secretary, 1859–65. In 1865 he again became Prime Minister, leaving office in 1866. Russell failed to achieve the union of Whigs and Peelites which he desired during his first premiership, and was unable to establish the control he would have wished over his Cabinet and the Commons. During his second administration he proved a bold advocate of electoral reform and alarmed some of his colleagues by his 'rapidity'.

St Aldwyn, Earl: See Hicks Beach, Sir Michael.

Salisbury, 3rd Marquis of, Robert Arthur Talbot Gascoyne-Cecil (1830–1903): Cecil was Conservative MP for Stamford, 1853–68. In 1865 he became Viscount Cranbourne. He served as Secretary for India in 1866, resigning in protest at the 1867 Reform Bill. In 1868 he succeeded as Marquis of Salisbury. He returned as Secretary for India, 1874–76, and as Foreign Secretary, 1878–80. He was leader of the opposition in the House of Lords and joint leader of the Conservative Party, 1881–85. In 1885 he became Prime Minister and sole party leader. He acted as Prime Minister and Foreign Secretary, 1885–86, Prime Minister in 1886, Prime Minister and Foreign Secretary, 1887–92 and 1895–1900. He was Prime Minister and Lord Privy Seal, 1900–02. Salisbury was a remarkably able diplomat, while in the domestic sphere he had an incisive knowledge of the Conservative Party. As a Tory and a High Church Anglican he was able to control an unruly party, and by moderate social reform and opposition to Home Rule he succeeded in forging the Unionist alliance which dominated British politics between 1886 and 1906.

Scott, Charles Prestwich (1846–1932): Journalist, editor and politician. Extremely influential and long-serving editor of the *Manchester Guardian*, 1872–1929. Liberal MP for Leigh, 1895–1906.

Shaftesbury, 7th Earl, Anthony Ashley Cooper, Baron Ashley (1805–85): MP for Woodstock, 1826–30; Dorchester, 1830–31; Dorset, 1833–46; champion of measures to improve factory conditions, including various Factory Acts between 1833 and 1850, and Owners Act of 1842; he was a noted philanthropist and evangelical, interested in Bible Society movements at home and abroad.

Shaw, George Bernard (1856–1950): Playwright and socialist publicist. Edited *Fabian Essays* (1889) and wrote numerous tracts on socialism for the Fabian Society. Awarded the Nobel Prize for Literature, 1925.

Sherbrooke, Viscount: See Lowe, Robert.

Sidmouth, 1st Viscount, Henry Addington (1757–1844): Addington was MP for Devizes, 1784–1805. In 1805 he was created Viscount Sidmouth. Addington was Speaker of the House of Commons, 1789–1801, Prime Minister and Chancellor of the Exchequer, 1801–04, Lord President of the Council, 1805, Lord Privy Seal, 1806, Lord President of the Council, 1806–07 and 1812. He was Home Secretary, 1812–22 and was a member of the Cabinet without ministerial office, 1822–24. Although an able administrator, Sidmouth proved a mediocre Prime Minister. He proved an efficient but repressive Home Secretary.

Smith, William Henry (1825–91): Conservative MP, 1868–91; First Lord of the Admiralty, 1877–80; First Lord of the Treasury and Leader of the House, 1887–91; founder of W.H. Smith Booksellers; opposed Lord Randolph Churchill's (*q.v.*) budgetary proposals for economies and succeeded him as Leader of the House.

Solly, Henry (1813–1903): Social reformer who sponsored workmen's education. Founder of the Workingmen's Club and Institute Union.

Somerset, Lord Fitzroy James Henry: See Raglan, Lord.

Spring-Rice, Thomas (1790–1866): Whig politician. His senior posts included terms as Colonial Secretary, 1834, Chancellor of the Exchequer, 1835–39 and subsequently Comptroller-General of the Exchequer, 1839–65. Created first Baron Monteagle (1839).

Spurgeon, Charles (1834–92): Leading Nonconformist. As Baptist minister of the Metropolitan Tabernacle in London he was the most popular preacher of the Victorian age.

Stacy, Enid (1868–1903): Pioneer socialist publicist and lecturer who was a prominent campaigner for women's suffrage.

Stanley, Edward: See Derby, Earl of.

Stead, William Thomas (1849–1912): Journalist and author. Editor, Darlington *Northern Echo*, 1871–80, *Pall Mall Gazette*, 1883–89. Founder and editor, *Review of Reviews*, from 1891. Author of various propagandist works, including *Maiden Tribute of Modern Babylon* (1885).

Stephens, James (1824–1901): Irish revolutionary. Member of the Young Ireland movement. Founded the Fenians in 1858.

Stephenson, George (1781–1848): Engineer and locomotive designer. Built *Locomotion* for Stockton and Darlington Railway, 1825. Famous for his locomotive *Rocket*.

Temple, Henry: See Palmerston, Viscount.

Tillett, Benjamin (1866–1943): Trade Union leader. Labour MP for N. Salford, 1917–24, 1929–31; chairman, TUC General Council, 1928–29; helped organise unionisation of dockworkers; secretary of Dock, Wharf, Riverside and General Workers' Union, 1887–1922; one of leaders of 1889 London dock strike; initiative led to formation of National Transport Workers' Federation; alderman of London County Council, 1892–98; a founder of the Independent Labour Party and Labour Party; member TUC General Council, 1921–31.

Trent, 1st Baron (Sir Jesse Boot) (1850–1931): Businessman and philanthropist. Founder of Boots the Chemist.

Trevor, John (1855–1930): Unitarian minister. Founder of the Labour Church movement (see p. 297).

Tuckwell, Gertrude Mary (1861–1951): Women's trade union leader. Secretary, Women's Trade Union League, 1892–1904; later its president. President, Women Public Health Officers' Association. Chairman, National Association of Probation Officers.

Vansittart, Nicholas: See Bexley, Baron.

Victoria, Queen: See p. 27.

Ward, Mary Augusta (1851–1920): Novelist and social worker. Founded the Passmore Edwards Settlement and the Play Centres for London, 1897. A founder of the Women's National Anti-Suffrage League in 1908.

Watson, Robert Spence (1837–1911): Liberal politician. Political, social and educational reformer. Helped found Armstrong College, Durham, 1871; first President, 1910. Pioneer of university extension teaching in North of England. President of the National Liberal Federation, 1890–1902. President of the Peace Society.

Webb, (Martha) Beatrice (1858–1943): Born Beatrice Potter. Political scientist and socialist author. Contributed to Charles Booth's *Life and Labour of the People*. Member of Royal Commission on the Poor Law and Unemployment, 1905–09, and joint author of the Minority Report. Member of various government committees. With her husband Sidney Webb wrote numerous works of social investigation and labour history.

Webb, Sidney James, 1st Baron Passfield (1859–1947): with his wife Beatrice (*q.v.*), a pioneer of British social and economic reform; they were joint authors of numerous influential works on labour history, including *The History of Trade Unionism*, 1894, and *Industrial Democracy*, 1897; and were founders of the London School of Economics and of the *New Statesman*; Sidney Webb helped in reorganisation of University of London and provision of public education legislation, and held various offices: MP for Seaham, 1922–29; President of the Board of Trade, 1924, Secretary of State for Dominion Affairs, 1929–30 and Secretary of State for Colonies, 1930–31; elevated to peerage as 1st Baron Passfield, 1929.

Wellesley, Arthur: See Wellington, Duke of.

Wellington, 1st Duke of, Arthur Wellesley (1769–1852): Military leader and politician. Wellesley was MP for Trim, 1790–95, for Rye in 1806, for Mitchel in 1807 and for Newport, 1807–09. In 1812 he was created Earl Wellington and then Marquis. In 1814 he was created Duke of Wellington. Between 1807 and 1809 he acted as Chief Secretary for Ireland. He was Master-General of the Ordnance, 1819–27. He was Prime Minister, 1828–30 and was Secretary of State of all departments and Prime Minister Nov.–Dec. 1834. He served as Foreign Secretary, 1834–35, and Minister without Portfolio, 1841–46. After rising to pre-eminence as a military leader during the Napoleonic Wars, culminating in his victory at Waterloo in 1815, Wellington found it difficult to adapt to the necessities of compromise and expediency concomitant on political life. He viewed his premiership simply as fulfilling the duty of carrying on the King's government and was on uneasy terms with many of his Cabinet. His reluctance to countenance franchise reform led to the break-up of his government in 1830.

William IV: See p. 26.

Willoughby de Broke, Baron, Richard Greville Verney (1869–1923): Conservative politician who came to prominence as a leading die-hard in defence of the traditional powers of the House of Lords.

Wolseley, Viscount, Garnet Joseph Wolseley (1833–1913): Army career. Worked with Cardwell to further Army reform. Commanded the punitive expedition into Ashanti, 1873–74. Promoted to Major-General and sent to Natal in a political post, 1875. High Commissioner in Cyprus, 1878. Supreme civil and military commander in Natal and the Transvaal, 1879. Returned to Britain, 1880, and appointed Quartermaster-General. Adjutant-General responsible for training in the Army, 1882. Sent in Aug. 1882 to Egypt to put down Arabi's revolt; defeated him at Tel-el-Kebir, 13 Sept. 1882. In Jan. 1885 the relieving force under Wolseley reached Khartoum two days after Gordon's death. Returned to War

Office as Adjutant-General; Commander-in-Chief in Ireland, 1890–94. Commander-in-Chief of the Forces, 1895–1900.

Wood, Sir Charles (1800–85): First elected as Whig MP, 1826. He served as Chancellor of the Exchequer, 1846–52; President of the Board of Control, 1852–55; First Lord of the Admiralty, 1855–58 and Secretary for India, 1859–66. Created Viscount Halifax, 1866. Lord Privy Seal, 1870–74.

Wood, Sir Henry Evelyn (1838–1919): Army commander. Entered Royal Navy, 1852, and served in the Crimea with the Naval Brigade. Transferred to the Army, and served as a cavalry officer in the Indian Mutiny. Served with Wolseley in the Ashanti War of 1873, and commanded a column in the Zulu War. Second-in-command to Sir George Colley in the First Boer War, and came to terms with the Boers in Mar. 1881 on government orders. Commanded a brigade in Egypt, 1882, and was Commander of the Egyptian Army, 1882–86. Went to the War Office as Quartermaster-General, 1893. Adjutant-General to the forces, 1897, and responsible for mobilisation at the outbreak of the South African War. Field-Marshal, 1903.

SECTION SIX

Glossary of terms

Adullamites   A term used by John Bright on 13 Mar. 1866 to describe the independent attitude of Robert Lowe (Lord Sherbrooke), Horsman and their Liberal supporters who were opposed to the 1866 Reform Bill. The 'cave of Adullam' is a biblical reference.

Alabama Dispute   After the US civil war, the American government claimed compensation from Britain for damage done by the *Alabama*, a privateer fitted out in England to raid the commerce of the northern states. Britain eventually paid out substantial damages.

Anti-Corn Law League   See p. 8 and p. 198.

Anti-Parnellites   The term for the majority of the Irish Parliamentary Party, who removed Parnell (q.v.) from the leadership after the O'Shea divorce case.

aristocracy of labour   Collective term for members of skilled trades whose earnings and superior status gave them a distinctive political stance in Victorian Britain and later, and made them often more inclined to reformist and labourist (q.v.) policies.

Arrow War   Alternative name for the second Opium War (see p. 222). So-called when the Hong Kong-registered ship *Arrow*, flying the British flag, was boarded at Canton by the Chinese, who arrested most of the crew for piracy, causing outrage in London.

artisan   Term applied to skilled craft workers, traditionally associated with independence, higher earnings, superior status and greater political involvement than the general mass of labourers.

bag and baggage   Famous phrase used in the policy advocated by Gladstone in 1876 (while in opposition), at the time of the Bulgarian Atrocities. It was to the effect that if the Ottoman Empire failed to reform the administration of her Christian provinces, she must be turned out of Europe 'bag and baggage'.

balance of power   Doctrine of maintaining a European system in which no single power was dominant. Britain was traditionally concerned to support coalitions opposing one power gaining hegemony over Europe.

Ballot Act   The legislation which introduced a secret ballot in place of the hitherto open voting at parliamentary elections (see p. 70).

Bank Charter Act   See Banking, p. 193.

Bedchamber crisis   The episode in May 1839 when Melbourne offered to resign, advising Queen Victoria to appoint a Tory administration under Peel. Peel refused office when Victoria refused to dismiss certain Whig-sympathising Ladies of the Bedchamber.

Bering Sea controversy   Dispute between the United States and Great Britain over the extension of American territorial waters in the Bering Sea. The United States had purchased Alaska from Russia in 1867 and claimed that the territorial rights transferred to her included control over the eastern part of the Bering Sea, from which she sought to exclude British seal fishing ships. The dispute went before an international arbitration tribunal in 1893 which awarded damages to the British sealers.

Black Friday   The financial panic of 11 May 1866 caused by the failure of Overend and Gurney.

Blanketeers   Lancashire textile workers, mainly handloom weavers, who attempted to march on London in March 1817 to petition the Prince Regent and highlight distress resulting from post-war economic crises. The military arrested 200, and stopped the march.

Bloemfontein convention   The 1854 Convention under which Britain abolished the Orange River Convention and recognised the independence of the Orange Free State.

Bloody Sunday   See Trafalgar Square Riots, p. 309.

Boers   Literally 'farmers' (Afrikaans). Descendants of Dutch settlers in South Africa. Two wars were fought between British and Boers in 1881 and 1899–1902, known as First and Second Boer Wars.

Boxers   Young Chinese provoked in 1900 to engage in anti-foreign violence by the expansion of European commerce and territorial acquisitions in China by Germany, Russia and Britain. Major Boxer disturbances occurred in Peking and the provinces of Shensi and Manchuria.

boycott   Organised refusal to buy goods and services. Originated by Parnell during Irish land agitation of 1880, when peasants effectively ostracised an estate manager, Captain C.C. Boycott, to protest against land evictions.

Captain Swing   The signature put on threatening letters sent to farmers and magistrates during the so-called 'Swing' riots. The riots started with the destruction of threshing machines in Kent in 1830 and quickly spread.

The most affected counties in the 'Swing' riots were the most rural areas of southern England where wages were lowest and unemployment highest. The rioters smashed threshing machines, fired ricks, and demanded higher wages and an end to tithes. 19 were hanged and over 500 transported before the riots were finally put down.

Catholic Emancipation   See p. 248.

Cato Street Conspiracy   The name of the plot organised by Arthur Thistlewood (1770–1820) and his fellow conspirators to assassinate the Tory Cabinet in February 1820. Most of the conspirators were arrested at their Cato Street base after the plot had been infiltrated by a government agent. Five of the leaders were hanged and five transported.

Charge of the Light Brigade   Famous incident during the Crimean War at the Battle of Balaklava, 25 Oct. 1854. Lord Raglan (see p. 279) ordered his cavalry commander Lord Lucan to retrieve Turkish guns captured by Russians. Misunderstanding the order, Lucan deployed the Light Brigade in a frontal attack on the main Russian position, and a third of the Brigade were killed or wounded in its capture.

Chartist   One who advocated fulfilment of the People's Charter of 1838, the cardinal aims of which were universal male suffrage, annual parliaments, vote by ballot, payment for MPs, equal electoral districts, and abolition of property qualifications for MPs. From 1839 to 1848 the Chartists engaged in petitioning Parliament and demonstrations. The entire phase of activity is referred to as Chartism. (See p. 154.)

Christian Socialism   A movement led by Ludlow and Kingsley with the object of fostering the social principles of the Gospels. (See p. 181.)

Clan na Gael (Gaelic 'Family of Gael')   Irish revolutionary organisation founded among immigrants to the US by Jerome Collins in 1867. In 1876 the organisation mounted a successful mission to rescue six Fenian prisoners from transportation to Australia and in the following year affiliated to the Irish Republican Brotherhood. Clan na Gael activists were instrumental in securing weapons from Germany for the 1916 Easter Rising.

Coffin ships   The overcrowded and insanitary vessels used to carry Irish emigrants across the Atlantic during the 1845–49 famine. In 1847 alone, over 17,000 people died from cholera and typhoid as a result of conditions on the ships.

Combination Acts   The legislation of 1799 and 1800 which prohibited workers 'combining' in trade unions. For details, see p. 151.

Condition of England question   Phrase used to describe concern for social conditions in the manufacturing districts in the 1830s and 1840s and fears of social unrest, reflected in the novels of Charles Dickens, Mrs Gaskell and Benjamin Disraeli and major parliamentary enquiries into social problems such as child and female labour.

confessional state   Phrase used to describe Britain in the period prior to 1832 when support for the Anglican Church and opposition to Catholic Emancipation (see p. 248) and full toleration for dissenters are seen as the ideological foundations of an English Ancien Régime. Largely developed in Professor J.C.D. Clark's *English Society, 1688–1832* (1985) it elevates the ideological character of pre-1832 politics.

Corn Laws   Used to describe Corn Law of 1815, which prevented the import of foreign grain until the domestic price reached 80s per quarter, and its successor of 1828 which introduced a sliding scale of tariffs. The abolition of the Corn Laws in 1846, following the Irish famine of 1845, was to divide the Tory party for a generation. For a detailed discussion, see p. 198.

Cotton famine   Term current in the early 1860s to describe the distress caused in Lancashire in 1862 following the cessation of cotton shipments from America during the Civil War, by which thousands of cotton workers were made redundant.

Dark Continent   Victorian term for the continent of Africa, partly because it was not fully explored until late in the nineteenth century, partly because of the perceived 'uncivilised' condition of the people.

disestablishment   Process of separation of church and state, implying end of state support for the Anglican Church and of any attempt by the state to enforce religious duties or discriminate in its favour. Usually adopted in relation to the moves to disestablish the Anglican Church in Ireland, completed in 1871, and later moves to disestablish the Anglican Church in Wales, passed in 1914 and coming into effect after the First World War.

Don Pacifico affair   David Pacifico was a Portuguese Jew, but British citizen. Palmerston used an incident over his property in Athens to gain great popularity.

durbar   Hindustani word signifying ceremonial court of audience. Used to refer to formal assemblies such as that on the occasion of Queen Victoria's proclamation as Empress of India (1876), and the famous Delhi Durbar of December 1911 when King George V announced restitution of Bengal as united province.

Durham report   Report of 1839, produced by Lord Durham as Governor-General of Canada, which recommended the union of Upper and Lower Canada and the introduction of responsible government. It was a landmark in the development of modern Canada.

Eastern Question   Nineteenth-century term, reflecting concern about the future of the Balkan territories belonging to the declining Ottoman Empire. Britain was fearful of the expansion of Russian influence over the Balkans, Constantinople, the Dardanelles and the eastern Mediterranean and the consequent threat to the route to India. Britain often supported Turkey against Russian 'aggression' and sought arbitration of the disputes in the area.

Emancipation   See Catholic Emancipation, p. 248.

Entente Cordiale   French: 'cordial understanding'. Description of relationship between Britain and France following Anglo-French *entente* reached in 1904, and continuing in spite of foreign policy differences until 1940.

Evangelicals   Group within Church of England who in the late eighteenth century sought to combat clerical apathy, while accepting Anglican discipline. Emphasised importance of moral earnestness and proclaimed salvation by faith. They gave rise to important philanthropic movements in the nineteenth century.

Fabian   Follower of a largely middle-class group established in Jan. 1884 to spread socialist ideas in Britain. The society played an important role in founding the Labour Party. Among its early leaders were Graham Wallas, G.B. Shaw, Sidney and Beatrice Webb. *Fabian Essays in Socialism* in 1889, edited by Shaw, displayed what became the distinctive Fabian emphasis on gradualism. During the 1890s the characteristic policy was one of 'permeating' the major parties with socialist ideas, but in the years just before and during World War I the Society drew closer to the Labour Party.

Factory Acts   A series of Acts providing for the inspection and regulation of factories. For details, see p. 119.

Famine, the See Potato Famine, p. 303.

Fashoda Incident Crisis in Anglo-French relations as a result of rival claims to Sudan. A French detachment under Colonel Marchand had marched to the town on the Upper Nile from French West Africa, reaching it in July 1898, just before the arrival of General Kitchener, fresh from his defeat of the Mahdi's forces at Omdurman, with a large Anglo-Egyptian army. France's claim to the area by right of prior conquest was hotly disputed by Britain who wished to retain control of the Nile Valley. A 'war scare' was fanned in both countries by the popular press, but France's distraction by the Dreyfus affair and lack of support from Russia forced her to back down. Marchand withdrew from Fashoda in November 1898 and France agreed in March 1899 to renounce all claims to the Nile Valley. Now known as Kodok.

Fenians Supporters of an Irish revolutionary movement which was formed in the USA in 1858 and spread to Ireland in 1865. Fenian disturbances in Chester (February 1867) and bomb attacks on Clerkenwell prison and other places helped make Gladstone aware of the urgency of the Irish problem.

Force, physical and moral Phrases used in the nineteenth century to describe methods of popular agitation; moral force denoting peaceful agitation, physical force, resorting to arms.

Fourth Party See under Randolph Churchill, p. 263.

Free trade See *laissez-faire*.

Gaelic League Organisation established in Ireland in 1893 by Douglas Hyde (1863–1947, first President of Ireland) and Eoin MacNeill (1867–1945) to encourage the spread of the Irish language to counter English cultural influence. By 1902, the League had at least 400 branches and took on an increasingly radical stance. In 1915 Padraic Pearse, who was executed following the 1916 Easter Rising, became president of the League.

general unions Phase of trade union activity in the 1830s marked by attempts to achieve a 'General Union of Trades', under the influence of the ideas of Robert Owen (see p. 158) and the leader of the Lancashire cotton spinners, John Doherty. Early attempts in 1810, 1818 and 1829 culminated in the formation of the Grand National Consolidated Trades' Union of Great Britain and Ireland in Feb. 1834. Achieving a maximum of 50,000 members drawn mainly from London and Lancashire, the scheme collapsed after a series of strikes in spring and summer 1834.

Grand Old Man (GOM)   Popular nickname of Gladstone, through his towering position in Victorian political life.

Great Depression   Phrase applied to the period of low agricultural prices, slower industrial growth and cyclical economic depressions in the late nineteenth century, contrasting with the rapid and almost continuous expansion of the mid-Victorian period. Some historians doubt the validity of the term for a period which continued to show overall growth in the economy.

Great Exhibition   The 1851 exhibition of arts and manufactures held in Hyde Park, which attracted six million visitors. The idea of the Prince Consort, it seemed to demonstrate the confidence and technological achievement of Victorian Britain.

Great Trek   The mass emigration of Boer settlers from Cape Colony in 1836 and 1837, caused primarily by the inadequate compensation received when Britain emancipated the black slaves. It resulted in the first colonisation of southern Africa beyond the Orange River. Other Boers crossed the Drakensberg into Natal and established a republic there in 1838. A second trek occurred in 1844–45 when Boer farmers left the area between the Orange River and the Vaal and founded the South African Republic, in order to avoid British rule established in 1848 in the Orange River Sovereignty.

Gunboat diplomacy   Conduct of foreign policy by use of naval power, usually associated with Palmerston's (q.v.) time as a jingoistic Foreign Secretary.

Hansard   Colloquial term for official report of debates in Houses of Parliament. From 1812 Hansard family published parliamentary debates, and even after the family sold the undertaking it continued to be known as Hansard.

High Church   Section within the Church of England upholding belief in sacraments and ritual, the authority of the church hierarchy, and the close relationship between church and state. In the seventeenth and early eighteenth centuries it was associated with political support for the monarch as head of church and state, and later with opposition to the removal of civil disabilities on dissenters and Roman Catholics and to disestablishment (*q.v.*). In the nineteenth century, the 'Anglo-Catholic' movement represented High Churchmen nearest to Roman Catholic doctrine and liturgy.

High farming   Period of great agricultural prosperity in the interval between the repeal of the Corn Laws and the flood of cheap agricultural produce from abroad which began in the 1870s, characterised by heavy investment in new techniques, including the large-scale application of machinery.

high politics school   View of politics which places emphasis upon the relationships between the top politicians as the crucial determinants of policy-making and action.

Highland clearances   Term for the removal of the crofters (tenants of small farms) in the Scottish Highlands during the Victorian period. The landowners could make higher returns from large-scale sheep farming. Forcible eviction of crofters took place, causing widespread anger. Some crofters turned to violence in the 1880s in the 'Crofters' War'. They finally gained security of tenure in 1886.

Home Rule   Policy of granting partial self-government to Ireland, including the re-creation of an Irish parliament. Home Rule Bills were introduced in 1886, 1893 and 1914.

Hungry Forties   The 1840s, so described not only because of famine in Ireland, 1845–49, but because of depression and unemployment in Britain which provoked widespread discontent, including the Chartist and Anti-Corn Law movements. Widespread concern with the 'Condition of England' question (see p. 292) was reflected in contemporary literature.

hustings   Booths where votes were cast at parliamentary elections, or platforms from which candidates spoke. Synonymous with electioneering and political campaigns.

Indian Mutiny   See p. 224.

International   The First International Workingmen's Association was formed by Marx in London in 1864. It aimed to co-ordinate efforts by the working classes in different countries to establish socialism. Disputes between the anarchists and Marxists culminated in the final break between Marx and Bakunin in 1872. The First International moved its headquarters to New York. It was finally dissolved in 1876.

International Co-operative Alliance   See p. 166.

Invincibles   An Irish secret society, based in the USA, notorious for the murders in May 1882 of the Chief Secretary for Ireland, Lord Frederick

Cavendish, and the Under Secretary, T.H. Burke, while they were walking in Phoenix Park in Dublin. Those immediately involved in the crime were brought to trial, but the leaders of the society, including Tynan, the 'Number 1', were never relinquished to British justice.

Irish question Term for the vexed and seemingly insoluable problem of Britain's relationship with Ireland, a problem exacerbated by Protestant immigration into Ulster in the seventeenth century. There were religious aspects of the problem (most of Ireland was Roman Catholic), economic aspects (the problems of Irish agriculture and especially land ownership) but above all political. Attempts by Liberal governments to grant Home Rule were thwarted in 1886, 1892 and 1914. (See p. 253.)

Irvingites Name given to members of the Catholic Apostolic Church founded in 1832 by a Scottish minister, Edward Irving (1792–1834) and the MP Henry Drummond (1786–1860). The sect's main tenet was the imminence of Christ's Second Coming. By the end of the nineteenth century it had little influence.

Jameson raid The ill-fated expedition against the Transvaal in January 1896 organised by the forces of the British South Africa Company which was supposed to come to the assistance of the Uitlanders. Jameson led a detachment of British South Africa Police into the Transvaal, but they were quickly defeated and arrested by a force of Boer commandos. The Kaiser's subsequent telegram of congratulation to Kruger greatly soured Anglo-German relations.

Jewel in the Crown India, following the proclamation of Queen Victoria as Empress of India on 1 Jan. 1877. So called because it was the most valuable of Britain's colonial possessions.

Jingoes Party in England in favour of the Russo-Turkish war of 1877–78. The term was derived from a music-hall song whose chorus began 'We don't want to fight, but by jingo if we do, we've got the ships, we've got the men, we've got the money too.' In the last decade of the nineteenth century the term jingoism came to be applied to any aggressive expression of nationalism or imperialism.

Kilmainham treaty The agreement between Parnell and Gladstone in 1882 (see p. 252).

Labour Church movement The movement was started by John Trevor, a former Unitarian minister who believed that in a spiritually exhausted age the Labour movement provided the focus for a non-sectarian replacement of organised religion. The first Labour Church was established in Manchester in 1891, and during the early 1890s scores of such churches were established, particularly in the Midlands and North of England. A Labour Church Union was established in 1893. During the late 1890s the movement declined. Trevor left the Union in 1898, and by the eve of World War I the movement had all but disappeared. The similar Socialist Sunday School movement opened its first branch in Battersea in 1892. The movement aimed to provide, through a socialist education, an ethical alternative to Christianity for young people, and attempted to inculcate a morality which would make socialism more than just a series of administrative changes.

Labourism   Phase of working-class activity after 1850 characterised by pursuit of limited objectives of wage bargaining and strengthening trade union organisation. More generally, a phrase used to characterise the more cautious traditions of the Labour movement.

laissez-faire   Doctrine of non-interference of state in economic affairs derived from teachings of classical political economists like Adam Smith, Malthus and Ricardo, and from Benthamite tradition (see Utilitarianism p. 311). It was a fundamental tenet of British liberalism for most of the nineteenth century.

Liberal Toryism   Reforming Toryism associated with the later years of Lord Liverpool's administration (see pp. 3–5) and his leading ministers, Canning, Peel and Huskisson (see pp. 261, 278, 271 respectively).

Lib-Lab   Term applied to those representatives of labour, usually trade unionists, who were returned to Parliament as Liberal MPs before the foundation of the Independent Labour Party. In the 1870s and 1880s opposition to them grew among the representatives of labour, partly because the Liberal Party organisation grew more rigid and local associations, dominated by the middle classes, became reluctant to adopt working-class candidates. Furthermore, many of the working class were disillusioned by the attitude of Gladstone and other Liberal leaders during the 1880s and 1890s to questions of social reform such as the 8-hour day. In 1893, the Independent Labour Party was founded and, following changes in trade union law, the unions largely agreed to the formation of a Labour Representation Committee in 1900, which became the Labour Party in 1906 (see p. 161). But it was not until 1909 that the bulk of the remaining Lib-Lab MPs, the nominees of the miners' unions, joined the Labour Party. The miners' reluctance to renounce 'Lib-Labism' stemmed from their power, through the number of votes they commanded, to force candidates of their choice on the Liberals in mining areas.

Little Englander   In the 1890s and early twentieth century, one who opposed expansion of the British Empire and the establishment of a federal system of imperial rule, based on close economic and commercial ties with the colonies, arguing that Britain should rather address herself to social reform and to the industrial development of the domestic sector.

Local Government Acts   See pp. 146–7.

local option   A popular Nonconformist and Liberal demand whereby the majority of ratepayers in each locality would have the power to determine the number of outlets allowed to sell alcoholic drink. A similar system could be found in various states of the USA.

Luddism   Phase of widespread machine-breaking in the North and Midland counties of England between 1811 and 1817. Machine-breaking was said to be carried out on the orders of a mythical 'Ned Ludd' or 'General Ludd'. Machine-breaking began in Nottinghamshire as part of the campaign of the framework-knitters for greater regulation of their trade and higher wages for work in a period of high prices and unemployment. Disturbances spread to Yorkshire where shearing-frames were destroyed by the wool-croppers and to Lancashire where power looms were attacked. The main disturbances were over by the end of 1812 when some 10,000 troops were deployed in the manufacturing districts.

Mafeking, relief of   On 13 Oct. 1899 5,000 Boer troops attacked the British garrison at Mafeking. With only 700 soldiers and 600 armed civilians Colonel Baden-Powell resisted the assault, forcing the Boers to lay siege to the town. The outnumbered British resisted for 217 days until the siege was lifted on 17 May 1900 by a column of British cavalry. The Boers suffered 1,000 casualties to 273 British. The 'relief of Mafeking' became the most celebrated event of the Boer War in Britain.

Mahdi   Title claimed by the nationalist Islamic leader in the Sudan, Mohammed Ahmed, who headed the rising in eastern Sudan in 1881 and captured Khartoum.

Manchester school   Political and economic school of thought which originated in the meetings of the Manchester Chamber of Commerce (founded 1820). Their leaders included Cobden and Bright and their attitudes dominated the Liberal Party in the mid-nineteenth century. Many adherents of their philosophy of free trade, free competition and freedom of contract were businessmen, rather than economic theorists or politicians. They advocated an individualistic policy, were usually isolationist regarding foreign affairs and tended towards pacifism. See also *laissez-faire*.

Marxist history   Interpretation of history which follows the ideas of Karl Marx (1818–83) and Friedrich Engels (1820–95) and is implied by their writings. Although many variations of Marxist theory exist, they follow broadly the view of Marx and Engels that 'all history is the history of class struggle', giving primacy to the economic forces which mould society and determine its divisions into bourgeoisie (*q.v.*) and proletariat (*q.v.*). This 'materialist conception of history' assumes inevitable progression from feudalism, through capitalism, to communism.

Maynooth grant   Grant to the Roman Catholic College of Maynooth in Ireland by Peel's administration in 1846. It aroused considerable Protestant opposition.

Midlothian campaign   The famous electoral campaign undertaken by Gladstone beginning in November 1879.

Model unionism   See 'New Model' unionism, p. 301.

Molly Maguires   Irish agrarian society, formed in 1843, in opposition to distraint for rent. Named after Cornelius Maguire (a leader of the 1641 Irish Rebellion). The 'Molly' was added because members frequently disguised themselves in women's clothes.

Moonlighters   In Ireland, agrarian secret society, similar in constitution and methods to an earlier secret society, the Whiteboys, and guilty of many acts of violence in 1881.

Muscular Christianity   A derogatory description of those in favour of Christian Socialism (see p. 181).

Nanking, treaty of   See under Opium Wars, p. 222.

navvies   Popular term for the many thousands of manual labourers (mainly Irish) who worked to build the railways.

Newcastle programme   The political platform of 1892 based on resolutions passed at the meeting of the National Liberal Federation at Newcastle in Oct. 1891. The main points of the platform were abolition of the House of Lords, Home Rule, disestablishment of the Church in Wales, taxation of ground values and one man one vote.

new imperialism   Term applied to the renewed phase of imperial expansion in the latter part of the nineteenth century, to distinguish it from the eighteenth-century colonial expansion.

new Liberalism   Term applied to the philosophy and phase of progressive social reform undertaken by Liberal governments after 1908 and associated with Lloyd George and Winston Churchill, distinguished from traditional Liberalism by the greater readiness to countenance state intervention and increased government spending.

'New Model' unionism   Phase of trade union organisation in the mid-Victorian period marked by the formation of the Amalgamated Society of Engineers in 1851. It set a pattern of high fees and exclusiveness, national organisation and restriction to skilled craft workers. The 'New Model' unions pursued moderate, craft interests in contrast to the more ambitious aims of the General Unions (see p. 294) and had greater permanence than the purely local trade societies.

New Poor Law   Method of poor relief established in 1834 largely as a reaction against the Speenhamland system (see p. 120).

new unionism   A dramatic upsurge in unionisation among the unskilled in 1889–92, with a socialist-led London dock strike in the summer of 1889 at its centre. In 1890 the new unions – 'new' because unlike their predecessors they levied low dues, and depended for success on aggressive tactics – were 320,000 strong, but by 1896 this had fallen to 80,000.

'Nomination' boroughs   See 'Pocket' boroughs.

no popery agitation   Term for the anti-Catholic ferment in 1851 when the Pope created Cardinal Wiseman Archbishop of Westminster. In order to appease the Protestant opposition an Ecclesiastical Titles Bill was introduced (which proved ineffective).

Old Corruption   Term used to describe the unreformed political and ecclesiastical system before the 1832 Reform Act and the beginning of reform in the Church of England, characterised by patronage and influence.

'open door' policy   Term describing principle of equal trading opportunities for great powers in parts of Africa, as adopted by the Berlin Conference, 1884–85; a policy later used by the USA towards its involvement in China.

Orange card   Expression first used by the Conservative Lord Randolph Churchill (1849–95) of his use of extreme Protestantism in Ulster to thwart the Irish Home Rule Bill introduced by W.E. Gladstone in 1886. Churchill had decided, he wrote, 'the Orange card would be the one to play'. Irish Liberals were pushed into the Unionist camp, riots were fomented in Ulster, the Bill was defeated and Gladstone's Liberals lost the ensuing general election. The term is more widely used to describe, for example, attempts to divide the Irish (and later Northern Irish) working class on sectarian lines.

Orangemen   Members of the Orange Order, a society formed in Ulster in 1795 to preserve Protestantism in Ireland, named after William III, former Prince of Orange.

Oxford Movement   Group within Church of England from the 1830s seeking to restore the High Church (see p. 295) traditions of the seventeenth century. The movement arose out of anxiety over the implications of Catholic emancipation (see p. 248) and the Parliamentary Reform Act of 1832. It was led by three Fellows of Oriel College, Oxford, and led to a strong Anglo-Catholic revival. Though Keble and Pusey (see pp. 272, 279) remained in the Church of England, Newman (see p. 276) became a Roman Catholic.

Parnellites   Followers of Charles Stewart Parnell (see p. 278), the Irish politician who launched a campaign to secure Home Rule for Ireland. Parnell lost influence in 1890s following involvement in a sensational divorce case.

Pax Britannica   Period of Britain's maritime and diplomatic supremacy (and hence 'peace') in the nineteenth century, associated particularly with Palmerston's periods as Foreign Secretary.

Peelite   Policies associated with Sir Robert Peel (see p. 278) of sound, efficient government dominated by concern for national rather than party interests.

People's Budget   Introduced in 1909 by Liberal Chancellor of the Exchequer Lloyd George, the budget proposed redistributive super-tax and land value duties. Its rejection by the Lords provoked a clash between the Commons and peers over their respective rights, leading to a general election and to the 1911 Parliament Act which reduced the power of the Lords to delay legislation.

People's Charter   Document published in 1838 which gave its name to Chartism. Largely drafted by William Lovett (1800–77), founder in 1836 of the London Working Men's Association, it made six demands: annual parliaments; universal male suffrage; equal electoral districts; voting by ballot; payment of MPs and an end to the property qualification for MPs.

Peterloo 'Massacre'   Name for the break-up of a peaceful reform demonstration in St Peter's Fields, Manchester, on 16 Aug. 1819, when the local magistrates sent in troops to arrest the radical orator, Henry Hunt (see p. 271). Eleven people were killed and over 400 injured. 'Peterloo' was a pun on Waterloo.

Phoenix Park Murders   The Dublin park murders of Lord Frederick Cavendish (who had just been appointed Chief Secretary for Ireland) and his Under-Secretary, Thomas Henry Burke, on 6 May 1882. The murders precipitated widespread revulsion. A Coercion Act was introduced. Five of the 'Invincibles' were subsequently hanged.

Plan of Campaign   A combination of tenants in Ireland who united to refuse to pay rents on those estates where the rent reductions they demanded were not conceded. In April 1888 the Vatican declared the plan unlawful.

'pocket' boroughs   Boroughs directly controlled by a patron, sometimes the government, who could dominate representation and 'nominate' its MPs. (See also 'Rotten' boroughs.)

Potato famine   In 1845 and 1846 three-quarters of the Irish potato crop, the staple diet of the four million population, was destroyed by blight. The disaster was compounded by a European corn harvest failure and British maladministration, causing a million deaths from starvation and the enforced migration of a further million people.

potwalloper   Franchise qualification prior to Reform Act of 1832. In some boroughs, every man who had a family and boiled a pot there qualified for the franchise, if resident for six months, and not in receipt of poor rates. Such voters were considered susceptible to bribery and instructions from borough patrons.

Pretoria Convention   The agreement of 1881 which ended the first Boer War (see p. 225) and gave limited independence to the Transvaal.

Primrose League   Conservative Party organisation founded in 1883 by the Fourth Party as part of their attempt to democratise the party by broadening its base of support and reforming its organisation. The name was chosen because the primrose was the favourite flower of the great Conservative leader, Benjamin Disraeli (1804–81).

Princely States   Expression used to describe the 570 states in British India that remained under the rule of princes rather than under direct colonial government. Following the 1857–58 Indian revolt, the British preserved the privileges of the Indian aristocrats in return for their collaboration. The territories controlled by the princes were annexed by India and Pakistan on independence in 1947.

Protestant Ascendancy   Expression used to describe the Protestant landowning class in eighteenth- and nineteenth-century Ireland which dominated cultural, economic, political and social life. Members of the Ascendancy – who were members of the Church of Ireland – were not exclusively English and viewed with suspicion increasing toleration of Catholicism in England.

Puseyite   Follower of Dr Edward Pusey (1800–82), one of the leaders of the Oxford Movement, so called because its leaders were members of Oxford University. Its adherents sought to reassert the authority of the Anglican Church to counter the spread of 'liberal theology' in the nineteenth century. The movement dated from July 1833 when John Keble preached a sermon criticising a Bill for the suppression of ten Irish bishops. Between 1833 and 1841 Keble, Newman and Hurrell Froude issued a series of pamphlets, *Tracts for the Times*, stating their position. (From the title, adherents also became styled 'Tractarians'). The movement saw the Church of England as threatened by secular power. Emphasis was laid on it as a divine institution and on ritual and the continuity of the Catholic faith. In Tract 90 Newman showed that the 39 Articles could be made to square with Roman doctrine. In Oct. 1845 Newman, followed by many of his supporters, was received into the Roman Catholic Church but Pusey and Keble remained within the Anglican Church.

Quadruple Alliance   Term used to describe the alliance formed in 1813 by Austria, Britain, Prussia and Russia, and renewed in 1815, to prevent the return of Napoleon and preserve European peace. In 1818 France joined, transforming the grouping into the Quintuple Alliance. The Alliance held conferences at Aix-la-Chapelle (1818), Troppau and Laibach (1820–21), and Verona (1822) but Britain's reluctance to accept the right of its members to intervene in the internal affairs of other states to prevent revolution forced its collapse in 1825.

radical   First used to describe the supporters of universal suffrage, annual parliaments and secret ballot. Major Cartwright contrasted 'radical' and 'moderate' parliamentary reform as early as 1776 in *Take Your Choice*, and in 1792 the London Corresponding Society promulgated a 'Plan of Radical Reform'. Proposals for 'radical' reform were taken up by MPs such as Sir Francis Burdett (see p. 261) and popular writers and speakers such as William Cobbett and Henry Hunt (see pp. 264, 271). The campaign for 'radical' reform continued after 1832 in the Chartist movement. In the later nineteenth century the term became associated more broadly with sweeping social and economic reform.

Railway mania   Term for the over-rapid and often speculative building of railways in the 1840s.

Raj   Literally 'rule' or 'sovereignty'. Refers to period of British rule in India.

Rebecca riots   South Wales protests in 1843 against turnpike gates in which rioters dressed in women's clothes, the leader and his followers being known as 'Rebecca and his daughters', an allusion to Genesis 24: 60. Troops and London police imposed order and the riots ended with a government pledge to enquire into the Turnpike Laws.

ribbonism   Agrarian movement in the South and West of Ireland *c*.1869, whose main purpose was to agitate for security of tenure. Its methods, initially innocuous, soon degenerated into terrorism.

Rochdale pioneers   See pp. 164–5.

'rotten' boroughs   Boroughs where, prior to the 1832 Reform Act, the electorate had shrunk almost to nothing. Among the most notorious were Gatton and Old Sarum. They were a source of political influence for borough owners. (See also 'pocket' boroughs.)

Round Table Conference   The series of meetings held in 1887 with the objective of trying to reunite the Liberal Unionists and the Gladstonian Liberals after the events of 1886. The four main participants were Sir George Trevelyan, Joseph Chamberlain, John Morley and William Harcourt. The meetings were inconclusive.

Sand River Convention   The agreement in 1852 under which Britain acknowledged the independence of the Boers beyond the Vaal River in South Africa. The Convention was followed in 1874 by the Bloemfontein Convention in which Britain relinquished authority over the Orange River Sovereignty.

Sheffield disturbances   Also called the Sheffield outrages. The term describes the violence against non-union labour in the Sheffield cutlery industry in 1866–67. The establishment of the Royal Commission on Trade Unionism was a direct response to these events. (See p. 159.)

Six Acts   Repressive legislation passed by Lord Sidmouth (see p. 282) in 1819 in the aftermath of Peterloo (see p. 303), prohibiting meetings of more than 50 people, preventing military drilling, increasing newspaper duties, permitting magistrates to search for arms and seditious writings, and to speed up judicial proceedings.

Social Democratic Federation   Organisation founded in 1881 by H.M. Hyndman as the Democratic Federation. It was reorganised as a clearly socialist organisation in 1883 when it adopted its traditional name. The SDF introduced a distinctive Marxist approach into British politics but never succeeded in becoming a mass movement and was subject throughout its existence to various schisms. Towards the end of 1884 the Socialist League, led by William Morris, broke away, and the early twentieth century saw further splits which led to the formation of the Socialist Labour Party and the Socialist Party of Great Britain. In 1911 the Socialist Democratic Party, as it had become in 1909, provided the major constituent of the British Socialist Party.

Socialist League   Organisation founded in 1884 as a breakaway from the Social Democratic Federation, dominated by H.M. Hyndman. The League, of which William Morris was the leading personality, objected to elements in Hyndman's personal dominance of the SDF and the opportunist politics it pursued. But during its brief existence the League displayed fissiparous tendencies, with elements moving from Marxism towards anarchism. After Morris's break with the League in 1890 he founded the Hammersmith Socialist Society, which survived until 1896. The League itself faded away in the early 1890s.

souperism   Expression used in Ireland during the great famine to describe Catholics who changed their religion in return for food. There were suggestions that Protestant bodies organising relief during the famine of 1845–49 insisted on conversion to the Church of Ireland before providing assistance.

Special men   Term applied to Irish political prisoners in England in the 1880s. Special men were subjected to especially hard treatment. Prominent among them were Thomas Clarke (1858–1916, imprisoned for attempted bombings in 1883), John Daly (1845–1916, imprisoned for possession of dynamite in 1884), and Thomas Gallagher (1851–1925, imprisoned for attempted bombings in 1883). Gallagher became insane as a result of his treatment in prison.

Speenhamland system   See pp. 120–1.

Splendid isolation   Phrase used to describe period of British foreign policy prior to entering the system of alliances in 1902 when a treaty was concluded with Japan.

'standard of living' debate   Debate over the course of living standards during the Industrial Revolution between 'optimists' who see a general real rise in living standards and the 'pessimists' who see a fall. Main protagonists include J.H. Clapham, T.S. Ashton and R.M. Hartwell ('optimists'), and J.L. and B. Hammond, E. Hobsbawm and E.P. Thompson ('pessimists').

Straits question   The issue of rights of passage through the Dardanelles and the Bosphorus which was disputed between the Great Powers and Turkey at several points in the nineteenth and twentieth centuries. Under the 1841 Straits Convention the passage from the Bosphorus to the Dardanelles, which links the Black Sea to the Mediterranean, was placed under international control.

Suffragette   Supporter of Women's Social and Political Union, founded in 1903, and dominated by Emmeline and Christabel Pankhurst. Between 1906 and 1914 it undertook militant action to further the cause of women's enfranchisement. Women over 30 were enfranchised in 1918, and women between 21 and 30 in 1928. (See pp. 128–9.)

Suffragist   Supporter of National Union of Women's Suffrage Societies. Believed in constitutional methods to obtain women's suffrage, and adult suffrage in general. Mrs Millicent Fawcett was the best-known suffragist leader. (See p. 266.)

'Sweated' trades   Domestic trades such as tailoring, hat-making and flower-making where child, female and foreign labour were often grossly underpaid for work in poor conditions. The conditions of 'sweated' workers became a major cause for concern in the late nineteenth and early twentieth centuries, leading to government legislation in 1909, and the Trade Boards Act, which set minimum wages.

Swing riots   See under Captain Swing, pp. 290–1.

Syndicalist   Supporter of principle of ownership and running of industry by workers directly. Syndicalism was influenced by writings of

Proudhon and Sorel, and obtained some following in Britain 1910–14, for which Tom Mann was a spokesman.

Taff Vale In July 1901 the House of Lords granted the Taff Vale Railway Company an injunction against the Amalgamated Society of Railway Servants for damages caused by picketing in an official strike, enabling the company to win £23,000 compensation. The result, seen as an attack on the right to strike, encouraged increased union support for the Labour Representation Committee, the forerunner to the Labour Party, and prompted a Liberal government to give unions immunity from similar actions by the 1906 Trades Disputes Act.

Tamworth Manifesto Name given to a speech made by Sir Robert Peel (1788–1850) in his constituency of Tamworth, Staffordshire in 1834. Peel's speech enunciated many of the new Conservative principles of reform, and signalled his party's shift from a position defending aristocratic and landowning interests to a stance more representative of the rising industrial middle classes.

Tariff Commission Established in 1903 by Joseph Chamberlain. It consisted of a cross-section of businessmen, and had the task of investigating the conditions of British industry and of recommending how tariffs might be used to promote production, discourage unfair competition, and develop imperial trade. W.A.S. Hewins was secretary of the Commission, 1903–17 and chairman, 1920–22.

Tariff Reform League Established in mid-1903 on the initiative of Joseph Chamberlain. Originally intended as a propaganda organisation for Chamberlain's advocacy of Imperial Preference, it became a focal point for protectionist feeling.

'taxes on knowledge' Newspaper and stamp duties were attacked by radicals in the early nineteenth century as 'taxes on knowledge'. The 'unstamped' or 'pauper' press were those publications which avoided or evaded such duties. Stamp duties were abolished in 1855.

temperance movement Movement to restrict or ban the consumption of alcohol. Temperance societies were started as early as the 1820s, soon achieving support from Methodist and other Nonconformist churches. Temperance became a major feature of the Liberal Party's programme in the latter half of the nineteenth century and resulted in Licensing Acts in 1872 and 1902. (See p. 181.)

Ten Hours Act Part of the Factory Act legislation (see p. 119). It came after a prolonged campaign to limit the normal working day for women and children in factories to 10 hours.

'**Three acres and a cow**' Famous phrase used by Liberal politician Jesse Collings in the 1885 election. It was part of his programme that all agricultural labourers should have free allotments of land.

'**Three Fs**' A frequently used political abbreviation for the programme of the Irish Land League in 1880: fixity of tenure, fair rent, free sale.

Tolpuddle Martyrs Name given to the 6 agricultural workers from Tolpuddle in Dorset who formed a union branch in 1834. They were found guilty of taking a seditious oath and were given the maximum sentence of transportation to Australia for 7 years. A widespread public outcry led to their pardon in 1836. They have a place as icons in the history of the trade union movement.

Tory Name which became current in the Exclusion Crisis of the early 1680s for a supporter of hereditary succession, the royal prerogative, divine right and loyalty to the Church of England. After the deposition of James II many became Jacobites, and the taint of Jacobitism excluded them from office for 30 years after 1715. By the end of the eighteenth century, the term was being applied to those who upheld the prerogatives of George III, resisted the removal of disabilities from Dissenters and Roman Catholics, and opposed parliamentary reform. The name 'Tory' was revived by Canning (see p. 261) in the early nineteenth century for the natural party of government which was opposed by the Whigs (see p. 312). In the mid-nineteenth century, the Tories also came to be called the Conservative Party.

Tory democracy Description of policies advocated by Disraeli (see p. 265) and Lord Randolph Churchill (see p. 263), combining maintenance of established institutions with cautious social reform in an attempt to win working-class support for the Conservative Party.

Tractarians Name applied to supporters of the Oxford Movement (see p. 302), following J.H. Newman's *Tracts for the Times*. The revived liturgical ceremonial and the emphasis on the social obligations of the church led to the introduction of religious communities within the Church of England. Many Tractarians became Roman Catholics, including Newman who became a cardinal in 1879.

Trafalgar Square riots A series of disturbances following meetings of the unemployed in Trafalgar Square. After the gatherings were banned by Sir Charles Warren, the Chief Commissioner of Police, violence ensued on Sunday 13 Nov. 1887. The riots petered out after arrests ended the violence.

transportation   Deportation of convicts to overseas penal colonies practised in England until 1868. After the American War of Independence (1775–84) it was decided to transport convicts to Australia, often for minor offences. Transportation to New South Wales ended in 1840, to Tasmania in 1853 and to Western Australia in 1868. (See also p. 144.)

Treaty ports   The ports on the coast of China and on main rivers which were opened to Western influence under the unequal treaties. The first five – Amoy, Canton, Fuzhou, Ningbo and Shanghai – were opened by the 1842 Treaty of Nanking and by the end of the nineteenth century over 50 ports had been established. The advantage of the ports was that they enabled foreigners to trade and establish enterprises free from Chinese taxation.

Trent affair   Incident during the United States civil war. The forcible removal by the US sloop *Jacinto* of two envoys of the southern Confederate states (Mason and Sliddell), who were en route to Europe from the English vessel, the *Trent*. Although they were later released, the incident inflamed opinion on both sides of the Atlantic.

Truck Acts   Acts of 1831 and 1887 prohibiting the payment of wages, either wholly or in part, by goods rather than money.

'Two nations'   Phrase used by Benjamin Disraeli (see p. 265) to describe the polarisation of early Victorian society into rich and poor. In his novel *Sybil*, of 1845, he wrote of 'two nations: between whom there is no intercourse and no sympathy; who are ignorant of each other's habits, thoughts and feelings, as if they were dwellers in different zones, or inhabitants of different planets . . .' A powerful strain in Conservative philosophy since Disraeli has emphasised its commitment to 'one nation Toryism' by stressing the need to better the condition of the people as a whole and prevent the emergence of a divided society. As well as Disraeli, Conservative leaders such as Baldwin, Macmillan and Heath were seen as operating within this tradition.

Ultra-Tories   Section of the Tory Party active from the 1820s through to the 1850s which opposed Catholic emancipation (see p. 248) and supported the Corn Laws (see p. 198). Their opposition contributed to the downfall of the Tory government in 1830, precipitating the Reform Crisis of 1830–32, and they subsequently opposed Peel over the Maynooth grant in 1845 and voted against repeal of the Corn Laws in 1846.

'Unauthorised programme'   Radical programme adopted by Joseph Chamberlain (see p. 262) during the 1885 election campaign which called for free education, housing reform and a programme of small-holdings to relieve unemployment. Although Chamberlain campaigned as a Liberal the programme was not official party policy.

Unionist Supporter of the constitutional union between Britain and Ireland, dating from the Act of Union of 1800, and by implication an opponent of Home Rule or Irish independence. In 1886 used by Lord Randolph Churchill (see p. 263) to describe opponents in Ireland and Britain of attempts to include Ulster in Home Rule proposals. In 1912, the Conservative Party adopted the title Conservative and Unionist Party when it formally absorbed those Liberals opposed to Home Rule.

Unitarianism Religious movement, whose members believe in the single person of God. They were excluded from the Toleration Act of 1689 and from the Dissenters' conference at Salter's Hall, London in 1719. From 1812 they were legally tolerated, but attempts were made to turn them out of their chapels on the grounds that their preachers did not hold the same views as the founders of the endowments. This conflict ended with the 1845 Dissenting Chapels Act. In 1825 the British and Foreign Unitarian Association was founded though it issued no authoritative confession of faith.

Utilitarianism School of moral philosophy in the nineteenth century whose main proponents were James Mill, John Stuart Mill and Jeremy Bentham. The utilitarians were a strong intellectual force for reform in the first half of the nineteenth century and their doctrines helped shape the Liberal Party. Theirs was one of the strands of thought represented in demands for *laissez-faire*. Bentham's theory was based on the principle that the greatest happiness of the greatest number is the criterion of the highest good. Mill (*Utilitarianism*, 1861) suggested rather that the social consequences of an act be taken as the criterion of good and also that intellectual pleasures rank higher than sensory ones.

Venezuela boundary dispute In January 1895, Venezuelan troops crossed the Cuyuni river into British Guiana, and hoisted the Venezuelan flag in territory which had been occupied by Britain for several years. The ensuing Anglo-Venezuelan dispute caused a crisis in relations with America (the USA forcing Britain to go to arbitration before the dispute was finally settled in 1899).

Vereeniging Location of the conference of Boer leaders in May 1902 which agreed to accept the terms of surrender in the Boer War (see p. 226).

Waitangi   Name of the treaty of 1840 by which the Maoris ceded sovereignty over New Zealand to Britain.

Webster-Ashburton Treaty   The Anglo-American agreement of 1842 establishing the frontier between Canada and the northeastern United States.

Whig   Parliamentary party which emerged in the late seventeenth century, dominated British politics in the first half of the eighteenth century and evolved into the Liberal Party in the middle of the nineteenth century. Whigs were defenders of parliamentary government, ministerial responsibility and Protestantism. The 'Glorious Revolution' of 1688–89 was regarded as a triumph of Whig principles and the Whigs monopolised power following the Hanoverian succession in 1714. In the later eighteenth century they fell from favour under George III and became associated with religious toleration, economic reform and opposition to the revival of monarchical authority. Divided by the French Revolution, they became supporters of moderate parliamentary reform in the 1820s and passed the Reform Act of 1832. The Liberal Party was formed in the mid-nineteenth century out of a fusion of Whigs, radicals and Peelites. More generally, the term has been used to refer to a paternalist, but moderately reforming, approach to politics.

Whig history   Interpretation of history as a process of improvement from earliest times to the present, and involving viewing the past from contemporary moral assumptions. Thomas Macaulay (1800–59) and Lord Acton (1834–1902) are considered principal exponents of the Whig interpretation of history.

white rajahs   Name given to the Brooke dynasty who effectively ruled the territory of Sarawak (in present-day Malaysia).

Who? Who? ministry   Nickname given to the administration formed by Lord Derby in 1852. Many of the Cabinet were new to high office. Apparently the very deaf Duke of Wellington would ask 'Who?' after each unfamiliar name.

Women's Labour League   Founded in 1906 as an organisation of women to work for independent Labour representation in connection with the Labour Party, and to obtain direct representation of women in Parliament and on local authorities. Margaret MacDonald was a prime instigator of the League, and other women involved included Mary Middleton, Dr Marion Phillips and Katherine Bruce Glasier.

Young England   Movement led by younger Tories including Disraeli (see p. 265) in the late 1830s and 1840s in opposition to Peel's reforming tendencies; sometimes known as 'Throne and Altar' conservatism from its professed attachment to the monarchy and the established church. Other members included George Smythe (1818–57) and Lord John Manners (1818–1906).

Young Ireland   Predominantly middle class and intellectual Irish nationalist movement founded in 1842 but which attracted less moderate supporters during the famine of 1845–49. Under pressure of these members' demands for action, Young Ireland split in 1847, leading to the formation of the Irish Confederation which mounted a badly organised insurrection under William Smith O'Brien (1803–64) in 1848. In the wake of the rising's defeat, Young Ireland leaders were arrested or fled.

Young Ulster   A secret organisation formed by Frederick Crawford (1861–1952) in 1892 to oppose Home Rule for Ireland. Ownership of a weapon and a hundred rounds of ammunition was a condition of membership. After a brief existence, Young Ulster dissolved itself into larger Unionist organisations. Crawford went on to become a founder member of the Ulster Volunteer Force (UVF) in 1913.

SECTION SEVEN

Topic bibliography

Topic bibliography

Topics

1. Lord Liverpool's administration, 1812–27
2. Radicalism and popular protest, 1815–32
3. The Reform Act crisis, 1832
4. Peel and the Corn Laws
5. The Chartist movement
6. Ireland 1815–68: Emancipation and famine
7. The movement for social reform
8. The development of early trade unionism
9. British foreign policy, 1815–84
10. British colonial policy, 1815–84
11. Women and society in the Victorian era
12. Religion and society
13. Gladstone and Liberalism
14. Disraelian Conservatism
15. Irish nationalism and the Home Rule crisis
16. The new imperialism
17. The Conservative ascendancy, 1886–1905
18. The rise of Labour
19. Edwardian Liberalism
20. The Suffragette crisis
21. Britain and the origins of the First World War

List of abbreviations

AgH	Agricultural History
AmHR	American Historical Review
BIHR	Bulletin of the Institute of Historical Research
CHJ	Cambridge Historical Journal
E	Economica
EH	Economic History
EconHR	Economic History Review
EHR	English Historical Review
H	History
HJ	Historical Journal

HT	History Today
HW	History Workshop
IHS	Irish Historical Studies
IRSH	International Review of Social History
JBS	Journal of British Studies
JEccIH	Journal of Ecclesiastical History
JEconH	Journal of Economic History
JHI	Journal of the History of Ideas
JMH	Journal of Modern History
LHSB	Labour History Society Bulletin
NH	Northern History
OH	Oral History
PH	Parliamentary History
PP	Past and Present
SH	Social History
SHR	Southern History Review
THAS	Transactions of the Hunter Archaeological Society
TRHS	Transactions of the Royal Historical Society
VS	Victorian Studies
WHR	Welsh History Review

Introductory note

This bibliography is arranged in rough chronological order and is intended to represent a fair selection of the major topics in British history for the period 1815–1914. The reading is deliberately greater than would be required for an average essay, but does reflect the wealth of bibliographical material now available for most of these subjects and allows a degree of specialisation on particular aspects of a topic. Similarly, the article literature mentioned, while not an exhaustive list, is intended as guide to some of the most important material from which a selection can be made according to preference.

Background texts

Those seeking an introduction to the period are advised to consult the various general texts that are available. The nineteenth century is now served by a good range of modern texts, including E. Evans, *The Forging of the Modern State: Early Industrial Britain, 1783–1870* (2nd edn, 1995); N. Gash, *Aristocracy and People, 1815–65* (1980); R. Shannon, *The Crisis of Imperialism 1865–1915* (1974); D. Read, *The Age of Urban Democracy: England, 1868–1914* (revised edn, 1994); E.J. Feuchtwanger, *Democracy and Empire: Britain, 1865–1914* (1985); and M.J. Bentley, *Politics without Democracy*

(1984). A number of texts carry the story through from the nineteenth century into the twentieth: M. Pugh, *The Making of Modern British Politics, 1867–1939* (1986) and his *State and Society: British Political and Social History, 1870–1992* (1994) and K. Robbins, *The Eclipse of a Great Power, Modern Britain, 1870–1992* (2nd edn, 1994). For those seeking works on economic history, C.H. Lee, *The British Economy since 1700; A Macroeconomic Perspective* (1986); and P. Mathias, *The First Industrial Nation: An Economic History of Britain, 1700–1914* (1969) are helpful. One-volume social histories dealing with this period are E. Royle, *Modern Britain: A Social History, 1750–1985* (1987) and F. Bedarida, *A Social History of England, 1851–1975* (trans. 1976). A helpful volume in the Pelican Social History of Britain is J. Harris, *Private Lives, Public Spirit: A Social History of Britain, 1870–1914* (1993). F.M.L. Thompson (ed.), *The Cambridge Social History of Britain, 1750–1950* 3 vols. (1990) is a major contribution.

Scotland and Wales are now better served than they were. For the former see the two volumes by T.C. Smout, *A History of the Scottish People, 1560–1830* (1969) and *A Century of the Scottish People, 1830–1950* (1986). A good introduction can be found in S. and O. Checkland, *Industry and Ethos: Scotland, 1832–1914* (1984). Wales has been well served by G.A. Williams, *When Was Wales? A History of the Welsh* (1985); K.O. Morgan, *Rebirth of a Nation: Wales, 1880–1980* (1982); G.E. Jones, *Modern Wales: A Concise History of Modern Wales, 1485–1979* (1984) and P. Jenkins, *A History of Modern Wales, 1536–1990* (1992).

For Ireland, see K. Theodore Hoppen, *Ireland since 1800* (2nd edn, 1998); R.F. Foster, *Modern Ireland, 1600–1972* (1988); F.S.L. Lyons, *Ireland since the Famine* (1973); and A. O'Day and J. Stevenson, *Irish Historical Documents since 1800* (1992).

1. Lord Liverpool's administration, 1812–27

Ministerial politics are best considered in N. Gash, *Aristocracy and People* (1979) and *Lord Liverpool* (1984). There is detailed treatment of the post-war period in J.E. Cookson, *Lord Liverpool's Administration: the Crucial Years, 1815–1822* (1975). Also of importance are J.C.D. Clark, *English Society, 1688–1832* (1986), ch. 6 and B. Hilton, *Corn, Cash Commerce* (1977) and *The Age of Atonement* (1988), esp ch. 5. For other ministerial figures, see D. Gray, *Spencer Perceval, 1762–1812* (1963); N. Gash, *Mr. Secretary Peel: the Life of Robert Peel to 1830* (1961); P. Ziegler, *Addington, a Life of Henry Addington, First Viscount Sidmouth* (1965); and C.J. Bartlett, *Castlereagh* (1966). The Whigs are discussed in A. Mitchell, *The Whigs in Opposition, 1815–1830* (1967). The principal Whig personalities are discussed in E.A. Smith, *Lord Grey, 1764–1845* (1990); and Earl Fitzwilliam in E.A. Smith, *Whig Principles and Party Politics* (1975). See also J.J. Sack, *The Grenvillites* (1979) and P. Jupp, *Lord Grenville, 1759–1834* (1985).

Among a wealth of useful articles are B. Hilton, 'Lord Liverpool. The art of politics and practice of government', *TRHS* (1988). J. Dinwiddy, 'Luddism and politics in the North', *SH* (1979) is a judicious survey of the upheaval of those years. T.M. Parssinen, 'The revolutionary party in London 1816–20', *BIHR* (1972) shows the genuine revolutionaries at work. For the North, see F.K. Donnelly and J.L. Baxter, 'Sheffield and the English revolutionary tradition, 1791–1820', *IRSH* (1974). Important radical personalities are discussed in J.R. Dinwiddy, 'Sir Francis Burdett and Burdettite Radicalism', *H* (1980) and J.C. Belchem, 'Henry Hunt and the evolution of the mass platform', *EHR* (1978).

2. Radicalism and popular protest, 1815–32

For those seeking sources and documents, G.D.H. Cole and A.W. Filson, *British Working Class Movements: Select Documents, 1789–1875* (1951) has documents on trade union and radical groups. For secondary works, students should consult the later sections of A.D. Harvey, *Britain in the Early Nineteenth Century* (1979). Also of much help are J.W. Derry, *Politics in the Age of Fox, Pitt and Liverpool* (1990), ch. 4 and F. O'Gorman, *Voters, Patrons and Parties: the Unreformed Electorate of Hanoverian England, 1734–1832* (1989), chs 5 and 6. An important appreciation of radicalism is J.R. Dinwiddy, *From Luddism to the First Reform Bill* (1986). See also D.G. Wright, *Popular Radicalism: the Working-class Experience 1780–1800* (1988). On radicalism, see also E.P. Thompson, *The Making of the English Working Class* (2nd edn, 1968), Pt III.

Popular disturbances of the period are discussed in M.I. Thomis, *The Luddites* (1970); A.J. Peacock, *Bread or Blood* (1965); M.I. Thomis and P. Holt, *Threats of Revolution in Britain, 1789–1848* (1977); and J. Stevenson *Popular Disturbances in England, 1700–1832* (1992). D. Read, *Peterloo: The 'Massacre' and its Background* (1958) remains the best account of the famous event and its background. G. Spater, *William Cobbett: the Poor Man's Friend* (1982) supersedes the older life by G.D.H. Cole, but see also J.W. Osborne, *William Cobbett: his Thought and his Times* (1966). For other reformers see J. Belchem, *'Orator' Hunt* (1985), W. Thomas, *The Philosophic Radicals* (1979) and J. Dinwiddy, *Christopher Wyvill and Reform, 1790–1820* (Borthwick Paper No. 39, 1971).

For the rise of public opinion, see D. Read, *The English Provinces, c. 1760–1960* (1964) and *Press and People, 1790–1850* (1960) and R.K. Webb, *The British Working Class Reader, 1790–1848* (1955).

For the 'standard of living' debate, see R.M. Hartwell, 'The rising standard of living in England, 1800–50', *EconHR* (1961); E.J. Hobsbawm, 'The British standard of living, 1790–1850', *EconHR* (1958); and E.J. Hobsbawm and R.M. Hartwell, 'The standard of living during the Industrial Revolution – a discussion', *EconHR* (1963).

3. The Reform Act crisis, 1832

M. Brock, *The Great Reform Act* (1973) is the best modern single-volume study. A broader survey can be found in J. Cannon, *Parliamentary Reform, 1640–1832* (1973); see also J.C.D. Clark, *English Society, 1688–1832* (1986) for a view of the durability of the old order. One of the issues which produced the break-up of the Tory dominance is discussed in G.I.T. Machin, *The Catholic Question in English Politics, 1820 to 1830* (1964), while J.A. Phillips, *The Great Reform Bill in the Boroughs: English Electoral Behaviour, 1818–1841* (1992) examines the Reform Act in relation to electoral developments over the period. The Whig Party is treated in A. Mitchell, *The Whigs in Opposition, 1815–1830* (1967) and the role of Grey in E.A. Smith, *Lord Grey, 1764–1845* (1990). The rise of 'public opinion' is discussed in D. Read, *Press and People, 1790–1850* (1960) and P. Hollis, *The Pauper Press: a Study in Working Class Radicalism in the 1830s* (1970).

On the reform crisis J. Hamburger, *James Mill and the Art of Revolution* (1965) pursues the important argument that the radicals 'worked up' a crisis in order to force through the Bill. This argument is considered in J. Stevenson, *Popular Disturbances in England, 1700–1870* (1979). See also D. Fraser, 'The agitation for parliamentary reform', in J.T. Ward (ed.), *Popular Movements, c. 1830–1850* (1970).

The effects of the Reform Bill on the structure of politics are analysed in N. Gash, *Reaction and Reconstruction in English Politics, 1832–52* (1965). See also G.B.A.M. Finlayson, *England in the Eighteen Thirties: Decade of Reform* (1969) and H.J. Hanham, *The Reformed Electoral System in Great Britain, 1832–1914* (Historical Association Pamphlet, 1968). The impact of the Reform Act on Whig and Liberal politics is discussed in P. Mandler, *Aristocratic Government in the Age of Reform: Whigs and Liberals, 1830–1852* (1990); R. Brent, *Liberal Anglican Politics: Whiggery, Religion and Reform, 1830–1841* (1987); I.D.C. Newbould, *Whiggery and Reform: the Politics of Government* (1990); T.A. Jenkins, *The Liberal Ascendency, 1830–1886* (1994) and his *Parliament, Party and Politics in Victorian Britain* (1996), ch. 2.

There is also a wealth of article material. A. Briggs, 'Middle-class consciousness in English politics, 1780–1846', *PP* (1956); 'Thomas Attwood and the economic background of the Birmingham Political Union', *CHJ* (1947–49); 'The background of the parliamentary reform movement in three English cities, 1830–32', *CHJ* (1950–52) are important. Also relevant are J. Milton-Smith, 'Earl Grey's cabinet and the objects of parliamentary reform', *HJ* (1972); D.C. Moore, 'The other side of reform', *VS* (1961) and 'Concession or cure: the sociological premises of the first Reform Act', *HJ* (1966); G. Rudé, 'English rural and urban disturbances, 1830–31', *PP* (1967); and D.J. Rowe, 'Class and political radicalism in London, 1831–2', *HJ* (1970). For more recent discussions of the reform, see L. Mitchell, 'Foxite politics and the Great Reform Bill', *EHR* (1933); E. Wasson, 'The great Whigs and parliamentary reform, 1809–1830', *JBS* (1985); J. Phillips, 'The many faces of reform. The electorate and the Great Reform Act', *PH* (1932); W. Rubinstein, 'The end of "Old Corruption" in Britain, 1780–1860', *PP* (1983); and J.A. Phillips and C. Wetherell, 'The Great Reform Act of 1832 and the political modernization of England', *AHR* (1995).

4. Peel and the Corn Laws

For one of the most absorbing of topics A. Briggs, *The Age of Improvement, 1783–1867* (1959), ch. 6, is still a good brief introduction to the politics of the 1840s; see also the section in N. Gash, *Aristocracy and People: Britain 1815–1865* (1980). There is a useful discussion in W.H. Chaloner, 'The agitation against the Corn Laws', in J.T. Ward (ed.), *Popular Movements c. 1830–1850* (1970). More detailed studies include N. Gash, *Politics in the Age of Peel* (1953) and *Reaction and Reconstruction in English Politics, 1832–52* (1965). R. Blake, *The Conservative Party from Peel to Thatcher* (1985) has a brief outline, but see R. Stewart, *The Foundation of the Conservative Party, 1830–1867* (1979) for a more detailed study. N. Gash's *Peel* (1976) or his *Sir Robert Peel* (1972) are the standard lives. See also D. Read, *Peel and the Victorians* (1987) and E.J. Evans, *Sir Robert Peel: Statesmanship, Power and Party* (1991). N. McCord, *The Anti-Corn Law League* (1958) is essential on the famous pressure group. D.G. Barnes, *A History of the English Corn Laws* (2nd edn, 1961) analyses the long-term history of the Corn Laws. F.M.L. Thompson, *English Landed Society in the Nineteenth Century* (1963) is valuable on the position of the landed interest. G. Kitson Clark, *The Making of Victorian England* (1962), especially ch. 7, has a masterly analysis of the repercussions of the repeal of the Corn Laws. R. Stewart, *The Politics of Protection: Lord Derby and the Protectionist Party 1841–1852* (1971) discusses one strand of Tory reaction to the Corn Law issue.

There are many useful articles. G. Kitson Clark, 'The repeal of the Corn Laws and the politics of the forties', *EconHR* (1951); B. Kemp, 'Reflections on repeal of the Corn Laws', *VS* (1961–62) and S.S. Fairlie, 'The nineteenth-century Corn Law reconsidered', *EconHR* (1965) are of general relevance. G. Kitson Clark, 'The country gentlemen and the repeal of the Corn Laws', *EHR* (1967) and 'The electorate and the repeal of the Corn Laws', *TRHS* (1951) are also relevant. The party political dimension is discussed in N. Gash, 'Peel and the party system', *TRHS* (1951) and A. Aydelotte, 'The House of Commons in the 1840s', *H* (1954). The reactions of the landed interest are discussed in A. Aydelotte, 'The country gentry and the repeal of the Corn Laws', *EHR* (1967); W.R. Ward, 'West Riding landowners and the Corn Laws', *EHR*

(1966); and D. Spring, 'Earl Fitzwilliam and the repeal of the Corn Laws', *AgH* (1954).

5. The Chartist movement

E. Royle, *Chartism* (2nd edn, 1996) is a useful introduction as is A. Briggs, *Chartism* (1998). J.T. Ward, *Chartism* (1973), D. Jones, *Chartism and the Chartists* (1975) and D. Thompson, *The Chartists* (1986) are also helpful. A. Briggs, *Chartist Studies* (1958) is essential on the regional background and G.D.H. Cole, *Chartist Portraits* (1940) on the leaders.

The social background of the 1840s is discussed in J. Rule, *The Labouring Classes in Early Industrial England, 1750–1850* (1986) and M.I. Thomis, *The Town Labourer in the Industrial Revolution* (1974). D. Bythell, *The Handloom Weavers* (1969) deals with a group prominent in Chartist activity. J. Stevenson, *Popular Disturbances in England, 1700–1870* (1979), ch. 12, discusses the public order side.

The ideological background to Chartism is discussed in D. Thompson, *The Early Chartists* (1971); E.P. Thompson, *The Making of the English Working Class* (2nd edn, 1968), ch. 16; P. Hollis, *The Pauper Press: a Study in Working-class Radicalism of the 1830s* (1970), chs 6 and 7; and G. Stedman Jones, 'Rethinking Chartism', in his *Languages of Class* (1984). See also D. Thompson and J. Epstein (eds), *The Chartist Experience* (1982).

Individual biographies include J. Epstein, *The Lion of Freedom: Feargus O'Connor and the Chartist Movement* (1982); A. Plummer, *Bronterre: a political biography of Bronterre O'Brien* (1971); D. Williams, *John Frost: A Study in Chartism* (1939); and A.R. Schoyen, *The Chartist Challenge: a portrait of George Harney* (1958).

The last phase of Chartism is discussed in J. Saville, *1848: the British State and the Chartist Movement* (1987) and his *Ernest Jones: Chartist* (1952). See also M. Taylor, *The Decline of British Radicalism, 1847–1860* (1955).

For the large and growing literature of regional studies of Chartism, see the bibliography in D.J.V. Jones, *Chartism and the Chartists* (1975), but two important contributions are D.J.V. Jones, *The Last Rising: The Newport Insurrections of 1839* (1985) and D. Goodway, *London Chartism* (1982).

For relevant documents, see G.D.H. Cole and A.W. Filson (eds), *British Working Class Movements, 1789–1870* (1951); D. Thompson (ed.), *The Early Chartists* (1971); P. Hollis (ed.), *Class and Conflict in Nineteenth Century England, 1815–1850* (1973); and F.C. Mather (ed.), *Chartism and Society* (1980).

Important articles include D.J. Rowe, 'The failure of London Chartism', *HJ* (1968); I. Prothero, 'Chartism in London', *PP* (Aug. 1969) and 'London Chartism and the Trades', *EconHR* (May 1971); H. Weisser, 'Chartist internationalism, 1845–8', *HJ* (1971); D.J. Rowe, 'Some aspects of Chartism in the north-east', *IRSH* (1971); and T.R. Tholfsen, 'The Chartist crisis in Birmingham', *IRSH* (1958).

6. Ireland 1815–68: Emancipation and famine

For an excellent recent introduction, see R.F. Foster, *Modern Ireland, 1600–1972* (1988) but the older histories, J.C. Beckett, *The Making of Modern Ireland, 1603–1923* (1969) and F.S.L. Lyons, *Ireland since the Famine* (2nd edn, 1973) still offer reliable accounts. See also D.G. Boyce, *Nationalism in Ireland* (3rd edn, 1995). Two valuable other perspectives are J.E. Lee, *The Modernisation of Irish Society, 1848–1918* (1973) and R. Dudley Edwards, *An Atlas of Irish History* (1973) with invaluable material on political, economic and social questions. There are useful documents in A. O'Day and J. Stevenson, *Irish Historical Documents since 1800* (1992).

The Repeal period can be studied through O. MacDonagh, *O'Connell: the Life of Daniel O'Connell, 1775–1847* (1991 edn); A.D. Macintyre, *The Liberator: Daniel O'Connell and the Irish Party, 1830–1847* (1965); R.B. McDowell, *The Irish Administration, 1801–1914* (1964); K.B. Nowlan, *The Politics of Repeal: a Study in the Relation between Great Britain and Ireland, 1841–50* (1965); G. O'Tuathaigh, *Ireland before the Famine, 1798–1848* (1972) and O. MacDonagh, 'O'Connell and Repeal, 1840–45,' in M. Bentley and J. Stevenson (eds), *High and Low Politics in Modern Britain* (1983). On the land question, see R.D. Collison Black, *Economic Thought and the Irish Question, 1817–1870* (1960). R. Dudley Edwards and T. Desmond Williams (eds), *The Great Famine* (1956) is a more scholarly treatment than C.B. Woodham-Smith, *The Great Hunger* (1962). J. Mokyr, *Why Ireland Starved* (1983) is a difficult but important analysis of the pre-famine Irish economy, while popular unrest in Ireland is examined in M. Beames, *The Whiteboy Movements and Their Control in Pre-Famine Ireland* (1985). For the mid-century, see K. Theodore Hopper, *Elections, Politics and Society in Ireland, 1832–85* (1984).

7. The movement for social reform

D. Englander, *Poverty and Poor Law Reform in Nineteenth Century Britain, 1834–1914* (1998), J.P. Roach, *Social Reform in England, 1780–1880* (1978) and U.R.Q. Henriques, *Before the Welfare State: Social Administration in Early Industrial Britain* (1979) are comprehensive modern studies of the problem. H. Perkin, *The Origins of Modern English Society, 1780–1880* (1969) is relevant, especially ch. 8. Specific reform movements are discussed in J.T. Ward, *The Factory Movement, 1830–1855* (1963); J. Burnett, *A Social History of Housing, 1815–1970* (1979); M.E. Rose, *The English Poor Law, 1870–1930* (1971) and *The Relief of Poverty, 1834–1914* (1972); G.W. Oxley,

Poor Relief in England and Wales, 1601–1834 (1974), D. Fraser (ed.), *The New Poor Law in the Nineteenth Century* (1976); J.J. Tobias, *Crime and Industrial Society in the Nineteenth Century* (1967); C. Emsley, *Crime and Society in England, 1750–1900* (2nd edn, 1996); J. Hurt, *Education in Evolution* (1972); and A.T. Scull, *Museums of Madness: the Social Organisation of Insanity in Nineteenth Century England* (1979).

There is an important local study in E.C. Midwinter, *Social Administration in Lancashire, 1830–1860* (1969) and of the problems which remained to be solved in G. Stedman Jones, *Outcast London: A Study in the Relationship between Classes in Victorian Society* (1971). The role of state intervention is discussed in A.J. Taylor, *Laissez-faire and State Intervention in Nineteenth Century Britain* (1972). For administrative consequences see O. MacDonagh, *Early Victorian Government* (1977) and D. Roberts, *Victorian Origins of the British Welfare State* (1960). The 'social control' theme is discussed in A.P. Donajgrodzki (ed.), *Social Control in Nineteenth Century Britain* (1977) and P. McCanny (ed.), *Popular Education and Socialisation in the Nineteenth Century* (1977). See also D.N. Chester, *The English Administrative System, 1780–1870* (1981); V. Cromwell, *Revolution or Evolution: British Government in the Nineteenth Century* (1977); and J. Prest, *Liberty and Locality: Parliament, Permissive Legislation and Ratepayers' Democracies in the Mid-Nineteenth Century* (1990). There is also an excellent overview by P. Thane, 'Government and Society in England and Wales, 1750–1914', in F.M.L. Thompson (ed.), *The Cambridge Social History of Britain, 1750–1950*, vol. 3 (1990).

There is a large article literature which can be followed from the secondary works. See especially W.O. Aydelotte, 'The Conservative and Radical interpretations of early Victorian social legislation', *VS* (1967) on general issues. On poverty, see U.R.Q. Henriques, 'How cruel was the Victorian Poor Law?', *HJ* (1968); D. Roberts, 'How cruel was the new Poor Law?', *HJ* (1963); M. Blaug, 'The myth of the old Poor Law', *JEconH* (1963) and 'The Poor Law re-examined', *JEconH* (1963). More general issues are discussed in G. Kitson Clark, 'Statesmen in disguise', *HJ* (1959); J. Hart, 'Nineteenth-century social reform: a Tory interpretation of history', *PP* (1965); B. Harrison, 'Philanthropy and the Victorians', *VS* (1966) and 'Religion and recreation in nineteenth century England', *PP* (1967); O. MacDonagh, 'The nineteenth-century revolution in government: a reappraisal', *HJ* (1958–59); V. Cromwell, 'Interpretations of nineteenth-century administrations: an analysis', *VS* (1966); H. Parris, 'The nineteenth century revolution in government: a reappraisal reappraised', *HJ* (1960). Two recent discussions are D. Eastwood, '"Amplifying the Province of the Legislature": the flow of information and the English State in the early nineteenth century', *HR* (1989) and his 'Men, morals and the machinery of social legislation, 1790–1840', *PH* (1994).

8. The development of early trade unionism

H. Pelling, *A History of British Trade Unionism* (new edn, 1987), E.H. Hunt, *British Labour History, 1815–1914* (1981) and K.O. Brown, *The English Labour Movement, 1700–1951* (1982) are broad histories. A highly suggestive interpretation is A. Fox, *History and Heritage: The Social Origins of the British Industrial Relations System* (1985).

The early history of trade unions is discussed in C.R. Dobson, *Masters and Journeymen: a Prehistory of Industrial Relations, 1717–1800* (1980), J. Rule, *The Experience of Labour in Eighteenth-century Industry* (1981), E.P. Thompson, *The Making of the English Working Class* (2nd edn, 1968); and J.L. and B. Hammond, *The Skilled Labourer, 1760–1832* (1919, new edn with introduction by J. Rule, 1980). G.D.H. Cole, *Attempts at General Union, 1818–1834* (1953) and J.F.C. Harrison, *The Early Victorians, 1832–51* (1971), especially chs 2 and 6, are important on the 1830s and 1840s.

Biographies of early trade union leaders include G. Wallas, *The Life of Francis Place, 1771–1854* (5th edn, 1951); R.G. Kirby and A.E. Musson, *The Voice of the People: John Doherty, 1798–1854* (1975); I. Prothero, *Artisans and Politics in Early Nineteenth Century London: John Gast and his Times* (1979).

On the Victorian years, R. Harrison, *Before the Socialists: Studies in Labour and Politics 1861–1881* (1965); D. Kynaston, *King Labour* (1976); A. Briggs, 'Robert Applegarth and the trade unions' in *Victorian People* (1954); K. Burgess, *The Origins of British Industrial Relations: the Nineteenth Century Experience* (1975) and *The Challenge of Labour: Shaping British Society, 1850–1930* (1980).

There are a number of important collections of essays, especially E.J. Hobsbawm (ed.), *Labouring Men* (1964); A. Briggs and J. Saville (eds), *Essays in Labour History*, vol. 1 (2nd edn, 1967); and B. Pimlott and C. Cook (eds), *Trade Unions in British Politics* (1982), chs 1 and 2. For the overlap between formal trade unionism and violence, see M.I. Thomis, *The Luddites* (1970); J. Stevenson, *Popular Disturbances in England, 1700–1870* (1979), chs 11–14; and for Wales, D.J.V. Jones, *Before Rebecca: Popular Protests in Wales, 1793–1835* (1973), chs 3–4.

For particular trades and areas see the bibliography in A.E. Musson, *British Trade Unions, 1800–1875* (1972), to which can be added H. Hikins, *Building the Union* (Merseyside) (1973); E. Ellen, N. McCord, J.F. Clarke and D.J. Rowe, *The North-East Engineers' Strikes of 1871* (1971); G.J. Barnsby, *The Working Class Movement in the Black Country, 1750–1867* (1979); B. Trinder, *The Industrial Revolution in Shropshire* (1973); B. Glen, *Urban Workers in the Early Industrial Revolution* (Stockport) (1984); G. Crossick, *An Artisan Elite in Victorian Society: Kentish London, 1840–80* (1978); and G. Stedman Jones, *Outcast London* (1971). For agriculture see P. Horn, *Joseph Arch* (1971); and J.P.D. Dunbabin (ed.), *Rural Discontent in Nineteenth Century Britain* (1974).

For the ideology of trade unionism, see J.F.C. Harrison, *Robert Owen and the Owenites in Britain and America* (1969); J. Foster, *Class Struggle in the Industrial Revolution* (1974); H.J. Collins and C. Abramsky, *Karl Marx and the British Labour Movement: Years of the First International* (1965); and G. Stedman Jones (ed.), *Languages of Class* (1984). There are also useful sections in H. Perkin, *The Origins of Modern English Society, 1780–1880* (1969) and S.G. Checkland, *The Rise of Industrial Society in England* (1964). The role of the 'aristocracy of labour' is discussed in E.J. Hobsbawm, 'The labour aristocracy in nineteenth-century Britain', in his *Labouring Men* (1964) and R.Q. Gray, *The Aristocracy of Labour in Nineteenth Century Britain, 1850–1914* (1981); see also B. Harrison, 'Traditions of respectability in British labour history', in his *Peaceable Kingdom: Stability and Change in Modern Britain* (1982) and P. Joyce, *Work, Society and Politics: the Culture of the Factory in later Victorian England* (1980).

Among a large number of articles are the following. Hobsbawm's four articles, 'The labour aristocracy', 'The machine-breakers', 'Economic fluctuations and some social movements' and 'Custom, wages and workload', reprinted in *Labouring Men*, are all important. R.N. Price, 'The other face of respectability: violence in the Manchester brickmaking trade, 1859–1870', *PP* (1975) and S. Pollard, 'The ethics of the Sheffield outrages', *THAS* (1953–54) bear upon the place of violence in trade disputes. R.V. Clements, 'British trade unions and popular political economy, 1850–1875', *EconHR* (1961); A.E. Musson, 'The Webbs and their phasing of trade-union development between the 1830s and the 1860s', *LHSB* (1962); and S.W. Coltham, 'George Potter, the Junta and the Beehive', *IRSH* (1965) are also relevant.

9. British foreign policy, 1815–84

K. Bourne, *The Foreign Policy of Victorian England, 1830–1902* (1970) and J.B. Joll, *Britain and Europe: Pitt to Churchill, 1793–1940* (1950) are particularly helpful collections of relevant diplomatic documents. M. Chamberlain, *'Pax Britannica?' British Foreign Policy, 1789–1914* (1989) is a useful introduction. P.M. Hayes, *The Nineteenth Century, 1814–80* (1975) has a general outline of foreign policy; see also the opening chapters of R.W. Seton-Watson, *Britain in Europe, 1789–1914* (2nd edn, 1955). The essential work on post-1848 diplomacy is A.J.P. Taylor, *The Struggle for Mastery in Europe, 1848–1918* (1954). See also H.A. Kissinger, *A World Restored: Metternich, Castlereagh and the Problems of Peace, 1812–1822* (1957).

Biographical studies include C.J. Bartlett, *Castlereagh* (1966); J.W. Derry, *Castlereagh* (1976); P.J.V. Rolo, *George Canning: Three Biographical Studies* (1965) and W. Hinde, *George Canning* (1973). On Palmerston, see K. Bourne, *Palmerston: the Early Years, 1784–1841* (1982) and D. Southgate, *'The Most English Minister . . .' The Policies and Politics of Palmerston* (1966).

C.K. Webster, *The Foreign Policy of Palmerston, 1830–41* (2 vols, 1951) deals with the early period. J. Ridley, *Lord Palmerston* (1970) offers a general biography. D.C.M. Platt, *Finance, Trade and Politics: British Foreign Policy, 1815–1914* (1968) is an overall interpretative study.

Among useful articles are G.B. Henderson, 'The foreign policy of Lord Palmerston', *H* (1938) and M. Beloff, 'Great Britain and the American Civil War', *H* (1952). See also as case studies, M.M. Robson, 'Liberals and "vital interests": the debate on international arbitration, 1815–72', *BIHR* (1959); F.G. Weber, 'Palmerston and Prussian Liberalism, 1848', *JMH* (1963); K.A.P. Sandiford, 'The British cabinet and the Schleswig-Holstein crisis, 1863–4', *H* (1973).

10. British colonial policy, 1815–84

For imperial and colonial issues, B. Porter, *The Lion's Share: A Short History of British Imperialism, 1850–1970* (3rd edn, 1996) and R. Hyam, *Britain's Imperial Century, 1815–1914: a Study of Empire and Expansion* (1976) provide general outlines. B. Semmel, *The Rise of Free Trade Imperialism: Classical Political Economy, the Empire of Free Trade and Imperialism, 1750–1850* (1970) and D.K. Fieldhouse, *Economics of Empire, 1830–1914* (1976) discuss the economic dimension. C.A. Bodelsen, *Studies in Mid-Victorian Imperialism* (1924) is an important study, now amplified by W.P. Morrell, *British Colonial Policy in the Age of Peel and Russell* (1930, rev. edn, 1970). A.P. Thornton, *The Imperial Idea and its Enemies* (1959) discusses policy, as does K.E. Knorr, *British Colonial Theories: 1570–1850* (1963). The later period is treated in J. Gallagher and R. Robinson, *Africa and the Victorians: the Official Mind of Imperialism* (1961) and C.C. Eldridge, *Victorian Imperialism* (1978). J.M. Ward, *Colonial Self-Government: the British Experience, 1759–1856* (1976) offers a view of colonial government.

P.M. Kennedy, *The Rise and Fall of British Naval Mastery* (1976) is particularly useful on the military aspects of the Pax Britannica; see also C.J. Bartlett, *Defence and Diplomacy: Britain and the Great Powers, 1815–1914* (1993). A classic article remains J. Gallagher and R. Robinson, 'The imperialism of Free Trade', *EHR* (1953).

11. Women and society in the Victorian era

General works which examine the position of women in society include S. Rowbotham, *Hidden from History* (1977), M. Hartmann and L. Banner (eds), *Clio's Consciousness Raised* (1974) and L. Davidoff et al., *The Family Story: Blood, Contract and Intimacy 1830–1960* (1998).

The early history of feminist ideas is discussed comparatively in J. Rendall, *The Origins of Modern Feminism: Women in Britain, France and the United States, 1780–1860* (1985). The use of demographic material to study assumptions about family size, age of marriage, and household structure in pre-industrial society has been pursued into the industrial period by M.S. Anderson, *Family Structure in Nineteenth-Century Lancashire* (1971). Two studies of marriage which have attracted attention are A. Macfarlane, *Marriage and Love in England: Modes of Reproduction, 1300–1840* (1986) and J.R. Gillis, *For Better For Worse: British Marriages 1600 to the Present* (1986).

An early attempt to examine the impact of industrialisation on family structure was N.J. Smelse, *Social Change in the Industrial Revolution* (1959), but the wider effects of industrialisation are discussed in I. Pinchbeck, *Women Workers and the Industrial Revolution, 1750–1850* (1969), and there are relevant chapters in the more recent studies by J. Walvin, *The English Urban Worker, 1776–1851* (1984) and J. Rule, *The Labouring Classes in Early Industrial England, 1750–1850* (1986). A case study of one group of working women is A.V. John, *By the Sweat of their Brow: Women Workers at Victorian Coal Mines* (1980) and another is J.R. Walkowitz, *Prostitution and Victorian Society: Women, Class and the State* (1980).

The role of middle-class women in entrepreneurial families is explored in L. Davidoff and C. Hall, *Family Fortunes: Men and Women of the English Middle Class, 1780–1850* (1986). M. Vicinus (ed.), *Suffer and Be Still: Women in the Victorian Age* (1980) and *A Widening Sphere: Changing roles of Victorian Women* (1980) are two collections of essays on the position of Victorian women. N. Boyd, *Josephine Butler, Octavia Hill, Florence Nightingale: Three Victorian Women who Changed their World* (1982) examines women who achieved a national reputation in the Victorian era, while F. Prochaska, *Women and Philanthropy in Nineteenth-Century England* (1980) looks at the important role of women in that sphere. B. Caine, *Destined to be Wives: the Sisters of Beatrice Webb* (1986) is a fine portrait of the lives of the other Potter daughters. P. Jalland, *Women, Marriage and Politics, 1860–1914* (1986) is a study of women in the later Victorian era, but see also P. Hollis, *Women in Public: The Women's Movement, 1850–1900* (1979).

A spate of more recent studies includes C. Bolt, *The Women's Movement in the United States and Britain from the 1790s to the 1920s* (1993); L. Bland, *Banishing the Beast: English Feminism and Sexual Morality, 1885–1914* (1995); J. Purvis (ed.), *Women's History: Britain, 1850–1945* (1995) and R. Watts, *Gender Power and the Unitarians in England, 1760–1860* (1998). The experiences of women in Wales and Scotland are examined in A.V. John (ed.), *Our Mothers' Land: Chapters in Welsh Women's History, 1830–1939* (1991) and E. Breitenbach and E. Gordon (eds), *Out of Bounds: Women in Scottish Society, 1800–1945* (1992).

Women's role in the radical and labour movements is attracting more attention. D. Thompson, *The Chartists* (1984) has a section on women, and on the unions see S. Lewenhak, *Women and Trade Unions* (1977), N.C. Soldon, *Women in British Trade Unions, 1874–1976* (1978) and S. Boston, *Women Workers and the Trade Union Movement* (1980). Women's generally shabby treatment in employment by both employers and male colleagues is examined in a number of studies, such as A. John (ed.), *Unequal Opportunities: Women's Employment in England, 1800–1918* (1986), L. Davidoff and B. Westover (eds), *Our Work, Our Lives, Our Words* (1986) on women in work from 1880 to 1939, and E. Roberts, *Women's Work, 1840–1940* (1987). See also S.S. Holton, *Feminism and Democracy: Women's Suffrage and Reform Politics in Britain, 1900–1918* (1986).

Much of the broader work on the position of women leads into the twentieth century: see J. Lewis, *Women in England: Sexual Divisions and Social Change* (1984), J. Lewis (ed.), *Labour and Love: Women's Experience of Home and Family, 1850–1940* (1986), and E. Roberts, *A Woman's Place: an Oral History of Working-class Women, 1890–1940* (1984). The crucial question of family size and welfare is discussed in J. Lewis, *The Politics of Motherhood: Child and Maternal Welfare in England, 1900–39* (1980). See also D. Gittins, *Fair Sex: Family Size and Structure, 1900–1939* (1982).

The development of attitudes towards sexuality is the subject of J. Weeks, *Sex, Politics and Society: The Regulation of Sexuality since 1800* (2nd edn, 1989). The collection by S. Cartledge and J. Ryan (eds), *Sex and Love* (1983) has a number of useful studies including L. Bland, 'Purity, motherhood, pleasures or threats? Definitions of female sexuality, 1900–1970'. The development of family planning and its place in early feminist causes is discussed in J.A. and O. Banks, *Feminism and Family Planning in Victorian England* (1964) and A. McLaren, *Birth Control in Nineteenth-Century England* (1978).

On the general question of the range and nature of women's history, see the articles in 'What is Women's History?' in *HT* (1985). On the family see M.S. Anderson, 'Sociological history and the working-class family: Smelser revisited', *SH* (1976) and on women's work see E. Richards, 'Women in the British economy since about 1700: an interpretation', *H* (1974) and K.D.M. Snell, 'Agricultural seasonal unemployment, the standard of living and women's work in the south and east: 1690–1860', *EconHR* (1981). For the link between work and family limitation see A. McLaren, 'Women's work and regulation of family size', *HW* (1977). Two broad perspectives on women's history in a European context are L. Tilly and J. Scott, 'Women's work and the family in nineteenth-century Europe', *Comparative Studies in Society and History* (1975) and L. Tilly, J. Scott and M. Cohen, 'Women's work and European fertility patterns', *Journal of Interdisciplinary History* (1976). See also J. Bourke, 'Housewifery in working class England, 1860–1914', *PP* (1994) and J. Vellacott, 'Feminist consciousness and the First World War', *HW* (1987).

12. Religion and society

There is an excellent survey by J. Obelkevitch, 'Religion', in F.M.L. Thompson (ed.), *The Cambridge Social History of Britain, 1750–1950* vol. 3 (1990), while both A. Armstrong, *The Church of England, the Methodists and Society, 1700–1850* (1973) and W.G. Ward, *Religion and Society in England, 1790–1850* (1972) are good general accounts. A.D. Gilbert, *Religion and Society in Industrial England: Church, Chapel and Social Change, 1740–1914* (1976) provides the essential data on church-going and denominational affiliation. K.S. Inglis, *Churches and the Working Class in Victorian England* (1963) poses the major problem of urban growth, a theme taken up by H. McLeod, *Religion and the Working Classes in Nineteenth Century Britain* (1984) and his edited collection *European Religion in the Age of Great Cities, 1830–1930* (1995).

The great study of the Anglican Church is O. Chadwick, *The Victorian Church* (Part 1, 1966, Part 2, 1970). See also G. Kitson Clark, *Churchmen and the Condition of England, 1832–85* (1973); J.D. Haydon, S. Taylor and J.D. Walsh (eds), *The Church of England, 1688–1833* (1993); J. Wolffe (ed.), *Evangelical Faith and Public Zeal: Evangelicals and Society in Britain, 1780–1980* (1995).

For the Oxford Movement see G. Faber, *Oxford Apostles* (1936); R.W. Church, *The Oxford Movement. Twelve Years 1833–45* (2nd edn, 1932); and Y.T. Brilioth, *The Anglican Revival, Studies in the Oxford Movement* (new imp., 1934). See also D. Newsome, *The Parting of Friends* (1966). D. Hempton, *Methodism and Politics, 1750–1850* (1984) is an excellent modern study. R.F. Wearmouth, *Methodism and the Working-Class Movements of England, 1800–1850* (1937) and *Methodism and the Struggle of the Working Classes, 1850–1900* (1954), and E.R. Taylor, *Methodism and Politics, 1791–1851* (1935) are all relevant to the later history of Methodism, if somewhat uncritical. R. Moore, *Pit-men, Preachers and Politics* (1974) is more sophisticated in its approach, and see also the excellent case study J. Obelkevitch, *Religion and Rural Society, South Lindsey, 1825–1875* (1976). On Nonconformity, see C. Binfield, *So Down to Prayers: Studies in English Nonconformity, 1780–1920* (1977).

The Roman Catholic community can be studied through J. Bossy, *The English Catholic Community, 1570–1850* (1975) and G.A. Beck (ed.), *The English Catholics, 1850–1950* (1950). The important theme of anti-Catholicism is covered by G. Best, 'Popular protestantism in Victorian Britain', in R. Robson (ed.), *Ideas and Institutions of Victorian Britain* (1967) and E.R. Norman, *Anti-Catholicism in Victorian England* (1968).

For Scotland, see T.C. Smout, *A Century of the Scottish People, 1830–1950* (1986), ch. 8; A.L. Drummond and J. Bulloch, *The Church in Victorian Scotland, 1843–1874* (1975) and *The Church in Late Victorian Scotland 1874–1900* (1978); A.C. Cheyne, *The Transforming of the Kirk* (1983),

S.J. Brown, *Thomas Chalmers and the Godly Commonwealth of Scotland* (1982); and C.G. Brown, *Religion and Society in Scotland since 1730* (1987).

There are several important articles. See K.S. Inglis, 'Patterns of worship in 1851', *JEcclH* (1960); D.M. Thompson, 'The 1851 Religious Census', *VS* (1967); A. Smith, 'Popular religion', *PP* (1968); W.L. Arnstein, 'The Murphey riots: a Victorian dilemma', *VS* (1975); and K.T. Hoppen, 'The Oxford Movement', *HT* (1967).

13. Gladstone and Liberalism

On Gladstone himself, an excellent one-volume study can be found in R. Jenkins, *Gladstone* (1995). Other studies include H.C.G. Matthew, *Gladstone, 1809–74* (1986) and *Gladstone, 1874–98* (1995), while P. Adelman, *Gladstone, Disraeli and Later Victorian Politics* (3rd edn, 1997) is also valuable. Shorter works include E. Feuchtwanger, *Gladstone* (1975) and P. Stansky, *Gladstone* (1979). There is a valuable detailed study in J.P. Parry, *Democracy and Religion: Gladstone and the Liberal Party, 1867–75* (1986).

On the background history of the Liberal Party, see J.R. Vincent, *The Formation of the British Liberal Party, 1857–1868* (1966), D.G. Southgate, *The Passing of the Whigs, 1832–1886* (1962) and M. Bentley, *The Climax of Liberal Politics: British Liberalism in Theory and Practice, 1868–1918* (1987), chs 2–4. J.R. Vincent, *Pollbooks: How Victorians Voted* (1967) is an important illustration of how politics worked at the local level. H.J. Hanham, *Elections and Party Management: Politics in the time of Disraeli and Gladstone* (1959) is important for the development of parties. For Palmerston's contribution see E.D. Steele, *Palmerston and Liberalism, 1855–1865* (1991). A recent perspective on the development of Liberal politics is T.A. Jenkins, *The Liberal Ascendency, 1830–1886* (1994).

The Second Reform Bill is discussed in F.B. Smith, *The Making of the Second Reform Bill* (1966) and M. Cowling, *1867: Disraeli, Gladstone and Revolution: The Passing of the Second Reform Bill* (1967). R.T. Shannon, *Gladstone and the Bulgarian Agitation, 1876* (1963) examines the domestic repercussions of the Bulgarian crisis. The later stages of Gladstone's career are discussed in D.A. Hamer, *Liberal Politics in the Age of Gladstone and Rosebery* (1972); J.R. Vincent and A. Cooke, *The Governing Passion: Cabinet Government and Party Politics in Britain, 1885–86* (1974); and M. Barker, *Gladstone and Radicalism: the Reconstruction of Liberal Policy in Britain, 1885–94* (1975).

The popular basis of Liberal politics is discussed in E. Biagini, *Liberty, Retrenchment and Reform: Popular Liberalism in the Age of Gladstone* (1992); see also J.P. Parry, *The Rise and Fall of Liberal Government in Britain* (1993).

On major Liberal figures, see W. Hinde, *Cobden* (1987); D. Read, *Cobden and Bright* (1967); R. Jay, *Joseph Chamberlain: a Political Study* (1981); D. Judd, *Radical Joe: a Life of Joseph Chamberlain* (1977); P. Fraser, *Joseph*

Chamberlain: Radicalism and Empire, 1868–1914 (1966); and R. Rhodes James, *Rosebery* (1963).

Local political allegiances are discussed in H. Pelling, *The Social Geography of British Elections 1885–1910* (1967); K.O. Morgan, *Wales in British Politics, 1868–1922* (1963); A. Briggs, *Victorian Cities* (1963); P. Waller, *Democracy and Sectarianism: a Political and Social History of Liverpool, 1868–1939* (1981); G.S. Messinger, *Manchester in the Victorian Age* (1985); I. Adams, *The Making of Urban Scotland* (1978); and S.G. Checkland, *The Upas Tree: Glasgow 1875–1975* (1976).

Among important articles are T.R. Tholfsen, 'The transition to democracy in Victorian England', *IRSH* (1961); F.H. Herrick, 'The Second Reform movement in Britain, 1850–65, *JHI* (1948); R. Harrison, 'The British working class and the general election of 1868', *IRSH* (1960); W.H. Mael, 'Gladstone, the Liberals and the election of 1874', *BIHR* (1963); J. Parry, 'Religion and the collapse of Gladstone's first government, 1870–74', *HJ* (1982); C.H.D. Howard, 'Joseph Chamberlain and the Unauthorised Programme', *EHR* (1950); R. Kelly, 'Midlothian', *VS* (1960); J. Dunbabin, 'Parliamentary elections in Great Britain 1868–1900: a psephological note', *EHR* (1966); W.C. Lubenow, 'Irish Home Rule and the social basis of the great separation in the Liberal Party in 1886', *HJ* (1985).

14. Disraelian Conservatism

R. Blake, *The Conservative Party from Peel to Thatcher* (1985) puts Disraeli in context, but Disraeli's place in the earlier history of the party can also be examined in R. Stewart, *The Foundation of the Conservative Party, 1830–1867* (1978). The standard life is R. Blake, *Disraeli* (1966), but I. Machin, *Disraeli* (1994) is of interest. P. Adelman, *Gladstone, Disraeli and Later Victorian Politics* (3rd edn, 1997) is helpful and R. Blake, 'The rise of Disraeli', in H. Trevor-Roper (ed.), *Essays in British History presented to Sir Keith Feiling* (1965) is also relevant.

H.J. Hanham, *Elections and Party Management: Politics in the time of Disraeli and Gladstone* (1959) discusses the political machinery of the period. The Second Reform Act is treated in F.B. Smith, *The Making of the Second Reform Bill* (1966) and M. Cowling, *1867. Disraeli, Gladstone and Revolution: The Passing of the Second Reform Bill* (1867). See also the chapter on 1867 in R. Harrison, *Before the Socialists: Studies in Labour and Politics, 1861–1881* (1965) for a view which stresses the popular pressure for reform.

P. Smith, *Disraelian Conservatism and Social Reform* (1967) and E.J. Feuchtwanger, *Disraeli, Democracy and the Tory Party* (1968) examine some of the wider aspects of Disraelian conservatism. R. McKenzie and J. Silver, *Angels in Marble* (1968) has an appraisal of the appeal of working-class Toryism, as does P. Joyce, *Work, Society and Politics* (1980). H.J. Hanham, *The Nineteenth Century Constitution, 1815–1914. Documents and Commentary* (1969) and P. Adelman, *Gladstone, Disraeli and Later Victorian Politics* (1970) also have some relevant documents.

Among important articles to consult are C.J. Lewis, 'Theory and expediency in the policy of Disraeli', *VS* (1960–61); E.J. Feuchtwanger, 'The Conservative Party under the impact of the Second Reform Act', *VS* (1959); J. Cornford, 'The transformation of conservatism in the late nineteenth century', *VS* (1963–64); J.P. Dunbabin, 'Parliamentary elections in Great Britain, 1868–1900: a psephological note', *EHR* (1966). There is a review of the debate on the Second Reform Act in G. Himmelfarb, 'The politics of democracy: the English Reform Act of 1867', *JBS* (1966). On party organisation see E.J. Feuchtwanger, 'J.E. Gorst and the central organisation of the Conservative Party, 1870–1882', *BIHR* (1959).

15. Irish nationalism and the Home Rule crisis

For the Home Rule period J.L. Hammond, *Gladstone and the Irish Nation* (1938) represents the traditional view of Gladstone's involvement with Ireland. D.A. Hamer, *The Liberal Party in the Age of Gladstone and Rosebery* (1972) explains policy towards Ireland in terms of Liberal politics. J.R. Vincent and A. Cooke, *The Governing Passion: Cabinet Government and Party Politics in Britain, 1885–86* (1974) is important.

On the influence of Parnell, C. Cruise O'Brien, *Parnell and his Party, 1880–90* (1957) is essential, but see also D.G. Boyce and A. O'Day, *Parnell in Perspective* (1991). F.S. Lyons, *Charles Stewart Parnell* (1978) is the standard biography; see also A. O'Day, *The English Face of Irish Nationalism: Parnellite Involvement in British Politics, 1880–86* (1977).

The relationship between the land question and the rise of the Home Rule issue is examined in P. Bew, *Land and the National Question in Ireland, 1858–1882* (1977). The attitude of the Conservatives is reviewed in L.P. Curtis, *Coercion and Conciliation in Ireland, 1880–1892: A Study in Conservative Unionism* (1963) and P. Bew, *Conflict and Conciliation in Ireland, 1890–1910* (1986). The rise of Unionism is discussed in P. Buckland, *Irish Unionism 1885–1923: A Documentary History* (1973); P. Gibbon, *The Origins of Ulster Unionism* (1975); A.T.Q. Stewart, *The Narrow Ground: Aspects of Ulster, 1609–1969* (1977); P. Bew, *Ideology and the Irish Question* (1994); A. Jackson, *The Ulster Party: Irish Unionists in the House of Commons, 1884–1911* (1989); and J. Loughlin, *Gladstone, Home Rule and the Ulster Question* (1986). The later aspects of the Irish crisis are discussed in A.T.Q. Stewart, *The Ulster Crisis* (1967).

Among articles on the Irish question, see D.A. Hamer, 'The Irish Question and Liberal politics, 1886–1894', *HJ* (1969); M. Hurst, 'Ireland

and the Ballot Act of 1872', *HJ* (1965); L.J. McCaffrey, 'Home Rule and the general election of 1874', *IHS* (1954–55). For the later period see D.G. Savage, 'The origins of the Ulster Unionist Party, 1885–6', *IHS* (1960–61); G.P. Taylor, 'Cecil Rhodes and the Second Home Rule Bill', *HJ*, (1971); F.S.L. Lyons, 'John Dillon and the plan of campaign, 1886–90', *IHS* (1964–65); L.P. Curtis, 'Government policy and the Irish Party crisis, 1890–92', *IHS* (1962–63); H.W. McCready, 'Home Rule and the Liberal Party, 1899–1906', *IHS* (1962–63); D.G. Boyce, 'British Conservative opinion, the Ulster Question and the partition of Ireland, 1912–21', *IHS* (1970–71).

16. The new imperialism

M.A. Chamberlain, *The New Imperialism* (Historical Association pamphlet, 1967) is a good survey of mid-twentieth-century thinking on the question of imperial expansion. Of the general histories, see especially B. Porter, *The Lion's Share: a Short History of British Imperialism, 1850–1970* (3rd edn, 1984); R. Hyam, *Britain's Imperial Century, 1815–1914: a Study of Empire and Expansion* (1976); and P.J. Cain and A.G. Hopkins, *British Imperialism: Innovation and Expansion, 1688–1914* (1993). J. Gallagher and R. Robinson, *Africa and the Victorians: The Official Mind of Imperialism* (1961) is an important series of case studies of how expansion occurred. On the 1860s and 1870s see also C.C. Eldridge, *Victorian Imperialism* (1978).

D.K. Fieldhouse, *The Colonial Empires* (1966) and *Economics and Empire, 1830–1914* (1976) reconsiders the economic arguments for imperialism. D.C. Platt, *Finance, Trade and Politics in British Foreign Policy, 1815–1914* (1968) is an important study which places imperialism in the context of British foreign policy. More recent are P.J. Cain, *Economic Foundations of British Overseas Expansion* (1980); L. David and R. Huttenback, *Mammon and the Pursuit of Empire: the Political Economy of British Imperialism* (1986); and A. Porter and R.F. Holland, *Money, Finance and Empire, 1790–1960* (1985). On investment see A.R. Hall (ed.), *The Export of Capital from Britain, 1870–1914* (1968); S.B. Saul, *Studies in British Overseas Trade 1870–1914* (1960); and P.L. Cottrell, *British Overseas Investment in the Nineteenth Century* (1975).

On the diplomatic repercussions of imperialism see P. Kennedy, *The Rise of the Anglo-German Antagonism, 1860–1914* (1980) and W. Langer, *The Diplomacy of Imperialism, 1890–1902* (1935), which also has an interesting chapter on the public psychology of imperialism. This theme is followed up in R. Price, *An Imperial War and the British Working Class: Working-class Attitudes and Reactions to the Boer War, 1899–1902* (1972). Attitudes to empire are also the theme of H. Pelling, 'British labour and British imperialism' in his *Popular Politics and Society in Late Victorian Britain* (1968). A.P. Thornton, *The Imperial Idea and its Enemies* (1959)

and *Doctrines of Imperialism* (1965) discuss ideologies of empire; see also
J. Kemp, *Theories of Imperialism* (1967) and W. Mommsen, *Theories of
Imperialism* (1980).

On the political repercussions of empire see D. Judd, *Balfour and the
British Empire* (1968); and H.G. Matthew, *The Liberal Imperialists: the Ideas
and Politics of a Post-Gladstonian Élite* (1973). Chamberlain's role is discussed
in R.V. Kublicek, *The Administration of Imperialism: Joseph Chamberlain at
the Colonial Office* (1969).

On the Boer War see T. Pakenham, *The Boer War* (1979); J.S. Marais,
The Fall of Kruger's Republic (1961); E. Pakenham, *Jameson's Raid* (1960);
S. Koss (ed.), *The Pro-Boers* (1973); and A.N. Porter, *The Origins of the
South African War: Joseph Chamberlain and the Diplomacy of Imperialism* (1980).

The collection of essays by C.J. Bartlett (ed.), *Britain Pre-Eminent* (1969)
has several useful contributions; see especially D. Southgate, 'Imperial
Britain'. Other collections of relevance are R. Hyam, *Reappraisals in British Imperial History* (1975); D.A. Low, *Lion Rampant: Essays in the Study
of British Imperialism* (1974); P. Kennedy, *The Realities Behind Diplomacy:
Background Influences on British External Policy, 1865–1980* (1981) and
C.C. Eldridge (ed.), *British Imperialism in the Nineteenth Century* (1984).

Among a wealth of articles, of particular value are H. Cunningham,
'Jingoism in 1877–78', *VS* (1971); J. Gallagher and R. Robinson, 'The
imperialism of Free Trade', *EconHR* (1953); D.C. Platt, 'Economic
factors in British policy during the "New Imperialism"', *PP* (1968); and
P. O'Brien, 'The costs and benefits of British imperialism 1846–1914',
PP (1988). Among a number of more detailed articles, see W.D. McIntyre,
'British policy in West Africa: the Ashanti Expedition of 1873–4', *HJ*
(1962); R.L. Tignor, 'Lord Cromer: practitioner and philosopher of
imperialism', *JBS* (1962–63); E. Stokes, 'Milnerism', *HJ* (1962); W. Strauss,
'Joseph Chamberlain and the theory of imperialism', *PA* (1942).

17. The Conservative ascendancy, 1886–1905

Among a wealth of studies are M. Pugh, *The Tories and the People, 1880–
1935* (1985) and H. Pelling, *Popular Politics and Society in Late Victorian
Britain* (1968). H. Pelling, *The Social Geography of British Elections, 1885–
1910* (1967) has a mass of information on local politics. The major
personalities of the late Victorian Conservative Party can be examined in
R. Taylor, *Salisbury* (1975), P. Marsh, *The Discipline of Popular Government:
Lord Salisbury's Domestic Statecraft, 1881–1902* (1978) and J. Cornford,
'The parliamentary foundations of the Hotel Cecil', in R. Robson (ed.),
Ideas and Institutions of Victorian Britain (1967). Lord Randolph Church-
ill's influence on the Tory Party is discussed in R. Foster, *Lord Randolph
Churchill* (1982). Joseph Chamberlain's gradual movement towards the

Conservatives can be followed in P. Fraser, *Joseph Chamberlain, Radicalism and Empire, 1868–1914* (1966); H. Browne, *Joseph Chamberlain, Radical and Imperialist* (1974); D. Judd, *Radical Joe: a Life of Joseph Chamberlain* (1977) and R. Jay, *Joseph Chamberlain* (1981).

Among important articles are R. Quinault, 'Randolph Churchill and Tory democracy', *HJ* (1979). The role of the Liberal Unionists and Chamberlain is discussed in P. Fraser, 'The Liberal Unionist alliance: Chamberlain, Hartington, and the Conservatives, 1886–1904', *EHR* (1962). See also P.R. Ghosh, 'Disraelian Conservatism. A financial approach', *EHR* (1984).

18. The rise of Labour

H. Pelling, *The Origins of the Labour Party, 1880–1900* (2nd edn, 1965) is the standard account. See also F. Bealey and H. Pelling, *Labour and Politics, 1900–1906: A History of the Labour Representation Committee* (1958). E.H. Hunt, *British Labour History, 1815–1914* (1981), K.D. Brown, *The English Labour Movement, 1700–1851* (1982) and J. Hinton, *Labour and Socialism: A History of the British Labour Movement, 1867–1974* (1983) are alternative general treatments. Trade union attitudes are discussed in H. Pelling, *A History of British Trade Unionism* (4th edn, 1986); J. Lovell and B.C. Roberts, *A Short History of the T.U.C.* (1968); R. Gregory, *The Miners and British Politics, 1906–1914* (1968); and H. Clegg, A. Fox and A.F. Thompson, *A History of British Trade Unions since 1889* (Vol. I, 1964, Vol. II, 1985). E. Hobsbawm, *Labouring Men* (1964) has a number of important essays; see especially 'General labour unions in Britain, 1889–1914' and 'Trends in the British Labour Movement since 1850'. The early political fortunes of Labour are discussed in P. Thompson, *Socialists, Liberals and Labour: The Struggle for London, 1885–1914* (1967) and H. Pelling, *The Social Geography of British Elections, 1885–1910* (1967).

The intellectual influences on the early socialist movements are discussed in E.P. Thompson, *William Morris: Romantic to Revolutionary* (1955); C. Tsuzuki, *H.M. Hyndman and British Socialism* (1961); H. Pelling, *America and the British Left* (1956); M. Cole, *The Story of Fabian Socialism* (1961); A.M. McBriar, *Fabian Socialism and English Politics, 1884–1918* (1966); E.R. Pease, *The History of the Fabian Society* (2nd edn, 1963); N. and J. MacKenzie, *The First Fabians* (1977); S. Pierson, *Marxism and the Origins of British Socialism* (1973) and W. Wolfe, *From Radicalism to Socialism* (1975).

R. McKibbin, *The Evolution of the Labour Party, 1910–1924* (1974) discusses the growth of labour organisation, while the argument that Labour's position was weakening prior to 1914 is made by R. Douglas, 'The strange death of Labour England, 1910–14', in K. Brown (ed.), *Essays in Anti-Labour History* (1974); see also K. Brown, *The First Labour*

Party, 1906–14 (1986), D. Tanner, *Political Change and the Labour Party, 1900–18* (1990), and K. Laybourn and J. Reynolds, *Liberalism and the Rise of Labour, 1890–1918* (1984). The rise of a more militant socialist movement is discussed in W. Kendall, *The Revolutionary Movement in Britain, 1900–21* (1969) and R. Holton, *British Syndicalism, 1900–1914: Myths and Realities* (1976).

The character of the Labour Party representatives in Parliament is discussed in D.E. Martin, ' "The instruments of the people"?: The Parliamentary Labour Party in 1906', in D.E. Martin and D. Rubinstein (eds), *Ideology and the Labour Movement: Essays presented to John Saville* (1979). On prominent Labour personalities see I. McLean, *Keir Hardie* (1975); K.O. Morgan, *Keir Hardie: Radical and Socialist* (1975); F. Reid, *Keir Hardie: the Making of a Socialist* (1978) and the early chapters of D. Marquand, *Ramsay MacDonald* (1977).

Documents and articles are also highly important on this topic. E. Hobsbawm (ed.), *Labour's Turning Point 1880–1900* (2nd edn, 1974) has a range of documents on trade union and radical politics at the end of the nineteenth century. R. Tressell, *The Ragged Trousered Philanthropists* (1955) is a remarkable novel of Edwardian working-class life. Among important articles are R.I. McKibbin, 'James Ramsay MacDonald and the problem of the independence of the Labour Party, 1910–1914', *JMH* (1970); K.O. Morgan, 'The New Liberalism and the challenge of Labour', *WHR* (1973); G.A. Phillips, 'The triple industrial alliance in 1914', *EconHR* (1971); P.F. Clarke, 'The electoral position of the Liberal and Labour parties, 1910–14', *EHR* (1975); and H.C.G. Matthew, R.I. McKibbin and J. Kay, 'The franchise factor in the rise of the Labour Party', *EHR* (1976).

19. Edwardian Liberalism

K.O. Morgan, *The Age of Lloyd George: the Liberal Party and British politics, 1890–1929* (1971) has an excellent selection of documents bearing directly on this topic. During the Edwardian period, the question of the rise of Labour and the downfall of the Liberal Party has generated one of the major historical debates of our time. There is a good survey of this debate in G.R. Searle, *The Liberal Party: Triumph and Disintegration, 1886–1929* (1992), K.O. Morgan, *The Age of Lloyd George*, chs 1–5 and M. Bentley, *The Climax of Liberal Politics* (1987), chs 7 and 8; see also H. Pelling, 'Labour and the downfall of Liberalism', in his volume of essays *Popular Politics and Society in Late Victorian England* (1968). G. Dangerfield, *The Strange Death of Liberal England* (1936) argues the case for the decline of 'Liberalism' by 1914. P.F. Clarke, *Lancashire and the New Liberalism* (1971) argues in favour of a 'new Liberalism' by 1914; see the informative review by K.O. Morgan in *History* (1972) and W. Arnstein, 'Edwardian politics: turbulent spring or Indian summer?', in A. O'Day (ed.), *The Edwardian Age: Conflict and Stability, 1900–1914* (1984). R. McKibbin, *The Evolution of the Labour Party, 1910–24* (1974) in essence contradicts this view, as does K. Laybourn and J. Reynolds, *Liberalism and the Rise of Labour, 1890–1918* (1984); see also T. Wilson, *The Downfall of the Liberal Party, 1914–35* (1966) which locates the crucial period of decline after 1914. H. Pelling, *The Social Geography of British Elections, 1885–1910* (1967) is a mine of information. See also K.D. Brown (ed.), *Essays in Anti-Labour History* (1974) and C. Cook, *A Short History of the Liberal Party, 1900–1997* (1998). H.W. Emy, *Liberals, Radicals and Social Politics, 1892–1914* (1973); H.G. Matthew, *The Liberal Imperialists: the Ideas and Politics of a post-Gladstonian élite* (1973); C. Wrigley, *David Lloyd George and the British Labour Movement* (1976); and B.K. Murray, *The People's Budget 1909/10: Lloyd George and Liberal Politics* (1980) deal with important themes.

The ideology of Liberalism has attracted increasing attention; see especially M. Freeden, *The New Liberalism: an Ideology of Social Reform* (1978); and P.F. Clarke, *Liberals and Social Democrats* (1978).

There are several biographies of Lloyd George; see especially M. Pugh, *Lloyd George* (1988); K.O. Morgan, *Lloyd George* (1974); P. Rowland, *Lloyd George* (1975); J. Grigg, *Lloyd George* (3 vols, 1973–). Also available are F. Owen, *Tempestuous Journey* (1954); A.J.P. Taylor, *Lloyd George: Rise and Fall* (1961) and C.L. Mowat, *Lloyd George* (1964).

For other prominent figures, see R. Jenkins, *Asquith* (rev. edn, 1978) and S. Koss, *Asquith* (1976). Churchill's early career is covered in R.S. Churchill, *Winston S. Churchill*, vols I and II (1966 and 1967). See also K. Robbins, *Sir Edward Grey* (1971); D.A. Hamer, *John Morley* (1968); and A. Briggs, *Seebohm Rowntree* (1961).

Among the article literature major topics are dealt with in J.F. Harris and C. Hazlehurst, 'Campbell-Bannerman as prime minister', *H* (1970); F. Bealey, 'Negotiations between the Liberal Party and the L.R.C. before the general election of 1906', *BIHR* (1956) and 'The electoral arrangement between the L.R.C. and the Liberal Party', *JMH* (1956); M. Peter, 'The progressive alliance', *H* (1973); P.F. Clarke, 'The progressive movement in England', *TRHS* (1974); P. Thompson, 'Liberals, Radicals and Labour in London, 1880–1900', *PP* (1964); J. Howarth, 'The Liberal revival in Northamptonshire, 1880–95', *HJ* (1969); J.G. Kellas, 'The Liberal Party in Scotland, 1876–1895', *SHR* (1965); C. Hazlehurst, 'Asquith as prime minister, 1908–16', *EHR* (1970); K.O. Morgan, 'Lloyd George's premiership', *HJ* (1970). For the influence of franchise arrangements on party support, see H.C.G. Matthew, R.I. McKibbin and J.A. Kay, 'The franchise factor in the rise of the Labour Party', *EHR* (1976); and P.F. Clarke, 'Liberals, Labour and the franchise', *EHR* (1977).

20. The Suffragette crisis

The development of the women's suffrage movement is traced in
H. Smith, *The British Women's Suffrage Campaign, 1886–1928* (1998) and in
M.D. Pugh, *Women's Suffrage in Britain, 1867–1928* (Historical Associa-
tion pamphlet, 1980), but see also A. Rosen, *Rise up Women! The Militant
Campaign of the Women's Social and Political Union, 1903–14* (1974) and
J. Liddington and J. Norris, *One Hand Tied Behind Us: the Rise of the
Women's Suffrage Movement* (1978). C. Rover, *Women's Suffrage and Party
Politics in Britain, 1866–1914* (1967) complements the detailed overview
dealing with electoral reform before and after 1914 in M.D. Pugh, *Electoral
Reform in War and Peace, 1906–1918* (1978). D. Morgan, *Suffragists and
Liberals* (1975) examines the relationship of the women's movement
with its most likely supporters in Parliament, but much the most considered treatment of the women's suffrage question at Westminster is
B. Harrison, 'Women's Suffrage at Westminster', in M. Bentley and
J. Stevenson (eds), *High and Low Politics in Modern Britain: Ten Studies*
(1983) and his *Separate Spheres: The Opposition to Women's Suffrage in Britain* (1978). See also J. Rendall (ed.), *Equal or Different? Women's Politics,
1800–1914* (1987) and J. Lewis (ed.), *Before the Vote was Won: Arguments
for and against Women's Suffrage, 1864–1896* (1987).

21. Britain and the origins of the First World War

B. Schmitt, *The Outbreak of War in 1914* (Historical Association pamphlet,
1964) is a good overview of the traditional interpretation that the alliance system was to blame for the outbreak of war, a view increasingly
under attack; see, for example, H.W. Koch (ed.), *The Origins of the First
World War: Great Power Rivalry and German War Aims* (1972) and the
more recent overview by J. Joll, *The Origins of the First World War* (1985).
A.J.P. Taylor, *The Struggle for Mastery in Europe, 1848–1918* (1954) is a major
diplomatic study. Z.S. Steiner, *Britain and the Origins of the First World War*
(1977) is the most detailed analysis of British involvement. The classic
study of Anglo-German naval rivalry is E.L. Woodward, *Great Britain and
the German Navy* (1935), now updated on the naval side by A.J. Marder,
From the Dreadnought to Scapa Flow. Vol. 1: *The Road to War, 1904–14*
(1961) and on the political by P. Kennedy, *The Rise of the Anglo-German
Antagonism, 1860–1914* (1980). Military preparations are discussed in
M. Howard, *The Continental Commitment: the Dilemma of British Defence
Policy in the Era of Two World Wars* (1972), ch. 2, and S.R. Williamson, *The
Politics of Grand Strategy: Britain and France Prepare for War, 1904–1914* (1969).
    Among important document collections are J.B. Joll (ed.), *Britain and
Europe: Pitt to Churchill, 1793–1940* (1950); J.H. Wiener (ed.), *Great Brit-
ain: Foreign Policy and the Span of Empire* (4 vols, 1972) and C.J. Lowe and
M.L. Dockrill, *The Mirage of Power: British Foreign Policy, 1902–22* (3 vols, 1972).

Index